THE ECONOMIC AND SOCIAL ORIGINS OF GNOSTICISM

SOCIETY
OF BIBLICAL
LITERATURE

DISSERTATION SERIES

William Baird, Editor

Number 77
THE ECONOMIC AND SOCIAL ORIGINS
OF GNOSTICISM
by
Henry A. Green

Henry A. Green

THE ECONOMIC AND SOCIAL ORIGINS OF GNOSTICISM

Scholars Press
Atlanta, Georgia

THE ECONOMIC AND SOCIAL ORIGINS
OF GNOSTICISM

Henry A. Green

Ph.D., 1982
St. Mary's College
St. Andrew's University
Scotland

Advisor:
R. McL. Wilson

©1985
Society of Biblical Literature

Library of Congress Cataloging-in-Publication Data

Green, Henry A.
  The economic and social origins of Gnosticism.

  (Dissertation series / Society of Biblical
Literature ; no. 77)
  Bibliography: p.
  1. Gnosticism. I. Title. II. Series: Dissertation
series (Society of Biblical Literature) ; no. 77.
B638.G64   1985   299'.932   85-18259
ISBN 0-89130-842-3 (alk. paper)
ISBN 0-89130-843-1 (pbk. : alk. paper)

Printed in the United States of America
on acid-free paper

TO JORDAN

You saw the Spirit, you became Spirit. . . .
What you see is yourself; and what you see
you shall become.

(*Gospel of Philip* 61.29-35)

We shall begin with the fact that the same
concept means very different things when
used by differentially situated persons.

(Mannheim, *Ideology and Utopia*, 245)

v

Contents

List of
Tables and Map

Tables

Map

x

Preface

In 1970 while studying in Jerusalem, I was introduced to the writings of the Gnostics. Their message of self-discovery, of an interior path of *gnosis*, I found most appealing. Trained as a sociologist, I wondered if I could marry theology and sociology and understand the emergence of Gnosticism. Following Max Weber, I wanted to continue the dialogue between the two disciplines. Religious movements, however spiritual in character, have social form.

Professor R. McL. Wilson, my supervisor, encouraged and supported me from the very beginning. He provided me with a way of understanding Gnostic writings and sensitively guided me. He continually challenged me to go beyond the history of past scholarship and to find a new resolution that accounted for the socio-economic environment. Francis Schmidt, in Paris, furnished me with a model for interpreting the economy of Egypt in relation to the origins of Gnosticism. His exploratory studies in the material world of Judaism and early Christianity have been a constant help. Jonathan Cloud, my dear friend, who with kindness and patience oversaw the project in the final stages, sharpened my sociological arguments, and helped me to cultivate an interdisciplinary approach. To all of them, my indebtedness is immeasurable.

I am also very grateful to friends and colleagues who during the course of the writing have read and criticized all or parts of the manuscript. Charles Rachlis contributed much to my sociological thinking and Steve Wilson conscientiously advised me on theological pitfalls. For other advice and criticism on drafts of individual chapters, I wish to acknowledge with gratitude the assistance of Stephen Emmel, Ithamar Gruenwald, Phil Lockhart, Birger Pearson, Hannah Safrai, Alan Segal, Guy Stroumsa, Richard Stursberg, Michel Tardieu, Zvi Werblowsky and David Wolfe.

I am also obliged to Professor William Baird, editor for New Testament and Cognate Areas, SBLDS, who has aided me in the publication of the dissertation. On his recommendation Chapter One of the dissertation (a study in methodology) has been eliminated. An earlier version can be found in *Numen* 24 (1977), 95-134, entitled "Gnosis and Gnosticism: A Study in Methodology."

My thanks also go to Bruce Collins who codified the data, Sue Beninger who typed the early drafts, Norma Rankin who did the typing of the final dissertation manuscript, and Eileen Hirsch who prepared the text for publication.

The research and writing of this dissertation would have been impossible without the financial support of the Canada Council, the Social Sciences and Humanities Research Council of Canada, St. Leonards College, St. Andrews University, the Government of Israel and the Hebrew University of Jerusalem. The Judaic Studies Program of the University of Miami provided the financial support for the publication of this volume.

Finally, during the many years of the maturation of the dissertation, my wife Elizabeth has had to arrange homes in many different countries and to accommodate herself to my research. Her loving faith has continually inspired me.

October 1984
Tishrei 5745
Coral Gables, Florida

Abbreviations and Methods of Citation

The abbreviations of Gnostic, rabbinic, Christian, and classical literatures used in this thesis, as well as those of series and periodicals, follow those set out by the *Journal of Biblical Literature*. See "Instructions for Contributors," *JBL* 95 (1976), 331-346. Additional abbreviations are listed below with full references provided in the bibliography.

Biblical texts are usually quoted according to the Revised Standard Version; and Gnostic texts, for the most part, according to the translations provided in James Robinson, ed., *The Nag Hammadi Library in English* (New York, 1977). When the tractate is first mentioned its location in the library is noted in the text—e.g., *The Gospel of Philip* (NHC II,3). Full references are always provided in the footnotes (i.e., location in the library, page and line numbers—e.g., NHC II,3:69,10-18).

In some cases, however, I have given my own translations, either when I disagreed with those provided in the Robinson edition, or simply for the sake of establishing consistency in the rendering of Greek or Coptic terms.

Other Gnostic texts, as well as Christian and Jewish sources, are quoted according to the standard scholarly editions, listed in the bibliography. Classical sources are quoted according to the Loeb Classical library whenever possible. For references to classical authors' writings on the Jews, see M. Stern, *Greek and Latin Authors on Jews and Judaism* (Jerusalem, 1974, 1980), 2 vols. Standard reference works such as lexicons, works of grammar or encyclopaedias have not been included in the bibliography.

For papyrological publications the standard abbreviations have been employed. The non-expert may consult E. G. Turner, *Greek Papyri. An Introduction* (Princeton, 1968), 154ff., or M. David and B. A. van Groningen, *Papyrological Primer* (Leiden, 1965⁴), 6ff.

Modern scholarly works are identified in full only the first time they

xiii

are cited in the footnotes; short titles are used thereafter. The full reference may be found in the bibliography.

Abot R. Nathan	*Abot de Rabbi Nathan*
Adv. Haer.	Irenaeus, *Adversus Haereses*
Adv. Val.	Tertullian, *Adversus Valentianos*
Ant.	Josephus, *Antiquities of the Jews*
Apol.	Justin Martyr, *Apology*
Aug.	Suetonius, *Augustus*
Authors	M. Stern, *Greek and Latin Authors on Jews and Judaism*
CII	J. B. Frey, *Corpus Inscriptionem Judaicarum*
Conf.	Philo, *De Confusione Linguarum*
CPJ	V. A. Tcherikover et al., *Corpus Papyrorum Judaicarum*
Dam. Doc.	*Damascus Document*, see Ch. Rabin, *The Zadokite Document*
De Jos.	Philo, *De Josepho*
De Off.	Cicero, *De Officiis*
De Opif. Mundi	Philo, *De Opificio Mundi*
De Prof.	Philo, *De Providentia*
De Spec. Leg.	Philo, *De Specialibus Legibus*
De Virt.	Philo, *De Virtutibus*
De Vita Cont.	Philo, *De Vita Contemplativa*
Epist.	Pliny the Younger, *Epistulae*
Exc. ex Theod.	Clement of Alexandria, *Excerpta ex Theodoto*
Flacc.	Philo, *In Flaccum*
GCS	*Griechische christliche Schriftsteller*
Gen. Rab.	Genesis Rabbah, see J. Theodor, *Bereshit Rabbah*
Geog.	Strabo, *Geography*
Haer. Fab.	Theodoret, *Haereticarum Fabularum Compendium*
Hom.	Pseudo-Clementine, *Homilies*
Lam. Rab.	*Lamentations Rabbah*, see H. Freedman, *Midrash Rabbah*
LCL	*Loeb Classical Library*
Leg. ad Gaium	Philo, *De Legatione ad Gaium*
Leg. All.	Philo, *Legum Allegoriae*

IQS	F. M. Cross et al., *Scrolls from Qumran Cave I*
Migr. Abr.	Philo, *De Migrationa Abrahami*
NHC	Nag Hammadi Codices, see J. M. Robinson, ed., *The Nag Hammadi Library in English*
Or.	Dio Chrysostum, *Oratio*
Pan.	Epiphanius, *Panarion*
Prep. Evang.	Eusebius, *Preparatio Evangelica*
Quis Rerum Div. Heres	Philo, *Quis Rerum Divinarum Heres*
Quod Omn. Prob.	Philo, *Quod Omnis Probus*
Ref.	Hippolytus, *Refutatio Omnium Haeresium*
SC	Sources chrétiennes
SEHHW	M. Rostovtzeff, *The Social and Economic History of the Hellenistic World*
SEHRE	M. Rostovtzeff, *The Social and Economic History of the Roman Empire*
Sib. Or.	Sibylline Oracles
Strom.	Clement of Alexandria, *Stromata*
Vesp.	Suetonius, *Vespasian*

1

Sociology and Gnosticism

1.1 Introduction

In the study of Gnosis and Gnosticism there has been a noticeable absence of a sociological perspective. With the exception of E. Michael Mendelson's paper, "Some Notes on a Sociological Approach to Gnosticism" presented at the Messina Colloquium in 1966,[1] Hans Kippenberg's article, "Versuch einer soziologischen Verortung des antiken Gnostizismus" in *Numen* in 1970,[2] and K. Rudolph's "Das Problem einer Soziologie und 'sozialen Verortung' der Gnosis" in *Kairos* in 1977,[3] sociological studies are absent. Mendelson, a social anthropologist, suggested for consideration a number of sociological questions but unfortunately left them unanswered. Instead he proceeded to present examples from his own field of research, Buddhism, as an analogous situation. His sociological analysis of Gnosticism, therefore, is severely limited and neither substantive nor theoretical. His suggestion that an analysis of Gnosticism move from the ideological level of analysis to that of sectarian conflict with special consideration given to "patterns of social relations"[4] still has to be explored.

Kippenberg, a theologian with sociological interests, attempts to demonstrate that the ideological elements of Gnosticism are a reflection

---

[1]E. M. Mendelson, "Some Notes on a Sociological Approach to Gnosticism," in *Le Origini dello Gnosticismo*, ed. U. Bianchi (*Numen*Sup 12, Leiden, 1967), 668-676.

[2]Hans Kippenberg, "Versuch einer soziologischen Verortung des antiken Gnostizismus," *Numen* 17 (1970), 211-232.

[3]K. Rudolph, "Das Problem einer Soziologie und 'sozialen Verortung' der Gnosis," *Kairos* 19/1 (1977), 35-44.

[4]Mendelson, "Notes," 669f. and 673f.

of a socio-political reality in which the Gnostics felt repressed and alienated. His thesis is that the sects of the Gnostic movement were bred
among the impotent Hellenized intellectual elite of the eastern fringes of
the Roman Empire.

Kippenberg's argument emphasizes the ideological roots of philosophical systems, drawing on the theoretical work of the German neo-positivist
sociologist, E. Topitsch.[5] Following Topitsch's model, Kippenberg posits
that structural similarities exist between metaphysical doctrines and
everyday experience and hence that the former can be conceived as
analogous to and arising out of the latter. Kippenberg also uses Eric
Fromm's psychological assumption that every image of God is a projection
of political authority.[6] By integrating the two, Kippenberg begins to
address some of the ways in which Gnostics may have interpreted the
social reality of Imperial Rome and transformed it into a new world-view
for their own interpretations of God, man and the world.

Kippenberg's novel interpretation has been criticized by Peter Munz on
a number of points.[7] Methodologically, Munz considers Kippenberg's
framework to be itself ideological, and suggests that instead of looking
from either end of the continuum—metaphysical-religious beliefs or
socio-political experience—the social scientist search for a mediating link
between social forms and thought forms.[8] Second, Munz criticizes
Kippenberg's theoretical position that ideologies are constructed from
human experience. According to Munz, this assumption leads Kippenberg
to suggest that the Evil Demiurge is analogous to Roman Imperial tyr-
anny, in spite of the fact that no data exist to support such a conclusion.
Leaving aside the epistemological problem, Munz has misinterpreted the
thrust of Kippenberg's thesis: it is not the Evil Demiurge that is central
for the Gnostics, it is their passion for freedom through *gnosis*.[9]

---

[5]Kippenberg, "Versuch," 213f. For E. Topitsch's view see his
Sozialphilosophie zwischen Ideologie und Wissenschaft (Luchterhand,
1961), especially 261-296.

[6]Kippenberg, "Versuch," 230f. For E. Fromm's ideas see his *Das
Christusdogma und andere Essays* (Munich, 1965), especially 9-91.

[7]Peter Munz, "The Problem of *'Die Soziologische Verortung des antiken
Gnostizismus,'*" *Numen* 19 (1972), 41-51.

[8]Munz's suggestion is closely aligned with that of Mary Douglas in her
book *Natural Symbols* (London, 1970). Munz ("Problem," 49ff.) favours
Douglas' suggestion that the human body might be that missing link, the
vehicle through which social forms and religious beliefs are connected.

[9]Kippenberg, "Versuch," 225: the intention of the Gnostics is "ein
herrschaftsfreies Seinsverhältnis" and "sich durch Rekurs auf seine Ver-
nunft ausserhalb des irrationalen Machtsystems zu begeben."

Like Kippenberg, Rudolph also is a theologian with sociological interests. As early as 1963 he had called for a sociological analysis of Gnosticism,[10] and in several subsequent articles he has used sociological concepts.[11] Yet although he seems enthusiastic, he remains sceptical of their
worth: "Aus Überlieferungsbestimmten Gründen, aber auch aus solchen
der Forschungsorientierung und method heraus, waren soziologische
Überlegungen in der Gnosisforschung nicht sehr opportun."[12]
Rudolph's "Das Problem einer Soziologie. . .der Gnosis" is more of a
preliminary discussion with sweeping speculative generalizations than a
detailed and theoretically argued sociological analysis. It suggests answers
but provides little or no socio-economic data. Rudolph addresses three
themes: the social composition of Gnostic communities, social and ideological features of Gnosticism, and the origin of the first social carriers
of the Gnostic religion. In each case he presents a series of premises
followed by general conclusions. Gnostic leaders were amateur intellectuals who had been Hellenistically trained and educated. Their communities represented all strata. Gnostic ideology advocated equality of sexes,
a brotherhood of man, and the elimination of social differences and private property. The first Gnostics were Jewish wisdom *literati* who represented a politically powerless lay intellectualism.

In many ways Rudolph's arguments follow Kippenberg's earlier analysis.
Like Kippenberg he accepts the position that the ideological elements of
Gnosticism reflect socio-political reality. However, Rudolph has refined
Kippenberg's thesis. He views Gnosticism as a reaction by Jews of the
Hellenized Orient who felt both demoralized and estranged by Roman
conquest. Recoiling from Rome's political power, they re-evaluated the
cosmos as a miscarriage, and critically re-interpreted Hellenistic and
Jewish values and ideology. Perceiving themselves as an elite who had
exclusive knowledge, they advocated brotherhood, equality and individual-
ism as means of escaping the clutches of a Roman dominated world.
Gnosticism became the vehicle for creating a new identity.

---

[10]K. Rudolph, "Stand und Aufgaben in der Erforschung des Gnostizismus," in the Tagung für allgemeine Religionsgeschichte, *Sonderheft des
Wissenschaftlichen Zeitschrift der Friedrich-Schiller-Universität* (Jena,
1963), 89-102.
[11]See, for example, K. Rudolph, "Randerscheinungen des Judentums
und das Problem der Entstehung des Gnostizismus," *Kairos* 9 (1967), 109ff.
and "Soziologische Bemühungen," *TRu* 36 (1971), 119ff. See also his *Die
Gnosis* (Göttingen, 1977), 219ff.
[12]Rudolph, "Problem einer Soziologie," 35.

However appealing Rudolph's argument might be, the fundamental problem remains: where are the supporting social data? Rudolph's analysis therefore suffers from several of the same defects as Kippenberg's. It posits structural similarities between metaphysical doctrines and everyday experiences without providing a detailed analysis of either the material conditions of daily life or how these inter-act with ideological development. Nor are the implications of the sociological concepts fully developed. Rudolph's use of such variables as class, education and urban-rural conflict is suggestive but does not provide a solid causal illustration of the social context from which Gnosticism evolved. To state that, in the evolution of Gnosticism, Gnostics took advantage of trade openings and cultural exchanges,[13] is no more than conjecture unless socio-economic data are used to identify geographical, historical and cultural categories of investigation. The problem is not Rudolph's conclusions; rather, his lack of adequate documentation, and incomplete use of sociological theory prevent classifying his work as a theoretical or methodological contribution to the sociology of Gnosticism.

The work of Elaine Pagels should also be noted. Pagels has progressively moved towards adopting a sociological perspective in her analysis of Gnosticism. In contrast to her earlier works which emphasized motifs in literary contexts,[14] The Gnostic Gospels focuses on the relationship between society and religion and examines how several ideological battles between Gnostic-Christians and Catholic-Christians affected the developing structure of the early Catholic Church.[15] Certain themes such as the participation of women, the organization of authority and martyrdom clearly indicate that ideology influenced social relationships. Yet, in spite of her sociological orientation, most of her source material remains exclusively theological and her analysis lacks an integration of social scientific theory and methodology. Nevertheless, Pagels is the first scholar of Gnosticism to confront the data from Nag Hammadi from a perspective that is more than a combination of historical-philological-literary motifs. She attempts to draw relationships between non-empirical concepts and concepts of human action as they are ideologically manifested. However, in The Gnostic Gospels Pagels is not addressing the more difficult problem of origins. Her purpose is to draw out significant ideological

---

[13]Ibid., 42.
[14]For example, see E. Pagels, The Johannine Gospel in Gnostic Exegesis (Nashville, 1973) and The Gnostic Paul (Philadelphia, 1975).
[15]E. Pagels, The Gnostic Gospels (New York, 1979).

confrontations between Catholic Christians and Gnostic Christians in order to explain aspects of what may be called the institutionalization process in early Catholic Christianity. The relationship of Gnosticism to its non-Christian contemporary environment is not explored, nor are social-cultural indicators delineated.

Nevertheless, these attempts at a sociological analysis of Gnosticism should be compared with the experimental investigations of physical scientists: pioneering work often provokes negative reactions. The need for sociological investigation remains. This has been explicitly stated by several Gnostic scholars;[16] in 'Proposal Six' of the Messina Colloquium in 1966: "the Collquium expresses the hope that further study will deepen the . . . sociological aspects of the movements of Gnosticism";[17] and, most recently, by the International Conference on Gnosticism in 1978, which viewed sociology as a pertinent contribution.[18]

This dissertation is a response to the call for a sociological analysis of Gnosticism. It consolidates economic and social phenomena that contributed to the emergence of Gnosticism. It examines the particular socioeconomic context that gave rise to Gnosticism, and the particular audience the Gnostic authors wished to address. By locating the precursors of Gnosticism within a specific geographical, economic and social context, we can see ideology as rooted in historical reality and reflecting the material conditions of life.

---

[16]For example, in 1963 Rudolph ("Stand und Aufgaben," 98) called for a sociological analysis with special emphasis placed on the socio-economic causes of Gnosticism. Th. P. van Baaren in a Messina paper mentioned the "almost complete ignorance of sociological aspects of Gnostic communities" and advocated research into the consequences of Gnostic belief systems on everyday life ("Towards a Definition of Gnosticism," in Bianchi, ed., *Origini,* 177); in 1973 Petr Pokorný recommended an examination of the social background and environment of the Gnostics ("Der soziale Hintergrund der Gnosis," in *Gnosis und Neues Testament,* ed. Karl-Wolfgang Tröger (Berlin, 1973), 77ff.); and in 1978 G. Stroumsa has again reiterated the need for such an undertaking. See his *Another Seed: Studies in Sethian Gnosticism* (Cambridge, 1978), 12, fn. 29.

[17]Bianchi, ed., *Origini,* xxix.

[18]See the comments in "Le Congrès de Yale sur le Gnosticisme," *Revue des études augustiniennes* 24 (1978), 203 of M. Tardieu, who implicitly suggests the importance of putting 'Proposal Six' of the Messina Colloquium into practice; the brochures forwarded to participants at the Conference; and the remarks in the preface to Volume One of the Conference's proceedings (*The Rediscovery of Gnosticism,* ed. B. Layton (Leiden, 1980), v. 1, xi).

1.2   Sociology and Theology

The use of social scientific paradigms in the study of early Christianity has gained numerous supporters over the last decade. Theissen, in a series of studies in New Testament sociology, has investigated the Corinthian congregation[19] and the Jesus movement.[20] Gager, in *Kingdom and Community*, has examined "specific problems (in early Christianity) in terms of theoretical models from recent work in the social sciences," in the hope that there will emerge a new constituency of social scientists as well as a new paradigm.[21] Malherbe, in *Social Aspects of Early Christianity*, has considered the relationship between different social strata and theological disputes that splintered the community in Corinth;[22] B. Holmberg, in *Paul and Power*, has studied the exercise of authority in the early church;[23] and Kee, in *Christian Origins in Sociological Perspective*, has applied a number of sociological models to the study of early Christianity.[24] More recently, Wayne Meeks in *The First Urban Christians* has presented a comprehensive social description of early Christians, and in particular Paul, and the social networks that were generated by his missionary efforts in urban environments.[25] All these studies point to the usefulness of applying a social-scientific approach to the study of the New Testament.[26] In a similar fashion, this dissertation

---

[19]See G. Theissen, *Studien zur Soziologie des Urchristentums* (Tübingen, 1979).

[20]See G. Theissen, *The First Followers of Jesus*, trans. J. Bowden (London, 1978). For a critique of Theissen's work see J. H. Schütz, "Steps toward a Sociology of Primitive Christianity: A Critique of the Work of Gerd Theissen," paper presented at the annual meeting of the Society of Biblical Literature/American Academy of Religion, San Francisco, 1977.

[21]J. Gager, *Kingdom and Community: The Social World of Early Christianity* (Englewood Cliffs, N. J., 1975), 12 and 14.

[22]A. J. Malherbe, *Social Aspects of Early Christianity* (Baton Rouge and London, 1977).

[23]B. Holmberg, *Paul and Power: The Structure of Authority in the Primitive Church as Reflected in the Pauline Epistles* (Lund, 1978).

[24]See H. C. Kee, *Christian Origins in Sociological Perspective: Methods and Resources* (Philadelphia, 1980).

[25]W. Meeks, *The First Urban Christians* (New Haven and London, 1983).

[26]For recent bibliographies and analysis of social interpretations of early Christianity see R. Scroggs, "The Social Interpretation of the New Testament: The Present State of Research," *NTS* 26 (1980), 164-179, E. A. Judge, "The Social Identity of the First Christians: A Question of Method

applies social-scientific concepts and techniques to the study of Gnosticism.

In contrast to theology, which addresses religious questions and produces religious answers, sociology examines its subject matter in terms of social facts and provides secular interpretations. For the sociologist it is axiomatic that man's consciousness is determined by his social being.[27] The sociological enterprise rests on the assumption that the subjective and objective dimensions of human experience are inextricably intertwined; ontology and history are fused together within the existence of social individuals. Biologically and socially, man is compelled to externalize himself. Collectively, human beings produce a social world that takes the form of an objective reality which the individual apprehends as external to himself. Human ontology is given concrete expression in linguistic, cultural and social norms and institutions. The social world provides the context for the interpretation of human existence. Through socialization, this objective reality is internalized and becomes part of the subjective awareness of the socialized individual. Through socialization, man accepts the world around him as "taken for granted" and acts out roles according to age, sex, occupation, geographical location and social identity.

> Man and his social world interact with each other. . . . Externalization and objectivation are moments of a continual dialectical process. . . . Society exists only as individuals are conscious of it . . . and individual consciousness is socially determined. . . . Society is a human product; society is an objective reality; man is a social product.[28]

Sociology addresses itself to human events in the historical development of the world; theology to God's creation of man and man's subsequent development in relation to God. The sociological enterprise is horizontal, that of theology vertical. Sociology interprets human experience in terms of the phenomenal realm, theology in terms of the noumenal one. Sociology is compatible with ethical relativism, whereas

---

in Religious History," *JRH* 7/2 (1980), 201-217 and D. J. Harrington, "Sociological Concepts and the Early Church: A Decade of Research," *TS* 41 (1980), 181-190.

[27] Z. A. Jordan, *Karl Marx: Economy, Class and Social Revolution* (London, 1972), 198.

[28] Peter Berger and Thomas Luckmann, *The Social Construction of Reality* (Garden City, N. Y., 1966), 61.

theology speaks to ethical absolutes. In other words, because of different philosophical assumptions and historical traditions, sociology and theology employ different methods and criteria for analysis, and 'map' their data in radically different ways.

1.3   Geographical, Economic and Social Considerations

1.3.1   Geographical Considerations

The appearance of Gnosticism is distributed over a wide geographical area, including parts of Italy, Egypt, Palestine, Syria, Asia Minor and Persia. However, for the purposes of this study only Egypt has been considered. Apart from the fact that any comprehensive sociological study of these various socio-economic locations would be unwieldly, Egypt stands out as the most logical starting point for tracing the origins of Gnosticism. Many of the Church Fathers designate Egypt as a source of Gnostic teachings and locate a number of the earliest Gnostics there. Two Fathers (Clement of Alexandria and Origen) lived there during the Valentinian period. According to the Pseudo-Clementine writings, Simon (c.50 A.D.)—the originator of the Gnostic heresy according to the Church Fathers—acquired his Gnostic knowledge (i.e., magic) in Egypt.[29] There is a tradition that Cerinthus, who was active in the late first century A.D., had also been trained in Egypt.[30] Two other well-known Gnostics, Carpocrates and his son Epiphanes, are mentioned by Clement of Alexandria[31] and Theodoret[32] as being from Egypt and practising their religion there in the first third of the second century A.D. According to Irenaeus, Basilides and his son Isidore were active in Egypt in the second quarter of the second century A.D.[33] Valentinus, the most prominent of the Gnostics, was born in Egypt and in all likelihood became familiar with Gnosticism there before coming to Rome.[34] Moreover, several of his disciples, such as Theodotus and Julius Cassianus, came from Egypt,[35] and Apelles,

---

[29]Pseudo-Clementine, *Hom.*, 2.22 and 24.
[30]Hippolytus, *Ref.*, 7.7.33 and 10.21.
[31]Clement of Alexandria, *Strom.*, 3.2.
[32]Theodoret, *Haer. Fab.*, 1.5.
[33]Irenaeus, *Adv. Haer.*, 1.24.1.
[34]Epiphanius, *Pan.*, 31.7.
[35]A. Harnack, *The Mission and Expansion of Christianity in the First Three Centuries*, trans. J. Moffatt (London, 1908[2]), v. 2, 159ff. There is also a tradition that Marcus was an Egyptian. See Jerome, *Epistle, 75.3.*

the pupil of Marcion, was also active in Egypt.[36] Yet in spite of the fact that this evidence points toward a common conclusion, Patristic comments concerning the origins of Gnosticism are of limited historical value and cannot be considered wholly reliable. Later writers tend to lack first-hand knowledge of Gnostic teachings and to follow earlier ones; hence it is difficult to distinguish fact from fiction or hearsay in their writings. Nonetheless, in spite of these limitations, a conclusion can be drawn that Gnostic traditions in Egypt are contemporary with Christianity and were a constant preoccupation of the Church Fathers.

The evidence of the Church Fathers is supplemented by the Nag Hammadi library, a collection of Gnostic writings, which was discovered in Egypt in 1945. Although the library itself dates, at the earliest, from the second half of the fourth century A.D.,[37] the overwhelming majority of the individual tractates were composed before this time. The provenance of nearly one-third of the tractates has been identified as Egyptian.[38] The

---

[36]Tertullian, *De Praescriptione Haereticorum* 30.

[37]See J. W. Barns' dating of the codex covers in "Greek and Coptic Papyri from the Covers of the Nag Hammadi Codices," in *Essays on the Nag Hammadi Texts in Honor of P. Labib*, ed. M. Krause (NHS 6, Leiden, 1975), 9-17. See also *The Nag Hammadi Library in English*, ed. J. M. Robinson (New York, 1977), 15ff. and more recently, Charles Hedrick, "Gnostic Proclivities in the Greek Life of Pachomius and the Sitz im Leben of the Nag Hammadi Library," *NovT* 22 (1980), 78-95.

[38]In the introductions to the specific tractates of *The Nag Hammadi Library in English*, ed. Robinson, seven tractates have been identified as most likely of Egyptian composition. See *Ap. James* (NHC I, 2), *Hyp. Arch.* (NHC II, 4), *Orig. World* (NHC II, 5 and XIII, 2), *Great Pow.* (NHC VII, 4), *Melch.* (NHC IX, 1), *Norea* (NHC IX, 2) and *Testim. Truth* (NHC IX, 3). In addition, another seven tractates whose provenance was not identified in Robinson, ed., *Nag Hammadi Library*, have been placed in Egypt. See *Ap. John* (NHC II, 1, III, 1 and IV, 1)—H.-Ch. Puech, "Gnostic Gospels and Related Documents," in E. Hennecke and W. Schneemelcher, eds., *New Testament Apocrypha*, trans. R. McL. Wilson (London, 1963), v. 1, 330; *Dial. Sav.* (NHC III, 5)—Puech, "Gnostic Gospels," in Hennecke and Schneemelcher, *New Testament Apocrypha*, v. 1, 250; *Thund.* (NHC VI, 2) —G. Quispel, "Jewish Gnosis and Mandaean Gnosticism," in *Les textes de Nag Hammadi*, ed. J. E. Ménard (NHS 7, Leiden, 1975), 86; *Disc. 8-9* (NHC VI, 6)—K.-W. Tröger, "Die sechste und siebte Schrift aus Nag-Hammadi Codex VI," *TLZ* 98 (1973), 497; *Asclepius* (NHC VI, 8)—J. P. Mahé, "Remarques d'un Latiniste sur l'Asclepius Copte de Nag Hammadi," *RSR* 48 (1974), 136-155; *Steles Seth* (NHC VII, 5)—M. Tardieu, "Les Trois Stèles de Seth," *RSPT* 57 (1973), 558; and *Gos. Egy.* (NHC III, 2 and IV, 2)

Nag Hammadi tractates exhibit several forms of Gnosticism including
Simonian, Basilidean, Sethian and Valentinian. Furthermore, other Gnostic
writings not included in the Nag Hammadi library have been identified as
being of Egyptian origin: The Pistis Sophia,[39] the two Books of Jeu,[40] and
the Poimandres.[41]

Evidence of Gnosticism in Egypt is also extant from classical writers.
For example, Plotinus' acquaintance with Gnosticism resulted in a treatise
against the Gnostics.[42]

In addition to the evidence of Gnostic activity, Egypt is a natural
choice for a number of other reasons. Ptolemaic Egypt was the heart of
the Mediterranean papyrus industry and corn production. Its largest city,
Alexandria, was the leading cultural and intellectual centre in the Hellenistic Age. Its library was renowned, as were its philosophical schools.
Tourists and merchants, scribes and priests, the aristocracy and the
dispossessed, gravitated to Alexandria. All ethnic groups and social
classes would have been present. Thus, in many ways, Alexandria represents a microcosm of the ancient world in this period.

Given this emphasis of the Church Fathers in Egypt, the presumption
that many Gnostic writings were written there, the finding of the Nag
Hammadi library, and the wealth of literary and papyrological evidence
from Egypt, it seems most appropriate to begin there.

1.3.2   Economic Considerations

The Gnostic writings provide little information concerning
economic life. Conversely, a knowledge of the ancient economy may
provide clues regarding the origins of Gnosticism. Mediterranean states
favoured private ownership of land and production. The Graeco-Roman
state depended on the landowner both as a source of capital and as an
indirect manager of the economy. Social structure became increasingly

---

—P. Bellet, "The Colophon of the Gospel of the Egyptians: Concessus and
Marcarius of Nag Hammadi," in R. McL. Wilson, ed., Nag Hammadi and
Gnosis (NHS 14, Leiden, 1978), 50. Thus fourteen of the forty-six trac-
tates listed in the Nag Hammadi Library point to Egypt as a source of
Gnosticism.

[39]Puech, "Gnostic Gospels," in Hennecke and Schneemelcher, New
Testament Apocrypha, v. 1, 252.

[40]Ibid., v. 1, 260.

[41]See R. Reitzenstein, Poimandres (Leipzig, 1904).

[42]Plotinus, Enneads, 2.9.

differentiated and more complex. Many have interpreted this as evidence that the Graeco-Roman world was characterized by a predominance of the slave mode of production.[43] However, Egypt stands out as an exception. In Egypt, the state monopolized property, production and economic management. Only with Roman rule, beginning in 31 B.C., did a trend towards privatization occur, based on individual property ownership, initiative and accountability. Consequently, in the first century A.D., Egypt was economically transformed, and the new economic relations that were created—in particular, the integration of state and slave modes of production—were alien to those which had existed in the Ptolemaic era. This economic transformation in Egypt is unique in the Mediterranean world.

From a sociological point of view, emphasis on the economy serves two important functions: (1) it grounds the analysis in evidence that is not dependent on religious literary sources; and (2) it establishes the sociological roots of the thesis that ideologies are constructed from human experience and that modes of production are correlated to the rise of new *Weltanschauungen*.

1.3.3 Social Considerations

Wherever Gnosticism arose, it was the product of a specific social group or class. Since the discovery of the Nag Hammadi library, there has been an increasing emphasis on the Jewish contribution to Gnosticism. In the nineteen-fifties, Wilson studied the relationship between the thought of Diaspora Judaism and second century Gnosticism and concluded that Judaism "provided a bridge across the gulf which separates the Graeco-Oriental and the Jewish-Christian worlds of thought. Its contribution to the development of Gnosticism was not only direct, through the absorption of Jewish ideas into Gnostic thought, but also in part indirect, since it was through the medium of Jewish speculation that certain pagan elements came into Gnosticism."[44] In particular, Wilson focused on the role of Philo and Alexandrian Judaism, and sought to trace Jewish theories of a syncretistic nature which bore the germs of later Gnostic ideas. In his final summation, however, Gnosticism is a second-century phenomenon, "a phase of heathenism."[45]

---

[43]For example, see P. Anderson, *Passages from Antiquity to Feudalism* (London, 1974), 18-28.
[44]R. McL. Wilson, *The Gnostic Problem* (London, 1958), 182.
[45]Ibid., 256ff.

Since Wilson's study, the incorporation of data from the Nag Hammadi library has led several scholars to re-examine the links between Judaism and Gnosticism. The leading figures of this group are Pearson, Quispel and MacRae. Pearson, in several articles over the last decade, has argued that Gnosticism originated in a Jewish environment, as an expression of alienation from Judaism, and has focused on apostate Jews in Egypt and Syria-Palestine as possible sources.[46] Pearson's position strongly supports Friedländer's thesis[47] of nearly a century ago that pre-Christian sects of an antinomian Gnostic character existed in Alexandria, and "that Gnosticism is not, in its origins, a 'Christian' heresy, but that it is, in fact, a 'Jewish' heresy."[48] Similarly, Quispel has long argued that Gnosticism stems from a Jewish heresy, and attributes its origin to rebellious and heterodox Jews in Palestine or Egypt in the first century A.D.[49] MacRae

---

[46]B. Pearson, "Friedländer Revisited: Alexandrian Judaism and Gnostic Origins," *Studia Philonica* 2 (1973), 23-39; "Jewish Haggadic Traditions in the Testimony of Truth from Nag Hammadi (CG IX.3)," in *Ex Orbe Religionum: Studia Geo Widengren oblata,* ed. J. Bergman, K. Drynjeff and H. Ringgren (*Numen*Sup 21, Leiden, 1973), v. 1, 457-470; "The Thunder: Perfect Mind (CG VI.2)," paper given at Graduate Theological Union, Berkeley, 1973; "The Figure of Melchizedek in the First Tractate of the Unpublished Coptic-Gnostic Codex IX from Nag Hammadi," in *Proceedings of the XIIth International Congress of the International Association for the History of Religions* (Leiden, 1975), 200-208; "Biblical Exegesis in Gnostic Literature," in *Armenian and Biblical Studies,* ed. M. Stone (Jerusalem, 1976), 70-80; "The Figure of Norea in Gnostic Literature," in *Proceedings of the International Colloquium on Gnosticism,* ed. G. Widengren (Stockholm, 1977), 143-152; "Some Observations on Gnostic Hermeneutics," in *The Critical Study of Sacred Texts,* ed., W. D. O'Flaherty (Berkeley, 1979), 243-256; "Gnostic Interpretation of the Old Testament in the Testimony of Truth," *HTR* 73 (1980), 311-319; and "Jewish Elements in Gnosticism and the Development of Gnostic Self-Definition," in *Jewish and Christian Self-Definition,* ed., E. P. Sanders (London, 1980), v. 1, 151-160.

[47]M. Friedländer, *Der vorchristliche jüdische Gnosticismus* (Göttingen, 1898).

[48]Pearson, "Friedländer Revisited," 35.

[49]G. Quispel, "Der gnostische Anthropos und die jüdische Tradition," in *Gnostic Studies* (Istanbul, 1974), v. 1, 173-195; "Gnosticism and the New Testament," in J. P. Hyatt, ed., *The Bible in Modern Scholarship* (Nashville, New York, 1965), 252-271; "The Origins of the Gnostic Demiurge," in *Kyriakon,* ed. P. Granfield and J. A. Jungmann (Münster, 1970), v. 1, 271-276; and "Jewish Gnosis" in Ménard, ed., *Les textes,* 82-122. For a

has advanced the thesis that Jewish origins can explain the fall of Sophia, and connects this fall to a revolt within Judaism.[50] In his words, "no theory today can adequately account for the origins of Gnosticism if it does not give a prominent place—one is tempted to say the most prominent place—to Hellenistic Judaism whether in Alexandria or elsewhere in the Diaspora or even in Palestine. . . . The Gnosticism of the Nag Hammadi documents is not a Christian heresy but if anything a Jewish heresy."[51]

Rudolph,[52] Böhlig[53] and Pokorný[54] have also contributed studies emphasizing the role of heterodox Judaism in the development of Gnosticism. For all these scholars, some variety of heterodox Judaism was transformed and shifted toward a position antithetical to its source. However, a number of other scholars have expressed reservations about the role of Judaism in the origins of Gnosticism. Jonas, for example, refers only to "a zone of proximity,"[55] and Wisse states that "we need no

collection of Quispel's essays, including many which deal with Judaism, see his *Gnostic Studies*.

[50]G. MacRae, "The Jewish Background of the Gnostic Sophia Myth," *NovT* 12 (1970), 86-101. See also "The Coptic Gnostic Apocalypse of Adam," *HeyJ* 6 (1965), 27-35, and "The Apocalypse of Adam Reconsidered," in *Society of Biblical Literature, 1972 Proceedings*, ed., L. C. McGaughy (Missoula, 1972), v. 2, 573-579.

[51]G. MacRae, "Nag Hammadi and the New Testament," in B. Aland, ed., *Gnosis: Festschrift für Hans Jonas* (Göttingen, 1978), 150.

[52]K. Rudolph, "Randerscheinungen des Judentums," 105-122; "Gnosis und Gnostizismus, ein Forschungsbericht," *TRu* 34 (1969), 121-175, 181-231; *Die Gnosis*, especially 291ff; and "Problem einer Soziologie," 35-44.

[53]A. Böhlig, "Der jüdische und jüdenchristliche Hintergrund in gnostischen Texten von Nag Hammadi," in Bianchi, ed., *Origini*, 109-140; A. Böhlig and P. Labib, *Koptisch-gnostische Apocalypsen aus Codex V von Nag Hammadi im koptischen Museum zu Alt-Kairo* (Halle-Wittenberg, 1963); and Böhlig and Labib, *Die Koptisch-gnostische Schrift ohne Titel aus Codex II von Nag Hammadi im koptischen Museum zu Alt-Kairo* (Berlin, 1962).

[54]P. Pokorný, "Der Ursprung der Gnosis," *Kairos* 9 (1967), 94-105 and "Hintergrund," in Tröger, ed., *Gnosis*, 77-87.

[55]Hans Jonas, "Response to G. Quispel's 'Gnosticism and the New Testament,'" in Hyatt, ed., *Bible in Modern Scholarship, 293.*

Jewish Gnosticism nor a virulent anti-Judaism to account for the Jewish elements in gnostic writings."[56]

The view that Gnosticism may be indebted to heterodox Judaism places Egypt in a central position. Egypt is contiguous with Palestine. It had a large and significant Jewish population. Jews in Egypt had economic and religious contact with Palestine and were familiar with Palestinian traditions. A great deal of Jewish heterodox literature was produced in Egypt and a number of Jewish philosophers are well-documented. Philo, in particular, lived in Alexandria and was a contemporary of Jesus. Moreover, there is sufficient papyrological and literary evidence of Jews in Egypt to undertake a sociological analysis. Thus, an examination of the social and economic conditions of Jews in Egypt may shed some light on their role in the emergence of Gnosticism.

1.4   Sociological Considerations

This dissertation is also an attempt to speak to certain methodological and theoretical issues in sociology. Although the founders of sociology made liberal use of *Historismus* and historiography, historical sociology (the testing of hypotheses about social behaviour using data from the past) only has recently become fashionable again. The character of the two disciplines is complementary; as Hughes states, "the systematic elaboration of sociology (although) subordinate to the procedures of historical knowledge (offers) a conceptual apparatus designed to make possible the understanding of human behaviour in the concrete 'becoming' of . . . individual events in the world of history."[57] History is "the shank of social study."[58]

The study of historical phenomena poses methodological issues for the sociologist. The ontological distinction between *Geist* and *Natur,* between the cultural and the natural sciences, requires the student of history to take account of more than the material underpinnings of human experiences. Sociology can draw on natural-science models of explanation, but

---

[56]F. Wisse, "Do the Jewish Elements in Gnostic Writings Prove the Existence of a Jewish Gnosticism?", paper presented at the annual meeting of the Society of Biblical Literature/American Academy of Religion, New York, 1979, 11.

[57]H. Stuart Hughes, *Consciousness and Society* (New York, 1961), 325. For a recent account of how the two disciplines are complementary see Peter Burke, *Sociology and History* (London, 1980).

[58]C. W. Mills, *The Sociological Imagination* (Oxford, 1959), 143.

stands apart from them in seeking to employ an interpretive mode. For
"all knowledge of cultural reality . . . is always knowledge from particular
points of view."[59]

Max Weber's empirical studies of religion are the classic examples of
how the sociology of religion can both remain firmly rooted within the
framework of history and at the same time incorporate an understanding
of human behaviour into the context of unique events. Weber's studies are
part of a comparative historical examination of religion and social structure in Europe, China, India and Palestine.[60] The themes of these studies
reflect his fundamental preoccupation with the relationship between
socio-economic conditions and ideology, and especially with the way ideas
function as independent variables in social change. In *The Protestant
Ethic and the Spirit of Capitalism* Weber sought to explain the emergence
of capitalism and concurrently to challenge Marx's historical materialism.
According to Birnbaum, in one sense "Weber made explicit what Marx left
implicit."[61] Weber tried to demonstrate the intimate relationship between
the predominant psychological state and the historical process, in order to
show that values and meanings are as potent considerations in societal
evolution as material factors. As Weber puts it:

> We only wish to ascertain whether and to what extent reli-
> gious forces have taken part in the qualitative formation and
> the quantitative expansion of that spirit [i.e., capitalism] over
> the world, [and] what concrete aspects of our capitalistic
> culture can be traced to them [i.e., the Reformation]. . . . We
> can only proceed by investigating whether and at what points
> certain correlations between forms of religious belief and
> practical ethics can be worked out . . . [and] clarify the
> manner and the general direction in which, by virtue of those

[59]M. Weber, *The Methodology of the Social Sciences*, trans. E. Shils
and H. Finch (New York, 1949), 84.

[60]Max Weber, *The Protestant Ethic and the Spirit of Capitalism*, trans.
T. Parsons (New York, 1958), *The Religion of China-Confucianism and
Taoism*, trans. and ed. H. H. Gerth (New York, 1964), *The Religion of
India-The Sociology of Hinduism and Buddhism*, trans. and ed. H. H. Gerth
and D. Martindale (Glencoe, 1958) and *Ancient Judaism*, trans. and ed.
H. H. Gerth and D. Martindale (New York, 1952).

[61]N. Birnbaum, "Conflicting Interpretations of the Rise of Capitalism:
Marx and Weber," *British Journal of Sociology* 4/2 (1953), 125-141.

relationships, the religious movements have influenced the development of material culture.[62]

Weber's aim was to demonstrate how "ideas become effective forces in history"[63] by documenting how an ethic originally formulated for other-worldly purposes became transmuted, even if unintentionally, into a stimulus for material gain. His conclusion, after studying the relative effects of material and ideological factors in the rise of capitalism in the West among Catholics and Protestants, was that the dynamic force of Puritanism was the decisive factor. By drawing attention to the differences between Protestants and Catholics in terms of their inclination toward technical, industrial and commercial occupations, Weber argued that the former were to a greater degree oriented towards "economic rationality."

For Weber, "the principal explanation of this difference between Protestanism and Catholicism must be sought in the permanent intrinsic character of their religious beliefs, and not only in their temporary external historico-political situations."[64] Lutheranism produced the concept of *Beruf*, a 'calling' which referred to the morally dutiful fulfillment of a task assigned by God; but Luther's concept of 'calling' was totally opposed to usury and "economic rationality." Rather it was Calvin's teaching of 'predestination' that unintentionally transformed Luther's doctrine into an ethical form conducive to capitalist enterprise. According to Weber, Calvin's doctrine of 'predestination' created a psychological dilemma for the believer. To avoid the existential burden of this dilemma a 'sign' was required which would designate the 'elect.' Thus, good works became the 'sign' of 'election.' Luther's individualistic 'calling' was transformed and secularized by Calvin and became for 'predestination' what the confession was to free will. To Weber, the Protestant Ethic meant "work, the morally dutiful pursuit of a calling and a belief that God helps those who help themselves."[65] In Puritanism the spirit of religious asceticism came to fruition. "Puritanism carried the ethos of the rational organization of capital . . . in which the Puritan idea of the calling and the premium it placed upon ascetic conduct was bound directly to influence the development of a capitalistic way of life."[66] Protestant asceticism not only

---

[62]Weber, *Protestant Ethic*, 91f.

[63]Ibid., 90.

[64]Ibid., 40.

[65]I. Zeitlin, *Ideology and the Development of Sociological Theory* (Englewood Cliffs, N. J., 1968), 128.

[66]Weber, *Protestant Ethic*, 166.

restricted the consumption of goods and their enjoyment, but also freed the acquisition of goods from the inhibitions of traditional ethics.[67] Work as a 'calling' was the highest means to asceticism, proof of 'election' and the lever for the rise of the spirit of capitalism.

Weber's innovative combination of religious data (e.g., Luther, Calvin, Franklin, Baxter and Wesley), with secular data (from Germany, Switzerland, England, the Netherlands and France) demonstrated that spiritual manifestations can play active or passive roles in social change. His subsequent analysis of the role of religious ideologies in ancient China, India and Palestine was designed to show that his conclusions in The Protestant Ethic were valid in other historical contexts. In each case he concluded that the characteristics of these religions were obstacles to the development of capitalism. Buddhism and Hinduism lacked an ethic that endorsed the life of rationally-oriented commerce and industry; Confucianism taught traditionalism and moderation; and Judaism was a marginal religion marked by an ethical dualism that was unfavourable for the rise of a capitalist ethos.

Weber's efforts to integrate historicism with sociology are acknowledged and supported in this dissertation; but the dissertation adopts a different and non-Weberian theoretical orientation. Following Marx, ideas are treated in this study as dependent variables in social change; socioeconomic contexts are taken as the crucial independent variables.[68] The forces and relations of production are viewed as central to the production of life.

From a Marxist perspective the mode of production in Egypt can be described as Asiatic.[69] The state is powerful, centralized and based on hydraulic agriculture. However, the notion of the Asiatic mode of production as it is now used is diffuse and unwieldly. Anderson has

---

[67]Ibid., 171.

[68]For a methodological discussion regarding the various approaches of economic history and the role of the social scientist see E. Tuma, Economic History and the Social Sciences (Berkeley, Los Angeles, 1971).

[69]For a short comprehensive overview of the Asiatic mode of production, including bibliography, see P. Anderson, Lineages of the Absolutist State (London, 1974), Note B, "The 'Asiatic Mode of Production,'" 462-549. For a collection of essays, see Sur le 'mode de production asiatique', Centre d'études et de recherches marxistes (Paris, 1969) and D. Seddon, ed., Relations of Production (London, 1978).

eloquently summarized the consequences of its indiscriminate application to non-Western civilizations.

> To mix such immensely disparate historical forms and epochs under a single rubric is to end with the same *reductio ad absurdum* produced by an indefinite extension of feudalism; if so many different socio-economic formations, of such contrasting levels of civilization, are all contracted to one mode of production, the fundamental divisions and changes of history must derive from another source altogether, that has nothing to do with the Marxist conception of modes of production. The inflation of ideas, like coins, merely leads to their devaluation.[70]

Godelier has argued that given this predicament "the theoretical task is to draw up a typology of the various forms of this mode of production" including those that would evolve "from certain forms of the Asiatic mode of production to certain forms of feudalism, without going through a slave stage."[71] The economic argument presented in this study contributes to this typology by examining a particular historical example—the Ptolemaic mode of production—from the conquest of Egypt by Alexander the Great to the end of the first century A.D. Or, stated more generally, it is a case study of certain pre-capitalist social and economic formations, through an examination of the modes of production which characterized them, and of their transformation.

This dissertation, therefore, should be regarded as a pilot study, an attempt to apply social-scientific paradigms to the examination of ancient religions, and specifically Gnosticism. Through its use of sociological analysis, new insights as well as a different way of understanding religious texts may be achieved.

1.5   Hypotheses and Outline

The dissertation has two central theses: (1) that the transformation in the Ptolemaic mode of production towards privatization was

---

[70] Anderson, *Lineages,* 486f.

[71] M. Godelier, "The Concept of the 'Asiatic Mode of Production' and Marxist Models of Social Evolution," in Seddon, ed., *Relations of Production,* 242 and 245.

structurally related to the ideology of individualism embodied in Gnosticism; and (2) that certain Jews in Egypt, experiencing this change in the mode of production, acted as catalysts in the sectarian development of Judaism and hence played a pivotal role in the emergence of Gnosticism. The dissertation is placed within the context of both the sociology of knowledge and the sociology of religion. It is concerned with understanding the emergence of a religious movement in terms of the dialectical relationship between social and institutional factors, culture and consciousness. It follows Weber's historical sociology of socio-cultural processes but approaches the subject matter from a materialist rather than an idealist perspective. It posits that there is a "significant equivalence" between the spirit of privatization within the Ptolemaic mode of production and the Gnostic ethic of individualism.[72]

The remaining chapters of the dissertation are organized as follows: Chapter 2 describes the Ptolemaic mode of production under both the Greeks and the Romans, and the corresponding change in the management of the economy from state domination to privatization. It analyses the division of labour in Egyptian society and the changes in status of minority social groups. Finally, it comments on the effect of technology, and the role of Alexandria as a cosmopolitan centre in antiquity.

Chapter 3 examines the presence, role and significance of the Jews in Egypt and the effects of the transformation in the Ptolemaic mode of production on Egyptian Jewry. The economic, social and cultural links of these Jews to Palestine, as well as their efforts to accommodate themselves to Hellenistic society, are explored in order to show the material context of their alienation.

Chapter 4 provides a typological model of the possible responses to this alienation, and looks at the Jewish origins of Gnosticism. It relates the process of economic privatization to the theme of individualism in the Gnostic ethos, behaviour and social organization. Chapter 5 presents the conclusions.

---

[72]The sense in which 'individualism' is used can be understood more clearly in the French word *individualité* (or the German *individualität*) implying personal independence or self-realization. See Steven Lukes, *Individualism* (Oxford, 1973).

2
The Material Presence

2.1   Introduction

This chapter is focused on the interrelationship of economic structures and social change. It is concerned with changes in the pattern of property holding, production, and economic management that occurred in the Ptolemaic state before and after the Roman conquest in 31 B.C. These changes took place over several centuries. However, their impact was felt fully only after the conquest of Egypt by Augustus and the integration of Ptolemaic and Roman economic relations; then these transformed economic relations became elements of a new social formation[1] alien to that which had existed in the Ptolemaic period.

To understand the socio-economic circumstances in which Gnosticism developed, it is necessary to examine the nature of economic life in antiquity, and in particular the Ptolemaic mode of production. The foundations of economic activity in the ancient world were qualitatively different from our own. Although agriculture was the basis of economic life for all classes and the foundation for commercial and industrial development, "rationalized agriculture" was unknown;[2] nor was there "an enormous conglomeration of interdependent markets"[3] constituting a

---

[1]A social formation is a "concrete combination of different modes of production, organized under the dominance of one of them." See P. Anderson, *Passages from Antiquity to Feudalism* (London, 1974), 22, fn. 6.

[2]G. Mickwitz, "Economic Rationalism in Graeco-Roman Agriculture," *The English Historical Review* 52 (1937), 577-589. See also M. I. Finley, *The Ancient Economy* (Berkeley and Los Angeles, 1973), 117ff.

[3]Finley, *Ancient Economy*, 22 and 33; in contrast, for example, to F. M. Heichelheim, *An Ancient Economic History*, trans. J. Stevens (Leiden, 1970), v. 3.

single complex economic unit. More profoundly, this analysis is guided by an important methodological consideration. The economy of antiquity was not simply one involving fewer people and less commerce and manufacturing than that of modernity. Nor can it be interpreted by transferring the "categories of . . . capitalist production and exchange, . . . class structure, [and] ideological configurations."[4] Essentially, Ptolemaic and Roman Egypt did not experience "the same process of development"[5] as that of Western Europe today.

It is also necessary to examine certain developments involving the Ptolemaic state in the period surrounding the Roman conquest. These developments are important in indicating a trend towards privatization under Roman rule. This trend is manifested in the transformation of the Ptolemaic state's monopolization of property, production, and economic management and the introduction of new patterns based on individual ownership, initiative and accountability. A comparative examination of the modes of production of Ptolemaic Egypt and Roman Egypt through the first century A.D. shows that the Roman conquest initiated a three-fold transition: from state to private ownership of property; from state monopolization of production and distribution to a mixture of private initiative and state monopolization; and from state (bureaucratic) management of economic life and revenue collection to policies reflecting a degree of decentralization and private accountability. In many cases, these developments were very gradual, and some of the seeds were planted by the Ptolemies themselves. However, these seeds remained dormant. They germinated only after the conquest by Augustus and attained fruition in the development of a social formation alien to the intrinsic nature of the Ptolemaic mode of production.

2.2   The Ptolemaic Mode of Production

2.2.1   Theoretical Description and Suggested Features

As outlined in Chapter 1, the Asiatic mode of production needs to be given greater specificity in its historical application. The following section examines the Ptolemaic mode of production as an instance of the

---

[4]M. Reinhold, "Historian of the Classic World: A Critique of Rostovtzeff," *Science and Society* 10 (1946), 363.

[5]In contrast to M. Rostovtzeff; see his *A History of the Ancient World* (Oxford, 1945[2]), v. 1, 10.

Asiatic one in the context of current scholarly opinion that "l'économie ptolémaique relève plus du mode de production asiatique que du mode de production esclavagiste."[6] Subsequent sections examine the historical application of this concept through an examination of the social and economic data as well as of later historical literature. The Asiatic mode of production arose in countries with great stretches of desert, where climate and soil conditions required public irrigation and hydraulic works and where a centralized state had a monopoly over land production. "Artificial irrigation is here the first condition of agriculture and this is a matter for . . . the central government. . . .[Hence,] the absence of private property in land is indeed the key to the whole of the East. Herein lies its political and religious history. . . ."[7]

In a situation of monopoly state land ownership, the direct producer is not the legal owner, but only the possessor of the usufruct of the land. The state "stands over them [the possessors] as their landlord and simultaneously as sovereign. . . . rents and taxes coincide. No private ownership of land exists, although there is both private and common possession . . . of land."[8] As the owner of the land, the state also controls the means of production and distribution, and acquires the surplus labour and surplus product of the producers either by tax or rent. These two elements—ownership of land and ownership of production—are the two necessary conditions for the performance of the state's economic management function.

State management of the economy is based on the fact that the state is personified in and identified with the king. Those who manage the economy on the king's behalf benefit from his surplus. Hence, class differentiation develops as the managerial class appropriates the labour and production of the class of direct producers.[9] Although both classes can

---

[6]See Modrzejewski's comments to D. Bonneau's paper, "Esclavage et irrigation d'après la documentation papyrologique," in *Actes du Colloque 1973 sur l'esclavage* (Annales Littéraires de l'Université de Besançon 182, Paris, 1976), 327.

[7]K. Marx and F. Engels, *Selected Correspondence* (New York, 1942), 66ff.

[8]K. Marx, *Capital* (New York, 1967), v. 3, 791. See also 30ff. below for the significance of 'ownership' and 'possession' of land in Ptolemaic law.

[9]For the development of class structures in the Asiatic mode of production see M. Godelier, "The Concept of the 'Asiatic Mode of Production' and Marxist Models of Social Evolution," in Seddon, ed., *Relations of Production*, 209-257. Lukács states that in pre-capitalist societies "status

possess land, the majority of the population (the productive class) have no
right to their own surplus. In addition, the producers are not protected
from taxation, compulsory labour and expropriation, and are subject to
direction by the state's representatives.[10] These representatives, who
manage the economy on behalf of the king, are elements of the central
bureaucracy that guarantees irrigation, high agricultural productivity and
the payment of taxes to the royal treasury.

In the Asiatic mode of production there is no pronounced division of
labour. As always, the stage of production and the character of the division of labour are related. Specialization in agriculture and crafts is
circumscribed by the lack of applied technology. Most products are consumed at the village level, with the surplus being forwarded to the owner
(i.e., the king) or those who represent his interests (e.g., aristocrats,
bureaucrats). Consequently, it is the state that transforms the surplus of
natural resources into industrial commodities. For the most part, this
development takes place in the cities or administrative centres where
labour is more plentiful and where the wealthier families reside. These
sites are also the major centres for the consumption of surplus products
and industrial commodities. The larger the population centre the greater
the hinterland of rural villages required to support it, and the more intensive the industry and commerce within the centre.

In the following analysis several of these characteristics will be applied
to the Ptolemaic mode of production and investigated in some detail to
support the hypothesis that the Ptolemaic state's monopolization of
property, production and management of the economy was transformed
under Rome's authority. Those of primary importance include: (1) state
monopoly of land and the absence of private ownership; (2) the existence
of public irrigation; (3) state control of the means of production and
distribution; (4) the city as industrial producer and major consumer;
(5) state management of the economy through a centralized bureaucracy;
and (6) class stratification.

---

consciousness . . . masks class consciousness"; see G. Lukács, *History and
Class Consciousness*, trans. R. Livingstone (Cambridge, 1971), 58.
  [10] Marx called this "general slavery" since exploitation of man by man
occurred. However, "general slavery" is distinct from Roman slavery as it
is not a bond of dependence on another individual; personal freedom still
exists. See Marx, *Pre-Capitalist Economic Formations*, ed. E. Hobsbawm
(London, 1964), 95.

2.2.2   The Historical Application

Since prehistoric times, Egypt's lifeline has been the Nile river. Irrigation farming to this day remains necessary in order to nourish the dry soil and to encourage the collection of silt along the natural tributaries and man-made canals. Without irrigation, climate and soil conditions would inevitably create a vast desert (see table 1). Nearly every village or city during the Ptolemaic-Roman epoch was therefore in proximity of its banks (see map 1). To describe Egypt as no more than a ribbon of inhabited land bordering the Nile would be no exaggeration—even at its peak when Josephus claimed that its population, exclusive of Alexandria, was seven and a half million.[11] Nevertheless, these villages produced enough wheat to supply both domestic and foreign markets. The surplus of wheat, however, was directly dependent upon the proper maintenance of the irrigation system. Further, the proper maintenance of the irrigation system was dependent on the dominant class being able to control the means of production.

Ptolemaic Egypt lent itself to state ownership of property; geography facilitated centralized management. Under the Pharaohs the state had been personified in and identified with the king. Egypt was his private property, his personal estate, his dwelling. The exploitation of the country's resources and their distribution were for him to decide. The inhabitants of the country were personally bonded to him and obliged to honour his requisitions (e.g., the *corvée*). Thus, the early Ptolemies, by adopting policies that favoured state ownership, in many ways were responding only to the demands of the natural terrain and re-establishing the Pharaonic tradition. In Egypt productivity had always depended on state intervention. Under the Ptolemies, such intervention was embodied in a variety of measures. They enlarged the available areas of cultivation,[12] ensured public irrigation, instituted an intricate web of royal monopolies over farm implements, seeds and other necessities, diversified agricultural production, introduced new technology and further centralized and bureaucratized the management of the economy.

---

[11]Josephus, *War*, 2.385.

[12]Enlarged areas of cultivation in the Philadelphia area resulted in the erection of 114 new villages of which nearly two-thirds had Greek names. See M. Avi-Yonah, *Hellenism and the East* (Jerusalem, 1978), 197.

Table 1
Conditions of Irrigation in Ptolemaic-Roman Egypt*

climate	semi-tropical
rainfall per year	20.3—30.5 cm per year
average summer temperature	$43^{\circ}C$
average winter temperature	$12^{\circ}C$
months of the floods	August to early October
season after the floods	winter
increase in water quantity	4x
rise of water	5—7m
surrounding countryside	lime and sandstone hills
type of silt	clay with up to 20% sand
profile of river valley	concave, slope towards sea, 1:13,000
system of irrigation	basin
effects of irrigation	tendency to extract salt; very slow silting up of canals

*Source: R. J. Forbes, *Studies in Ancient Technology* (Leiden, 1965), v. 2, 5 and 15.

Map 1
Urban Centres in Ptolemaic-Roman Egypt*

*Source: J. A. Wilson, "Buto and Hierakonpolis in the Geography of Egypt," *Journal of Near Eastern Studies* 14 (1955), 211-213.

Map 1 (continued)

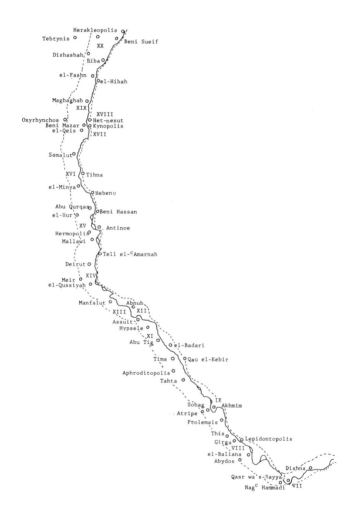

Map 1 (continued)

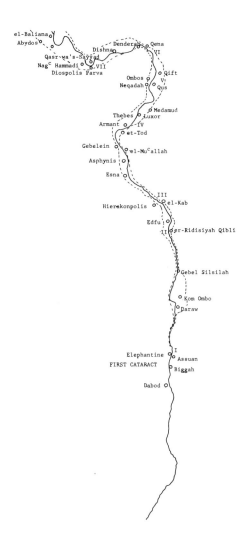

Under the Ptolemies all agricultural land was owned by the king. This principle is clearly established in Ptolemaic law where ownership and possession are distinguished. "Private property of land was not featured in Ptolemaic law . . ."[13] as "legal ownership of all land in Egypt resided in the king."[14] For administrative purposes, however, land fell into two main categories: royal (βασιλικὴ γῆ—under the direct administration of the king or his agents) and land under grant (γῆ ἐν ἀφέσει—under the indirect administration of the king or his agents). Land under grant can be further divided into temple (ἱερά), cleruch or veteran (κληρουχική), gift estate (γῆ ἐν δωρεᾶ) and private (ἰδιόκτητος).[15]

Royal land comprised most of the land in Egypt. Owned by the king, this land was leased according to its productive category[16] on short term leases to free Egyptian peasants.[17] Administrative agents of the king informed the lessee as to what and how much was to be planted on the land. The royal tenant had to swear an oath to remain present from the sowing to the harvesting and not to desert the land.[18] He was also bound to keep the land from deteriorating. All necessary means of production had to be leased from royal monopolies (e.g., agricultural implements and seed). The lessee was not entitled to a percentage of the harvest; the state's share "was a pars quanta, not quota."[19] The lessee was also liable for the corvée and responsible for a variety of taxes such as "one artaba of wheat for each arura cultivated; half an artaba for surveying, fees for guards, for storage, for using the threshing-floor, for cleaning the wheat for transport, dues to officials, etc. etc."[20] Invariably, with such a tax burden, in hard economic times the peasant deserted the land, productivity fell and the irrigation system was not properly maintained. During the Ptolemaic period the total amount of royal land increased due to

---

[13]R. Taubenschlag, The Law of Graeco-Roman Egypt in the Light of the Papyri (Warsaw, 1955²), 232ff.

[14]S. LeRoy Wallace, Taxation in Egypt (Oxford, 1938), 1.

[15]Taubenschlag, Law, 233ff. (based on P. Tebt. 27.54). Cf. M. Rostovtzeff, SEHHW, v. 1, 276ff. and C. Préaux, L'Économie royale des Lagides (Brussels, 1939), 459ff.

[16]For a discussion of productive categories, see below 42 and fn. 88.

[17]Prosopographic statistics indicate that the majority of the royal tenants were from the native population. See Avi-Yonah, Hellenism, 109 and 157ff.

[18]Rostovtzeff, SEHHW, v. 1, 279ff.

[19]Ibid., loc. cit.

[20]Avi-Yonah, Hellenism, 206.

confiscations (e.g., *doreae* or gift estates), the abandonment of land by *cleruchs* and the passing of land from individuals who died intestate.[21] Temple land belonged to the king who assigned it to the gods. The priests, as the gods' civil servants, possessed the land[22] and were given long term leases. Priests were granted the right to grow crops of their own choosing but like royal peasants, had to lease the means of production from royal monopolies. Temple land was sometimes liable for taxes at a rate similar to that assessed on *cleruch* land and sometimes free.[23] Temple industries were re-defined and by the time of the Revenue Laws of Ptolemy Philadelphus had lost their monopolistic rights on oil and textile manufacture to the state.[24] Henceforth they were permitted to service the needs of the temples but were not allowed to compete with the industries of the state. These industries were subject to state taxes and were watched closely. Priests were not liable for the *corvée*.[25] Temple land was more extensive in Upper than Lower Egypt. Otto estimated that in the second century B.C. in Upper Egypt one-tenth of the total cultivated land belonged to the temples.[26]

Cleruch land refers to land that was allotted to soldiers in return for military service and served in lieu of salaries. Land allotments were regulated by rank and nationality of the holder and ranged from approximately 5 to 120 *arurae*.[27] For example, the normal allotment of a native Egyptian *machimos* was 7 *arurae*,[28] compared to that of a Macedonian

---

[21]A. S. Saad similarly has postulated that the majority of cultivated land at the end of the Ptolemaic period was royal. See "Le Mode de production asiatique et les problèmes de la formation sociale Égyptienne," *La Pensée* 189 (October, 1976), 27.

[22]Rostovtzeff, *SEHHW*, v. 1, 280ff.

[23]Wallace, *Taxation,* 3.

[24]J. A. S. Evans, "A Social and Economic History of an Egyptian Temple in the Graeco-Roman Period," *Yale Classical Studies* 17 (1961), 211.

[25]Taubenschlag, *Law,* 618ff.

[26]See Max Weber, *The Agrarian Sociology of Ancient Civilizations,* trans. R. I. Frank (London, 1976), 241, for Otto's estimation. Although the total area of temple land in Lower Egypt was less, individual temple estates may have been quite large. Evans ("Egyptian Temple," 213) states that the temple of Soknebtunis "had an estate of at least 630$\frac{1}{4}$ *arurae* during the latter years of the Ptolemaic dynasty. . . ."

[27]Avi-Yonah, *Hellenism,* 106ff.

[28]Ibid., 110.

who averaged 80 *arurae* in the second century B.C.[29] A *cleruch* was not
constrained by administrative agents regarding the cultivation of his land
(excluding oil-producing plants) although, like the peasant on royal land,
all means of production necessary for agricultural purposes had to be
leased from the royal monopolies. A *cleruch* was also responsible for
several taxes (e.g., guard fees, upkeep of embankments) but was not liable
for the *corvée* except in times of emergency.[30] Greek *cleruchs* tended to
employ local labour or lease their lands to Egyptian peasants in contrast
to the Egyptian *machimoi* who worked their own land.[31] In spite of the
fact that these grants passed from father to son on condition that the heir
would accept his father's military duties as incumbent upon himself, the
claim of a statutory successor was not recognized by the state until the
last quarter of the third century B.C.[32] Before this period the *cleruch*
legally "had no right to sell, mortgage, or bequeath his allotment."[33]
Another century and more was to pass before this right "passed over to
the *proximi agnati*."[34] Thus, for the greater part of the Ptolemaic period
the state could confiscate the land for a variety of legal and political
reasons (e.g., no heir, deserted, non-compliance of duties).

   Cleruch land never amounted to a large percentage of the total arable
land and Avi-Yonah has postulated that even at its peak (third century)
only "about two million *arurae* were held by the military settlers, most of
them foreigners."[35] Evidence suggests that until the mid-second century
B.C. preference for land allotments was given to foreigners (mostly
Greeks) with individual Macedonians having the largest holdings and
accredited the highest social status, although as a group, they held less

---

[29]Ibid., 107.
[30]Taubenschlag, *Law*, 618 and fn. 38.
[31]Avi-Yonah, *Hellenism*, 144.
[32]Rostovtzeff, *SEHHW*, v. 2, 727.
[33]Ibid., v. 1, 286.
[34]Taubenschlag, *Law*, 237. See, for example, BGU 1185.
[35]Avi-Yonah, *Hellenism*, 111. Avi-Yonah's estimation of two million
arurae is too high if the total amount of cultivated land in Ptolemaic
Egypt was more or less identical to that of Roman Egypt. See below 62ff.
and G. M. Parassoglou, *Imperial Estates in Roman Egypt* (American
Studies in Papyrology 18, Amsterdam, 1978), 44, who has suggested
approximately seven million *arurae* as the total area of cultivable land in
the first century A.D. Nevertheless, Avi-Yonah's basic assumption
remains cogent.

than 10% of the total *cleruch* allotments.[36] Thereafter the total number of Greek *cleruchs* considerably declined and Persians of the *Epigone* (i.e., Semites) were granted increasing status.[37] In the third century Greeks totalled 31% of the military population; in the first less than 2%. In contrast, Semites totalled 4% of the military population in the third century and over two-thirds in the first.[38] Upward mobility and Semite military settlement are highly correlated. This rise in status became solidified for certain ethnic minorities in the following century and a half (e.g., Jews) and coincided with the loosening of property laws with regard to *cleruchs*. However, *cleruchs* were never given the "unrestricted right of disposal until the Roman era."[39]

Gift estates (i.e., *doreae*), refer to land that was allotted to the king's chief advisors (military or civilian) for political patronage. Most of this land was distributed in the third century to Macedonians or other Greek nationals.[40] These estates tended to be quite large. For example, Apollonius at Philadelphia in the Fayum had an estate of 10,000 *arurae*. As with the *cleruchs*, these allotments served in lieu of salaries and thereby contributed indirectly to the wealth of the king. Those granted *doreae* were free to manage their estates as they saw fit (e.g., lease it, plant a variety of crops, etc.) although they were dependent on government monopolies for the means of production. For example, in the above-mentioned estate of Apollonius, "every phase of [agricultural] activity in Philadelphia is regulated by the administrative machine of the Ptolemies. . . ."[41] Like the *cleruchs* these land-holders were not liable for the *corvée* except in an emergency.[42] Yet in spite of these privileges the king retained ownership of the land and could confiscate it if he thought his interests were being abused.[43]

---

[36]Avi-Yonah, *Hellenism*, 107.

[37]Ibid., 107ff. and Weber, *Agrarian Sociology*, 238. For the identification of Persians of the *Epigone* with Semites see Avi-Yonah, *Hellenism*, 107.

[38]Avi-Yonah, *Hellenism*, 109.

[39]Taubenschlag, *Law*, 238.

[40]According to Avi-Yonah's data (*Hellenism*, 158 and fn. 142), out of a total of 47 *doreae*, only 5 were granted outside of the third century A.D. For a discussion of the *doreae* see M. Rostovtzeff, *A Large Estate in the Third Century B.C.* (New York, 1979 [1922]), 42ff.

[41]Rostovtzeff, *Large Estate*, 127.

[42]Taubenschlag, *Law*, 618 and fn. 38.

[43]For example, Apollonius' estates were confiscated by Ptolemy III and

Although ἰδιόκτητος falls under the category of land under grant both Rostovtzeff[44] and Taubenschlag[45] contend that the true meaning of the term is still obscure. On the one hand, there seems to be some consensus that non-agricultural land (e.g., building lots) and in certain cases vineyards and garden plots could be privately owned.[46] On the other hand, according to the nature of Ptolemaic law the king *de jure* owned all arable land and had the right of confiscation. Rostovtzeff has suggested that the conditions surrounding the ἰδιόκτητος with regard to arable land "probably existed in Pharaonic times . . . [and] the Ptolemies did not resort to confiscation or similar measures in respect of this land, but accepted the *de facto* situation."[47] He points out, however, that the land was taxed, that the state monitored the cultivation of crops and had recourse to confiscation and sale of the land in lieu of taxes.[48] Consequently, one can only surmise that if private ownership of arable land existed, it was marginal. Its importance therefore lies, in conjunction with the changes in *cleruch* land, in demonstrating that "the possession of arable land underwent a transitory stage . . ."[49] in the Ptolemaic era, and that the seeds of private ownership were planted before the Roman conquest.

Since the king (i.e., the state) owned all the agricultural land and since land was the basis of production in antiquity, intervention in the functioning of the economy was not difficult. This was embodied in state policy in two fundamental ways: by controlling labour and by controlling production. The state controlled labour by maintaining that the divinity of the king invested him with the right to requisition the services of his subjects. Thus, through the method of the *corvée*, the agricultural population was obliged in one way or another to build and repair the canals and dikes necessary for cultivation and transportation.[50] The state was therefore instrumental in the maintenance and the expansion of the irrigation

---

most likely incorporated within the royal land in the area. See T. Frank, *An Economic History of Rome* (New York, 1962[2] rev.), 386.

[44]Rostovtzeff, *SEHHW*, v. 1, 289ff.

[45]Taubenschlag, *Law*, 233ff.

[46]Ibid., loc. cit.

[47]Rostovtzeff, *SEHHW*, v. 1, 289ff.

[48]Ibid., v. 1, 290.

[49]Taubenschlag, *Law*, 235.

[50]See above 30ff. regarding the discussion of the administrative categories of land and those liable for the *corvée*. Cf. Taubenschlag, *Law*, 618ff. The *corvée* required the individual to devote five days of his labour to the state without pay. See Frank, *Economic History*, 383.

system and hydraulic works. Secondly, in terms of production, the state merely prefixed the word royal before anything it wished to control. Consequently there were royal granaries, industries, woods, ponds, and so on. In fact everything produced, directly or indirectly, was viewed as a means of providing revenue for the king. Thus the state, as owner, manager and distributer of production, left little room for private initiative. "In the Ptolemaic kingdom, we have no written record of any sector of the economy, of which the state did not take full advantage for its own ends. . . ."[51] "Complete free trade . . . did not exist in any branch of the economic activity of the subjects of the Ptolemies."[52] If he participated in the industrial or commercial sectors of the economy the inhabitant of Egypt encountered a monopolistic state enterprise.

The complex web of monopolies instituted by the Ptolemies touched all branches of economic life.[53] For example, with regard to wheat the state had a monopoly of the means of production (e.g., seeds, agricultural tools, ability to provide labour to keep the canals open, etc.) and its distribution. The royal peasant, the *cleruch*, the possessor of the gift estate and the priest were all dependent on the state. Furthermore, everyone's harvest was delivered to royal granaries (tax or rent in kind) and from there by royal ships to royal warehouses. For those who leased royal land, state intervention was even greater. They were informed as to what and how much to plant and were constantly under the supervision of royal bureaucrats. Consequently, the royal peasant had to contend with state supervisors, taxes, rents and the *corvée*. For example, on an average wheat yield of 10 *artabae* to an *arura*, half the peasant's surplus was due to the state outright, and the other half had to be sold to the state at a price which was previously set by the state.[54]

Major industries were monopolized and directed to varying degrees (e.g., oil from sesame, beer from barley, paper from papyrus, aromatic products from flowers). The state would decide how much oil would be needed in a given year and prescribe how much sesame each farmer had to grow. State seeds would then be sold to royal bureaucrats *(sitologoi)* in charge of the state stores who would distribute them and supervise the cultivation and harvesting. The farmer would plant, harvest and deposit

---

[51]Heichelheim, *Ancient Economic History*, v. 3, 189.

[52]Rostovtzeff, *Large Estate*, 142.

[53]See Avi-Yonah, *Hellenism*, 194-218; Taubenschlag, *Law*, 658-684; Rostovtzeff, *SEHHW*, v. 1, 255-422 and Préaux, *Économie royale*.

[54]Avi-Yonah, *Hellenism*, 206.

the crop in a royal store. Then oil would be produced in state-owned village mills. The labourers in these mills were compelled to produce a specified amount each day and were paid a state salary. Once produced, the oil was distributed to local merchants who had previously bought a retail concession (i.e., a licence) for a particular village. These merchants would then sell the oil to the villagers at a price set by the state. Thus, the state not only controlled all aspects of the production and distribution process (seeds, planting, harvesting, milling, retailing) but also made the state officials liable by having them buy the royal seeds and thereby become personally responsible for oil revenues.

The list of full or partial state monopolies during the Ptolemaic period is impressive: hunting and fishing that took place in royal woods or on royal rivers and lakes; the sale of timber; banking and foreign exchange; the production of textiles (hemp, linen, wool), nitre, alum, leather, or spices; and arboriculture, among others.[55] Similarly, the ability to control the distribution process also must be viewed as a considerable achievement. This was done by restricting trading activity to those who had bought concessions at auction; a concession allowed a trader only to sell commodities at a price fixed by the king. Monopolization of the means of production by the Ptolemies also meant control over distribution and the retail trade. "The trade in almost all the goods was carried out not by free merchants but by *concessionaires* of the king in a certain limited district, for a certain time, and for a certain kind of goods. . . ."[56] As a result, the state reaped in every possible way a surplus (in kind or coin) at the expense of the wage-earner's or farmer's labour. The extent of this surplus is staggering. With regard to wheat, for example, Heichelheim has postulated that taxation in kind and rents could account for as much as 90% of Ptolemaic wheat exports.[57] Fraser has summarized the monopolization of the Ptolemaic economy as follows:

> The economic life of Egypt was therefore dominated by the monopolistic system, in which both natural products themselves and the products of industries practised on a large

---

[55] Even baths were on principle monopolized by the state; Greeks and Egyptians had to pay a capitation tax for their maintenance. See C. Préaux, "La Taxe des bains dans l'Égypte Romaine," *Chronique d' Égypte* 9 (1934), 128.

[56] M. Rostovtzeff, "Roman Exploitation of Egypt in the First Century A.D.," *Journal of Economic and Business History* 1/3 (1929), 341.

[57] Heichelheim, *Ancient Economic History*, v. 3, 45.

scale . . . were the property of the Crown, which disposed of them as it wished: by direct sale on the retail market, by sale to retailers, or by storing them or exporting them. . . .[58]

The development of the royal monopoly in banking is of particular importance. Before the Ptolemies, the Egyptian economy was predominantly based on a natural economy. Kind was more important than coin. However, with the arrival of the Ptolemies, a monetary economy was introduced and all monetary transactions had to be executed with royal coin. Foreign coin was never allowed to circulate in Egypt.[59] Thereafter the two economies, monetary and kind, co-existed.[60] Some taxes and rents could be paid in kind (e.g., wheat, oil) whereas others had to be paid in coin (e.g., vineyards, fruitlands).[61] Payment of taxes varied according to how the state viewed the importance and scarcity of the commodity.

Several consequences resulted from the monetarization of the economy. Salaries rose more slowly than the decline in the value of the currency (due to debasement); and wage-earners were not able to keep abreast with the cost of living.[62] Royal bureaucrats were also affected, as governments in antiquity operated on a strictly cash basis. Over time, this produced greater inequality in the distribution of wealth and a wider gap between rich and poor. In addition, the revenue base of the state was greatly increased through the sale of surpluses (e.g., wheat, linen, paper) to the Aegean or Greek mainland. However, since the coin received was rarely circulated it had the same effect as hoarding. The development of a coin economy also encouraged redistribution rather than local bartering.

Foreign competition was displaced by the monopolistic enterprises of the state. In order to protect domestic industries "extraordinarily high custom rates were regularly exacted in the interests of the royal exchequer."[63] All important commodities were subject to a customs tax according to the class of merchandise. A customs rate of 50% protected

---

[58]P. M. Fraser, *Ptolemaic Alexandria* (Oxford, 1972), v. 1, 134.

[59]T. Mommsen, *The Provinces of the Roman Empire*, trans. W. P. Dickson (New York, 1899), v. 2, 257.

[60]For the growth of a money economy in Egypt over the next four centuries see Weber, *Agrarian Sociology*, 226ff.

[61]There are some examples that vine and garden land could be paid for in kind although it was not the norm. See Wallace, *Taxation*, 47.

[62]Avi-Yonah, *Hellenism*, 209ff.

[63]Fraser, *Ptolemaic Alexandria*, 135.

the oil industry, a duty of 20% on wool protected the weaving industry and foreign wine cost 400% more than domestic wine.[64]

A policy of increasing productivity went hand in hand with the Ptolemaic monopolization of production. The Ptolemies experimented with new crops and new methods of growing. Land was sown twice, sheep were imported, wine was cultivated and attempts were made to grow olives and garlic.[65] Marsh land was drained and trees were planted on the embankments to prevent erosion. Red Sea trade was resumed and roads leading to the Nile were developed (e.g., Coptos to Myos Hormos, Syene to Bernice).

In addition, new technological inventions were promoted. According to Jope, "the highest development of ancient Mediterranean agriculture was seen in the last centuries before Christ, especially in Italy and Ptolemaic Egypt, where great attention was devoted to the choice and improvement of agricultural tools and methods."[66] Under the Ptolemies Egypt moved from the bronze age into the iron age. Iron tools became customary. The toothed wheel and screw press were invented, new technical methods were introduced to make glass and irrigation became more efficient with the shadoof, snail, sakiyeh and water-wheel.

Yet in spite of these technological developments Tarn's assessment that "too much must not be made of Hellenistic science,"[67] still remains valid in terms of what is known today. Technology remained primitive as the only power harnassed was human or animal. Greek science was more theoretical than applied. Nature was studied to acquire wisdom and not for its practical value. So in spite of the fact that mechanical equipment for transmitting power was invented (toothed wheels, cam shafts, cranks, pulleys, winches and counter weights) it was never applied in conjunction with some motive power to agricultural or industrial production. Labour-

[64]P. Zenon 59.012. Cf. Fraser, *Ptolemaic Alexandria,* 148ff. and Préaux, *Économie royale,* 371ff.

[65]P. Zenon 59.033, 59.142, 59.155, PSI 428 and Strabo, *Geog.,* 17.1.35. Cf. Avi-Yonah, *Hellenism,* 197ff.

[66]E. M. Jope, "Agricultural Implements," in *A History of Technology,* ed. C. Singer, E. Holmyard, A. Hall and T. Williams (Oxford, 1956), v. 2, 81.

[67]W. W. Tarn and G. T. Griffith, *Hellenistic Civilization* (London, 1952³), 308. Cf. M. I. Finley, "Technical Innovation and Economic Progress in the Ancient World," *The Economic History Review* second series 18/1 (1965), 29: "The Greeks and Romans together added little to the world's store of technical knowledge." Van Groningen's analysis of Gnosticism should be viewed with these comments in mind.

saving devices, apart from water-driven grindstones and water-lifting arrangements, were not developed. The yoke, regularly used for animals, when harnessed to a horse, choked it if the horse pulled too hard.[68] Avi-Yonah has argued that this lack of development was due to the Greek ideal which promoted leisure among the upper classes and the educated rather than an inclination to maximize productivity.[69] Although this interpretation may account for part of the value system of the period, it does not explain the relationship between technology and mode of production. The fact is that technology had no effect on the relations of production and only traces of influence on the means of production in Ptolemaic Egypt. If in spite of the above technological changes most needs were still met by one's own labour and most goods were consumed locally, the impact of technology on production and consumption patterns must be said to have remained virtually negligible. A natural economy still predominated. Finley adopts the same point of view with regard to the means of production: "there was no selective breeding (of plants and animals), no noticeable change in tools or techniques, whether of ploughing or exploiting the soil or harvesting or irrigation" for the Ptolemies or Romans.[70] Among the upper class technology was viewed only as a means of further draining the wealth of the Ptolemaic kingdom by unproductive expenditures, not as a means of maximizing productivity or of changing the relations of production. Hellenistic science failed to induce a revolution in the mode of production.

Finally, attempts to increase productivity are also manifested in Ptolemaic attempts to persuade cleruchs and royal leaseholders to irrigate unflooded and dry land.[71] Public irrigation and hydraulic works on such land were futile unless someone undertook to use it for agricultural production. However, from the perspective of the cleruch and royal peasant such a commitment always may not have been worthwhile. Quality of land is directly related to expenditure of labour and productivity. Much of the land offered to cleruchs, for example, was of low quality and

---

[68] A. Burford, Craftsmen in Greek and Roman Antiquity (London, 1972), 114ff. and especially 117.

[69] Avi-Yonah, Hellenism, 250ff. Finley (Ancient Economy) has adopted a similar rationale to explain the Roman failure to maximize productivity. See below 46f. and fn. 102 for slavery being a negligible economic factor in the development of Ptolemaic Egypt.

[70] Finley, "Technical Innovation," 29.

[71] Unflooded land refers to land subject to irrigation by ditching. See below 42 and fn. 88.

even government incentives (low rents, use of reclaimed land) did not redress the balance.[72] Taxes still had to be paid even if the land proved unproductive, and they "rested legally upon the landowners [i.e., the *cleruch*] or direct lessee of government land [i.e., the royal peasant], rather than upon the tenant."[73] Moreover, full legal title could never be attained. Consequently, motivation to increase productivity rested with the state and not with the individual.

Although lack of technology and the burden of taxes impeded a revolutionary jump in levels of productivity, growth did occur as a result of the introduction of water-driven grindstones and water-lifting arrangements. Furthermore, monopolization of production and centralized management of the economy were instrumental in stimulating the growth of urban centres. During the Ptolemaic period there were 42 *nome*-capitals (20 and 22, in Lower and Upper Egypt respectively)[74] and three autonomous cities, two of which were founded by the Ptolemies themselves (Ptolemais and Alexandria). These centres attracted a variety of inhabitants (e.g., wealthy landowners, priests, *cleruchs*, scholars, skilled and unskilled labourers, artisans, merchants, soldiers, etc.) because of their administrative importance as provincial capitals and their economic significance, as surpluses were temporarily held in the *nome*-capitals before being shipped to Alexandria. Increased population led to increased consumption, increased capital expenditures and the establishment of industries. It was in these urban areas that citizens congregated, that absentee landlords parted with their rents, that wage-labourers came to find work in industries and that production rose "to anything of the size of an export industry."[75] Nevertheless, the urban centres (excluding Alexandria) remained small in comparison to today, and according to Sjoberg the total urban population of agrarian societies in antiquity probably constituted no more than 10% of the total population.[76]

---

[72]For example, the decree of Euergetes II, who granted five years of tax exemption and four years of reduced taxes for those planting vines or gardens on unflooded and dry land. See P. Tebt. 5.

[73]W. L. Westermann, "The 'Uninundated Lands' in Ptolemaic and Roman Egypt," Part II, *Classical Philology* 16 (1921), 178.

[74]J. A. Wilson, "Buto and Hierakonpolis in the Geography of Egypt," *Journal of Near Eastern Studies* 14/4 (1955), 209-236.

[75]R. J. Forbes, *Studies in Ancient Technology* (Leiden, 1965[2]), v. 2, 102.

[76]G. Sjoberg, *The Pre-Industrial City* (New York, 1960), 83. For differences between the pre-industrial and the industrial city see 17ff.

There is very little information about the growth of these centres with the exception of Alexandria.[77] Along with Rome and Athens it is considered one of the three great cities of antiquity. As the capital of Egypt, Alexandria was the home of the king, the royal court, the senior bureaucrats (mostly Greeks) and the most wealthy citizens. With a population, according to Diodorus, of 300,000 free inhabitants in the first century B.C.,[78] intra-urban production, circulation and consumption must have been substantial. Several of the country's major industries were situated there including metal work, glassware, the manufacture of textiles, pottery, perfumes and unguents.[79] However, it should be noted that industries in antiquity did not require sophisticated specialization. In fact, "everything we know about ancient production argues against extensive division of labour. . . ."[80]

Alexandria thrived by exploiting the *chora* (countryside). Raw resources nourished the industries, and wheat, barley, wool, and other commodities were shipped to the city to support the needs of the urban population.[81] For example, a special office for the feeding of Alexandria was created to ensure supply.[82] In consequence, the *chora* became a hinterland to be exploited by city-dwellers to meet their consumer demands. Alexandria's survival depended on the appropriation of agricultural surpluses from an alienated rural labour force.[83] Moreover, within the city, the distribution of commodities, and in particular of industrial goods, remained far from equitable. Whereas the wealthy could afford to purchase whatever appealed to them, the purchasing power of the mass of the urban population remained too low to acquire anything beyond the most immediate

---

[77]Rostovtzeff (*SEHHW*, v. 2, 1137ff.) has suggested that during the reign of Soter and during the life of Diodorus Egypt had approximately 30,000 villages. In the interim (early fourth to mid-first century B.C.) population fluctuations occurred because of the periodic neglect of the irrigation system.

[78]Diodorus 17.52.6. See Fraser's discussion of the data (*Ptolemaic Alexandria*, v. 2, 171, fn. 358).

[79]Ibid., v. 1, 135ff.

[80]Finley, "Technical Innovation," 38.

[81]Fraser, *Ptolemaic Alexandria*, v. 1, 147ff.

[82]Taubenschlag, *Law*, 631.

[83]W. Sombart, *Der moderne Kapitalismus* (Leipzig, 1902), v. 1, 142ff. and v. 2, 222ff. Cf. Finley "The Ancient City: From Fustel de Coulanges to Max Weber and Beyond," *Comparative Studies in Society and History* 19 (1977), 317.

necessities.[84] Similarly, other urban benefits were unequally distributed. These included citizen privileges (exemption from certain obligations), the right to collect taxes, the acquisition of advantages in state monopolies, or membership in the royal bureaucracy.[85]

The advantage of becoming a royal bureaucrat should not be underestimated. Ptolemaic Egypt exemplifies one of the most rigidly centralized bureaucracies known.[86] All economic activities had to be coordinated and supervised. A bureaucratic career was salaried and frequently was a means to upward mobility. Intervention by the state in the productive process or in the collection of revenues would have been impossible without these individuals.

In order to simplify these functions, Egypt was planned as a unitary state within which each village was a microcosm of the whole. Each *nome* or province was divided into *toparchies* and villages and each bureaucracy resembled that of the central bureaucracy in Alexandria. A *nome* was presided over by a Greek governor (*strategus*) and he was assisted by a cluster of Greek officials who had specific institutional functions (e.g., justice, law and order, finance). This same format was duplicated at the lower levels although native Egyptians had a greater opportunity of being recruited for certain positions. The division into *nomes, toparchies* and villages was interconnected with the organization of the irrigation system and of the state monopolies. Consequently, all bureaucratic transactions (e.g., the *corvée*, permits, licences, leases, authorizations) between even the smallest village and the king proceeded in a manner that promoted universalistic state-supervised practices.[87]

The most notable universalistic practice was the registration of land. Registration involved the location and size of the land, the name of the possessor or leaseholder and the category of production based on the quality of the land (flooded, unflooded, dry).[88] These production

---

[84]Weber, *Agrarian Sociology*, 356. In contrast, see Rostovtzeff's preface to the first edition of the *SEHHW*.

[85]Taubenschlag, *Law*, 596ff.

[86]A. H. M. Jones, *The Cities of the Eastern Roman Provinces* (Oxford, 1971²), 297.

[87]For a general survey of Ptolemaic administration see E. R. Bevan, *A History of Egypt under the Ptolemaic Dynasty* (Chicago, 1968 [1927]), 132-138.

[88]See W. L. Westermann, "The 'Uninundated Lands' in Ptolemaic and Roman Egypt," Part I, *Classical Philology* 15 (1920), 120-137 and II, 16 (1921), 169-188. See also his "The 'Dry Land' in Ptolemaic and Roman Egypt," *Classical Philology* 17 (1922), 23-36.

categories were then employed as a means of assessing tax rates. In practice this required each village scribe to define the administrative category of the land (e.g., *cleruch*, temple, royal) and their category of production. The data would then be forwarded to the *nome* scribe who in turn would pass them on to Alexandria.[89] Thus, each year the state was able to forecast agricultural yields, to compare yearly yields for all production categories and to take remedial action should it wish to further enhance productivity, "so that nothing [would] be lost to the royal treasury."[90] Moreover, registration of land provided the state with a continuous appraisal of the adequacy of the public irrigation system. Without royal bureaucrats to undertake this work the revenues of the state would have fallen sharply since the rulers of Ptolemaic Egypt depended on agricultural production for their wealth.

Royal bureaucrats, as noted above, were also employed to collect the state's revenues. In contrast to the systems of such countries as Greece or Italy, the Ptolemies invented a form of collection that reflected their penchant for state management. They imported the concept of the tax-farmer from Greece but instead of leasing out the collection of taxes to the wealthy who guaranteed the state its taxes, the Ptolemies leased out contracts to prosperous and upwardly mobile individuals who became *ipso facto* underwriters and who insured the royal treasury against loss. In Egypt the tax-farmer had to deposit sureties for his contract. Moreover, whereas the tax-farmer in Greece had the opportunity to exploit the taxpayer and increase his tax burden, thereby profiting from the difference between the government lease and what he collected, the tax-farmer in Egypt was not allowed to collect the taxes himself. Royal bureaucrats, under state salary, were responsible for its collection. Thus, the Ptolemaic tax-farmer became indirectly an agent of the state who oversaw the royal bureaucrats as they performed their duties. Consequently, the state profited whether the royal bureaucrats collected the taxes or not. In Egypt, "no one has the right to do what he likes but everything is managed in the best way."[91]

From the above analysis it is evident that social rank was largely determined by the importance of one's landholding. It was the vehicle to office (bureaucracy, tax-farming) which in turn helped these individuals to possess more land. Land was the key to wealth. The Greek who was

---

[89]Westermann, "Uninundated Lands."

[90]P. Tebt. 5.

[91]P. Tebt. 703.

presented with a gift estate or a military allotment, initially by virtue of his Greek identity had higher social status than other foreign *cleruchs* or the native Egyptians. He was allotted more land, had greater opportunity to be affiliated with the state bureaucracy or a state monopoly and to reside in an urban centre.[92] Greeks drew their strength from their land, from a Greek king, and a Greek ideology of hereditary status. As time passed, however, social mobility became more and more a product of structural differentiation, and the Persians of the *Epigone* began to replace many of the Macedonians or other foreign nationals and be accorded higher social status. In fact, the term Macedonian became divorced from its connotation identifying a certain ethnic group, and merely recognized the individual as having high status. Combined, these two groups—Greeks and Persians of the *Epigone*—stood apart from the native Egyptians as possessors of the land, not merely lease holders; as royal bureaucrats, not merely functionaries; and as urban consumers, not merely agricultural labourers.[93] Moreover, whereas the native Egyptian had minimal access to gaining citizenship, the Greek or Persian of the *Epigone* had ample opportunity to do so. Yet in spite of their high status, the Greek and *Epigone* population in Egypt remained proportionally small to the total population.[94]

Rostovtzeff indicated long ago that the Ptolemies "almost entirely ignored the essence of the Greek economic system: private property recognized and protected by the state as the basis of society, and the free play of economic forces and economic initiative. . . ."[95] Only in the last century and a half did the Ptolemies begin to act otherwise, to make concessions to the wealthy who were non-Greek, to relax some of the rigours of the economy and to allow *cleruchs* further hereditary rights. Possession of land began to undergo a transition and slowly to acquire the

---

[92]Compare Apollonius' 6,500 acres to the average Egyptian peasant in the Fayum who, according to Crawford, cultivated no more than an acre or two. See D. J. Crawford, *Kerkeosiris* (Cambridge, 1971). See also Finley, *Ancient Economy,* 98ff. and Rostovtzeff, *SEHRE,* v. 1, 278.

[93]J. Modrzejewski has expressed it as "les agriculteurs libres" against the King and "la bureaucratie royale." See Modrzejewski's comments in "Discussion sur les formations économiques et sociales dans l'Antiquité," in *Colloque 1973,* 90.

[94]Avi-Yonah (*Hellenism,* 157, 195) has postulated that the Greek population in Egypt "cannot have been more than one in fifteen," and could "hardly have exceeded half a million."

[95]Rostovtzeff, *SEHHW,* v. 1, 273.

character of private property.[96] Nevertheless, the overwhelming majority of the producers (royal leaseholders) were responsible to the state which also controlled the means of production. They, like all other inhabitants in Egypt, were compelled to buy their industrial goods from state monopolies and to sell their surplus to the state at pre-determined prices. Only with the Roman conquest of Egypt did the concentration of the means of production by the state, monopolistic practices, and land ownership become significantly altered.

2.3   The Slave Mode of Production in Roman Egypt

In 31 B.C. Octavian conquered Egypt and Egypt changed from an independent kingdom to a province of the Roman Empire. Land and agricultural labour continued to be the two most important constituents of wealth "and [land was] indeed the only respectable form of investment."[97] However, the Roman mode of production was slave labour.[98] The result was an integration of Roman practices with the Ptolemaic mode of production, and in due course significant changes occurred giving rise to a new social formation. Three changes in particular stand out: the emancipation of private ownership from any extrinsic restraints; the devolution of several state monopolies and the increase in private initiative; and the deintensification of the bureaucracy and an increase in private accountability.

In Ptolemaic Egypt, state and king had been viewed as identical; in contrast, under Rome, the state was viewed as an entity separate from the emperor. The Ptolemies had supported state control of production and distribution as well as monopolization of land-ownership; in contrast, the Romans encouraged private ownership of land and the separation, to some extent, of production and distribution from the authority of the state.

In Italy the Roman economy was based on the slave mode of production.[99] Agrarian slavery maintained the estates of the aristocrcy who owned the majority of land. In this mode of production man is converted into an inert tool, deprived of social and legal rights and reduced to a

---

[96]Taubenschlag, *Law*, 235 and Rostovtzeff, *SEHHW*, v. 2, 733 and v. 3, 1499, fn. 151.

[97]K. D. White, *Roman Farming (London, 1970), 11ff.*

[98]For slavery under the Ptolemies see below and fn. 102.

[99]On the slave mode of production see Marx, *Pre-Capitalist Formations* and Anderson, *Passages,* 18ff.

standard object of sale and purchase.[100] He neither controls his labour
power nor the means of production which he uses. He is a producer of
objects as well as an object (i.e., a commodity) himself. His entire product
is appropriated by another. Consequently, in antiquity the slave was
described as no more than an *instrumentum vocale,* a speaking tool.[101]

There is a consensus that slavery was a negligible economic factor,
both agriculturally and industrially, in Ptolemaic Egypt.[102] At the turn of
this century the sociologist Max Weber wrote that "production based upon
slavery, . . .played no role whatever . . ."[103] and this position continues to
be re-affirmed by scholars today: "il est absolument certain que l'économie agraire de l'Égypte n'est pas fondée sur le travail servile. . . .[104] Similarly, most scholars agree that in Roman Egypt there was neither a
widespread introduction of agrarian slavery nor did it become the predominant type of surplus extraction.[105] "In Egypt, where agricultural slavery
had never existed," writes A. H. M. Jones, "the land continued to be cultivated by free peasants as tenants either of the state, the temples or
private landlords."[106] Perry Anderson, a Marxist, also adopts this

---

[100] Anderson, *Passages,* 24ff.

[101] Varro, *On Agriculture, 1.17.*

[102] See Avi-Yonah, Hellensim, 246ff.; W. L. Westermann, *The Slave
Systems of Greek and Roman Antiquity* (Philadephia, 1955), 46-57; Fraser,
Ptolemaic Alexandria, v. 1, 73ff.; Rostovtzeff, *SEHHW,* v. 1, 321ff.;
Préaux, *Economie royale,* 303ff.; Anderson, *Passages,* 45-52; Saad, "Mode
de production asiatique," 30ff.; and I Biezunska-Malowist, "L'Esclavage
dans l'Égypte Gréco-Romaine," in *Actes du Colloque 1971 sur l'esclavage*
(Annales Littéraires de l'Université de Besançon 140, Paris, 1972), 81-92,
and "L'Esclavage à Aléxandrie dans la période Gréco-Romaine," in
Colloque 1973, 291-312.

[103] Weber, *Agrarian Sociology,* 247.

[104] See Modrzejewski's comments in response to Bonneau's paper,
"Esclavage et irrigation," in *Colloque 1973, 327.*

[105] Westermann, *Slave Systems,* 46-57, 86ff. and 120ff.; Préaux,
Économie royale, 303ff.; A. C. Johnson and L. C. West, *Byzantine Egypt:
Economic Studies* (Amsterdam, 1967), 24; A. C. Johnson *An Economic
Survey of Ancient Rome: Roman Egypt* (Paterson, N.J., 1959), 343ff.;
Biezunska-Malowist, "L'Esclavage dans l'Égypte," 81-92 and "L'Esclavage
à Aléxandrie," 291-312.

[106] A. H. M. Jones, "Slavery in the Ancient World," in *Slavery in
Classical Antiquity,* ed. M. Finley (Cambridge, 1960), 11. For a brief
discussion of the differences between the slave and the free labourer in
antiquity see M. Finley, *Ancient Slavery and Modern Ideology* (London,
1980), 67-92.

position: agrarian slavery remained "a residual phenomenon that existed on the edges of the main rural work force."[107] The slave mode of production, therefore, could not be the dominant element of the new social formation.[108]

But if the slave mode of production never gained ascendancy in Roman Egypt, nevertheless the Ptolemaic mode of production absorbed a set of principles alien to its nature. For example, in Ptolemaic times ownership and possession of property had been separated. In Roman law the concept of absolute property existed and this was equally applied throughout the Empire.[109] This signified that an individual could acquire full legal title to property and ownership was no longer dependent on collateral rights. "Roman civilization was the first to separate the pure colour of 'property' from the economic spectrum of opaque and indeterminate possession that had typically preceded it."[110]

Godelier has argued that this transition to absolute property occurred alongside the expansion of the Roman Empire and the appearance of the Roman slave mode of production.[111] War, tribute, and slaves led to new relations of production and to the legal consummation of a slave economy. "Economic relationships progressed constantly [thereafter] in the direction of the reinforcement of rights of private property. . . ."[112] The development of private ownership of land in Egypt therefore is simply a manifestation of one of the characterisitc features of the slave mode of production alien to the Ptolemaic system. The devolution of state monopolization of production and distribution can also be viewed from this perspective. The combination of the different modes of production (Ptolemaic and slave) resulted not in the substitution of one mode of production for another; rather it created a new social formation under the

[107]Anderson, *Passages*, 21.

[108]For a discussion of Graeco-Roman law regarding slaves see Taubenschlag, *Law*, 66-101.

[109]H. F. Jolowicz, *Historical Introduction to the Study of Roman Law* (Cambridge, 1954), 142ff.

[110]Anderson, *Passages*, 67.

[111]Godelier, "Marxist Models," 244ff. See also M. L. Gordon, "The Nationality of Slaves under the Early Roman Empire," in Finley, ed., *Slavery*, 173.

[112]A. I. Pavlovskaia, "On the Discussion of the Asiatic Mode of Production in *La Pensée* and *Eirene*," *Soviet Studies in History* 4/4 (1965), 43.

dominance of the Ptolemaic mode of production.[113] This integration allowed both for the development of private ownership and for the state to continue to play a leading role in the economy (see Table 2). The following section examines this integration and the new individual patterns of landowning, production, and management manifested in Roman Egypt up until the end of the first century A.D. Collectively these patterns are indicative of a transition towards privatization with the Roman conquest of Egypt.

Table 2
The Ptolemaic Mode of Production

Ptolemaic period	Roman period
absence of private property	private property
public irrigation	private and public irrigation
state control of the means of production	private and state control of the means of production
state control of distribution	private and state control of distribution
fertile period of technological development	technology almost stagnant
state management of the economy, salaried bureaucracy	some decentralization of state management of the economy, salaried and unsalaried bureaucracy
city as industrial producer and consumer	city as industrial producer and consumer
status stratification (Greeks, *Epigone*, other, Egyptians)	status stratification (Romans, Greek citizens, other, Egyptians, slaves)

[113] See Godelier ("Marxist Models," 245) for a discussion of the theoretical models addressing the laws of evolution of the Asiatic mode of production.

2.4   The Ptolemaic Mode of Production
          and the Roman Transformations

          An investigation of Octavian's policies regarding ownership of
land immediately testifies to the Roman ideology of privatization.
Through acquisition by conquest and confiscation Augustus attempted to
encourage private ownership and to increase the number of private landholders.[114] For example, cleruch land was designated as private (ἰδιόκτητος) and cleruchs were granted the unrestricted right of disposal of
their land (e.g., sale, intestate succession, etc.). Roman veterans were
offered private lots of land free or at reduced rates if intensive labour
was required. Temple land was confiscated and redistributed to private
owners. Imperial favourites were the recipients of imperial grants and
crown (royal) land was sold to private investors. According to
Rostovtzeff, "everybody was welcomed who had money and wished to
invest it in land . . ." (including the former bureaucrats and tax-farmers of
the Ptolemies, and Alexandrian merchants), and "unnecessary formalities
which hampered free dealing in private land . . ." were removed.[115]
     Under the early Roman Empire administrative categories of land in
Roman Egypt depended on ownership and judicial status. The divisions
included crown, temple, city, imperial and private.[116] Crown land was in
actual fact the royal land (βασιλικὴ γῆ) of the Ptolemies that was
absorbed by the Roman state when Egypt was conquered. It also included
abandoned cleruch land and confiscated temple land. Not surprisingly,
therefore most of the land in Roman Egypt fell in this category.[117] This
land was leased to tenants, who for the most part were free Egyptian
peasants. Their leases were for a short term and their rental fee was
dependent on the provisions of the lease (e.g., category of production,
projected agricultural yield, etc.).[118] Rents paid were higher than taxes

---

[114]See Heichelheim, *Ancient Economic History*, v. 3, 157; Rostovtzeff,
SEHRE, v. 1, 287; and Parassoglou, *Imperial Estates*, 4.

[115]Rostovtzeff, *SEHRE*, v. 1, 287.

[116]See R. P. Duncan-Jones, "Some Configurations of Landholding in
the Roman Empire," in *Studies in Roman Property*, ed. M. Finley
(Cambridge, 1976), 7-24; Johnson, *Roman Egypt*, 25ff.; and Wallace,
Taxation, 3ff.

[117]Johnson and West, *Byzantine Egypt*, 18. Cf. fn. 21 above.

[118]Johnson, *Roman Egypt*, 74ff. For further examples of leases see D.
J. Crawford, "Imperial Estates," in Finley, ed., *Roman Property*, 177, fn.
53.

assessed on private land.[119] In addition, the tenant was liable for a number of taxes (e.g., capitation taxes) that increased his burden. Therefore the peasant in Roman Egypt tended to carry the bulk of taxes on his shoulders just as he had done in Ptolemaic Egypt. However, in contrast to the Ptolemies, who totally controlled the means of production, the Romans demonopolized a number of elements in the production process. The tenant was able to use his own seeds to avoid interest charges, could own his own tools and had the option of using private sources to transport his grain to village threshing-floors.[120] According to Wallace, even the private ownership of animals gradually developed.[121]

The most revealing change, however, was the Roman policy of taking land out of the public (i.e., state controlled) sector in order to encourage private investors to purchase it. In fact, evidence suggests that a certain portion of crown was always reserved for private enterprise.[122] An early example of such a purchse is P. Oxy. 721 in 13/14 A.D.

> To Gaius Seppius Rufus, from Polemon son of Tryphon and Archelaus . . . we wish to purchase in the Oxyrhynchite nome of the crown land returned as unproductive . . . from the holdings which were confiscated. . . .[123]

Consequently, over time the total amount of crown land gradually diminished either by assignment to veterans or to imperial favourites or by private purchase.

The extent of temple land was also greatly transformed under Roman rule. In less than a decade after the Roman conquest a considerable portion of the total amount of temple land was confiscated by the prefect Petronius.[124] This land was either assimilated with existing crown land, sold to private investors or returned in permanent leasehold to the temple

---

[119]Wallace, *Taxation*, 11.

[120]Johnson, *Roman Egypt*, 460ff.

[121]Wallace, *Taxation*, 95.

[122]Ibid., 3. Cf. Johnson, *Roman Egypt*, 76, and Duncan-Jones, "Some Configurations," 7.

[123]H. MacLennan, *Oxyrhynchus: An Economic and Social Study* (Amsterdam, 1968), 16ff. See also P. Oxy. 635, PSI 320 and P. Amh. 68. This land was usually unproductive (unflooded or dry). See Parassoglou, *Imperial Estates*, 8 and fn. 20.

[124]See Wallace, *Taxation*, 4, 337; Duncan-Jones, "Some Configurations," 10; and Johnson, *Roman Egypt*, 122.

from which it was confiscated.[125] Temple land held by lease (i.e., confiscated and returned) was subject to rent, like tenancy on crown land; unconfiscated temple land only paid taxes. Even more importantly, unconfiscated temple land came to be viewed as private property and this practically amounted to legal ownership. According to Wallace, "owners could lease the land to their own advantage or perhaps even sell it."[126] Thus, although temple land did not have the juridical status of private property some of the land could be treated by its owners as identical to private land. In part this would have been facilitated by the Romans' loosening their control over the means of production and the demise of the Ptolemaic monopolies.

There are few data on city land. Alexandria owned property near Euhemeria (Fayum)[127] and Johnson has suggested that in the edict of Tiberius Julius Alexander certain lands in the Delta may have been part of city land.[128] Duncan-Jones has postulated that it was from these properties that the needs of local governments could be maintained.[129]

Imperial land refers to land owned by the emperor. Initially, land defined as imperial belonged to imperial favourites who had been granted estates under the *principate*.[130] However, either by confiscation or by inheritance these estates progressively became the property of the emperor. The point of transition to an imperial patrimony is uncertain. Johnson[131] has suggested that under Nero or the Flavians the ἰουσιακὸς λόγος was created and Parassoglou[132] in his recent study on imperial estates has pinpointed the reorganization of land and taxation to 70 A.D. when Vespasian and Titus were both in Alexandria. In all probability Octavian started the trend towards imperial land when he inherited the estate of Maecenas, although unlike later emperors he neither confiscated

---

[125]For example, the temple of Soknebtunis. See P. Tebt. 302 and Evans' discussion in "Egyptian Temple," 213ff. Cf. Taubenschlag, *Law*, 264ff.

[126]Wallace, *Taxation*, 4. Cf. Evans, "Egyptian Temple," 214.

[127]Wallace, *Taxation*, 5.

[128]Johnson, *Roman Egypt*, 28.

[129]Duncan-Jones, "Some Configurations," 8.

[130]Crawford, "Imperial Estates," 35-70. In contrast, see Parassoglou (*Imperial Estates*), who has suggested that the *ousiae* were purchased on the open market rather than being granted to imperial favourites. See below 53 and 57.

[131]Johnson, *Roman Egypt*, 27ff.

[132]Parassoglou, *Imperial Estates*, 29.

land from Romans nor did he retain for himself, in a private capacity, any of the land conquered.[133] Imperial land was concentrated in the Fayum (Arsinoite *nome*) where, under the Ptolemies, large scale agricultural reclamation had occurred. Estates also existed in the Delta, the Memphite, Herakleopolite, Hermopolite and Oxyrhynchite *nomes*.[134] The production process and rental conditions for a tenant were similar to those for crown land.[135] Crawford has suggested that the tenants who farmed the land would have varied according to the type of land. Whereas only Egyptian peasants would farm corn land, a cross-section of the population may have farmed orchard land.[136]

The total area of private land greatly expanded due to Roman initiatives to encourage private ownership. This development was probably stimulated by the institution of the registry of real property (βιβλιοθήκη ἐγκτήσεων) in the middle of the first century A.D., which was "designed to offer far reaching protection for prospective purchasers of real estates. . . ."[137] As discussed above, the only agricultural lands considered private under Ptolemaic rule were garden plots and vineyards. Due to state monopolization of arable land, private individuals could legally possess, but not own, land. Roman policy that made private ownership of land possible had the potential to alter the shape of the market. This opened the door to a radical transformation in the mode of production. Distribution of confiscated, abandoned and crown land to private investors, Roman veterans and imperial family members and friends, and the application of Roman rather than Ptolemaic laws of property, testify to the inauguration of this transformation. For example, *cleruch* land was designated as private. All extrinsic legal restraints were removed.[138] Roman veterans were granted private land for their service and/or could purchase cultivable land for the price of 20 *drachmae* per *arura*.[139] The size of allotments usually depended on military status and the fertility of

---

[133]Crawford, "Imperial Estates," 40.
[134]Ibid., 37.
[135]See above 49f.
[136]Crawford, "Imperial Estates," 45ff. Although Crawford's data are from second century Karanis, similar conditions would have existed in the preceding century. Crawford's argument is that "different sectors of the population [were] involved in different forms of agriculture" (46).
[137]Taubenschlag, *Law*, 222ff.
[138]Ibid., 238, and Parassoglou, *Imperial Estates, 7*.
[139]Rostovtzeff, *SEHRE*, v. 1, 287, and Frank, *Economic History*, 390.

the soil. In addition, as mentioned above, a certain portion of crown land was placed on the private market (e.g., P. Oxy. 721).[140] The distribution of land to imperial favourites contributed significantly to the development of private property (see Table 3). The land grants, similar to the Ptolemaic *doreae* but now called *ousiae*, frequently have been undervalued in importance.[141] In part, the reason lies in the fact that the word *ousia* can be applied to private estates with no imperial connections.[142] (See Table 4.) In part also it is due to the lack of clarity concerning estates of members of the imperial family, and to the tradition of classifying their land as illustrative of imperial gifts.[143] These reasons deflect and diminish recognition of the innovation in private ownership brought about by the Romans.

Several recent studies have tried to redress this imbalance. For example, Crawford has argued that where confusion reigns, estates of "members of the imperial family should . . . be excluded from a consideration of imperial estates [i.e., *ousiae*] proper except when by inheritance, . . . they became part of the emperor's property."[144] As a way of applying this rule, she has suggested that estates which passed from person to person without the intervention of an imperial authority be distinguished from those subject to such intervention.[145] Consequently, many of the examples cited in Table 3 as imperial *ousiae* may, in actual fact, be judged as referring to private estates if additional data were available. Moreover, the traditional view that *ousiae* refer to imperial grants, and that the emperor's family and associates were the recipients of these gifts, has been challenged by Parassoglou in the light of the fact that *ousia* could be used for private land with no imperial connections. Parassoglou has postulated that individuals such as Livia, Pallas, Narcissus and Seneca bought their land on the open market, at a time that witnessed

---

[140]See above 50 and fn. 123.

[141]The equation of *ousiae* with *doreae* was first suggested by Rostovtzeff; see *Studien zur Geschichte des römischen Kolonates* (Archiv für Papyrusforschung und verwandte Gebiete 1, Leipzig/Berlin, 1910), 128. With the exception of T. Frank ("On Augustus and the Aerarium," *JRS* 23 (1933), 146, fn. 7) and Parassoglou (*Imperial Estates*) scholars have followed Rostovtzeff.

[142]Parassoglou, *Imperial Estates*, 7, 10ff. Cf. Crawford, "Imperial Estates," 41, 51.

[143]Crawford, "Imperial Estates," 39ff.

[144]Ibid., 40.

[145]Ibid., loc. cit.

Table 3
Imperial Properties (*Ousiae*) in the Arsinoite *Nome*
in the First Century A.D.*

Date (A.D.)	Place	Ousia—Reference
15	Tebtunis	P. Mich. recto xix
25-26		PSI 1028
42		P. Mich. 121 recto I. xii
42		P. Mich. 121 recto III. x
43		P. Mich. 244
46-47	Ibion-Eikosipentarouron	P. Mich. 274-275
57		SB 7742
26	Philoteris	P. Mil. 6
26	Theadelphia	P. Mil. 6
26		P. Med. 6
87-88		P. Giss. Univ.—Bibl. 12
94-95		P. Lond. 900 (III, p. 89)
98-117		SB 10218
99		P. Würz. 11
22	Euhemeria	P. Osl. 123
28-29		P. Ryl. 126
29		P. Ryl. 127
30		P. Ryl. 129
34		P. Ryl. 134
34		P. Ryl. 138
36		P. Ryl. 140
37		P. Ryl. 141
40		P. Ryl. 148
54		P. Vindob Tandem 10
29	Dionysias	P. Ryl. 127
46-47	Herakleia	BGU 650
55		P. Lond. 280 (II, p. 193)
56-57		P. Ryl. 171
5	Bakkhias	SB 9150
14-15		P. Lond. 445 (II, p. 166)
57		BGU 181
25-26	Philadelphia	P. Sorbonne inv. 2364
26		P. Yale inv. 443

Table 3 (continued)

Date (A.D.)	Place	Ousia—Reference
33-34	Philadelphia	P. Weill inv. 108
35		P. Princ. 11
50-51		SB 9224
56		P. Princ. II, 53
74		P. Hamb. 3
90-96	Sebennytos	P. Strassb. 210
83-84	Arsinoe	Stud. Pal. XX, 1.6, 26
I cent.	Nilopolis	P. Lond. 194 (II, p. 124)
48	Soknopaiou Nesos	P. Ross-Georg. II, 12
54-68		WChr. 176
39	Karanis	P. Athen. 32
46		P. Mich. 560
53		P. Mich. 540
c. 53		P. Mich. IX. 539
71		P. Osl. 21
89-90		P. Mich. 382
98		P. Mich. 524
early I	Unspecified	SB 6019
early I		SB 4226
early I		P. Lond. 195 (II, p. 127)
14-37		P. Tebt. 401
22		P. Strassb. 118
44		P. Coll. Youtie 19
48-49		P. Aberd. 29
98		P. Iand 26
I cent.		P. Aberd. 151
I cent.		P. Ryl. 684

*Sources: G. M. Parassoglou, *Imperial Estates in Roman Egypt* (American Studies in Papyrology 18, Amsterdam, 1978), Appendix Two, 69f., D. Crawford, "Imperial Estates," in *Studies in Roman Property*, ed. M. Finley (Cambridge, 1976), 59f. and M. Rostovtzeff, *SEHRE*, v. 2, 669f., fn. 45.

Table 4
Private (Non-Imperial) *Ousiae* in the Arsinoite *Nome*
in the First Century A.D.*

Date (A.D.)	Place	Ousia—Reference
29	Karanis	P. Osl. 33
c. 30	Theogonis	SB 10535
34		P. Mich. 312
26	Euhemeria	P. Ryl. 166
c. 30		P. Ryl. 128
31		P. Ryl. 131
32-33		P. Ryl. 132, 133
34		P. Ryl. 135
39		P. Ryl. 167
39		P. Ryl. 146
42		P. Ryl. 152
34-35	Philadelphia	P. Sorbonne inv. 2367
65-66	Hermoupolis	P. Lond. 1213; 1214; 1215 (III, p. 121)
36	Arsinoite *nome*	P. Mich. 232
38		P. Ryl. 145

*Sources: G. M. Parassoglou, *Imperial Estates in Roman Egypt* (American Studies in Papyrology 18, Amsterdam, 1978), Appendix one, 65f., D. Crawford, "Imperial Estates," in *Studies in Roman Property*, ed. M. Finley (Cambridge, 1976), 59f. and M. Rostovtzeff, *SEHRE*, v. 2, 669f., fn. 45.

an increase in private land-ownership.[146] Crawford has attempted to deflate his theory although she concludes that "there is no positive evidence either for this or for the traditional view."[147] Both Parassoglou's and Crawford's work illustrate the growing transition towards individual ownership of private property in Roman Egypt.

There are many examples of imperial family members and friends owning land in Roman Egypt. Augustus' wife Livia had considerable holdings (e.g., Philadelphia, Karanis, Euhemeria)[148] as did Drusus and his wife;[149] and Claudius' wife, Messalina, had estates in the Hermopolite and Herakleopolite *nomes*.[150] Similarly, friends of the emperors such as Petronius,[151] Maecenas,[152] Lurius,[153] Seneca[154] and Doryphorus[155] owned

---

[146]See Parassoglou, *Imperial Estates*. If his thesis is accepted many of the imperial properties listed in Table 3 would be references to private estates and, accordingly, would have to be transferred to Table 4.

[147]Crawford, "Imperial Estates," 40.

[148]For example, see SB 9150, P. Lond. 445 (II, p. 166), P. Mich. 560, PSI 1028, P. Ryl. 126 and P. Mil. 6. Cf. Crawford, "Imperial Estates," 174, fn. 16; Rostovtzeff, *SEHRE*, v. 2, 670, fn. 45; and Parassoglou, *Imperial Estates*, 72f.

[149]For example, see P. Oxy. 244, P. Ryl. 140, 141 and 171, BGU 199 verso, 212, 277 and 653, P. Fay. 60. Cf. Crawford, "Imperial Estates," 175, fn. 22; Rostovtzeff, *SEHRE*, v. 2, 670, fn. 45; and Parassoglou, *Imperial Estates*, 70f.

[150]For example, see P. Ryl. 87 and 684, WChr. 367 and P. Flor. 40. Cf. Crawford, "Imperial Estates," 175, fn. 23; Rostovtzeff, *SEHRE*, v. 2, 671, fn. 45 and Parassoglou, *Imperial Estates*, 73.

[151]For example, see P. Ryl. 127 and BGU 650. Cf. Rostovtzeff, *SEHRE*, v. 2, 671, fn. 45, and Parassoglou, *Imperial Estates*, 81.

[152]For example, see BGU 181 and 889, P. Ryl. 171, 207 and 383, P. Tebt. 343, P. Bour. 42, P. Mich. 223, 224 and 357, P. Chic. 23, 42, 61, 65 and 81, SB 4414, 7742 and 9224 and P. Oslo 26a. Cf. Crawford, "Imperial Estates," 175, fn. 31; Rostovtzeff, *SEHRE*, v. 2, 671, fn. 45; and Parassoglou, *Imperial Estates*, 79f.

[153]For example, see P. Hamb. 3, BGU 284, P. Chic. 32, 36, 39, 41, 48, 49, 50, 78 and 87, P. Bour. 42, P. Mich. 224 and SB 10512. Cf. Crawford, "Imperial Estates," 176, fn. 32; Rostovtzeff, *SEHRE*, v. 2, 671, fn. 45; and Parassoglou, *Imperial Estates*, 78f.

[154]For example, see P. Ryl. 99 and 207, P. Hamb. 3, P. Lips. 115, BGU 104, 172 and 202, P. Bour. 42, P. Chic. 5, 16, 18, 26, 53, 62, 65, 67 and 71, P. Mich. 223, 224 and 225, PSI 448 and P. Oxy. 2873 and 3051. Cf. Crawford, "Imperial Estates," 176, fn. 37; Rostovtzeff, *SEHRE*, v. 2, 671, fn. 45; and Parassoglou, *Imperial Estates*, 82.

[155]For example, see P. Ryl. 99 and 171, SB 9205, 10512, P. Oslo. 21, P.

land in Egypt. These landholders rarely, if ever, became residents of Egypt or even visited their domains.[156] In addition, Rostovtzeff has indicated that aristocratic Alexandrians may also have been absentee owners of Egyptian *ousiae*.[157] Estates tended to be managed by agents and there is no evidence for wide-spread agrarian slavery. The state did not control the means of production and owners had full legal title (e.g., sale and intestate succession) and were not subject to land taxes.[158] Under the Flavians many of the *ousiae* were confiscated.[159] Consequently, in order to keep the land productive "large tracts of fertile land . . . [were] let or sold to peasants or to anyone who wished to be a small local landowner."[160]

Whereas *cleruch* and veteran land tended to be farmed by the landowner himself, *ousiae* were farmed by hired labourers or rented out to Egyptian peasants. Leases followed the pattern of crown leases, and were generally short-term with specified conditions of crop-cultivation. The average rental for private land between 26 and 100 A.D. approximated 7 3/4 *artabae* of wheat per *arura* in contrast to crown land which was considerably less than 7.[161] The sale value of private property between 27 B.C. and 99 A.D. averaged 185 *drachmae* per *arura* whereas the average wage of the ordinary peasant, according to Johnson's estimate, was only slightly higher at around 210 *drachmae* a year in the first century A.D.[162]

Regardless of the administrative category of land, irrigation continued to play the most important role in the economic prosperity of Roman Egypt. During the last century of Ptolemaic rule, irrigation was neglected due to a variety of domestic problems and productivity declined. Arable land became a partial desert and depopulation occurred. To rectify this problem and to increase productivity Octavian used military and *corvée*

Chic. 52, P. Bour. 42, P. Mich. 223 and 224 and P. Strassb. 210. Cf. Crawford, "Imperial Estates," 175, fn. 26; Rostovtzeff, *SEHRE*, v. 2, 671, fn. 45; and Parassoglou, *Imperial Estates*, 77.

[156]The senatorial class were strictly forbidden to visit Egypt.

[157]Rostovtzeff, *SEHRE*, v. 1, 293f. and v. 2, 672, fn. 45.

[158]Johnson, *Roman Egypt*, 504.

[159]See Crawford, "Imperial Estates," 53; Rostovtzeff, *SEHRE*, v. 2, 669, fn. 45; and Parassoglou, *Imperial Estates*, 29.

[160]Rostovtzeff, *SEHRE*, v. 1, 295. See also Parassoglou, *Imperial Estates*, 28.

[161]Johnson, *Roman Egypt*, 81, 504.

[162]Ibid., 147, 304ff.

labour to clear the silt and build new canals.[163] Village men were obliged
to work for five days a year on the public irrigation system. Thus, the
state still controlled labour and was instrumental in the maintenance and
expansion of the irrigation system and hydraulic works. However, according to Johnson, privately owned land was the responsibility of the individual owner.[164] Consequently, "leases of *catoecic* [i.e., a sub-classification
of *cleruch* land] and private land in the Fayum usually contain a clause
imposing on the lessee the necessity for repair of embankments and
maintenance of the system of irrigation."[165] The state therefore no
longer monopolized the maintenance of the irrigation system although it
could monopolize labour through the *corvée*. Private land was viewed as
separate from the other categories of land.

The transition from state to private ownership of land not only
affected the way the irrigation system was maintained but also, and more
importantly, how the economy was structured. In contrast to the Ptolemies who monopolized both the production and distribution processes, the
Romans demonopolized several industries as well as the distribution
processes, and adopted an economic policy that combined laissez-faire
with state control.[166] "State monopolies . . . [were] wholly or partially
abandoned . . . and the dearth of evidence for the organization of monopolies . . . may well indicate that their importance had suffered a
decline."[167] For example, the monopoly on brewing and the distribution of
beer developed into a system of leases of concessions to private individuals.[168] Similarly, the manufacture and sale of ointments and perfumes
were permitted through the leasing of concessions, with the possible
exception of the Fayum.[169] The oil and papyrus industries also entered
the private market for the first time. According to Johnson, "the Ptolemaic oil monopoly seems to have vanished in the Nile valley under Roman

---

[163]Suetonius, *Life of the Caesars*, 2.18.2 and Dio Cassius, *Hist. Rom.*,
51.18.1.
[164]Johnson, *Roman Egypt*, 13 and Taubenschlag, *Law*, 618, fn. 42.
[165]Johnson, *Roman Egypt*, 13.
[166]See Rostovtzeff, *SEHRE*, v. 1, 91; Frank, *Economic History*, 392ff.;
Wallace, *Taxation*, 181ff.; Johnson and West, *Byzantine Egypt*, 23; and
Saad, "Mode de production asiatique," 34.
[167]Wallace, *Taxation*, 182ff.
[168]See ibid., 187ff.; Johnson, *Roman Egypt*, 327ff.; and Taubenschlag,
Law, 669ff.
[169]See Taubenschlag, *Law*, 670 and Johnson, *Roman Egypt*, 340.

occupation."[170] Oil presses were owned or leased to individuals who personally controlled the manufacture and distribution of all oil.[171] In a parallel way, the papyrus industry was privatized. According to Strabo, the government no longer exercised control over the manufacture of papyrus[172] and early leases support this claim by indicating that the marshes of the Delta were under private ownership.[173] Furthermore, there is little evidence for government ownership of boats on the Nile. In Johnson's opinion, "shipping was largely a matter of private enterprise and wealthy Alexandrians were the chief owners."[174] Even baths were privatized to some degree. In Lower Egypt there is substantial evidence for both private and municipal baths.[175] For other industries such as the manufacture and sale of bricks there is contradictory evidence. The brick industry appears to be under state control in the Fayum yet "there is no other evidence for government control"[176] in other parts of the country.

In spite of this trend towards the devolution of Ptolemaic state monopolies, several nonetheless continued to exist in Roman Egypt. The state continued to control resource extraction in mines and quarries[177] as well as the production of alum, linen, wool and the fulling of cloth.[178] Fishing and hunting on crown lands remained under state control,[179] as did the ownership of trees and the sale of wood.[180] Banking also remained a government monopoly in some form, although Taubenschlag has suggested the coexistence of private banks.[181]

---

[170] Johnson, *Roman Egypt*, 328. See also Evans, "Egyptian Temple," 226, Wallace, *Taxation*, 186 and Frank, *Economic History*, 402, fn. 33.
[171] See, for example, P. Ryl. 128.
[172] Strabo, *Geog.*, 17.1.15. See also N. Lewis, *Papyrus in Classical Antiquity* (Oxford, 1974): "Privately owned papyrus plantations are in evidence . . . from the very beginning of Roman Rule" (121).
[173] Johnson, *Roman Egypt*, 329 (e.g., P. Mil. 6).
[174] Ibid., 400.
[175] See ibid., 334 and 547ff., and Wallace, *Taxation*, 155ff.
[176] Johnson, *Roman Egypt*, 331.
[177] See ibid., 241ff., and Wallace, *Taxation*, 189.
[178] See Wallace, *Taxation*, 189, and Johnson, *Roman Egypt*, 326ff.
[179] See Johnson, *Roman Egypt*, 335 and 374ff. (e.g., P. Giss. Univ-Bibl. 12 and PSI 901). See also Taubenschlag, *Law*, 663ff.
[180] Johnson, *Roman Egypt*, 335 (e.g., P. Oxy. 1112 and 1188). See also G. M. Parassoglou, "On *Idios Logos* and Fallen Trees," *Archiv für Papyrusforschung und verwandte Gebiete* 24-25 (1976), 91-99.
[181] Taubenschlag, *Law*, 677ff. In Roman Egypt Alexandrian coinage served in the place of the imperial coinage but was not permitted to circulate as legal tender outside of Egypt.

The transition from state to private control of the production and distribution processes also affected custom tariffs. The Romans, unlike the Ptolemies, wished to encourage trade and had little motivation to protect domestic industries. As a result tariff rates were significantly reduced to promote private initiative and free trade (transit duties ranged from 2%-4%).[182] The only exception was the duty on imports into Leuce Come (25%) which has been explained by Rostovtzeff as a way to divert trade from the overland route to the Red Sea ports of Egypt.[183] However, since overland transportation was extremely expensive (the price of commodities doubled for every one hundred miles hauled overland),[184] a more probable reason is that the imported commodities were luxuries from the East and aimed at the small segment of the population that could afford them.[185]

There were two immediate consequences of demonopolization: revenues were lost, and wealth began to be redistributed. In order to make up for the dismantling of state monopolies the Romans increased their revenue base by adding new taxes. All persons engaged in industry (including apprentices) were assessed a capitation tax rather than a percentage tax on profits or on the gross income of the industry. "Rates were based on the evidence of past experience . . . [with] the knowledge of industries in which the government had previously exercised a monopoly form[ing] a fair guide to the expected profits of private enterprise."[186] In addition, new taxes on land helped to replace lost revenues with rates and form of payment (kind or coin) varying with the category of land (private, crown, imperial, temple, city) and crop (e.g., wheat, corn, garden or vine cultivation).[187] Furthermore, a series of capitation taxes had to be paid in coin.

The imposition of taxes paid in money would have necessitated that the volume of trade increase to offset this tribute. Consequently, Egypt would have had to earn money to pay its taxes by exporting goods of equal value.

---

[182]Frank, *Economic History*, 394, and A. H. M. Jones, *The Roman Economy*, ed. P. A. Brunt (Oxford, 1974), 171.

[183]Cited in Wallace, *Taxation*, 256.

[184]R. J. Forbes, "Food and Drink," in Singer et al., eds., *Technology*, v. 2, 103.

[185]See G. Lenski, *Power and Privilege* (New York, 1966), 205, and Jones, *Roman Economy*, 171ff. for similar arguments.

[186]Wallace, *Taxation*, 192. See also W. L. Westermann, "Apprentice Contracts and the Apprentice System in Roman Egypt," *Classical Philology* 9 (1914), 295-315, and Johnson, *Roman Egypt*, 537.

[187]See Wallace, *Taxation*.

The expansion of trade with the Eastern and Western parts of the Empire indicates that the Red Sea ports and Alexandria would have become centres of redistribution. However, given the nature of the economy in antiquity, this redistribution would have been narrowly confined to a small segment of the population. Nevertheless, it testifies to a degree of circulation of commodities and small scale changes in patterns of distribution and consumption.[188]

Johnson,[189] Wallace[190] and Rostovtzeff,[191] among others, have maintained that Octavian was the restorer of economic prosperity to Egypt. His reclamation of large tracts of land, his restoration of the irrigation system and his imposition of a uniform fiscal system are all pointed to as evidence. Moreover, his policy of increasing productivity by privatizing property and industry traditionally has been viewed as an important stimulant. However, this increase in economic prosperity may be more a reflection of the degeneration of Ptolemaic economic life and state management than of Roman creativity. Without major technological developments or changes in the relations of production agricultural productivity in Egypt in the first century A.D. could at best have only modestly appreciated from the peak periods under the Ptolemies. Available technology creates limits of possibility for the extraction of surplus within a society.

Mossé, like Finley, has commented that in real terms technology hardly advanced at all in Roman Egypt.[192] Under the Romans tools for agricultural production remained relatively constant,[193] and industries which were confined to a small number of towns made little technological progress. Local self-sufficiency in agriculture went together with self-sufficiency in manufacturing.

The only significant industrial innovations were in the silk and glass industries.[194] According to Strabo the former greatly expanded.[195] This

---

[188]See K. Hopkins, "Taxes and Trade in the Roman Empire," *JRS* 70 (1980), 101-125.

[189]Johnson, *Roman Egypt*, 12.

[190]Wallace, *Taxation*, 136.

[191]Rostovtzeff, "Roman Exploitation," 345.

[192]Claude Mossé, *The Ancient World at Work*, trans. J. Lloyd (London, 1969), 31ff. See also above 38f. and fn. 70.

[193]See the comments of White, *Roman Farming*, 156ff.

[194]Changes in military engineering are significant but peripheral to the economic argument.

[195]Strabo, *Geog.*, 2.5.12 and 17.1.13.

development was directly related to the discovery by Hippalus of the tradewinds and, concomitantly, the demand by the aristocracy, including wealthy Alexandrians, for luxury goods from the East.[196] In fact, the demand by both sexes for silk became so great that during Tiberius' reign a law was passed to prevent men from wearing silk.[197] The purchase of luxury items became the measure of social stratification.

In contrast, the glass industry was transformed by new technical methods. Glass-blowing was introduced and revolutionized the industry. According to Harden, it would take another 1,800 years until machinery for mass production was invented and the industry again undergo a transition of similar magnitude.[198] In agriculture, all the major artefacts (e.g., shadoofs, snails and sakiyehs) were in use before the Roman conquest. Similarly, crafts like spinning and weaving showed little progress and remained mainly household occupations.[199]

The only significant change that occurred was that craftsmen could privately own their own tools. However, due to lack of technology,[200] they were not able to significantly expand production. Burford has drawn the same conclusions from her data:

> Methods of production altered comparatively little. Craftsmen might become more specialized. . . . It would, however, be a mistake to press the argument that specialization increased. . . . Neither the methods of production nor the degree of specialization . . . changed very much.[201]

For the Romans, as for the Greeks, the fertile interplay between science and technology was almost totally absent. Nature was studied to acquire wisdom, not to be applied. "In antiquity, 'only the tongue was inspired by the gods, never the hand.'"[202]

---

[196]For silk weaving in Alexandria see Johnson, *Roman Egypt,* 339. For trade with India see M. P. Charlesworth, "Roman Trade with India: a Resurvey," in *Studies in Roman Economic and Social History,* ed. P. R. Coleman-Norton (Princeton, 1951), 131-143.

[197]Tacitus, *Annals,* 2.33.

[198]D. B. Harden, "Glass and Glazes," in Singer et al., eds., *Technology,* v. 2, 337.

[199]Forbes, *Ancient Technology,* v. 2, 99.

[200]Ibid., 99f.

[201]Burford, *Craftsmen,* 61.

[202]Finley, "Technical Innovation," 34.

With no significant gains in agricultural technology, and free labour rather than slaves dominating the labour force, productivity could not have increased substantially. Even government attempts to sell crown, confiscated, or abandoned land that was unflooded or dry by offering it at low prices and with tax incentives to private investors would not have appreciably altered productivity levels.[203] Although legal title rather than possession was offered as a stimulant, increased productivity on this land still required intensive labour, and taxes remained legally tied to the landowner.[204] Consequently, it would have been the landed aristocracy who were better equipped to purchase this land. Indirectly, therefore, government policy encouraging private ownership did so at the expense of the hired labourer or tenant who sub-leased land. In contrast to the Ptolemies, therefore, motivation to increase productivity would have rested with a small segment of the private sector rather than with the state.

If traditional methods of technology, agricultural organization, and relations of production blocked any significant growth in productivity, then success in farming would have depended more on weather than on planting techniques or even labour.[205] Unflooded and dry land would have fluctuated continually between good and bad years and this would have been accompanied by movements of the population. For those owning land, increased productivity would have been dependent on the location and maintenance of the irrigation system. Productivity would have been "poised on a fine edge between underflooding and overflooding every year."[206] Consequently, the relative increase in economic prosperity in the first century A.D. in Roman Egypt may be due more to Octavian's restoration of the irrigation system, coinciding with a century of good floods, than to his policies of privatization.[207] Policies of private initiative and increased economic prosperity did not stop the peasant from

---

[203]For examples of government incentives see P. Oxy. 721 and P. Amh. 68. See Parassoglou, *Imperial Estates*, 8.

[204]Westermann, "Uninundated Lands," Part II, 178.

[205]For a similar argument with regard to Egypt in the third century A.D. see C. R. Whittaker, "*Agri Deserti*," in Finley, ed., *Roman Property*, 137-165.

[206]Ibid., 153.

[207]See C. E. P. Brooks, *Climate through the Ages* (New York, 1970[2]), 329ff., and in particular 331, for literary and statistical evidence that Egypt had good floods in the first century A.D.

fleeing the land which was endemic from A.D. 19 onward.[208] Thus, Tarn's conclusions regarding technological developments for Ptolemaic Egypt can be applied equally to Roman Egypt. As Forbes notes, "the lack of stimulants to industrialize [i.e., to create a new means of production] left ancient technology practically stagnant during the Roman Empire."[209] This observation is amplified by Brunt, who comments that after the time of Augustus agricultural technique stagnated and with the exception of religion the Roman world was uncreative.[210]

In spite of the fact that agricultural productivity may have increased only modestly the *nome* capitals and the three autonomous cities continued to grow and to attract those with wealth or bureaucratic inclinations. Rostovtzeff, for example, has described a typical metropolis as comprising absentee landlords, officials, tax-farmers, shopkeepers, artisans, retail-traders, and the indigenous poor.[211] In these centres there would "be a sufficient concentration of the wealthy . . . to provide an adequate market" for industry and commerce.[212] However, the argument of Rostovtzeff[213] and Wallace,[214] among others, that an urban movement occurred and that Far Eastern commerce "made industry and trade more attractive than agriculture"[215] cannot be supported. The nature of life in antiquity counteracted such developments, and both the Ptolemaic and slave modes of production were based on agriculture. Economic historians such as Hopkins have pointed out that over 80% of the labour force in pre-industrial societies was deployed in agriculture. "The bulk of the labour force in the Roman Empire, perhaps 80%-90%, were primarily peasants who produced most of what they themselves consumed and consumed most of what they produced."[216] Even Finley has commented that outside the city of Alexandria "almost everyone was totally involved

---

[208]See Whittaker, "*Agri Deserti*," 149. See also Wallace, *Taxation*, 136; Rostovtzeff, "Roman Exploitation," 350ff.; and Philo, *De Spec. Leg.*, 3.159.

[209]Forbes, *Ancient Technology*, v. 2, 99.

[210]See P. A. Brunt's book review of K. D. White's *Roman Farming*, in *JRS* 62 (1972), 156.

[211]Rostovtzeff, *SEHRE*, v. 1, 297ff.

[212]Jones, *Roman Economy*, 39.

[213]Rostovtzeff, *SEHRE*, v. 1, 273ff.

[214]Wallace, *Taxation*, 339ff.

[215]Ibid., 340.

[216]Hopkins, "Taxes and Trade," 104. See also his *Conquerors and Slaves* (Sociological Studies in Roman History 1, Cambridge, 1978), 15ff.

with agriculture, including the soldiers and the innumerable petty offi-cials."[217] Given these data it is difficult to accept Wallace's or Rostovtzeff's premises that an urban movement occurred and that indus-try and trade displaced agriculture.[218]

Nevertheless, Alexandria does not fit the norm. Strabo described the city as "the greatest trading-centre in the inhabited world,"[219] and Dio Chrysostom, a century later, as "a meeting place of the whole earth."[220] All ethnic groups (e.g., Greeks, Jews, Egyptians) and classes (e.g., land-holders, merchants, artisans, slaves) were represented in Alexandria. In an alleged letter of Hadrian, which can be applied equally to the first cen-tury A.D., Alexandria is described as follows:

> The city is rich, wealthy and prosperous. Some are glass blowers, some are making paper, and others are engaged in weaving linen; everybody at any rate seems to be engaged in some occupation. . . . They have only one god—money. . . . Everyone worship[s] this divinity. Would that this city were endowed with better morals. . . .[221]

However, Frazer's suggestion of a growth rate of 25% from the time of Diodorus (c. 60 B.C.) to that of Josephus (c. 80 A.D.) must be viewed as no more than conjecture.[222]

The reasons for Alexandria's economic prosperity are directly related both to the economic initiatives inaugurated under the *principate* (demonopolization of key industries such as papyrus, glassware, perfumes and ointments) and to increased trade with the East and the West.[223] Strabo's comments, in particular, emphasize the increased trade with the East:

> When I accompanied Gallus up the Nile . . . I learned that as many as a hundred and twenty vessels were sailing from Myos

---

[217]Finley, *Ancient Economy*, 97. See also fn. 76 above.

[218]R. MacMullen has come to the same conclusion; see his *Roman Social Relations* (New Haven and London, 1974), 48ff.

[219]Strabo, *Geog.*, 17.1.13.

[220]Dio Chrysostom, *Or.*, 32.36.

[221]*Scriptores Historiae Augustae*, Saturninus, 8, cited in Johnson, *Roman Egypt*, 336.

[222]Fraser, *Ptolemaic Alexandria*, v. 2, 172, fn. 358.

[223]See Johnson, *Roman Egypt*, 335ff. and 486; Jones, *Roman Economy*, 59ff.; and Mommsen, *Provinces*, v. 2, 325ff.

Hormos to India, whereas formerly, under the Ptolemies, only a very few ventured to undertake the voyage and to carry on traffic in Indian merchandise.[224]

The increased volume of trade to the West grew on account of the initiation of the *annona* programme[225] and the need to supplement income to pay taxes.[226] Inevitably, private Alexandrian merchants, exporters, importers and shipbuilders would have flourished, as an increase in the volume of both inter-regional and world trade depended in antiquity upon an increase in the volume of cash to finance it. In fact, according to Johnson, it was private Alexandrian companies that profited most from this as they had control of the lucrative trade to the East and the *annona*.[227] Their profit, if one can accept Pliny, came to a hundred fold by the time Eastern commodities reached Rome.[228] However, it should be emphasized once more that in antiquity "the quantitative contribution of trade and manufacture was tiny . . ."[229] and that the propertied classes maintained a traditional disdain for trade.[230] Individuals with capital preferred to invest their money in slaves and land rather than commerce, as opportunities in the latter were not equal to profits from owning land.[231]

As was the case under the Ptolemies, urban wealth therefore lay chiefly in rural holdings and most trade continued to flow from the country to urban centres.[232] It was in the city that primary products (wool,

---

[224]Strabo, *Geog.*, 2.5.12.

[225]Johnson, *Roman Egypt*, 401. The *annona* refers to the Roman policy of confiscating Egyptian grain for the consumption of those living in Rome.

[226]See above 61f.

[227]Johnson, *Roman Egypt*, 400ff. See also Frank, *Economic History*, 404.

[228]Pliny the Elder, *Natural History*, 6.101.

[229]Finley, "Technical Innovation," 40. See also Jones (*Roman Economy*, 138) who has postulated that in the late Roman Empire "trade and industry combined contributed something like 5 per cent of the national income, . . . and that the capital of a great Alexandrian merchant was about a twentieth of that a typical senatorial land owner."

[230]Finley, *Ancient Economy*, 35-61.

[231]R. J. Forbes, "Power," in Singer et al., eds., *Technology*, v. 2, 604.

[232]MacMullen, *Social Relations*, 48ff. "Land was by far the preponderant ultimate producer of wealth and that it and the cities in its midst were thus closely symbiotic" (49).

hides, flax) were processed and transformed into goods of higher value but lower volume (cloth, dyes, ropes). Alexandria remained the prototypical consumer city with the *chora* acting as a hinterland to support its needs.[233]

> The quantitative expansion in [population] . . . was never accompanied by any qualitative modification of the structure of overall production within it. Neither industry nor trade could ever accumulate capital or experience growth beyond the strict limits set by the economy of classical antiquity as a whole.[234]

The upper class, both landed and commercial, continued to consume most of the imported goods and according to Fraser "was probably far wealthier [in the Roman period] than [they] had been in the Ptolemaic."[235] They also continued to enjoy a variety of privileges. In contrast, the bulk of the urban population remained poor and were unable to purchase the over-whelming majority of non-subsistence commodities. In Hopkins' opinion their average consumption was near that of the rural peasant.[236]

The division into *nomes, toparchies* and villages continued into the Roman period. The Romans adopted the main features of Ptolemaic bureaucracy but adjusted them to their own administrative system.[237] The *prefect* took the place of the king and a handful of other high ranking Roman bureaucrats co-ordinated and supervised the most important functions of the state (e.g., finance, justice). Land taxes and rents were still based upon productive categories (flooded, unflooded, dry), together with new administrative classifications (e.g., imperial, private, crown, etc.). Government administrators continued to pressure tenants to irrigate more land and to increase their productivity. The Romans also preserved the land registration system.[238] However, several profound changes were

---

[233]Weber, *Agrarian Sociology,* 48: "Ancient cities were always much more centres of consumption than production. . . ." Cf. Finley, *Ancient Economy,* 125, and fn. 83 above.

[234]Anderson, *Passages,* 80. In contrast, see Rostovtzeff, *SEHRE,* v. 1, 349.

[235]Fraser, *Ptolemaic Alexandria,* v. 1, 800. In addition, see Hopkins ("Taxes and Trade," 104) who has argued that Roman levels of consumption were higher than those of the pre-Roman epoch.

[236]Hopkins, *Conquerors,* 15.

[237]See Wallace, *Taxation* and Johnson, *Roman Egypt.*

[238]See above fn. 88.

introduced that indicate new patterns of economic management. For example, "contrary to the practice of the Ptolemaic period, under the Roman system the annual assessment was made on the basis of declarations handed in by the lessees of the state domain or by the landowner. . . ."[239] These declarations were forwarded to the *comogrammateus* who undertook a preliminary inspection before passing the declaration to higher authorities.[240] By having owners and lessees declare their expected yields the Roman administrative system—although still state dominated—was subject to the testimony of private individuals who became personally accountable for their actions. Not surprisingly, inspectors frequently found errors[241] as landowners and tenants attempted to avoid taxes. The partial extrication of the individual from state management coincided with the government's policy to devolve state monopolies and to encourage private ownership of land.

The Romans also transformed the civil service and thereby influenced how state revenues were collected. In contrast to the Ptolemaic civil service, which consisted of volunteers who were eventually able to acquire permanent salaried positions, tenure in the Roman civil service was temporary, without remuneration, and often under compulsion. An examination of the Roman method of collecting taxes highlights this difference. Whereas the Ptolemies employed royal bureaucrats to collect taxes after tax-farmers had ensured the royal treasury against loss, the Romans in the first century A.D. initiated a new policy that compelled the tax-farmer to collect the taxes himself. The tax-farmer therefore had to adopt the role of civil servant without receiving any remuneration and simultaneously had to risk a capital loss on his investment. This policy of compulsory service arose as the number of tax-farmers willing to serve dwindled.[242] Paniscus, *strategus* of the Oxyrhynchite *nome*, indicates the seriousness of the problem of the government's inability to recruit tax-farmers in the first century A.D.:

> At the last sale of taxes . . . the farmers of the tax on sales and the farmers of the tax on goods in the market not only refused to bid, on the plea that they had already suffered

---

[239]Westermann, "Uninundated Lands," Part I, 134. For a dissenting argument see Wallace, *Taxation,* 7ff.

[240]Westermann, "Uninundated Lands," Part I, 134f.

[241]Wallace, *Taxation,* 8ff.

[242]See Rostovtzeff, *SEHRE,* v. 1, 388ff. and "Roman Exploitation," 358ff.

sufficient loss, but even seemed likely to abscond. . . . [I was requested] to examine the terms under which the taxes had previously been farmed, and as far as possible to lighten the burden of the farmers, in order to prevent the disappearance of those who were pressed to bid. . . . The taxes have been put up to auction several times. . . .[243]

The refusal of tax-collectors to volunteer was a direct result, according to Paniscus, of Roman taxation policies that created numerous delinquent accounts. Tax-farmers were personally liable for the payment of arrears, which frequently meant the loss of their private property as compensation. Not surprisingly therefore, tax-farmers resorted to profiteering in order to make up their losses. Both Philo[244] and the edict of Tiberius Julius Alexander[245] illustrate the gravity of this problem.[246] Brunt considered the practice so widespread that he concluded that "extortion and fraud were endemic in the administration of Egypt. . . ."[247] Hopkins arrived at the same conclusion: "taking private profit from public office was built into the Roman system of provincial administration."[248] This stands in sharp contrast to the Ptolemaic epoch where no less an authority than A. H. M. Jones has commented that extortion by tax-farmers was a rare occurrence.[249] Moreover, this administrative change resulted in less rather than more effective state supervision.[250] It promoted decentralization. Although the first steps leading to the institution of liturgy (i.e., civic service to the state) were taken by the Ptolemies, "the full development and perfection [of this system] belongs . . . to the Roman period."[251] And according to Jones this was the critical step in the degeneration of the centralized system of state management of economic

---

[243]P. Oxy. 44. Cf. MacLennan, *Oxyrhynchus,* 19ff.

[244]Philo, *De Spec. Leg.,* 2.92ff. and 3.159.

[245]OGIS 669.

[246]For further testimony see P. Oxy. 284, 285, 393 and 394.

[247]P. A. Brunt, "The Administrators of Roman Egypt," *JRS* 65 (1975), 125.

[248]Hopkins, *Conquerors,* 43.

[249]Jones, *Roman Economy,* 175.

[250]Johnson (*Roman Egypt*) describes this change as responsible for a "lack of uniformity" (492). Similarly, Brunt ("Administration") has adopted this position: the conception "that specialization was increasingly favoured in Roman imperial administration . . . is anachronistic" (142).

[251]Taubenschlag, *Law,* 616.

life.[252] Decentralization and changes in administrative structure are indicative of the trend towards new patterns of individualism.

> Social rank and status in Roman Egypt were identical to those in Ptolemaic Egypt in being determined by land. . . . Land was the basic form of wealth, for even money used for speculation was derived from it. . . . This was necessarily so, for land was needed as collateral by anyone wishing to engage in the most lucrative forms of speculation. . . .[253]

Merchants, as indicated above, always stood below the land-holding aristocracy and above artisans, labourers, peasants and slaves.[254] Mobility was possible only in a limited number of ways such as through the military (land grants, profiteering), the bureaucracy (extortion, favouritism) or by investing one's capital from trade or industry in land.[255] Merchants therefore, if they acquired a fortune, "soon converted [it] into land which was safer than trade and gave higher prestige."[256]

Since land remained the basis of status, little changed for the native Egyptian peasant. Foreigners remained their masters although the hierarchy was slightly altered from one comprising Greeks, Persians of the *Epigone* and Egyptians to one made up of Romans, Greek citizens, Greeks (broadly defined) and Egyptians. Those defined as Egyptian were still the largest group in the population but had the lowest status, could not attain citizenship and suffered the full burden of taxes, including the *laographia* (poll-tax) which identified them as outsiders.[257] If they owned land it tended to be a small plot and their surplus was continually drained either

---

[252]Jones, *Cities*, 347.

[253]Weber, *Agrarian Sociology*, 396.

[254]For a classic statement at the end of the Roman republic see Cicero, *De Off.*, *1.150f.*

[255]The typical illustration used in antiquity of the upwardly mobile individual is Trimalchio, who among other things, invested his profits in land. See Petronius, *Satyricon*, 48.3, 76.10 and 77.3. Cf. MacMullen, *Social Relations*, 49ff.

[256]K. Hopkins, "Elite Mobility in the Roman Empire," *Past and Present* 32 (1965), 12. Cf. Cicero (*De. Off.*, 1.151) who writes, "trade, if it is . . . on a large scale. . . .deserve[s] the highest respect, if those who are engaged in it . . . make their way from the harbour to a country estate. . . ."

[257]For a discussion of the *laographia* and capitation taxes in Roman Egypt see Wallace, *Taxation*, 116-214.

by the state or by absentee landlords.[258] If they worked, their annual wage was only slightly higher than the price of an *arura* and provided them with barely enough income to support themselves and their family. In contrast, the small minority of wealthy Romans and Greeks had the highest status, were citizens and were wholly or partially immune from the pressure of taxes. They held the majority of private land[259] and their cash flow continually increased either from leasing their land or through tax-farming. They preferred to live in urban centres and indulge in the consumption of wealth,[260] policing their estates rather than acting as entrepreneurs. Thus, in Roman Egypt as in Ptolemaic Egypt, two social worlds existed: one with a dirt floor, debts, and propertylessness (peasants, tenants, shopkeepers, wage-earners); the other with mosaics, capital and land (Roman and Greek landowners). The lower class infrastructure and the elite superstructure belonged to separate, encapsulated worlds.

In urban centres class differences were magnified. Native Egyptians were demeaned by their speech, dress, mode of life and manners, and inequalities in wealth and mobility opportunities were reinforced.[261] Legal distinctions solidified these class differences. Laws differed for the free and slaves, for citizens and non-citizens, for landowners and tenants, for wage-earners and industrial owners. The citizen was invariably a landholder, the free non-citizen a tenant or wage-earner. Class lines were firmly entrenched.

In summary, with the Roman conquest of Egypt significant changes occurred in the Ptolemaic mode of production. New patterns of land-owning, production, and management of the economy were manifested. Although the state still owned the majority of the land (i.e., as crown

---

[258]For the living conditions and average wage of the poor, see Johnson, *Roman Egypt*, 246 and above 58 and fn. 162. See also MacMullen, *Social Relations*.

[259]For example, in Theadelphia in the first century A.D. more than two-thirds of the vineyard and garden land belonged to ten Roman citizens and eighty-seven Alexandrians. See MacMullen, *Social Relations*, 20ff.

[260]MacMullen (*Social Relations*, 89 and 183, fn. 1) has postulated that a Roman senator had to have property worth 250,000 times a labourer's daily wage. Cf. Hopkins, "Elite Mobility" for a similar argument emphasizing the gap between rich and poor. See also his "Economic Growth and Towns in Classical Antiquity" in *Towns in Societies*, ed. P. Abrams and E. A. Wrigley (Cambridge, 1978), 49ff.

[261]MacMullen, *Social Relations*, 46. MacMullen's argument is with respect to the third century A.D. but is equally applicable to the first century. See his Appendix B, "The Lexicon of Snobbery," 138ff.

land) it was now legal for private individuals to own land; as a result the total amount of state land gradually decreased. The maintenance of irrigation—the umbilical cord of Egypt—was no longer completely the responsibility of the state. State monopolies were wholly or partially abandoned and private initiative was encouraged. Individuals were able to control the means of production and to distribute their surplus without government intervention. The central bureaucracy was adjusted to meet the needs of Rome, thereby creating a less efficient administrative structure and opening the doors to decentralization.

Collectively, these changes are indicative of a transition from the state to the individual and a transformation in the Ptolemaic mode of production. "The sale of land to landowners . . . meant the legalizaton of a practice which broke with age-old traditions."[262] Private ownership revolutionzied the mode of production. It was "the most radical change introduced in Egypt by the Romans, and the example most illustrative of the fundamental differences between Hellenistic and Roman tradition."[263] The new social formation integrated state domination with the flowering of individualism.

---

[262]Rostovtzeff, "Roman Exploitation," 348.
[263]Parassoglou, *Imperial Estates*, 6.

3

The Jewish Presence

3.1   Introduction

The economic transformations that occurred in Egypt during the Ptolemaic-Roman epoch affected all ethnic groups. Of these the Jews stand out. The literature, archaeological finds, inscriptions and papyri all suggest that the Jewish voice was disproportionate to the Jewish share of the total population. The aim of this chapter is to document the extent of the Jewish presence in Egypt. Several questions are addressed. What was the demographic significance of the Jews in Egypt? Did they develop unique institutional structures that responded to Jewish needs? Did they have socio-economic and religious contact with Palestinian Jews? Were Egyptian Jews faithful to Judaism?

A key element which emerges from an understanding of the Jewish presence in Egypt is the interrelationship of socio-economic circumstances with the life-experiences of the Jews. As was suggested by the previous chapter's focus on property, it will be argued that the material circumstances had a determining influence on Jewish ideology and behaviour. This chapter seeks to explore the lived texture of Ptolemaic and Roman institutions and the changing Jewish position within them, and to identify Egyptian Judaism as a set of historical and ideological responses to this experience.

For a believing Diaspora Jew, whatever his ideological orientation, Judaism meant three things: (a) ethnic identification with the people of Israel; (b) religious identification with a set of precepts symbolized by a central sanctuary in Jerusalem; and (c) ethnic and religious identification with a community that regarded Israel as its homeland. The expression of this identification took several forms, the most obvious being the abandonment of polytheistic beliefs and, concomitantly, the acceptance of monotheism, along with circumcision for a Jewish male. In addition, there were certain behavioural customs, such as not working on the Sabbath, the eating and avoidance of certain foods, and attending specially-prescribed houses of worship. But the practice of Torah in everday life implied a great deal more than behavioural patterns of *halakah*. It also entailed certain unique institutional structures, with elected and appointed administrators who organized and directed the local Jewish communities. To facilitate the practice of Torah and to be more closely identified with their own kind, Jews most likely would have settled in areas recognized as Jewish areas of settlement; these would have had Jewish merchants, craftsmen and retailers who catered primarily to Jewish· clients; they would have had Jewish administrators to interpret and act as mediators with government officials on behalf of the community; and they may even have had their own Jewish cemeteries. Thus, a situation may be hypothesized that would parallel Jewish development in the Western world today: apostates and proselytes, conservatives and liberals, reactionaries and zealots, orthodox and reform believers, interacting together in Jewish social organizations and through their interaction redefining the meaning and practice of the religion itself. One brief example will illustrate this point. How different were the values of Jewish pilgrims living in the time of Jesus from those of contemporary Jewish pilgrims? At the time of Christ, the religious believer was commanded by law to undertake this sacred journey, and offer a sacrifice at the Jerusalem Temple; while in the modern period, the pilgrimage is frequently seen as a return to the national homeland (i.e., as secular Zionism). Yet at the root, in each case, is the historical identification with Judaism, however expressed.

The themes of this chapter are twofold. First, it will be shown that the Jews had a strong demographic presence and a viable institutional matrix in Ptolemaic Egypt, and were influenced significantly by the changes in the mode of production which occurred with the Roman conquest. Second, by examining their contacts with Judaism in Palestine and with Hellenism, the extent of the behavioural and ideological identification of Egyptian Jews with Judaism will be demonstrated. Class composition and place of residence will be used as indicators of assimilation. The hypothesis argued is that the Jews acted as the catalysts for the development of new social movements, in the context of the Roman transformation of the Ptolemaic mode of production and the persistent bonds of Hellenism. By exploring the Jewish presence in Egypt, the Jews' contribution to the ideological development of Gnosticism may be uncovered.

3.2   Demography

3.2.1   Migration

According to the Biblical story of the Israelites, Jewish contact with Egypt began in the second millennium B.C. The story of Joseph, the years of slavery and Moses' leadership are all chronicled. There is also evidence of Jewish immigration to Egypt in the period preceding Alexander the Great's conquest, from the Aramaic papyri at Elephantine,[1] and from the prophet Jeremiah.[2] The Elephantine papyri document the political, social, religious and corporate economic life of the Jewish community there[3] and Jeremiah mentions that Jews during his day were living in Migdol (east of Daphne), Tahpanhes (Daphne), Noph (Memphis) and Pathros (Upper Egypt).[4] However, after Ptolemy I conquered Palestine (four times between 320 and 301 B.C.)[5] Jewish immigration to Egypt was greatly accelerated. Various factors, including military, political and economic considerations, contributed to the dispersion of the Jews and the growth of the Egyptian Jewish community, including the effects of war and the concomitant capture of prisoners, the need for escape from political and/or religious persecution, and finally, the Ptolemaic policy of land allotments to foreign mercenaries.[6] As a result, the Jewish population of Egypt began to increase numerically, and commercial contacts between Palestine and Egypt expanded.

During the Ptolemaic wars, numerous Jewish prisoners were captured, many of whom were taken back to Egypt to be employed on garrison duties or to be sold as slaves to Ptolemaic soldiers.[7] During the next century (301-198 B.C.) Palestine remained in Ptolemaic hands and intercourse between the two countries gained momentum. Commercial and

---

[1]See A. E. Cowley, ed., *Aramaic Papyri of the Fifth Century B.C.* (Oxford, 1923), 190-199 and E. G. Kraeling, ed., *The Brooklyn Museum Aramaic Papyri* (New Haven, 1953), Introduction 27-48 and 76-117.
[2]Jer 42-44.
[3]See B. Porten, *Archives from Elephantine* (Berkeley, 1968).
[4]Jer 44:1 and 46:14.
[5]*Ep. Arist.*, 12-14.
[6]Mary Smallwood in *The Jews Under Roman Rule* (Leiden, 1976), 221, has listed several additional possibilities—such as over-population and land-shortage—but considers them as tangential to her subject matter.
[7]See *Ep. Arist.*, 12-14 and Josephus, *Ant.*, 12.7-9.

governmental contacts were intensified,[8] and in particular the trade in slaves was expanded, if the Zenon papyri accurately represent Ptolemaic administrative performance.[9]

In 198 B.C. Palestine was conquered by Antiochus III and a new wave of Jewish immigration to Egypt began. This was accelerated by the Helleniz- ing program under Antiochus Epiphanes and the subsequent Maccabean revolt. Philometor, Egypt's Ptolemy, responded by encouraging the immi- gration of large numbers of Jews to Alexandria and elsewhere in Egypt.[10] One of the many refugees who fled to Ptolemaic Egypt to escape political persecution was Onias IV (162-160 B.C.), the son of the High Priest in Jerusalem. Onias IV had been deprived of his office by Jewish Hellen- izers.[11] Jerome states that Onias was accompanied by many followers[12] and Jewish inscriptions indicate that Leontopolis, the colony founded by Onias, played an important role in Egyptian-Jewish history.[13] Other political refugees also fled to Egypt, including a leader of the Pharisees escaping from the persecutions of a Sadducean king.[14]

The Ptolemaic policy of granting land allotments (κλῆροι) to foreign mercenaries in return for their military service was also directed at Jews.[15] Although not numerous, Jewish mercenaries took advantage of

---

[8]See below Section 3.4.2, "Socio-Economic Contact," 131ff.

[9]See CPJ, v. 1, 2, 115-118 and nos. 1-6; Rostovtzeff, SEHHW, v. 1, 343ff.; also M. Hengel, Judaism and Hellenism, trans. J. Bowden (London, 1974), v. 1, 41 and v. 2, 32, fn. 317.

[10]Fraser, Ptolemaic Alexandria, v. 1, 688.

[11]V. Tcherikover, Hellenistic Civilization and the Jews (New York, 1970), 276ff.; see also 497, fn. 24 for alternative interpretations.

[12]Jerome, in Daniel, 2.13-14, cf. CPJ, v. 1, 2.

[13]For Jewish inscriptions see CPJ, v. 3, nos. 1451-1530. See also v. 1, 20f. and Tcherikover, Hellenistic Civilization, 281ff. For the importance of Leontopolis see Fraser, Ptolemaic Alexandria, v. 1, 83 and v. 2, 162ff., fns. 302, 306 and 307; Josephus, Ant., 13.285ff. and Apion, 2.49ff.

[14]See CPJ, v. 1, 3. The Pharisee was either R. Joshua Perahiah or R. Judah b. Tabbai, (see b. Sota, 47a and b. Sanh., 107b).

[15]See above Chapter 2, 31ff. for the settlement of veterans under the Ptolemies. For Jewish cleruchs, see CPJ, v. 1, Section III, 147-178. Hengel (Judaism and Hellenism) has argued that Josephus' comments concerning the enlistment of Jewish mercenaries by Alexander the Great can be accepted at face value (v. 1, 15f.) and that "the Jews had an old mer- cenary tradition" (v. 2, 11, fn. 84). For the opposing view expressed here, see CPJ, v. 1, 12ff. and Smallwood, Jews, 221, fn. 7.

this policy and were assigned to "pseudo-ethnic" units.[16] The earliest Jewish ethnic unit and military settlement is the land of Onias.[17] Not known for their military prowess, Jewish mercenaries for the most part achieved only low military rank[18] and received smaller plots of land than the Greeks, in the range of 24-60 *arurae*.[19] Nevertheless, this was considerably more than the native Egyptian *machimos*.[20] This would have resulted in the settlement of a considerable number of Jews on the land throughout Upper and Lower Egypt and, in particular, in the military settlements of the Fayum.[21] A military-landholding tradition would have been established and the mercenaries' children would have been known as Persians of the *Epigone*.[22] These landholdings were viewed as part of the royal land under grant and were leased to the Jewish military settler.

Jews, like other *cleruchs*, only possessed the land, although "in the process of time these plots became more and more the property of the leaseholder . . . [and] began to be bequeathed from father to son."[23] Like other Greek *cleruchs* and Persians of the *Epigone*, they leased out their land to native Egyptian peasants and regarded themselves as landholders rather than tenants or farmers. Indeed, many had little to do with their

---

[16]*CPJ*, v. 1, 12f. See Josephus, *War*, 2.487 for a reference to Alexandria.

[17]See Tcherikover, *Hellenistic Civilization*, 275; *CPJ*, v. 1, 2f.; and O. Murray, "Aristeas and Ptolemaic Kingship," *JTS* 18 (1967), 362ff. Tcherikover (*Hellenistic Civilization*, 280) dates the founding of the *catoecia* to c.145 B.C.

[18]*CPJ*, v. 1, 13. For Jews as officers, see *CPJ*, v. 1, nos. 24, 27 and 28.

[19]*CPJ*, v. 1, 13. Officers would have received larger land-holdings (*CPJ*, v. 1, 13 and 147).

[20]See Chapter 2, 31f. above.

[21]See *CPJ*, v. 1, Section III, 147-178 for the location of these settlements. See also Table 5, 93. Only one location of Jewish military settlers (Diospolis magna) is documented in Upper Egypt (*CPJ*, v. 1, no. 27), but its geographical setting suggests other Jewish settlements in the area.

[22]For Jews as Persians of the *Epigone*, see *CPJ*, v. 1, nos. 18, 20, 21, 23, 24 and 26; and v. 2, nos. 146 and 149. For Persians of the *Epigone* in general, see Chapter 2 above.

[23]*CPJ*, v. 1, 15. Also see above, Chapter 2, 32 and the discussion between ownership and possession 30ff.

land as they were preoccupied with business transactions.[24] Many Jews became upwardly mobile in the second half of the second century B.C. (Helkias, a certain Dositheus and Ananias were Egyptian generals, another Dositheus was an Alexandrian priest and Onias IV may have been a *strategus*[25]), and by the turn of the century Jewish *cleruchs* had entrenched hereditary rights.[26] They also appear to have been involved actively in the cultivation of unflooded and dry land.[27]

The rise of Jews as possessors of *cleruch* land and high status corresponds with the rise of Semites in the military.[28] Jews, like other Semitic mercenaries, replaced many of the Greeks and were identified as Macedonians.[29] Their upward mobility was also associated with the loosening of property law. It should be remembered that by far the largest part of land in Egypt was royal land and that the relaxation of state ownership of property did not alter significantly the Ptolemaic mode of production. The development of private ownership did not reach fruition until after the Roman conquest. Jews therefore were historically present in Egypt as possessors of land and as absentee landlords during the economic change in ownership of property from public to private.

Although emigration from Palestine to Egypt continued under the Roman conquest, fundamental changes occurred that affected the prosperity of Jewish settlers. The Ptolemaic army was abolished; with its abolition Jewish *cleruchs* lost their status as military-landholders. While *cleruch* land was not legally designated as private the possibility of new Jewish mercenaries' joining the Roman army and being granted private land was significantly decreased. "Rome was not interested in engaging

---

[24]See *CPJ*, v. 1, nos. 23-27.

[25]For Helkias and Ananias as generals see Josephus, *Ant.*, 13.285ff. and 348ff.; for Dositheus as a general see Josephus, *Apion*, 2.49; for Dositheus as a Ptolemaic priest see *CPJ*, v. 1, nos. 127a-d and *3 Macc* 1:3; and for Onias as a *strategus*, see Tcherikover, *Hellenistic Civilization*, 281.

[26]See above, Chapter 2, 32 and fn. 34.

[27]See, for example, *CPJ*, v. 1, no. 29. Tcherikover's suggestion that these *cleruchs* were forced to cultivate unflooded and dry land is only an hypothesis, particularly in light of the low rents paid to the government. See Westermann, "Uninundated Lands," Parts I and II, and "Dry Land," for rents concerning unflooded and dry land; see also above Chapter 2, 39f.

[28]See above, Chapter 2, 32f. Cf. Hengel, *Judaism and Hellenism*, 16.

[29]For Jews who identified themselves as Macedonians, see for example, *CPJ*, v. 2, nos. 142 and 143. See also Josephus, *War*, 2.487ff.

Jews for military service, since throughout the Orient Jews were known as seditious people."[30] Thus, immigration was no longer motivated by the allotment of state land. Nevertheless, immigration continued for a variety of reasons including political and military considerations.

From the very first Roman venture into Egypt, Jewish Palestinian soldiers were involved in shaping Ptolemaic Egypt's destiny. Hyrcanus and Antipater supported Gabinius' attempt to restore the deposed Egyptian king Ptolemy XI Auletes in 55 B.C. by supplying him with money, arms and auxiliaries. They accompanied him to Pelusium and there persuaded the Jewish garrison to let the Roman troops pass peacefully.[31] In 48 B.C. Hyrcanus and Antipater sent troops to help Caesar in his Alexandrian campaign. Once again a Jewish garrison, this time at Leontopolis, although initially hostile to Caesar, was persuaded to support him. [32] In both these cases an appeal was made to the Egyptian Jewish soldiers' ethnic and religious identification with Judaism. According to Mary Smallwood, a further appeal was made in 30 B.C. resulting in the support for Rome of the Jewish soldiers in Egypt.[33] In all the above cases, military, personal and commercial bonds between Jewish soldiers from Egypt and from Palestine would have been promoted and it is reasonable to assume that since most of the fighting took place on Egyptian soil, some Palestinian Jewish soldiers decided to remain there.

After the Roman conquest of Egypt Jewish migration continued, although it is difficult to assess its magnitude. Many of Mariamme's Hasmonean sympathizers, including the Pharisees and Scribes as well as other rivals to Herod's dynasty, would have felt the urge to flee Palestine and may have found Egypt an attractive alternative. Fifty or sixty years later Claudius' letter to the Alexandrians mentions the emigration of Jews from Palestine to Egypt; and the policies of the procurators ruling Palestine, such as Pontius Pilate (26-36 A.D.),[34] Albinus (62-64 A.D.),[35] and Florus (64-66 A.D.),[36] easily could have contributed to emigration on the part of the Jewish population. In the aftermath of the Jewish revolt in 70 A.D. Josephus informs us of the *sicarii*, who in order to save their lives

---

[30] *CPJ*, v. 1, 52.

[31] Josephus, *Ant.*, 14.98ff. and *War*, 1.175ff.

[32] Josephus, *Ant.*, 14.127ff. and *War*, 1.187ff.

[33] Smallwood, *Jews*, 224 and fn. 17.

[34] See Josephus, *Ant.*, 18.55ff. and *War*, 2.169ff. as well as Philo, *Leg. ad Gaium*, 299ff.

[35] See Josephus, *Ant.*, 20.197ff. and *War*, 2.272ff.

[36] See Josephus, *Ant.*, 20.252ff. and *War*, 2.277ff.

fled to Egyptian Jewish communities.[37] Immigration was also supplemented by the homeless, military deserters, relatives and tax debtors.[38] In addition numerous Jewish prisoners of war also passed through Alexandria on their way to Rome.[39] Although some of these Jewish prisoners would have been redeemed,[40] and others would have been condemned to work as quarry-slaves,[41] the majority of the Jewish captives would have been sold as slaves to private landholders on the block in Alexandria or in Rome.

In summary, therefore, a great deal of historical, literary, papyrological and epigraphical evidence can substantiate the position that Jewish emigration from Palestine to Egypt was constant from Alexander the Great's conquest to the end of the first century A.D. The magnitude of migration at various times was dependent on political-economic circumstances, but there is ample evidence that there was a continuing trickle of Jews who were fleeing persecution, who were sold into slavery, or who were seeking new occupational opportunities. The data indicate that the flow of new immigrants appreciably altered during the reign of

---

[37] See Josephus, *War*, 7.410.

[38] Theissen, in *First Followers*, 42, has postulated that Jews in debt for taxes would have been "driven to leave their homeland." See also Hengel, *Judaism and Hellenism*, v. 1, 49.

[39] According to Jerome (in *Jeremiam*, 31.15), Jewish prisoners of war were transferred to Rome via Gaza and Alexandria. See also Josephus (*War*, 6.420) who estimates 97,000 prisoners of war were taken during the fall of Jerusalem. For the selling of Jews into slavery see Josephus, *Ant.*, 17.289, *War*, 1.180 and 6.418.

[40] See Philo's comments in *Leg. ad Gaium*, 155 that the Jews in Rome redeemed captive Jews. S. Zeitlin, in *The Rise and Fall of the Judaean State* (Philadelphia, 1969), v. 2, 34, has suggested that Herod's policy of selling Jewish people to foreigners, led Pharisaic leaders in Palestine to institute a new precept making it a moral duty for every Jew to ransom Jewish slaves. For an example of this occurring in Egypt, at a somewhat later date, see *CPJ*, v. 3, no. 473. For Jewish manumission in Palestine in the first century A.D., see P. R. C. Weaver, *Familia Caesaris: A Social Study of the Emperor's Freedmen and Slaves* (Cambridge, 1972), 29 and 64ff. See also Westermann, *Slave Systems*, 96, fn. 7 and G. Alon, *The Jews in Their Land in the Talmudic Age*, G. Levi, ed. and trans. (Jerusalem, 1980), 57.

[41] See Johnson, *Roman Egypt*, 242, C. N. Bromehead, "Mining and Quarrying to the Seventeenth Century," in Singer et al., eds., *Technology*, v. 2, 29; and *CPJ*, v. 1, 85 (in reference to Josephus, *War*, 6.418).

Philometor and that the Jewish population thereafter grew considerably stronger both numerically and in political importance.

3.2.2   Natural Increase[42]

Although it is impossible to arrive at an actual estimate of the numerical strength of the Jews in Egypt, one can surmise that fertility and mortality rates generally were high and Jewish migration to Egypt was continuous until the end of the first century A.D. Natural increase in the population in Egypt was stimulated by its climate, economic conditions, the pace of life, and relative political stability (in contrast, for example, to Palestine); while immigration increased steadily as Alexandria became the greatest *entrepôt* in the ancient world. Egypt was also a tourist's paradise. In all likelihood, then, Egypt enjoyed strong population growth from the second century B.C. to the end of the first century A.D. This assessment is supported by T. Walek-Czernecki, who has estimated that the population of Egypt expanded by one million inhabitants between the mid first century B.C. (8 million) and the end of the first century A.D. (9 million).[43]

The growth of the Egyptian population during the late Ptolemaic and early Roman Empire would have been supported by two important behavioural features of agrarian societies in antiquity. First, marriage patterns encouraged parents to betroth their daughters at an early age. Twelve years of age represented the coming of puberty. The Mishnah[44] and Codex Justiniani,[45] although of a later date, legitimate this tradition by viewing it as the appropriate age for the marriage of girls.[46] In Graeco-Roman as well as Jewish custom, this frequently meant marriages pre-arranged by

---

[42]Natural increase refers to births over deaths.

[43]As cited in P. Salmon, *Population et dépopulation dans l'empire romain (Latomus* 137, Brussels, 1974), 35. Rostovtzeff (*SEHHW*, v. 2, 1138) has arrived at the same conclusion. Josephus (*War*, 2.385) claims 7.5 million excluding Alexandria. In contrast see Hopkins ("Taxes and Trade," 117, fn. 49), who has suggested 5 million as the total population of Egypt in the first century A.D., following K.J. Beloch, *Die Bevölkerung des griechisch-römanischen Welt* (Leipzig, 1886), 258 and 307. For the population of Alexandria, see above Chapter 2, 41 and 66.

[44]*M. Ketub.*, 3.1 and *m. Qidd.*, 2.1.

[45]*Codex Justiniani, 5.4.24.*

[46]See K. Hopkins, "The Age of Roman Girls at Marriage," *Population Studies* 18 (1964-1965), 313 for a similar conclusion.

the male guardian, and as a result it is not uncommon to find betrothals and marriages at even younger ages. Josephus informs us that Agrippa I had betrothed two of his daughters at six and ten;[47] Dio Cassius[48] and Tacitus[49] provide further examples of which the most notable was the marriage of Octavia to Nero in 49 A.D. (engagement at age 7 and marriage at 11).[50] Moreover, the Mishnah provides numerous legal discussions arising from marriages before the age of 12.[51] "Soranus' medical advice, . . . Plutarch's characterization of the Romans, . . . and epigraphic evidence . . . [all point to] pre-pubertal marriages . . . on some scale."[52] By the age of 15 the majority of Roman girls of the respectable classes would have been married,[53] whereas the daughters of peasants were expected to marry sometime after they were 13 or 14.[54]

Females in antiquity were viewed as economic liabilities.[55] Mortality rates at birth were very high[56] and women tended to have shorter life-

---

[47]Josephus, Ant., 18.354f.

[48]Dio Cassius, Hist. Rom., 54.16.7.

[49]Tacitus, Annals, 12.58 and 14.64. Cf. Hopkins, "Girls," 313 for further examples.

[50]See Hopkins, "Girls," 314f.

[51]For example, see m. Yebam., 13.7-12; m. Ketub., 1.3, 4.2 and 4; m. Git., 5.5, and m. Qidd. 2.1: "A man may give his daughter in betrothal while she is still in her girlhood [i.e., before twelve years and one day] either by his own act or by that of his agent." For non-Jewish evidence see Hopkins ("Girls," 313), who has studied Roman marriage inscriptions and found that 8% were of marriages between ages ten and eleven.

[52]Hopkins, "Girls," 315.

[53]K. Hopkins, "On the Probable Age Structure of the Roman Population," Population Studies 20 (1966-1967), 260.

[54]Hopkins, "Girls," 318 and 326. Although Hopkins' data included only Italian peasants, marriage patterns in pre-industrial societies are generally similar, and Egyptian peasants probably followed comparable behavioural patterns. For a Jewish example in Egypt see CPJ, v. 2, no. 421.

[55]In Egypt new-born girls were frequently exposed upon birth. See, for example, P. Oxy. 744 and Westermann's data in Slave Systems, 86, fn. 43. For the general practice of infanticide see Tacitus, Histories, 5.5.2. and Suetonius, Aug., 65.4. Philo abhorred this practice (De Spec. Leg., 3.110ff.), as did Josephus (Apion, 2.202). Female slaves were also viewed as economic liabilities. See Hopkins, Conquerors, 158ff.

[56]See Salmon (Population, 97ff.), who estimates an infant mortality rate of 24% for the first five years of life; and Hopkins ("Probable Age," 263), who suggests 200 per 1,000. Hopkins' data take into account the agricultural mode of production and the lack of medical technology and knowledge.

spans than their male counterparts.[57] Furthermore, the social status of women was low. They had no political rights. They were not permitted to make wills[58] and were under the control of a male guardian.[59] A famous rabbinical quote best typifies this sentiment: "The world cannot exist without males and females; happy is he whose children are males and woe to him whose children are females."[60] Ben Sira's comments concerning women similarly acknowledge their low status: "woman is the origin of sin . . . if she does not accept your control, divorce her and send her away."[61] Or, as bluntly expressed by Josephus, "woman . . . is in all things inferior to the man."[62]

In addition, an important feature of the ancient world was the fact that women frequently had several children while still in their teenage years. Philous, 20 years old and the mother of two children (aged 5 and 1), was typical of the women of her day.[63] As in modern pre-industrialized agricultural societies, the woman's major role in life was childbearing. In an agrarian mode of production, children are economic assets, contributing to agricultural production at an early age and providing economic support for elderly parents. Thus early marriages would benefit the family unity, as the offspring would provide free labour. In fact, according to Jewish

---

[57] See Szilagyis' data as cited by Salmon, Population, 107ff. See also A. E. Samuel, Death and Taxes (American Studies in Papyrology 10, Toronto, 1971) and M. Hombert and C. Préaux, Recherches sur le recensement dans l'Égypte romaine (Leiden, 1952), 156ff.

[58] Taubenschlag, Law, 597.

[59] See H. F. Jolowicz, Roman Foundations of Modern Law (Oxford 1957), 113. For evidence in the Mishnah, see m. Ketub., 4.4-5; m. Sota, 3.8; and m. Qidd., 2.1. Philo also acknowledges that girls were under the charge of male guardians (De Spec. Leg., 3.67). See also CPJ, v. 1, nos. 19 and 26, and v. 2, nos. 144, 146, 148 and 149 for Jewish evidence in Egypt and Tcherikover's comments (v. 1, 35).

[60] B. Qidd., 82b. This is from a later period but corroborates the evidence above. See also b. Menah., 43b: "A man is obliged to offer three benedictions everyday—for not being created a heathen; for not being created a woman; and for not being created an ignoramus."

[61] Sir., 25.24-26.

[62] Josephus, Apion, 2.201.

[63] See CPJ, v. 2, no. 421.

law, the command to be fruitful and multiply[64] was interpreted in the
Mishnaic period to mean that "if a man took a wife and lived with her for
10 years and she bore no child," reasonable grounds for divorce existed.[65]
The birth rates of all pre-industrial societies are high, and Salmon's data
indicate that the average life-span of individuals in Egypt exceeded that
of individuals in Rome (28 vs. approximately 20).[66] Hence the rate of
natural increase would have been significant, with the bulk of the population in the lower age groups. Although sufficient data are not available
for comparing Roman and Egyptian Jews, one would assume that a similar
pattern prevailed.[67]

---

[64]Gen 1:28.

[65]*M. Yebam.*, 6.6. Philo disapproves strongly of marriages with barren
women and believes that their unfortunate husbands should divorce them
(*De Spec. Leg.*, 3.34ff).

[66]Salmon's conclusion (*Population,* 97ff.) depends on sophisticated
statistical generalizations from Blumenkranz's comparative but limited
data base. See also Hombert and Préaux (refs. below) who have offered
two sets of figures for the life expectancy of the Roman Egyptian population. The first, based on epitaphs, is 32.4 years of age ("Note sur la durée
de la vie dans l'Égypte Gréco-Romaine," *Chronique d'Égypte* 20 (1945),
139-146); the second, calculated from census returns, is 27.2 for men and
26.4 for women (*Recherches,* 156f.). With regard to Rome see W. R.
MacDonell (cited in Samuel, *Death and Taxes,* 7, fn. 3) who has utilized
epitaphs and has suggested an average age of 21.7, which approximates
Salmon's calculation. Nevertheless, despite the above estimates, one must
be cautious of all such projections of average age at death. See Hopkins
("Probable Age," 245-264), who discusses the various shortcomings of such
data and the methodology employed, and emphasizes the fact that the
available data are mostly from the upper class. His estimation of the
average expectation of life at birth in the Roman Empire is therefore
very broad—between 20 and 30 years.

[67]In contrast, see Tcherikover (*CPJ,* v. 2, 205) and Hombert and Préaux
(*Recherches,* 154ff.), who have argued that "Egyptian families in general
were not blessed with a great number of children" (*CPJ,* v. 2, 205). They
assume high infant mortality rates, the Egyptian practice of exposing
female babies, and that peasant women suckled their children for up to
three years (as referred to in 2 *Macc* 7:27) to avoid pregnancy. Although
high infant mortality rates were part of the natural rhythm of life in
antiquity (see above fn. 56), there is no reason to assume a declining rate
of natural increase or that Egypt's growth rate would have been significantly lower than Italy's. Preindustrial societies generally show high rates
of natural increase. While the rate of natural increase in modern industri-

3.2.3   Proselytism

A further variable affected the demographic composition of Jews in Egypt. Proselytism was encouraged in Judaism,[68] and this slowly but significantly would have increased their number. Non-Jewish evidence indicates that there existed numerous Jewish itinerant preachers and rhetoricians who travelled from city to city, expounding their particular definition of Jewish reality. Valerius Maximus[69] mentions the missionary activity of the Jews in the second century and Horace[70] corroborates his evidence in the first century B.C. Strabo, writing in the same period, comments that "this people [i.e., the Jews] has already made its way into every city, and it is not easy to find any place in the habitable world which has not received this nation and in which it has not made its power felt."[71] The well-known denunciation of the Pharisees by Matthew, a generation or two later, echoes this observation: "Woe unto you, scribes and Pharisees, hypocrites, for ye compass sea and land to make one

---

alized countries is under 10 births per 1,000 of total population (1978 figures), in the underdeveloped countries the birth rate is 25 per 1,000. See *World Population Data Sheet* (Washington, 1978), cited in R. Hagedorn, ed., *Sociology* (Toronto, 1980), 197. Second, while non-Jews practised infanticide in both Italy and Egypt (above, fn. 55), Jews did not. Tcherikover's suggestion that *m. Qidd.*, 4.2 and *m. Maks.*, 2.7, may refer to this practice is conjecture only. אסופים in both contexts is more likely to refer to foundlings that have been deserted. Third, Tcherikover is mistaken in assuming that prolonged breast feeding will prevent ovulation. At best, ovulation can only be postponed for a relatively short period (7 to 15 months) and even then "it is not true that you cannot become pregnant as long as you are nursing. . . ." For an informed book on breastfeeding see *The Womanly Art of Breastfeeding* (La Leche League, Franklin Park, 1963[2]), 10. Moreover, why would Egyptian peasants suckle their children longer than Roman peasants? Finally, in an historical epoch where children were viewed as economic assets, it is highly improbable that peasant mothers waited 3-4 years between children, especially in light of the fact that the average life expectancy in the Roman Empire was between 20-30 years of age (above fn. 66).

[68]For forced conversion during the Hasmonean epoch see Josephus, *Ant.*, 13.257 and 318.

[69]Valerius Maximus, *Facta et Dicta Memorabilia*, 1.3.3.

[70]Horace, *Sermones*, 1.4.142-143.

[71]Josephus, *Ant.*, 14.115.

proselyte."[72] Bamberger has shown how the rabbis were overwhelmingly in favour of conversion and converts to Judaism[73] and given the missionary evidence documented above, it appears that this policy was only an extension of common practice.[74] During this century there is also evidence from Seneca,[75] Juvenal,[76] Dio,[77] Philo[78] and Josephus.[79] Baron, accepting this evidence at face value, argues that during the early Roman Empire, it was "an advantage rather than an obstacle" to become a Jew.[80] It is hard to accept Baron's contention in the light of conflicting evidence. Jews frequently were viewed as seditious and morally debased,[81] and conversion for a male involved the disfigurement of the body,[82] an initiatory ritual that was considered demeaning.[83] Moreover, towards the end of the first century A.D., to become a Jew exposed the proselyte to a charge of atheism.[84] Thus, analysis of the data supports Hengel's conclusion that:

> the connection between nation and religion, . . . gave Judaism
> its tremendous strength in the Diaspora but with few

---

[72]Matt 23:15.

[73]B. J. Bamberger, *Proselytism in the Talmudic Period* (New York, 1968).

[74]See ibid., 274ff.

[75]Seneca, *De Superstitione*, apud: Augustine, *De Civitate Dei*, 6.11 and *Epistulae Morales*, 108.22.

[76]Juvenal, *Saturae*, 3.10-18, 14.96-106.

[77]Dio Cassius, *Hist. Rom.*, 57.5.

[78]Philo, *De Spec. Leg.*, 1.51-52 and *Flacc.*, 46.

[79]Josephus, *Apion*, 2.282f.

[80]S. W. Baron, *A Social and Religious History of the Jews* (New York, London, 1952[2]), v. 1, 174ff.

[81]This tradition extends in Egypt from Manetho in the third century B.C. to Apion in the first century A.D. See Stern, *Authors*.

[82]See Gen 17 for the covenant between Abraham and God. See also *m. Sabb.*, 19.5 and *m. Arak.*, 2.2.

[83]See, for example, Martial, *Epigrammata*, 7.30.5-8, 35.3-4, 82.5-6; 9.94.1-8 and Petronius, *Satyricon*, 68.8 and *Poems*, 24. See also Philo, *De Spec. Leg.*, 1.2f. and Josephus, *Apion*, 2.137.

[84]For example, the execution of Flavius Clemens by Domitian for atheism. See Dio Cassius, *Hist. Rom.*, 67.14.1-3, and Smallwood's excellent discussion in *Jews*, 379ff. and fn. 82.

exceptions, . . . prevented really extensive missionary success. . . . In antiquity, to be a Jew was never simply a religious action; it was also a political decision: on his conversion the Gentile became a member of the Jewish ethnos.[85]

In Judaism, a convert (i.e., a *ger*, a *proselytos*) designated a Gentile as a *bona fide* religious and ethnic member of the Jewish faith.[86] From the Maccabean revolt (165 B.C.) until the destruction of Jerusalem (70 A.D.), proselytes could identify themselves both with a growing Diaspora Jewish community and as members of a Jewish state. For these individuals Judaism conveyed a sense of exclusivity as it allowed them the opportunity to share in the unique revelation of Torah to Israel. On the other hand, they could also claim that the message (ethical monotheism) was universal.[87]

The evidence from Ptolemaic and early Roman Egypt indicates that Jewish missionaries received a warm welcome but not wide-spread or mass support. They flourished as an exclusive group and simultaneously appealed to the public. The rulers of Ptolemaic Egypt allowed Jews religious liberty,[88] and the Roman conquest brought little change. Hellenistic and Roman authorities tended to regard expressions of worship as supplements, not substitutes for what already existed.[89] Under Caesar, Judaism became unofficially a *religio licita*,[90] "an incorporated body with an

---

[85]Hengel, *Judaism and Hellenism*, v. 1, 307.

[86]See Zeitlin, *Rise and Fall*, v. 3, 326ff.; S. Applebaum, "The Social and Economic Status of the Jews in the Diaspora," in S. Safrai and M. Stern, eds., *The Jewish People in the First Century* (Philadelphia, 1976), v. 2, 622ff.; and J. R. Rosenbloom, *Conversion to Judaism* (Cincinnati, 1978).

[87]See Weber, *Ancient Judaism*, 362ff. Weber discusses the particularistic and universalistic features of Judaism.

[88]Tcherikover has suggested that Ptolemy Euergetes II granted many Jews Alexandrian civic rights to weaken the Greek lobby (*CPJ*, v. 1, 23). For a general discussion of Jewish religious liberty see Smallwood *Jews*, 120ff. and S. Applebaum, "The Legal Status of the Jewish Communities in the Diaspora," in Safrai and Stern, eds., *Jewish People* (Assen, 1974), v. 1, 420ff.

[89]A. D. Nock, in *Conversion* (London, 1961), 6, has expressed the same idea by the term "adhesion."

[90]Tertullian's classification, *Apology*, 21.1. Unofficially, because in Roman legal terminology "there appears to have been a recognized usage of *'collegia licita'* but not *'religio licita'* . . . until the early third century

authorized cult"[91] and its synagogues were classified as *collegia* with the privileges of Jewish associations spelt out.[92]

Proselytes could also come to Judaism in other ways: for example, through war and forced circumcision[93] or through marriage.[94] But for the most part the proselytes were seduced by Jewish rhetoricians and philosophers, who invariably were competing with the Greeks for centre stage. Much of Philo's work represents the cosmopolitan, well-educated, upper class, and believing Diaspora-Jewish philosopher locked in combat with Hellenistic philosophy over the interpretation of the cosmos. For Philo and similar writers, philosophy and missionary propaganda were like two sides of the same coin. The partial success of Jewish missionary efforts is attested to by Philo's reports of Greek attacks on Jews,[95] and by Suetonius[96] and Dio Cassius[97] who report that Domitian employed spies to find Jewish proselytizers fifty years later.

It has been suggested that the Ptolemaic rulers' favourable disposition towards the Jews, and Caesar's charter of rights, which protected Jews from Greek infringement of their legally confirmed religious liberty, indirectly helped to fertilize the ground for Jewish missionaries. As a consequence, it is not surprising that Hellenistic-Roman writers, as well as those of the New Testament, were aware of Jewish missionaries. Judaism was an acknowledged force that might be ridiculed, but could not be ignored.

A.D." See F. C. Grant, *Roman Hellenism and the New Testament* (New York, 1962), Appendix, "A Note on *'Religio Licita,'*" 172-178.

[91]Smallwood, *Jews*, 135.

[92]For example, the right to observe the Sabbath and festivals, to assemble for worship and common meals, to hold funds and to build synagogues. See Josephus, *Ant.*, 14.213ff. Moreover, Jews were exempted from the military service and from participation in the imperial cult. See Smallwood, *Jews*, 134ff. and J. Juster, *Les Juifs dans l'empire romain* (New York, 1914), v. 1, 353ff. and v. 2, 121ff.

[93]See above, fn. 68.

[94]For example, see Josephus, *Ant.*, 20.139.

[95]Philo, *Flacc.* and *Leg. ad Gaium*.

[96]Suetonius, *Domitian*, 12.2.

[97]Dio Cassius, *Hist. Rom.*, 67.14.1-3.

3.2.4   Population Projection and Distribution

The preceding analysis has examined three sociological variables that furnish evidence for a Jewish presence in Egypt. Since a Jewish census was not recorded in Egypt until after 70 A.D.[98] and history has not granted us extensive archival records, any estimation of the Jewish population in Egypt for the period under consideration remains no more than a deduction from scholarly opinion and scattered documentary evidence. If, as has been suggested, missionary activity was partially successful, migration to Egypt was common, and the rate of natural increase was high, then Avi-Yonah's and Baron's suggestion of 7 million Jews for the early Roman Empire—of which 1 million lived in Egypt and 2.5 million in Palestine—seems reasonable.[99] On this basis, between 10% and 15% of the Egyptian population was Jewish at the turn of the millennium.[100]

Without question, Alexandria had the largest number of Jews living in Egypt during this historical period. Arkin has estimated 200,000,[101] although Tcherikover and Rostovtzeff believe that there exists no satisfactory information on this point.[102] Mommsen has described Alexandria as "almost as much a city of the Jews as of the Greeks."[103] Two of its

---

[98]A Jewish census was only introduced after the imposition of the Jewish tax (71-72 A.D.). See Josephus, *War*, 7.218 and Dio Cassius, *Hist. Rom.*, 66.7.2. For an examination of the evidence see *CPJ*, v. 1, 80ff. and v. 2, 111ff.

[99]See M. Avi-Yonah, "Historical Geography of Palestine" in Safrai and Stern, eds., *Jewish People*, v. 1, 109 and Baron, *Social*, v. 1, 170 and 370, fn. 7. See Philo for the figure of one million Jews resident in Egypt (*Flacc.*, 43), although Tcherikover considers it inflated (*CPJ*, v. 1, 4 and 81). For the conventional estimation of the population of the early Roman Empire, see Beloch, *Die Bevölkerung*, 507, and D. M. Heer, *Society and Population* (Englewood Cliffs, N.J., 1968), 2, who have suggested 50-60 million.

[100]See above 83 and fn. 43 for Walek-Czernecki's estimate of the population of Egypt during the early Roman Empire. See also Juster (*Juifs*, v. 1, 209) for a similar estimation of the Jewish population in Egypt.

[101]M. Arkin, *Aspects of Jewish Economic History* (Philadelphia, 1975), 25.

[102]For Tcherikover see *CPJ*, v. 1, 4; for Rostovtzeff, *SEHHW*, v. 2, 113ff.

[103]Mommsen, *Provinces*, v. 2, 177.

five sections were Jewish[104] and there is a wide consensus among scholars, based on Josephus' and Philo's accounts, that Jews lived throughout the city.[105] In addition to Alexandria, Jewish communities were scattered up and down the Nile in both Upper and Lower Egypt (see Table 5). Philo writes that the Jews were "resident in Alexandria and the country from the slope into Libya to the boundaries of Ethiopia,"[106] and Jewish inhabitants in Alexandria, the Fayum, Edfu and the Oxyrhynchite *nome* are particularly well-documented.[107] The demographic distribution, in the light of the papyrological, epigraphical and literary evidence, indicates that the Jews not only were firmly established in Alexandria, in the *nome*-capitals, and villages, and in the outlying rural areas but indeed had twice the overall population of the Greeks.[108]

The strong Jewish presence in Egypt from the latter half of the second century B.C. tends to suggest that, like the Palestinian Jewish community, Jews in Egypt developed their own particularistic institutional structures. This would imply extensive community organization; a definite sense of a Jewish identity, be it secular or religious; firm bonds of social solidarity; and a continuously-transmitted knowledge of Judaism. Moreover, the development of such structures would have affected all classes, including those who enjoyed high status in the social and economic life of the Egyptian state. Indeed, class composition and the evolution of social institutions go hand in hand.

---

[104] Philo, *Flacc.*, 55.

[105] For Josephus see *War*, 2.494ff. and *Apion*, 2.33ff.; for Philo see *Flacc.*, 55 and *Leg. ad Gaium*, 132.

[106] Philo, *Flacc.*, 43.

[107] See, for example, *CPJ*, v. 2, nos. 142-159 for Alexandria; v. 1, nos. 7-17, 19-26, 28-41, 43-46, 125-131 and v. 2, 426-432 for the Fayum; v. 1, no. 140 and v. 2, nos. 160-229 for Edfu; and v. 2, nos. 410, 414, 418c, 422-423, 425, 447-448 and 450 for the Oxyrhynchite *nome*.

[108] See above, Chapter 2, 44 and fn. 94. This would also imply that the Jewish population of Alexandria may have approximated the Greek. Thus, Mommsen's comment (fn. 103 above) takes on even greater significance. However, Segré's postulation that the Jews of Alexandria comprised "not much less than 40 per cent of the total population" in the early Roman Empire is without support. See A. Segré, "Anti-semitism in Hellenistic Alexandria," *Jewish Social Studies* 8 (1946), 134ff.

Table 5
Jewish Communities in Ptolemaic-Roman Egypt *

Lower Egypt	Alexandria, Athribis, Busiris, Castra Judae-orum, Leontopolis, Memphis, Migdal, Nitriai, Pelusium, Schedia, Tachpanches, Teberkytis, Vicus Judaeorum, Xenephyris, and unspecified places within the *nomes* of Heliopolis, Mendesia, and Pharbetites.
Upper Egypt	Fayum: Alabanthis, Alexandrou-Nesos, Apias, Apollonias, Arepolis, Arsinoe (= Krokodilopolis), Bacchias, Berenike-Hormos, Bernikis, Aigialu, Boubastos, Embolu-topos, Euhemereia, Gurob, Hephaistias, Herakleia, Ibion Argaiou, Karanis, Kerkeosiris, Kerkesephis, Lisymachis, Neilupolis, Philadelphia, Philoteris, Psenyris, Samareia, Sebennytos, Soknopion-Nesos, Tebtunis, Theadelphia, Trikomia. Oxyrhynchos *nome:* Anteiis Pela, Oxyrhynchos, Phthochis, Sephtha, Sinary. Abydos, Antinoe, Antinoupolis, Apollinopolis-Heptakomia, Apollinopolis magna (= Edfu), Elephantine, Koptos, Lycopolis, Ombos, Ptolemais Hermion, Syene, Thebes (= Diospolis magna). Unspecified places within the *nomes* of Herakleopolis, Hermoupolis magna, Kynopolis.

*Source: V. Tcherikover, *The Jews in Egypt in the Hellenistic-Roman Age in the Light of the Papyri* (in Hebrew, Jerusalem, 1963[2]), iv and 28ff. with additional data included.

3.3   Social Class and Social Institutions:
         The Institutional Matrix

3.3.1   The Social Mosaic

         Egyptian Jews belonged to all social strata, ranging from the
aristocracy to the slave. The data collected in the *Corpus Papyrorum
Judaicarum* document this in some detail.[109] In the Ptolemaic period,
Jews were soldiers, inclusive of the officer rank, landholders (military
settlers), tenants (leaseholders, king's peasants), labourers (fieldhands),
vine-dressers, and shepherds. They were agents of the governmental
bureaucracy and served in administrative roles such as district governors,
tax-collectors, managers of government storehouses and banks, and
policemen. Some acted as influential advisors to the king or queen (e.g.,
Dositheus, Onias IV)[110] while others were slaves.[111] There is little evidence of Jewish commercial activity, and what there is informs us only of
petty trade and the advancement of small loans.[112] Despite the paucity
of the data, this probably constituted the general trend. Ptolemaic banks
were a government monopoly and the Ptolemaic mode of production
favoured state ownership of the means of production and distribution.
Thus Jewish activity would more likely reflect government employment
than private enterprise. The few pieces of data that have survived
indicate that Jews were employed in state industries such as banking[113]
and chaff-stores.[114] Jewish artisans are also, for the most part, absent

---

[109]See *CPJ*, v. 1, 113-256 and v. 2, 1-224. See also V. Tcherikover's
analysis of the data in *The Jews in Egypt in the Hellenistic and Roman
Age in the Light of the Papyri* (in Hebrew, Jerusalem, 1963²).

[110]For the political and military ascendancy of the Jews under
Philometor see above, fn. 25. Fraser (*Ptolemaic Alexandria*, v. 1, 699ff.)
has also suggested that the author of the *Letter of Aristeas* was a high-
ranking Jew at the Ptolemaic court of Philometor.

[111]It was common practice in pre-industrial societies that the proceeds
of victory were distributed among the conquerors. Slavery was a product
of conquest. Hence it is not unreasonable to assume that when Ptolemy I
conquered Palestine he brought back slaves for his personal household. For
the practice in general, see Hopkins, *Conquerors*. For Jewish prisoners of
war see above fn. 7.

[112]See *CPJ*, v. 1, 16 and nos. 20, 23, 24, 26 and 32.

[113]For example, see *CPJ*, v. 1, nos. 65 and 69.

[114]For example, see *CPJ*, v. 1, nos. 97, 99-103 and 105.

from the papyri. Nevertheless, Philo's comments,[115] the guilds of Jewish craftsmen listed in the Tosephta,[116] as well as the Talmud,[117] and a few papyrological fragments[118] indicate that professional organizations of Jewish artisans did exist, at least in Alexandria. Finally, with regard to literary or scholastic life, several Jewish authors are referred to, although there is little indication of the strata to which they belonged.[119]

Jews, therefore, were landholders (e.g., cleruchs,[120] tax-collectors[121]) and tenants on royal land[122] in Ptolemaic Egypt. Jews who were cleruchs had higher status than tenants and were freed from the corvée and from a variety of taxes.[123] Those who were tax-collectors had even higher status as they were chosen from among the more affluent and had to guarantee the state its taxes.[124] Only those with a large and regular income were able to serve in this capacity. There is also some evidence of Jews possessing or owning vineyards since they paid the apomoira (vineyard and orchard tax).[125] They too can be counted as part of the more affluent class in Ptolemaic Egypt. Consequently, there would have been a number of affluent Jews who acquired advantages in state monopolies due to their class status.[126]

In summary, Jews occupied all grades of wealth and social rank. During the reign of Philometor a transition is noticeable in which Jews enter higher social strata (e.g., the royal court, the bureaucracy) more

---

[115]Philo, Flacc., 57.

[116]See t. Sukk., 4.6 and t. Yoma, 1.5-6.

[117]See b. Sukk., 51b, b. Yoma, 38a and b. Arak., 10b.

[118]For example, see CPJ, v. 1, nos. 28, 45 and 95.

[119]See Y. Gutman, The Beginnings of Jewish Hellenistic Literature (in Hebrew, Jerusalem, 1958-1963), 2 vols. Also see 111f. below.

[120]For examples of Jews possessing land as cleruchs, see fn. 15 above.

[121]For examples of Jews as tax-collectors see CPJ, v. 1, nos. 90, 91, 107, 109 and 110. See also Tcherikover's commentary in CPJ, v. 1, 200ff.

[122]For examples of Jews as tenants on royal land see CPJ, v. 1, nos. 35 and 43, and Section V, 194-226.

[123]For differences between cleruchs and royal peasants see Chapter 2, 30ff. and 43f.

[124]See above, Chapter 2.

[125]See, for example, CPJ, v. 1, nos. 64, 70-72.

[126]There is, however, no available evidence that Jews possessed doreae.

frequently. In proportion to their numbers, the Jews, as part of the Persians of the *Epigone*, would have become socially mobile and been accorded higher social status. Without doubt, this development would have created conflict with the Greek population, who with lesser numbers wished to maintain the *status quo*. Nevertheless, many Jews became part of the new intelligentsia, were given citizen status and were perceived as members of the upper class. This transition marks the entry of Jews into the Greek establishment and provides the foundation on which the Jewish society of Roman Alexandria was built.[127] By the end of the Ptolemaic kingdom, Jewish military, political and economic influence was considerable,[128] although the material conditions of the average Egyptian Jew remained unaffected.

> Jews served and worked everywhere, in every branch of the economic life of the country, as soldiers and policemen, tax-farmers and State officials, as tillers of the soil, artisans and merchants. There were, of course, rich Jews, in Alexandria as well as in the *chora*, but the general impression resulting from a study of the documents is that of a hard-working people earning its living by tenacious labour. The limits of this activity were determined not by the Jews themselves but by the general conditions of the Ptolemaic state: the 'totalitarian' system, hostile to all private initiative.[129]

With Roman rule the opportunities for Jews to become upwardly mobile along traditional channels were greatly curtailed. The Ptolemaic army was abolished. Jews no longer were able to attain status or mobility by obtaining employment as soldiers or recruitment as military settlers.[130] As a result, they lost the chance to receive land grants in return for their service. The *Epigone* were not enlisted, and according to Applebaum, suffered the same fate as others designated as Persians of the *Epigone*— legal disabilities as well as being perceived as "members of the lowest

---

[127] Fraser, *Ptolemaic Alexandria*, v. 1, 85. For Jewish mobility via the *gymnasium* see below 124f. and 161f.

[128] Ibid., v. 1, 55, 83ff. and 281.

[129] *CPJ*, v. 1, 19.

[130] See *CPJ*, v. 1, 52f., in contrast to Juster, *Juifs*, v. 2, 273ff. There is only one piece of evidence of Jews serving in the Roman army in Egypt (*CPJ*, v. 2, no. 229).

class of the part of the population which claimed Greek culture."[131] In addition, Jews could no longer act as tax-collectors or perform civil service roles. Roman authorities preferred Greeks or Romans. Although there are exceptions (e.g., Tiberius Julius Alexander), the exclusion of Jews from the civil service is not surprising. As mentioned above, the official Roman attitude towards the Jews was one of tolerance (i.e., *religio licita*) while the unofficial attitude seemed to border on antipathy.[132] Moreover, entrance into Roman administrative posts required public participation in state cults. Hence a position in the governmental bureaucracy meant *ipso facto* a renunciation of the Jewish faith.

Although the ability of Jews to become upwardly mobile by entering the military or civil service decreased, Rome's change of policy with regard to private enterprise and ownership of land helped to compensate for this loss. Philo,[133] Josephus,[134] the Mishnah[135] and the papyri[136] all testify to the active involvement of Egyptian Jews in commercial undertakings. In particular, the demonopolization of the shipping industry and the reduction of custom tariffs[137] greatly benefited the Jews. Jewish Alexandrian merchants were active in the Red Sea trade and in the movement of the *annona*.[138] According to Saad, "les juifs jouèrent un grand rôle dans l'infiltration des échanges commerciaux monétaires reguliers dans la campagne égyptienne. . . ."[139] Jews also benefited from the designation of *cleruch* land as private.[140] Jews who had been granted land by the Ptolemies were now legally private owners. In areas such as

---

[131] Applebaum, "Legal Status," in Safrai and Stern, eds., *Jewish People*, v. 1, 429. See also *CPJ*, v. 2, nos. 146, 149 and 411.

[132] See above, Section 3.2.3, 87ff. and fns. 81 and 90; Cf. Stern, *Authors*.

[133] For example, see Philo, *Flacc.*, 57 and *Leg. ad Gaium*, 129.

[134] For example, see Josephus, *Ant.*, 18.159f. and *War*, 5.205.

[135] For example, see *m. Kil.*, 15.1 and *m. Ohol.*, 8.1.

[136] For example, see *CPJ*, v. 2, nos. 152, 413 and 414.

[137] See above, Chapter 2, 60f.

[138] See above Chapter 2, 66f.; D. Sperber, "Objects of Trade Between Palestine and Egypt in Roman Times," *Journal of the Economic and Social History of the Orient* 19 (1976), 146; and Johnson, *Roman Egypt*, 400. See also Josephus, *Apion*, 2.64. One of the firms engaged in Red Sea trade was owned by Marcus Julius Alexander (*CPJ*, v. 2, 197).

[139] Saad, "Mode de production asiatique," 24.

[140] See above, Chapter 2, 52 for the change in legal status of *cleruch* land.

Leontopolis and the Fayum this would have amounted to substantial parcels of land. In addition, there is evidence of Jews owning land who were not *cleruchs*,[141] and Gaius Julius Alexander may have been the owner of an *ousia*.[142] Furthermore, Jewish landowners attempted to purchase and cultivate crown land that was confiscated, unflooded or dry.[143] They also may have benefited from the Flavian reorganization and reclassification of the *ousiae*.[144] Many of these landowners were citizens and were not subject to the *laographia*.[145] Consequently, the evidence suggests that "the emancipation of private initiative from the heavy burden of state control"[146] was responsible for the upward mobility of a significant number of Jews. The privatization of property and de-monopolization of several industries as well as of the distribution process provided numerous opportunities for Jews to become—in diminishing proportions—property-owners, *epheboi*, citizens and members of the upper class.[147]

The wealthy commercial strata are especially noteworthy. Philo refers to several different strata, among which "men of business" and capital predominate.[148] Alexander, Marcus, and Tiberius Julius Alexander (the

---

[141]See *CPJ*, v. 2, nos. 142, 145, 420a, 445 and 448.

[142]See *CPJ*, v. 2, no. 420 (P. Ryl. 126 and 166). Cf. Rostovtzeff, *SEHRE*, v. 2, 672, fn. 44. However, see also Parassoglou's reservations (*Imperial Estates*, 17, fn. 12).

[143]For a Jewish landowner cultivating dry land see *CPJ*, v. 2, no. 142.

[144]See above, Chapter 2, 51 and 58.

[145]See, for example, *CPJ*, v. 2, nos. 418-420, and no. 142 with reference to Jews holding land in the Alexandrian *chora*. Urban non-citizens were not permitted to own land in the *chora* of Alexandria (see Jones, *Cities*, 305ff.). In addition, see Josephus, *Ant.*, 14.236f. Cf. also *CPJ*, v. 1, 14ff. and v. 2, 116ff. and 197ff., and Tcherikover, *Hellenistic Civilization*, 327ff.

[146]Rostovtzeff, *SEHHW*, v. 2, 733.

[147]For access to *epheboi* and citizen status see below, 124ff.

[148]Philo, *Flacc.*, 57. Tcherikover (*CPJ*, v. 1, 48, fn. 2) has translated the πορισtῶν in Philo's passage as "men of business" or, strictly speaking, "men of profit." This translation is acceptable providing that these "men of business" are not equated with today's capitalists, as Tcherikover has done. For other "men of business" see Philo, *Leg. ad Gaium*, 129, and *CPJ*, v. 2, 282, 362, 404 and 422. The Mishnah also mentions Alexandrian ships (*m. Kil.*, 15.1 and *m. Ohol.*, 8.1).

prefect of Egypt and Philo's nephew), the family of the *alabarchs* (customs-officials), had a great deal of commercial wealth and political power.[149] In addition, it seems probable that Dorotheus, son of Cleopatrides of Alexandria,[150] Simon, son of Boethus, and Jesus, son of Phiabi,[151] were of Egyptian origin and from affluent commercial families. Commerce on a large scale produced considerable capital, although, as noted in Chapter 2, opportunities in commerce were not as great as profits and investments in land. "Land-ownership was the bedrock of wealth. . . . Commerce and finance were only the cream on the cake, not the cake itself."[152] Thus, it would not be surprising that individuals such as Marcus Julius Alexander who had capital invested it in land. Even the rabbis acknowledged the importance of owning land: "Anyone who owns no land is no proper man."[153] In spite of the fact that commerce was profitable it was perceived as having less status than land-holding.

Although the data suggest that many Jews took full advantage of the transformations in the Ptolemaic mode of production and profited through commerce or land-ownership, the majority remained employed in agriculturally-related tasks,[154] primarily as tenants on crown land, as artisans,[155] or in the remaining state industries. Finally, it should be

---

[149]See *CPJ*, v. 2, nos. 418a-f, 419a-e and 420a-b; Josephus, *Ant.*, 18.159f., 19.276f., 20.100 and *War*, 5.205.

[150]See Josephus, *Ant.*, 14.236f.

[151]The families of Boethus and Phiabi are both from Egypt and are the first examples of high priests in Jerusalem from the Diaspora. They were recruited by Herod as a buffer against the remnants of the Hasmonean dynasty and as a new elite that would be loyal to him alone. See Josephus, *Ant.*, 15.320ff. and 19.297f.

[152]Hopkins, *Conquerors*, 49 and 52. According to Hopkins, wealthy businessmen were frequently also prosperous landowners (51). See above Chapter 2, 66f. and 71.

[153]*B. Yebam.*, 63a. Although this quote is from a later period, Rabbi Eleazar's statement can here be read as reflecting conventional opinion.

[154]For example, see *CPJ*, v. 2, Section IX, Part II, nos. 230-374. As outlined in Chapter 2, 65f. the overwhelming majority of the labour force (80% to 90%) was deployed in agricultural work.

[155]For evidence of artisans see Philo, *Flacc.*, 57, t. *Yoma*, 1.5-6, t. *Sukk.*, 4.6 and *CPJ*, v. 2, nos. 405 and 432. The emphasis upon Jews learning a trade was particularly strong and the *Tannaim* encouraged it (e.g., *m. Abot.*, 2.2 and *m. Qidd.*, 4.14). See also Josephus (*Apion*, 2.283) who emphasizes Jewish labour "in the crafts."

noted that Jews were also part of the slave population.[156]

The transition from state to private ownership of property facilitated the mobility of many Jews to positions of influence in the realms of economics, politics and culture. A Jewish commercial stratum became highly visible and took the place of the more traditional military and civil service occupations as an avenue for mobility. These individuals were concentrated in urban centres and, in particular, Alexandria which further promoted their opportunities for being mobile. If they owned land they adopted the Greek pattern of ownership practised by aristocratic Alexandrians.[157]

Yet in spite of the upward mobility of some (both in property ownership and urban-rural preference), the status of the average Jew remained much the same or worse in the early Roman period. The majority of Jews, like the Egyptians, were overburdened with taxes, liable for the *laographia* and the *corvée* and were demeaned for their behaviour, dress and speech. In a society where an individual's status could change only with wealth, the Jew, like the Egyptian peasant, still lived mainly by the sweat of his brow.

> The general impression of the economic condition of Egyptian Jews in the early Roman period is that of slow decline. . . . It is true that Jews could profit from the economic freedom inaugurated by the Romans and the abrogation of the 'totalitarian' principles of the Ptolemies; but the progress made by Alexandrian traders and money-lenders was counterbalanced by the very considerable damage done to Jews by their exclusion from military service and government offices.[158]

In times of economic hardship Jews, like other peasants from the *chora*, deserted the land. Many of these peasants converged on Alexandria, contributing to the city's high growth rate in the first century A.D.[159]

---

[156]See above Chapter 2, 46f. for the role played by slaves in Roman Egypt. For Jewish slaves see 82 above, and fns. 39-41. The suppression of Jewish uprisings in Alexandria would also have contributed to the number of Jewish slaves.

[157]For example, Gaius Julius Alexander. Cf. Chapter 2, 58 and fn. 157.

[158]*CPJ*, v. 1, 54.

[159]See above Chapter 2, 66 for the growth rate of Alexandria at the turn of the millennium.

Only there could they expect a sympathetic response to their material needs based on bonds of religious and ethnic identity. In short, the condition of the majority of the Jews of early Roman Egypt remained largely unchanged from that of the Ptolemaic period.

The social mosaic of Jews in Ptolemaic and Roman Egypt can thus be described as follows: at the top of the social class pyramid was a small but prominent aristocracy and land-holding class, split into those who were associated with the Ptolemaic royal house (e.g., Onias) or with Rome (Tiberius Julius Alexander) and those who were not associated with one or the other but were independently wealthy (Philo); at the bottom, was a large class of indigent, propertyless peasants; and between these two extremes was a heterogeneous group that included small landholders, those engaged in commerce, artisans, and wage-labourers. Class composition and ownership of land are the important keys to understand Jewish assimilation patterns. Landholding in particular is the material expression of social stratification.

3.3.2   The Role and Impact of Religious Institutions

Jewish religious institutions in Egypt reflect the continuing identification of Egyptian Jews with their religion. They signify religious solidarity, social organization and historical continuity, and indicate the existence of defined roles, standards of conduct and normative prohibitions. The records of customs, rituals, and behavioural norms all testify to the vitality of these religious institutions. The more developed the religious canopy, the more Judaism dominated the secular life of the individual. The more an individual manifested his Judaism, the more he identified and interacted with other Jews. By addressing the question of the extent to which Egyptian Jews developed unique religious institutions, the demographic presence of Jews is transformed from a statistic into an actuality.

The Ptolemaic rulers' relatively favourable disposition towards the Jews and Caesar's charter of rights provided an environment conducive to the establishment and development of institutions that catered specifically to the needs of the Jewish ethnic community. Of these institutions, the synagogue (proseyche— προσευχή) was the most important.[160] The

---

[160]For differing opinions regarding the origins of the synagogue and its development see J. Gutmann, ed., *The Synagogue: Studies in Origins, Archeology and Architecture* (New York, 1975). For the identification of

synagogue was a centre of prayer (בית תפילה) and study (בית המדרש), and a centre for communal assembly (בית הקנסת). It served as the focal point for religious life and promoted feelings of ethnic and religious identification. It was through active participation in the synagogue that religious patterns of behaviour came to be viewed as normative and legitimate in spite of their divergence from Palestinian practice in the Jerusalem Temple.

Beginning in the third century B.C., there is epigraphical evidence of synagogues in Egypt, and the comments of Philo, Josephus and the Talmud suggest that they remained a dominant force in Jewish life through the first century A.D. Dedicatory inscriptions during the Ptolemaic period refer to *proseuchae* in Schedia (Lower Egypt)[161] and Arsinoe (Fayum)[162] in the third century B.C., in Nitriai (Wadi Natrun),[163] Athribis (Lower Egypt),[164] Alexandria[165] and Xenephyris (Western Delta)[166] in the second century B.C., and in Alexandria[167] in the first century B.C. There is papyrological evidence of a synagogue in Alexandrou-Nesos in the Fayum in the third century B.C.[168], and from Arsinoe in the second century B.C.[169] In addition to these synagogues, Onias IV near the end of his career built a Temple in Leontopolis (c. 145 B.C.).[170] Although the Temple contradicted biblical precept[171] and was never more than a shrine that possessed a purely local significance for the military colony,[172] it testifies that Jewish institutional practice could simultaneously be modelled after Jerusalem yet abandon Palestinian tradition. Deviant forms of

---

proseuche with synagogue see M. Hengel, "Proseuche und Synagoge," in Gutmann, ed., *Synagogue*, 27-54.

[161] *CPJ*, v. 3, no. 1440.
[162] *CPJ*, v. 3, no. 1532a.
[163] *CPJ*, v.3, no. 1442.
[164] *CPJ*, v. 3, nos. 1443, 1444.
[165] *CPJ*, v. 3, no. 1433.
[166] *CPJ*, v. 3, no. 1441.
[167] *CPJ*, v. 3, no. 1432.
[168] *CPJ*, v. 1, no. 129.
[169] *CPJ*, v. 1, no. 134.
[170] See Josephus, *Ant.*, 12.387ff. and 13.62ff. For Jewish inscriptions from Leontopolis, see *CPJ*, v. 3, nos. 1451-1530. See also *CPJ*, v. 1, 45 and fn. 113 and Tcherikover, *Hellenistic Civilization*, 279ff.
[171] *M. Menah.*, 13.10.
[172] Since no Jewish Alexandrian writer, including Philo, has documented the temple of Onias, its religious and national significance could only have been marginal. Cf. Smallwood, *Jews*, 368.

religious practice were able to find fertile ground in Egypt. In the early Roman period Philo bears witness to several Jewish *proseuchae* in Alexandria,[173] and there is a reference in the Tosephta to the great synagogue of Alexandria.[174] Applebaum has suggested that these synagogues were organized into a federation which coordinated religious practices and handled administrative chores.[175] Finally, two synagogues are mentioned in Arsinoe in 113 A.D., which most likely were erected in the preceding century.[176] All these pieces of evidence collectively suggest that the Ptolemaic and Roman policy of toleration led to the establishment of synagogues by Jewish communities throughout Egypt, of which only a handful so far have come to our attention.[177]

The structural characteristics of the synagogue facilitated its role as a centralizing force within the Jewish community. On the one hand the synagogue had to provide the same character of spiritual experience as the Temple in Jerusalem yet not usurp its role. On the other hand, the synagogue had to legitimize the religious ideology of a Jewish community separated from Palestine and vulnerable to non-Jewish influences. The synagogue simultaneously had to create the feeling for both the individual and the community that they were a part of their local Egyptian setting as well as a part of the Jewish nation as a whole, a nation that looked to Palestine, Jerusalem and the Temple for direction.

The synagogue's central concern, therefore, was not merely the maintenance of Judaism, but more fundamentally the promotion of social

---

[173]For example, see Philo, *Leg. ad Gaium*, 132, 156 and *Flacc.*, 45.

[174] *T. Sukk.*, 4.6. Cf. *b. Sukk.*, 51b.

[175]S. Applebaum, "The Organization of the Jewish Communities in the Diaspora," in Safrai and Stern, eds., *Jewish People*, v. 1, 500. Smallwood (*Jews*, 133ff.) has also implicitly adopted this position.

[176]See *CPJ*, v. 2, no. 432.

[177]Other references to *proseuchae* include *CPJ*, v. 1, no. 138 and v. 3, nos. 1447 and 1449. The date and provenance of all these are problematic. See also P. Oxy. 840, which mentions a priest and suggests a synagogue in close proximity. For the prevalence of synagogues as an institution in Palestine during the late Second Temple period, see John Wilkinson, "Christian Pilgrims in Jerusalem during the Byzantine Period," *PEQ* 108 (1976), 76ff., who has postulated that there were 365 synagogues in Jerusalem. This figure is undoubtedly inflated. For archeological evidence of synagogues in Palestine in the first century A.D. see E. M. Meyers, "Ancient Synagogues in Galilee: Their Religious and Cultural Setting," *BA* 43/2 (1980), 99-108.

integration and social solidarity in the face of Hellenism. It symbolically represented the essence of community. The synagogue was a 'fence around the Torah,' that protected the community against contamination and eventual disappearance. In this manner the community was placed at the forefront of Judaism, de-emphasizing the role of the individual, with the synagogue serving as the primary catalyst for motivating religious behaviour and ideology.

During this epoch, synagogue worship had several standardized features and rituals, although the format and even the content often varied.[178] Worship, including Torah reading, required a quorum of ten men at fixed regular intervals.[179] The Sabbath was the most important gathering day and non-Jewish[180] as well as Jewish writers[181] testify to its significance for the community. Philo, for example, comments that the *Therapeutae* met once a week.[182] In addition to the Sabbath, meetings took place on public feasts (e.g., Passover, Pentecost, Feast of Tabernacles, the New Year, and the Day of Atonement) and on fast days (e.g., on the occasion of drought).[183] A complex set of rituals and special prayers accompanied these religious gatherings. For example, one of the papyri (from the second century A.D.) contains fragments attesting to ritual on the Day of Atonement.[184]

The synagogue's primary function, as inscribed in the Mount Ophel inscription, was "the reading of the Torah and the study of the commandments"[185] and one would assume that the synagogues in the Diaspora played a similar role if the statements of Philo are credible.[186] The

---

[178]For a general introduction to the synagogue, see I. Levy, *The Synagogue* (London, 1963).

[179]*M. Meg.*, 4.3.

[180]For example, see Seneca, *De Superstitione*, apud: Augustine, *De Civitate Dei*, 6.11 and *Epistulae Morales*, 95.47; Suetonius, *Aug.*, 76.2; Juvenal, *Saturae*, 14.96-106; Horace, *Sermones*, 1.9.60-72; Ovid, *The Remedies of Love*, 218-220 and *Art of Love*, 1.75-76, 413-416; Tacitus, *Histories*, 5.4.3; and Tibullus, *Carmina*, 1.3.15-18.

[181]For example, see Philo, *De Spec. Leg.*, 2.56ff., *De Vita Mosis*, 2.215-216 and *Leg. ad Gaium*, 158; Josephus, *Ant.*, 16.163 and *Apion*, 2.282.

[182]Philo, *De Vita Cont.*, 30.

[183]For the occasion of a drought see *m. Ta'an.*, 3.1ff.

[184]S. Safrai, "The Temple," in Safrai and Stern, eds., *Jewish People*, v. 2, 898.

[185]*CII*, v. 2, no. 1404.

[186]See Philo, *Leg. ad Gaium*, 157 and *Quod Omn. Prob.*, 81ff.

magnitude of attendance for the Sabbath or feast-days fluctuated according to belief and necessity, although it is interesting to note that, like today, those who were otherwise indifferent to their religion sanctified the Day of Atonement and sat in the synagogue the whole day.[187] However, the majority of the procedures were different from the established practices of the Temple in Jerusalem. Individuals from the congregation were asked to lead the congregation in prayers and scripture-reading. This procedure stood in sharp contrast to the practice in the Temple where only the priests could provide access to God through their hereditary right to perform sacrifices.[188] Participation was dependent on achievement and knowledge, rather than on ascription and tradition. Yet in spite of this process of decentralization and liberalization, very few people outside of Palestine had enough competence in Hebrew to read the Torah. The Talmud and Philo both highlight this predicament. The Talmud records that Jews living in the Hellenistic world did not have the luxury to call upon three, five, or seven readers but only one,[189] and Philo testifies that in Alexandria on the Sabbath the Torah was read by one person only instead of seven.[190] Moreover, the process of liberalization did not involve any change in the status of women. They took no active part as institutionalized representatives of the synagogue community nor were they allowed to read scripture.[191]

The liberalization process also affected the content of prayers. Prayers shifted in focus from petitions of need to divine worship.[192] Although there is little evidence to suggest that standardization occurred between or among synagogues in Alexandria, Egypt, or Palestine, the very fact of

---

[187]See Philo, De Spec. Leg., 1.186.

[188]Similarly, the priests in Leontopolis had a higher status than the laity. However, it should be pointed out that the priests in Jerusalem did not consider the priests in Leontopolis as legitimate. "If priests have ministered in the House of Onias they may not minister in the Temple of Jerusalem" (m. Menah., 13.10).

[189]For the number of readers see m. Moed, 4.1-2. For the difficulty of finding them see t. Meg., 4.12-13 and y. Meg., IV.75a.

[190]Philo, Hypothetica, 7.13.

[191]See ibid., loc. cit. and t. Meg., 4.11. The early Christian movement adopted similar stance (1 Cor 14:34f.).

[192]S. Safrai, "The Synagogue" in Safrai and Stern, eds., Jewish People, v. 2, 915.

the prayers themselves indicates that a liturgy existed. If there was any standardization, it would have included some version of the eighteen benedictions (*shemone esre*) and the *shema*.[193] Safrai's comment with regard to the evolution of the *shemone esre* may apply in general to the development of prayers:

> There was a variety of versions, which were elaborated in various circles and gradually took on a fixed structure, where blessings, introductions and conclusions were given set form, and were adopted into the prayers. The institutional authorities to whom the prayers are attributed were responsible, in the main, only for settling the order and deciding how a prayer should be structured and formulated.[194]

Hence the variegation and fluidity of prayers during this historical period. The absence of a centralized decision-making body, which would have established a uniform legitimate tradition, may have provided the opportunity for alternative formulations to be nourished. As a result, discourses (*midrashim*) based on the lessons from the Torah were open to alternative hermeneutics. The writings of Philo, the New Testament, as well as many Nag Hammadi tractates can all be viewed as representative examples that depend on the Torah for their initial narrative.

The institutionalization of rituals and prayers, even if locally circumscribed, indicates that there existed a division of labour within the synagogue community. Status stratifiction had to be present as some members had to be more influential in defining rules governing organizational behaviour and formulating ideology. Social control had to be perpetuated and sacred objects and locations had to be maintained. These individuals would share responsibility in determining which rituals and prayers would play an instrumental role in the socialization of old and new members.

In particular, the presence of scripture-reading on the Sabbath emphasizes the division of labour within the synagogue, and more generally, within the Jewish community with regard to religious institutional life. As mentioned above, few Diaspora Jews could read the Hebrew Torah. Similarly, few could understand it. Hence an accompanying translation into Greek was required during the Hebrew scripture-reading. This necessitated that the translator memorize each verse separately before the reading to insure that his interpretation would be as close as possible to

---

[193]Ibid., 916.
[194]Ibid., 925.

the original Hebrew.[195] Thus the translator needed access to a *Septuagint* to be employed as the vehicle to transmit God's word to his people. In addition to this translator, a number of other individuals also held organizational positions, including a president (ἀρχισυνάγωγός) who with others, possibly *archons*, and a clerk (γραμματεύς), may have formed some kind of executive committee.[196] According to Applebaum, the *archons'* responsibilities were primarily secular,[197] whereas the president would have been more involved in religious matters than administrative affairs.[198] The clerk probably kept records and handled correspondence.[199] The synagogue would also have had a *hazzan (neokoros)*[200] who could be identified as the executive director, the person who ran the administration from day to day and who acted as master of ceremonies during the liturgy. For example, in a synagogue in Alexandria in the second century A.D., it was the *hazzan* who waved a scarf to signal Amen at the end of a blessing.[201] It also was the responsibility of the *hazzan*, among other things, to purchase and maintain religious objects (e.g., candelabras), blow the horn to announce the Sabbath and provide a source of water for purification.[202]

Since all of these individuals needed to know how to read, as well as a knowledge of the Torah and an awareness of prevailing traditions, it would seem logical to assume that they enjoyed high status both within the synagogue and the religious-ethnic community.[203] In fact, it could be argued that given the educational requirements necessary to perform such

---

[195] *M. Meg.*, 4.4

[196] For a general discussion of the problems regarding synagogue organization see Applebaum, "Organization" in Safrai and Stern., eds., *Jewish People*, v. 1, 493ff.; Safrai, "Synagogue," 933ff.; and H. J. Leon, *The Jews of Ancient Rome* (Philadelphia, 1960), 167ff.

[197] Applebaum, "Organization," 495.

[198] Safrai, "Synagogue," 935.

[199] Applebaum, "Organization," 496.

[200] Ibid., loc. cit. See *CPJ*, v. 1, no. 129 (νακόρος).

[201] *T. Sukk.*, 4.6

[202] For the care of candelabras see *m. Pesah.*, 4.4; for the blowing of the horn see *t. Sukk.*, 4.11-13; for the link between the reading of scripture and ritual purity see *t. Ber.*, 2.13. Ceremonial purification is most important to Judaism, including the need for purifying oneself before prayer. For epigraphical evidence see, for example, *CII*, v. 2, no. 1404; for papyrological evidence see, for example, *CPJ*, v. 2, no. 432; and for literary evidence see Philo and the Dead Sea Scrolls.

[203] See Safrai, "Synagogue," 934 for supporting evidence.

roles, many of the members holding organizational positions may have been from the more affluent strata. The president and the *hazzan* would have had to be quite skilled, as they were responsible for judging the competence of those invited to read scriptures, translate, or give discourses.[204] Similarly whoever was permitted to participate in the procedures must have been differentiated by his knowledge in contrast to the believer who could neither read nor write, be it Hebrew, Aramaic or Greek.[205]

Synagogues in the ancient world were not only a place of worship. Because structural differentiation was minimal, synagogues provided a variety of additional institutional functions. Synagogues were also schools in which old members, new converts, novice schoolboys, and learned scribes were socialized in the meanings of Torah. By learning Torah and concomitantly the appropriate behaviour and ideology, the individual would enhance his membership in the ethnic and religious community. Instruction was therefore mandatory; it served both to transmit knowledge (concerning what to do and to think) and to ensure the preservation of the collectivity itself.

According to the Mishnah[206] education was to begin at age five. Drazin has argued that the Jewish educational system in Palestine evolved through several stages and that by the time of Simon b. Shetah (c. 90 B.C.) an educational program (for adolescents?) was established, and by the time of Joshua b. Gamla (c. 64 A.D.), it was greatly expanded (to include elementary students?).[207] Drazin, of course, is reading data of the late Roman Empire back into earlier times and assuming universal support in all Jewish communities throughout the Roman world.[208] Although it is plausible to argue that Jewish education was emphasized well before the codification of the Talmud, and that some formalized system was institutionalized both in Palestine and the Diaspora, the data are insufficient to

---

[204]Ibid., 935f.

[205]On the extent of illiteracy in Hellenistic Egypt see H. C. Youtie, "ΑΓΡΑΜΜΑΤΟΣ: An Aspect of Greek Society in Egypt," *Harvard Studies in Classical Philology* 75 (1971), 161-176.

[206]*M. Abot.*, 5.21.

[207]N. Drazin, *The History of Jewish Education from 515 B.C.E. to 220 C.E.* (Johns Hopkins University Studies in Education 29, Baltimore, 1940), 37.

[208]Similarly, Hengel has argued that the school system was established by the first century B.C. He has suggested that its founder was Joshua b. Perahiah (*Judaism and Hellenism*, v. 1, 82).

suggest either a date of origin or to assume that all Jewish communities in antiquity followed a standardized interpretation of the Torah.

Nevertheless, it is certain that instruction was one of the key services provided by the synagogue, and Philo testifies to their designation as "houses of instruction."[209] Moreover, Philo claims that in his day Jews "are instructed in them [i.e., the laws of the Torah] from their earliest youth, . . ."[210] and "are taught, so to speak, from the cradle by parents, teachers and educators. . . ."[211] Similarly, Josephus boasts how Jews considered the education of children as of prime importance[212] and the Mishnah continually emphasizes the importance of learning Torah.[213] Religious education therefore was viewed as both socially desirable and necessary for the development and reinforcement of Jewish identity. However, the learning of Torah was obligatory only for boys—teaching a girl Torah, at least according to one rabbi[214] was tantamount to encouraging intimacy between the sexes. All that can be stated with any conviction is that, by the first century A.D., there were some organized methods and schools for teaching children and/or adolescents in Egypt, and that Philo was a witness to their existence.[215]

In Egypt the language of instruction was Greek.[216] Whether students were taught Hebrew at an early age is a matter of conjecture, although Tcherikover's thesis is attractive. He argues that after the *Septuagint* had come into existence, "the study of Hebrew became obsolete, and . . .

---

[209]See Philo, *De Vita Mosis*, 2.215. Elsewhere Philo speaks of Sabbath schools (*De Spec. Leg.*, 2.62).

[210]Philo, *Leg. ad Gaium*, 210.

[211]Ibid., 115. However, it is interesting to note that while Philo informs his readers about his Greek education, he tells us nothing about his Hebrew education. See R. Marcus, "Rashe perakim beshitat ha-hinnukah shel Philon ha-Alexandroni," *Sefer Touroff* (Boston, 1938), 223-231.

[212]Josephus, *Apion*, 2.178, 204.

[213]See the Mishnah tractate *Abot*.

[214]*M. Sota*, 3.4.

[215]On the legendary founding of a school in Alexandria by R. Judah b. Tabbai in the first century B.C. see *b. Sanh.*, 107b. Cf. fn. 14 above. See also H. A. Wolfson, *Philo* (Cambridge, Mass., 1948), v. 2, 80, who asserts that organized schools existed during Philo's day.

[216]Compare the situation in Palestine where, according to Lieberman, the language of instruction was Hebrew. See S. Lieberman, *Hellenism in Jewish Palestine* (New York, 1962[2]), 100.

disappeared wholly from Jewish life in Egypt."[217] Tcherikover has based his conclusion in part on the fact that the *Septuagint* had been in circulation from well before the Maccabean revolt, and that Jewish literature (both everyday and religious) from Egypt thereafter was nearly exclusively in Greek.[218] According to Mussies, "if translations were necessary among Diaspora Jews, the first-class mastery of Hebrew needed for making them was hardly to be found outside Palestine."[219] Although Rabin has argued against such a position by suggesting that "language loyalty" would have preserved spoken and written Hebrew,[220] the above evidence does not support this conclusion. Rather Hebrew most likely would have been relegated to a role similar to that of Latin today: the language of the church and religious or academic scholars. At what stage of learning an individual would be able to study Hebrew and how he would acquire the knowledge is impossible to ascertain from the data. In Philo's time, "Hebrew was almost unknown in Egypt."[221]

In all likelihood, teaching methods were similar to those of the Hellenistic-Roman world.[222] Reading and recitation went together and the

---

[217] *CPJ*, v. 1, 31.

[218] According to the editors of *CPJ*, Hebrew epigraphical evidence from Egypt is rare. The handful of references include nos. 1424, 1425, 1437, 1438, 1533, 1534, and 1536. An examination of the apocryphal and pseudepigraphical literature from Egypt indicates that they were almost uniformly composed in Greek. See R. H. Charles, *The Apocrypha and Pseudepigrapha of the Old Testament* (Oxford, 1913) and J. Charlesworth, *The Pseudepigrapha and Modern Research* (Septuagint and Cognate Studies 7, Missoula, 1976).

[219] G. Mussies, "Greek in Palestine and the Diaspora," in Safrai and Stern, eds., *Jewish People*, v. 2, 1054. Corroborative support comes from the Aristeas legend of the origin of the *Septuagint*—the translators were sent from Egypt to Palestine.

[220] Ch. Rabin, "Hebrew and Aramaic in the First Century," in Safrai and Stern, eds., *Jewish People*, v. 2, 1034.

[221] *CPJ*, v. 1, 31. See also S. Sandmel, *Philo's Place in Judaism* (Cincinnati, 1956), 13. In contrast, see Wolfson (*Philo*, v. 1, 90), who has suggested that Philo's knowledge of Hebrew was sufficient to check the originals. For a brief discussion of the state of Hebrew, Aramaic and Greek at the turn of the millennium see Rabin, "Hebrew and Aramaic," 1007-1037 and Mussies, "Greek," 1040-1060.

[222] A comparison of non-Jewish school manuals from the third century B.C. in Greek to those in Coptic in the fourth century A.D. indicates an extraordinarily high similarity in teaching methods despite the fact that

Pentateuch and other texts were learned by rote.[223] Both exercise books
and literary works were expensive and scarce.[224] Thus education for the
most part was the privilege of the wealthy and the average Jew was able
neither to read nor write.[225] Tied to the land or his employer, he had
little time to engage in the luxury of education. Although a few might
have had a smattering of the Hebrew Torah, it clearly would be insufficient to understand the religious tradition in its original language.[226] The
level of education, like the magnitude of land-holdings, was primarily an
expression of social stratification.

It is probably the case that content closely adhered to the Palestinian
model—*Pentateuch,* Prophets, and Writings, followed by *halakah* and
haggadah.[227] Concerning Palestine, Safrai has suggested that as one
became more informed one learned in addition associated disciplines such
as astronomy and mystical-philosophical writings[228] and this also may
have been the situation in Egypt. Mystical-philosophical writings

---

two different languages and cultures were involved. Although there is no
evidence of teaching manuals for Jewish communities, the fact that Jews
in Egypt studied in Greek and that there was little change for 700 years in
non-Jewish manuals suggests that educational methods were uniform
regardless of ethnic affinity. See H. I. Marrou, *A History of Education in
Antiquity,* trans. G. Lamb (Toronto, 1964), 216.

[223] Ibid., 215.

[224] Ibid., 216. "A roll of papyrus cost the equivalent of one or two days'
wages. . . ." See Lewis, *Papyrus,* 133.

[225] Lewis, *Papyrus,* 133.

[226] Some Jews (like today) would have known certain sections by heart
(e.g., *shema*), and others would have found them familiar although in
neither case would the majority have been able to comprehend Hebrew.

[227] Although there is wide consensus that the Jewish canon was closed
in the mid-second century B.C. (the three components are mentioned in
the prologue to *Ecclesiasticus*), the earliest evidence for an established
form of canon is Josephus (*Apion,* 1.38ff.). By the time of Yavneh (end of
first century A.D.), the existence of the canon is already assumed (*m.
Yad.,* 3.5). For an overview see E. Schürer, *The History of the Jewish
People in the Age of Jesus Christ,* rev. and ed., G. Vermes, F. Millar and
M. Black (Edinburgh, 1979), v. 2, 314-321.

[228] S. Safrai, "Education and the Study of the Torah," in Safrai and
Stern, eds., *Jewish People,* v. 2, 959.

concentrated on the creation of the world in Genesis (מעשה בראשית) and the divine chariot in Ezekiel (מעשה מרכבה).

Although Egyptian Jewish educational curricula followed the Palestinian format, each individual teacher had a great deal of latitude concerning translation and exegesis, as approaches to teaching were neither standardized nor centrally coordinated from Jerusalem. Heterogeneity rather than homogeneity was the norm. Many of the aphorisms and stories in the Apocrypha or Pseudepigrapha probably are typical of those used by teachers for illustration and moralizations. Furthermore, Hellenized thought probably influenced many teachers, since Jewish people living in Egypt were exposed to Hellenistic culture and continuously had to accommodate themselves to its presence.[229] Philo's thought, for example, can be viewed as representative of one stream of hermeneutics that combined Hellenism and Judaism. In an age of legitimacy-creation, the number of possible interpretations rapidly increased, before receding behind the wall of orthodoxy.

In summary, the synagogue also served as an educational institution with a degree of formalization. However, the absence of wealth among the majority of the Jews in Egypt, the low status and wages of teachers endemic to the ancient world,[230] the agriculturally-related life-style of the average individual, and the lack of standardization and central coordination would have counterbalanced any universal and uniform system of education and interpretation as advanced by Drazin.

Synagogues, in addition to their primary role as educational and religious institutions, could serve a variety of other institutional roles. If the synagogue was a large building, it could act as a town hall (political), or a place to transact business (economic) or function as a court (judicial) or substitute as a place for holding community events (social). Synagogues could also provide lodging for travellers if required (service).[231] And according to Tcherikover, in small rural towns, "the synagogue probably also accommodated all the public institutions of the community."[232]

Synagogues, therefore, were indispensable for Jewish community life.

---

[229]See below Section 3.5, 153ff.

[230]Marrou, Education, 361.

[231]See S. Krauss, Synagogale Altertümer (Berlin-Wien, 1922), 182ff. for the use of synagogues as prayer houses, places of public meeting, tribunals, schools, hostels and so on. Cf. Safrai, "Synagogue," 924ff.

[232]CPJ, v. 1, 8. Compare Smallwood (Jews, 133), who views synagogues as "responsible for the organization and administration of all aspects of the life of the community . . ." even in the larger cities.

Bonds of solidarity were fused and through an organizational network social control over everyday religious matters was maintained. Services presented the opportunity for public participation and controlled individual action. As a place of assembly, synagogues provided for many institutional gatherings and it is not surprising that Rome considered them as *collegia*. Synagogues denoted to the non-Jewish world a religious community and an ethnic group apart from the norm.

The favourable dispensation towards the Jews by the Ptolemies and the Romans also permitted Jewish religious practices to permeate secular institutions, including the family and the economy, and fostered the notion that Judaism was a "superstition shackled by ceremonial worship."[233] Family relationships, personal and social ethics, as well as food and dress, were all influenced by religious ideology. In the family one was supposed to recite certain prayers at sunrise and sunset (e.g., the *shema*) and before and after eating (e.g., the washing of hands and the blessing over bread).[234] In addition, a series of benedictions (*shemone esre*) were to be recited either two or three times a day.[235] A *mezzuzah* was to rest on the doorpost indicating that one was entering a Jewish home, and it appears that some viewed it as a protective amulet.[236] A male child's birth needed to be accompanied by certain rituals (e.g., circumcision),[237]

---

[233]Seneca, *De Superstitione,* apud: Augustine, *De Civitate Dei,* 6.11.

[234]For the *shema* see *m. Ber.,* 1.1-3. The *shema* consists of Deut 6:4-9 and 11:13-21, and Num 15:37-41. For washing of hands see *m. Hag.,* 2.5; Matt 15:1-2; Mark 7:2-5; Luke 11:37-38. For blessings over bread see *m. Ber.,* 6.7 and *m. Yad.*

[235]For the evidence for three times see Daniel 6:11 and *2 Enoch* 51:4. For twice a day see Josephus, *Ant.,* 4.212.

[236]Amulets were fundamental to everyday life in antiquity (like the cross in Europe in the Middle Ages). For the *mezzuzah* in general, see *Ep. Arist.,* 158; Josephus, *Ant.,* 4.213; and the Mishnah (*m. Sabb.,* 6.2, 8.2, 3; *m. Seqal.,* 3.2; and *m. Miqw.,* 10.2) which records their use. According to J. Trachtenberg, *Jewish Magic and Superstition* (New York, 1970), 146, the *mezzuzah* "retained its original significance of an amulet despite rabbinic efforts to make it an exclusively religious symbol."

[237]For the commandment to circumcise see above fn. 82; for Egyptian Jewish evidence see Philo, *De Spec. Leg.,* 1.2ff; for non-Jewish evidence that circumcision was viewed as an important feature of Jewish ethnic and religious identity (see above fns. 82, 83).

and similarly, death and burial had to meet with specified practices.[238] Marriages were to proceed according to established customs including the presentation of a marriage contract by the husband to the wife.[239] Wives were to be virgins, remain covered in public or, if possible, not go out at all. [240] Similarly, divorces followed Jewish precedent and required a formal bill of divorce.[241] Men were to dress with fringes (ציצת) attached to the four corners of their cloak[242] and *tefillin* (phylacteries), which were attached to their heads and arms.[243] Before the Sabbath, special preparations were undertaken and the non-Jewish world came to label this day as the "Day of Preparation."[244] Similarly, during the Sabbath behaviour was governed by strict rules, which impinged on everyday family activities such as baking and boiling water.[245] Several of these customs, as well as additional ones, were required before Feast days such as Passover or the Feast of Tabernacles.[246] Finally, with regard to the institution of the family, it should be noted that women were subject to the prohibitions of the Torah but not to all the commandments.[247]

---

[238]See *CPJ*, v. 1, no. 138; Philo, *De Spec. Leg.*, 1.112ff.; Josephus, *Apion*, 2.205; Matt 9:23; John 19:39-40; Acts 9:37; *m. Sabb.*, 23.5; *m. Moed Qat.*, 317; *m. Sanh.*, 6.5 and *m. Ketub.*, 4.4.

[239]See *Tobit* 7:14 and *m. Ketub.*, 4.7-12.

[240]See Philo, *De Spec. Leg.*, 3.169ff. and *Flacc.*, 89; *4 Macc* 18:7ff., and J. Jeremias, *Jerusalem in the Time of Jesus*, trans. F. H. and C. H. Cave (London, 1969), "Appendix: The Social Position of Women," 359-376.

[241]See Josephus, *Ant.*, 4.253 and *m. Git.*, 9.3.

[242]Matt 23:5 and *m. Menah.*, 3.7-4.1.

[243]*Ep. Arist.*, 159; Matt 23:5; Josephus, *Ant.*, 4.213; *m. Ber.*, 3.3; and Y. Yadin, *Tefillin from Qumran* (Jerusalem, 1969), 7ff. *Tefillin* were also viewed by some as amulets (Zeitlin, *Rise and Fall*, v. 3, 300).

[244]See fn. 180 above and p. 167 below. For Jews celebrating the Sabbath as early as the time of Zenon see *CPJ*, v. 1, no. 10. See also Josephus, *Ant.*, 16.163; Matt 27:62; Mark 15:42; Luke 23:54; and John 19:31, 42.

[245]For the prevailing customs see *m. Sabb.*, *m. Erubin* and *m. Besa*.

[246]For the prevailing customs see *m. Pesah.*, *m. Sukk.*, *m. Moed* and *m. Besa*. For evidence that the Jews in Egypt knew of the Feast days see Philo, and Tcherikover, *Hellenistic Civilization*, 529, fn. 60.

[247]See *m. Qidd.*, 1.7, *m. Sukk.*, 2.8 and *m. Ber.*, 3.3 for examples of commandments not pertaining to women. According to *m. Qidd.*, 1.7, women need not observe the negative ordinances of Lev 19:27 and 21:1.

Economic institutions also felt the impact of religious prescriptions. The fact that one could eat and drink only certain foods and beverages[248] meant that the planting, growing, selling and consumption of food were curtailed by religious practices.[249] Moreover, several classes of work were forbidden on the Sabbath, thus reducing productivity and options for employment.[250] Furthermore, the practice of tithing affected the distribution and revenues of goods.[251] Religious customs that impinged on the economy had the effect of isolating the Jew from his non-Jewish neighbour. At the same time, religious practices impinging on the economic sphere benefited those Jews in the economy who catered specifically to the Jewish population. Administrators were needed to collect the tithes, craftsmen to create the sacred objects for the synagogue and the home, scribes to reproduce the Torah in such articles of faith as *tefillin* or a *mezzuzah*, and shopkeepers to prepare Kosher food.

Yet in spite of these customs, traditions, and rituals that affected a variety of institutions, there was no standardization. Egypt was not the theocratic Palestinian state and religious behavioral patterns varied even more widely according to faction, leaders and circumstances. Lacking a centralized decision-making body for all aspects of religious institutional life, Egyptian Jews looked to Jerusalem and to the Temple for direction. Yet direction was not always forthcoming, as the various religious groupings in Jerusalem were engaged in their own ideological battles concerning the meaning and practice of Torah. Judaism was experiencing a turning point in its history.

The average Jew in Egypt probably practised his religion by following only those parts of the religion that appealed to his convictions or

---

[248] For evidence of these practices in Alexandria as early as the second century B.C. see *Ep. Arist.*, 158, 182-183. See also Fraser's comments, *Ptolemaic Alexandria*, v. 2, 698, fns. 121, 122.

[249] Jacob Neusner has pointed out that "sixty-seven per cent of all legal pericopae deal with dietary laws." See *The Rabbinic Traditions about the Pharisees before 70 A.D.* (Leiden, 1971), v. 3, 304.

[250] See Philo, *De Vita Mosis*, 2.22 and *De Spec. Leg.*, 2.60; *Jub.*, 2.25-30, 50; Josephus, *War*, 2.147; and *m. Sabb.*, 7.2.

[251] Philo discusses several of these tithes in *De Spec. Leg.*, 1.131ff., *Leg. ad Gaium*, 156-157 and *De Virt.*, 95. Although in the Torah tithes were levied on grain, wine and oil (Lev 27:30; Num 18:27; and Deut 12:17)—agricultural products—by Philo's time they also included non-agricultural products (*Jub.* 32:2; Luke 18:12). Also see below 148.

community obligations. Only the very devout would have attempted to guide their everyday secular life by religious affirmation. Yet in spite of their fervour for the ritualistic application of Torah, it is evident from Philo's description of various rituals that these practices were not identical with those in Jerusalem.[252] For example, Philo omits the four species during the Feast of Tabernacles,[253] claims that the shofar was not blown on Rosh Ha-Shana[254] and that Nisan, not Tishrai, was the principal New Year.[255] In other words, traditions varied and devotion in one setting may not have corresponded to devotion in another. Zeitlin has expressed a similar view: "outside the Temple, prayer was not standardized, nor were definite times and places set for it."[256] Thus it could be argued that orthodoxy and heresy were relative terms dependent on social location and historical context.

In summary, the evidence suggests that religion permeated everyday life for Jews in Egypt. Institutions were established that catered to the community needs but there was no consensus regarding uniformity of ritual or religious behaviour between Egypt and Palestine. Individuals reacted differently to their religion based on their understanding, motivation, commitment and self-interests. Variation is the only constant. According to Safrai, this "did not always stem from differences of biblical exegesis or tradition. . . . [It was] the spontaneous outcome of religious vitality. . . ."[257] Expressed sociologically, this spontaneity is often described as sectarian formation and reflects the diversity of communities in Jewish life. Religious commitment in Judaism did not lend itself to a separation from community. It promoted ethnic solidarity but at the expense of integration in the larger society. Tacitus expressed this paradox for the Judaeans but it can equally be applied to all observing Jews in the Diaspora: "The Judaeans are extremely loyal to one another and always ready to show compassion, but towards every other people they feel only hate and enmity."[258]

---

[252]Tcherikover (CPJ, v. 1, 33 and fn. 84) questions the reliability of Philo's testimony, in contrast to G. Alon, Jews, Judaism and the Classical World, trans. I. Abrahams (Jerusalem, 1977), "On Philo's Halakha," 89-137.

[253]Philo, De Spec. Leg., 2.204ff. Cf. Alon, "Philo's Halakha," 133f.

[254]Philo, De Spec. Leg., 2.138ff. Cf. Alon, "Philo's Halakha," 124f.

[255]Philo, De Spec. Leg., 2.150ff. Cf. Alon, "Philo's Halakha," 130f.

[256]Zeitlin, Rise and Fall, v. 2, 340.

[257]S. Safrai, "Religion in Everyday Life," in Safrai and Stern, eds., Jewish People, v. 2, 795.

[258]Tacitus, Histories, 5.5.1.

3.3.3   The Role and Impact of Secular Institutions

Everyday life demanded that the Jew interact with the non-Jew and observe local customs and Ptolemaic or Roman laws. The observance of these socio-cultural and legal norms affected all classes of society. Social integration necessitated the creation of a variety of institutions to respond to secular problems (law, politics, economy) that encroached on religious territory. Distinctive secular institutions could both respond to the unique needs of the Jews and mediate, on behalf of the Jewish community, with Ptolemaic or Roman judicial and administrative officials. If, as suggested above, religious norms had important implications for economic and social life, then it is essential to establish: (a) whether Ptolemaic-Roman or Jewish institutions dominated secular Jewish life and (b) whether there were class and urban-rural differences in responding to non-Jewish institutions.

Jewish communities in the Hellenistic world were considered as *politeumata* (πολιτεύματα). Smallwood, basing her evidence on Hellenistic policy in the East, describes the *politeuma* as "the standard political organization of all Jewish communities of any size in the East."[259] Alexandria's Jewish community was viewed as a *politeuma*[260] and Robert has suggested that the Jews in Leontopolis similarly constituted a *politeuma*.[261] A *politeuma* was a quasi-autonomous judicial entity. It referred to a recognized alien and ethnic group enjoying certain civic rights (but not citizenship) and domiciled in a *polis*. According to Smallwood, "it had its own constitution and administered its internal affairs as an ethnic unit through officials distinct from and independent of those of the host city."[262] As Roman policy was one of accommodation rather than altercation, Rome in all likelihood would not have fundamentally altered the *politeuma* system established by the Ptolemies. Caesar's confirmation of these privileges as well as Augustus' and Claudius' ratification support this contention.

The data with regard to the *politeuma* are nearly exclusively from Alexandria, the leading centre of the Jewish community in Egypt. The major evidence is from Strabo who stated that the *ethnarch* was the most

---

[259]Smallwood, *Jews*, 226.
[260]See *Ep. Arist.*, 310; *CPJ*, v. 1, 6; Smallwood, *Jews*, 225ff.
[261]L. Robert, "Épigramme d'Égypte," *Hellenica* 1 (1940), 18-24.
[262]Smallwood, *Jews*, 225.

important political functionary and held total administrative and judicial power.[263] His tasks included the supervision of contracts, the settlement of internal disputes and the modification of Jewish legislative practice in the light of new governmental edicts.[264] Tcherikover[265] and Smallwood[266] both suggest that the political power of the *ethnarch* had been established during the second century B.C. although Applebaum places it somewhat later.[267] Unfortunately, Strabo does not inform us of the mechanisms of his appointment or how long he held office.[268] Nevertheless, such an official would require an administration to implement his decisions and to organize the decision-making processes. Thus, there must have existed some degree of bureaucracy and stratification. Furthermore, the creation of an office in which all legitimate authority is centralized is indicative of the hierarchical class structure of antiquity. The *ethnarch* represented the upper class of Alexandrian Jewish society and was aligned with their cultural and economic interests. However, whereas Tcherikover views this development as simply a rational strategy to promote the social solidarity of the upper class,[269] the character of politics in antiquity also points to it being an example of *traditional authority* as described by Weber. Recruitment was based on personal affiliation. The division of labour did not require a great deal of role specificity, and power was distributed by established traditions rather than impersonal universal norms.[270] The relationship of domination between *ethnarch,* administrative staff and community members can be summarized as maintenance of the *status quo.*

Notwithstanding the centralization of legitimate power in the Jewish community, the *ethnarch* and the *politeuma* remained subordinate to the

---

[263]Josephus, *Ant.,* 14.117. See also Philo, *Flacc.,* 74.

[264]Josephus, *Ant.,* 19.283.

[265]*CPJ,* v. 1, 9f. and fn. 24.

[266]Smallwood, *Jews,* 226ff.

[267]Applebaum, "Organization," in Safrai and Stern, eds., *Jewish People,* v. 1, 473ff. See also fn. 271 below.

[268]Tcherikover (*CPJ,* v. 1, 9) has suggested self-appointment, given the political and institutional structures of Jewish communities in the Hellenistic world.

[269]*CPJ,* v. 1, 10; Tcherikover, *Hellenistic Civilization,* 303.

[270]M. Weber, *The Theory of Social and Economic Organization,* trans. T. Parsons (New York, 1947), 59ff. and 341ff.

state sovereign. By serving as a respected and powerful spokesman for the religious-ethnic community, sharing common material interests with the ruling Greek elite, and acting as a symbolic figurehead who could promote Jewish needs, the *ethnarch* was able to maintain the fragile balance between the Greek and Jewish communities. Whether his policies sought to accommodate or to insulate Jews from Hellenistic patterns of behaviour was dependent on several factors, of which two are of particular importance: the interests of his stratum and the Ptolemaic and Roman perceptions of the Jews as hostile or friendly. Thus, just as landholding was the geographical expression of class stratification, the position of the *ethnarch* was the social expression.

During the early first century A.D. the political structure of the *politeuma* was altered by Augustus. The position of the *ethnarch* was abolished and the administration of the Alexandrian Jewish community passed to the *gerousia*, a council of seventy-one elders.[271] The evidence seems to indicate that they remained in control of the Alexandrian Jewish community for the remainder of the period under study.[272] Although there is no direct information as to how their authority was distributed or whether they were elected or appointed, with the exception of Philo's comment that there existed *archons*,[273] certain organizational processes and offical functions appear to be similar to those of the local Jewish community in Bernice. Applebaum has suggested that the community in Bernice consisted of a board of *archons* that met regularly, represented both the city and the countryside, sent delegations and complaints to authorities, was responsible for collecting certain taxes, and possessed

---

[271]See Philo, *Flacc.*, 74. Although Josephus in *Ant.*, 19.283 contradicts Philo, Box has suggested a reconciliation. See H. Box, *Philonis Alexandrini: In Flaccum* (London, 1939), 103. For 71 members, see Josephus, *Ant.*, 12.108, *t. Sukk.*, 4.6 and *b. Sukk.*, 51b. In Applebaum's opinion the *gerousia* existed at the time of Aristeas and the position and/or power of the *ethnarch* was a later development during the Ptolemaic period. Tcherikover, in contrast, has argued that "the existence of a 'council of elders' [i.e., *gerousia*] of the Jewish *politeuma* in Alexandria under the Ptolemies, though not improbable, is not supported by any literary evidence." See *CPJ*, v. 1, 9, fn. 24.
[272]See Philo, *Flacc.*, 74 for a reference to them in 38 A.D. and Josephus, *Ant.*, 12.121f. for a reference to Titus' refusal to permit its dissolution in 73 A.D.
[273]Philo, *Flacc.*, 117, referring possibly to an inner cabinet.

and maintained buildings.[274] In Alexandria, Philo's *De Legatione ad Gaium* and *The Acts of the Alexandrian Martyrs*[275] provide examples of official Jewish delegations to the Emperor. The *ethnarch* and the *gerousia* were responsible for the collection of the half-*shekel* for the Temple in Jerusalem and may have coordinated the collection of Ptolemaic and Roman taxes. Musurillo, for example, has suggested that the *politeuma* collected the *laographia* and accepted the responsibility of forwarding the poll-tax to the authorities on behalf of the Jewish community.[276] Yet even if the *ethnarch* or the *gerousia* were not officially responsible for tax collection, non-collection would have reflected a hostile attitude towards the Ptolemaic or Roman governments and blame would have been placed at their doorstep. Coordination, therefore, seems highly likely. The *ethnarch* and the *gerousia* would also have been responsible for the maintenance of public institutions such as the synagogue, as there is circumstantial evidence to suggest that they were defined as communal property.[277] These examples tend to support the assumption that Jewish secular institutions were highly organized, responded to unique Jewish needs, and mediated on behalf of the ethnic community with Ptolemaic or Roman authorities. Thus power continued to be distributed among the *gerousia's* members and specific roles continued to be performed as outlined by Strabo;[278] and their power base presumably remained the upper stratum of Alexandrian society.[279] The *gerousia* most likely consisted of individuals who benefited from the policies of de-monopolization, who were active in the Red Sea trade or in the movement of the *annona*, and who owned land and were citizens or claimed *epheboi* status.

---

[274]Applebaum, "Organization," 488.

[275]*CPJ*, v. 2, nos. 154-159 and p. 50, lines 90-91.

[276]H. Musurillo, ed., *The Acts of the Pagan Martyrs: Acta Alexandrinorum* (Oxford, 1954), 139.

[277]The fact that synagogues were desecrated in 38 and 66 A.D. throughout Alexandria would have given rise to a co-ordinating body to monitor and direct their rebuilding and re-dedication. It would appear from Josephus' and Philo's comments that in both cases the community was able quickly to rebuild itself, which suggests *gerousia* responsibility.

[278]See 117f. above and fn. 264.

[279]Tcherikover (*CPJ*, v. 1, 79) has implicitly adopted this position when he speculates that in the anti-Jewish riots of 66 A.D. Tiberius Julius Alexander may have protected the leading members of the *gerousia* because of their class interests.

In a very real sense the evolution of the *politeuma* paralleled the evolution of religious institutions, and in particular the synagogue. Both grew during the latter half of the Ptolemaic epoch and during the early Roman Empire; both depended on Ptolemaic and Roman toleration. In Alexandria, the *politeuma* was responsible for the secular life of Jews, while a network of synagogues controlled their religious activities. Yet, whereas in Palestine religious norms dominated most areas of secular life, in Egypt the impact of religion on everyday activities was circumscribed by a non-Jewish normative canopy. Jewish religious norms competed with Ptolemaic-Roman laws for loyalty. By focusing on jurisdictional practice as a reflection of social reality and as the principal authority in defining legitimate behaviour, we can identify the place of Jewish secular institutions.

The papyrological data clearly show that the socio-economic behaviour of the Jews in Egypt was dominated by Hellenistic law. Above and beyond Strabo's comment that the *ethnarch* (and later the *gerousia*) modified Jewish laws as new Ptolemaic (and later Roman) laws were proclaimed,[280] Tcherikover has pointed out how administrative procedures, form and content of documents, and place of jurisdiction were all regulated by Ptolemaic law. For example, commercial documents were drawn up in the standard Hellenistic manner; the office employed was a regular government office (i.e., non-Jewish); legal disputes were brought before Ptolemaic authorities; and the laws and regulations for business life were those of the Greeks in Egypt.[281] Even such a basic economic transaction as lending money to fellow Jews tended to follow Ptolemaic custom[282] rather than Biblical precept.[283] Tcherikover further comments that these laws and regulations would have affected all social institutions, and in particular, the family. As he notes, "it follows that the family life of Alexandrian Jews, their marriages and divorces, were regulated by Greek contracts in accordance with the principles of Hellenistic law."[284] As

---

[280]See 117f. above and fn. 264.

[281]*CPJ*, v. 1, 33.

[282]For example, see *CPJ*, v. 1, nos. 20, 24. In the light of Philo's comments (*De Spec. Leg.*, 2.74ff.) it is evident that many Jews did not follow the economic laws of the Torah. See also *CPJ*, v. 1, 35.

[283]Exod 22:25 and Deut 23:20. Other economic transactions, such as the sale of slaves, may also have copied Greek models and practices. See Westermann, *Slave Systems*, 124f.

[284]*CPJ*, v. 1, 34.

well, in conformity with Ptolemaic and Roman practice, women were not able to appear in court without male representation.[285] In fact, except for one papyrological document which mentions a Jewish archive, "the papyri do not bear any distinct mark of Jewish law or institutions" in Ptolemaic or Roman Egypt.[286] Jewish tribunals in Alexandria, therefore, may not have played an important secular role in spite of Goodenough's contention that Philo's *De Specialibus Legibus* reflected the real judicial practice of Alexandrian Jewish tribunals.[287] Rather the evidence supports the use of non-Jewish courts; concomitantly, this implies Hellenistic norms of jurisprudence rather than Jewish law as promulgated in the Torah.[288]

In summary, socio-economic behaviour was regulated by Ptolemaic and Roman customs and jurisdictional practice. Jewish secular institutions established by the *politeuma* may have acted as no more than a clearing house through which administrative procedures were outlined, advice offered and complaints forwarded to the appropriate authorities.[289] Jewish jurisdictional practice was confined solely to religious matters. Consequently, the religious practices of the Jews, whether they lived in the *chora* or in urban centres, had to be accommodated within a non-Jewish normative framework.[290] By accepting Ptolemaic-Roman laws and institutions that encroached on religous norms, the governing members of the *politeuma* in effect were secularizing the practice of Judaism. The recognition of a Jewish status by Ptolemaic and Roman rulers applied solely to the religious sphere, and the religious sphere had little impact on secular life. As today, the norms and laws of the State took precedence over minority religious dictates.

The rise of anti-semitism in Egypt is one significant indicator of the depth to which non-Jewish norms outweighed Jewish religious practices.

---

[285]See 85 above and fn. 59.

[286]*CPJ*, v. 2, 4 in reference to no. 143.

[287]E. R. Goodenough, *The Jurisprudence of the Jewish Courts in Egypt* (New Haven, 1929).

[288]See *CPJ*, v. 1, 32f. and Tcherikover, *Jews in Egypt*, 95-135.

[289]For petitions and complaints which could fall within this reconstruction see *CPJ*, v. 1, nos. 37, 43, 128, 129 and v. 2, 151.

[290]Exceptions did occur: for example, the Jew was excused from appearing before a Ptolemaic or Roman court after 3 p.m. on Fridays and on the Sabbath (Josephus, *Ant.*, 16.163).

From the second century B.C. onward, anti-semitic attitudes were increasingly pronounced and deeply affected the life of the Jews.[291] The development of anti-semitism coincided with the establishment of the first Jewish military settlement in Leontopolis and the founding of the *politeuma* in Alexandria. In other words, the growth of anti-semitism is associated with the rising status and visibility of the Jews.[292] After the Roman conquest, anti-Jewish ideologies began to be manifested in material terms (e.g., the *laographia*).

The *ethnarch's* and the *gerousia's* function, in part, was to defuse such volatile situations. They acted on behalf of the Jewish community but shared the class interests of well-placed Greeks and Romans. Continually pulled between conflicting interests (tradition versus secularizaton), their class affiliation predisposed them towards accommodation rather than confrontation; and despite their role as spokesman for the community, the independence of the Jews was increasingly narrowed. Moreover, their conciliatory posture was viewed by many Jews as undermining the interest of the ethnic community.

Roman rule of Egypt continuously eroded the integrity of the Jewish minority. A new social formation resulted from the convergence of the Ptolemaic mode of production with the slave economy, and corresponding structural changes in social organization occurred. Behavioural patterns were circumscribed by economic realities including further taxes, (such as the *laographia*) and Roman absentee landlords. As part of the alienated rural labour force, Jewish peasants were especially affected. Living in the *chora*, their socio-cultural patterns would be more typical of Egyptian peasants than of urban Greeks. Their contacts with new and subtle ideological developments in Judaism, whether in Alexandria or Jerusalem, would have been few. Their reference group would have been the Egyptian peasantry. Consequently, it is not surprising that differences between the city and the *chora* in life-style, language, culture, political orientation and observance of Judaism increased.[293]

This widening rift between city and country was paralleled by changes in class composition. Forced by higher taxes to desert the land, Jewish

---

[291]For a recent analysis of anti-semitism during the Graeco-Roman period, including bibliography, see J. L. Daniel, "Anti-Semitism in the Hellenistic-Roman Period," *JBL* 98/1 (1979), 45-65.

[292]See Hengel, *Judaism and Hellenism*, v. 1, 306.

[293]For a similar analysis for Palestine see Theissen, *First Followers*, 47-59 and L. Finkelstein, *The Pharisees* (Philadelphia, 1962[3]), 2 vols.

peasants migrated to Alexandria. Joining the ranks of the urban poor, they identified with the less Hellenized urban retailers, wage-labourers and artisans, and retained a traditionalist attitude towards Judaism. In contrast, upper-class Alexandrian Jews (those who constituted the *gerousia:* landowners and wealthy merchants) came to view themselves as Greeks, and expected similar rights and privileges. Certain individuals, such as Philo, attempted to bridge the rift and integrate Judaism and Hellenism philosophically; but the extreme positions of apostasy (e.g., Tiberius Julius Alexander) on the one hand, and the political rejection of Hellenistic institutions (e.g., the revolts of 41 and 66 A.D.) on the other, became increasingly attractive to those at the opposite ends of the political spectrum. City-country differences and class biases reflected different orientations in the development of Egyptian Judaism. Material conditions and structural changes gave rise to increasingly divergent ideological manifestations.

The problem of anti-semitism brought to the forefront class polarization and city-country prejudices. At issue was the shape of Egyptian Judaism. What was to be the dividing line between acceptance and rejection of Hellenistic behaviour and institutions? For those upwardly mobile this queston translated in practical terms into how to be a Jew and simultaneously a Greek (i.e., an Alexandrian) or a Roman citizen? For those of the lower class the question was how to be a Jew and tolerate the accommodative tendencies of other Jews.

Alexandrian citizenship was a rare commodity. To be considered a Greek citizen an individual's legal status was taken into account. He was identified as belonging to a particular ethnic group (e.g., Egyptians, Greeks, Jews) and assessed accordingly. Citizenship, therefore depended largely on heredity. The privilege of having a *politeuma* meant only jurisdiction over one's own ethnic laws, not the right to confer citizenship status, which corresponded to taxability and other obligations to the State such as the *corvée*. It merely publicly confirmed social status. As a result there were only a limited number of ways one could attain citizenship. During the Ptolemaic epoch these included the *polis* granting it to an individual, nomination by the king (queen) or entry through the *gymnasium* (i.e., by means of a Greek education).[294] Although the first two means were available to Jews as to other foreigners, the third option was by far the most attractive. Until the turn of the millennium, upwardly mobile Jews who resided in urban centres, and in particular in Alexandria, could

---

[294] *CPJ*, v. 1, 40ff.

provide their children access to Greek educational institutions by acquiring wealth or property.[295] Through this process Jews could be labelled *epheboi* and might eventually attain citizenship.[296] Nonetheless, there is wide consensus today among scholars that the great majority of Alexandrian Jews never attained Alexandrian civic rights.[297]

Greek education encompassed much more than the possible acquisition of Greek citizenship. It included an immersion in Hellenistic culture. "Its overall object was to fashion the ideal of Greek gentlemen."[298] Through exposure, the individual tended to adopt Greek behavioural patterns (e.g., dress, language, names, sports, etc.) and ideological values (e.g., religious beliefs, traditions, customs and loyalties). Philo, for example, as representative of Alexandrian Jews from the upper strata, was a member of the *epheboi*, was familiar with Greek athletics, and shared many of the values of the Greeks.[299] For Philo, Greek institutions and behaviour were readily accessible. Similarly, other Jews who participated in athletic events could not have done so unless they had received a *gymnasium* education.[300] Box has even speculated that some Alexandrian Jews were *gymnasiarchs*.[301] If this is indeed the case, their achievement would not have been possible

---

[295]See Hengel, *Judaism and Hellenism*, v. 1, 66, 71. In contrast, see Wolfson, *Philo*, v. 1, 79, who has argued that Jews did not attend the *gymnasium*.

[296]For the connection between a *gymnasium* education and citizenship see *CPJ*, v. 1, 40ff., 59ff. and v. 2, no. 153. Cf. Tcherikover, *Hellenistic Civilization*, 313ff.

[297]For a brief overview of the literature see Smallwood, *Jews*, 220ff.

[298]M. Hadas, *Hellenistic Culture, Fusion and Diffusion* (New York, 1959), 60.

[299]For Greek athletics see Philo, *De Spec. Leg.*, 2.230, 246; *De Opif. Mundi*, 78; *De Jos.*, 82; *Quod Omn. Prob.*, 26; and *De Prov.*, 2.58. For allusions to the theatre see *Quod Omn. Prob.*, 141; *Flacc.*, 38; *Leg. ad Gaium*, 368; and *De Ebrietate*, 177. For Philo's family being granted citizenship by Augustus or Caesar, see *CPJ*, v. 2, 197, 200. See also L. Feldman, "The Orthodoxy of the Jews in Hellenistic Egypt," *Jewish Social Studies* 22 (1960), 224ff.

[300]See *CPJ*, v. 2, no. 153. Comparative evidence outside of Egypt can be added to support this argument. See *CPJ*, v. 1, 39, fn. 99, 41 and 75f.; Hengel, *Judaism and Hellenism*, v. 1, 65ff. and v. 2, 48, fn. 84.

[301]See H. Box, *Philonis*, xxi.

without an ideological acceptance of the world of the Greeks.[302] Simply stated, Jews who were identified as *epheboi* shared class interests, educational experiences and Hellenistic normative customs and had numerous contacts with non-Jewish elites. Since it was primarily from this exclusive group that the leaders of the *politeuma* emerged, their acceptance of non-Jewish institutions that encroached on religious norms had the effect of secularizing the practice of Egyptian Judaism.

The rise of upwardly mobile, Greek-educated and landholding Jews into the Greek upper strata had two irreversible consequences. First, Jews from the country and the urban lower class felt further estranged from the elite that represented their interests. Their opportunities to become upwardly mobile were circumscribed by both poverty and the barriers of legal status. Greek privileges and rights were unattainable. Prevented from acquiring Greek education, their status and outlook remained closer to those of the native Egyptians. They retained traditional values and identified themselves fully with their ethnic origins.[303] Consequently, they began to view the accommodative policies of their leaders as detrimental to their interests. This development, along with Roman policies, led to recurrent social upheavals.

Secondly, the entry of Jews into more affluent positions threatened the Greek population—particularly those with higher status. Numerically fewer than the Jews in the first century B.C. and A.D., they viewed the growing demographic, political and economic power of the Jews as a significant danger. Upwardly mobile Jews "were proud to call themselves Macedonians . . ."[304] and to usurp Greek traditions, values and behaviour. As a result "there was strong opposition to Jewish influence at court, in the army, amongst government officials, and . . . among the Greek citizens of Alexandria.[305] By the end of the Ptolemaic period anti-semitism had evolved "from a literary phenomenon to a strong incentive to action of a political and social character. . . . Anti-semitism appears [in Roman Egypt] as a well organized programme for the removal of the Jews from all positions, political and social alike, attained during the Ptolemaic period."[306]

---

[302] See Feldman ("Orthodoxy," 224ff.) who comments on the kinds of compromises Jews would have had to make.

[303] Both Tcherikover (*Hellenistic Civilization*, 355ff.) and Feldman ("Orthodoxy," 230) have arrived at the same conclusion.

[304] Hengel, *Judaism and Hellenism*, 101.

[305] *CPJ*, v. 1, 24.

[306] *CPJ*, v. 1, 25. Tcherikover's argument is that the increase in anti-semitism is correlated with the defeat of the Greeks by the Romans and

The implementation of this policy is immediately apparent in the introduction of the *laographia* (poll-tax) in 24 B.C. Jews were classified as part of the provincial population (i.e., non-Greeks). Only those possessing Greek or Roman citizenship were exempted. However, Roman authorities were lax in developing criteria to establish who was or was not a Greek. Consequently, many Jews who were not legally Greeks were able to claim such status; but three decades later (5 A.D.) this loophole was closed. Only those individuals who could prove that they were educated as Greeks and were *epheboi* henceforth could be considered as of Greek origin, and not be liable for the *laographia*. Many Jews in Alexandria who were not legally *epheboi*, but who had claimed exempt status on the basis of their class standing or appelation as Macedonians, had to forfeit their civic privileges. Thus, a great number of Jews in Egypt who were upwardly mobile or of high status lost the opportunity to legitimate themselves as both Greeks and Jews. Papyrological data[307] and *3 Maccabees*[308] provide adequate testimony to this development.[309]

This change in policy by Roman rulers inaugurated reactions that culminated in a series of civil wars. Jews and Greeks hereafter allowed one another no peace. More importantly, the defining of Jews as non-Greeks indicates the depth of anti-semitism and simultaneously the ineffectiveness of the Jewish lobby in comparison with the Greek lobby in Alexandria. The inability of the *gerousia* to mediate on behalf of the

---

the subsequent frustration of nationalistic Alexandrians. A Segré ("Anti-semitism," 119-136), has independently come to the same conclusion. To this political analysis, however, must be added the economic and social dislocation of the Greeks. Conquest only set the drama in motion. See above Chapter 2, Section 2.4, 49ff.

[307] For examples of payment see *CPJ*, v. 2, no. 151 and nos. 230-374 (from Edfu). For indirect evidence see *CPJ*, v. 2, nos. 153 and 156c.

[308] In *3 Macc* 2:28ff. and 3:21ff., acceptance of paganism was the condition for citizenship. Without such acceptance, one had to pay the *laographia*.

[309] Nevertheless, there are examples of Jews retaining or acquiring *epheboi* status and citizenship. There are cases of Jews holding Greek municipal office including Philo's brother Alexander, and Demetrius (Josephus, *Ant.*, 18.259, 19.276, 20.100, 147). These offices required Alexandrian citizenship, and Josephus' account implies that this was not uncommon for upper class well-placed Jews. Cf. Box, *Philonis*, xxif. and *CPJ*, v. 2, no. 142 and fn. 145 above.

Jewish community, in spite of the fact that it was precisely *gerousia* members who would be most affected by this turn of events, testifies to their powerlessness.[310] Through the restriction of Greek education in jurisdictional and citizenship terms, rather than by social status and tradition as was the case under the Ptolemies, Jews became publicly designated as inferior to the Greeks. The consequences were many: occupational mobility was greatly curtailed;[311] jobs in the civil service were closed and the tax burden was increased. Moreover, the identity of those rejected as 'Greeks' would have been shattered.[312] Although socially stigmatized as outsiders, in their cultural, social and economic interests they remained more aligned to the Greeks than the Jews. Advocating accommodation, secularization or even assimilation, they were now set adrift between Hellenism and Judaism.

Greek opposition to Jewish interests also contributed to Roman policies of anti-semitism. The *boule* papyrus, according to Tcherikover, indicates that "from the very beginning of Roman rule, the Greeks were anxious to quash every attempt on the part of the Jews to penetrate into their ranks and attain equality of citizenship with them"[313] The polemical arguments of Apion, Isidorus[314] and others in the years to follow serve to confirm this attitude. Rome's policies tended not only to aggravate further the fragile situation in Egypt between Jews and Greeks but also tipped the scales in favour of the Greeks. Henceforth, Jews could only attain citizenship by manumission from slavery, by an individual grant by the Emperor or through prior possession of Greek citizenship.[315] Further-

---

[310]As additional supporting evidence see *CPJ*, v. 2, no. 153, lines 90-91, where Claudius chastises the Alexandrian Jews for sending two embassies. Internal discord amongst the Alexandrian community contributed to the *gerousia*'s powerlessness. Cf. *CPJ*, v. 2, 50ff.

[311]See 96f. above.

[312]For example, in *The Acts of the Alexandrian Martyrs (CPJ*, v. 2, no. 156c) Agrippa I is denounced by Isidorus and identified with Egyptians paying the *laographia*. If the king was demeaned no doubt the average Alexandrian Jew also suffered such taunts, insults and indignities.

[313]*CPJ*, v. 1, 64 and v. 2, no. 150.

[314]See *CPJ*, v. 2, nos. 156a-d.

[315]Applebaum, "Legal Status," in Safrai and Stern, eds., *Jewish People*, v. 1, 445 and *CPJ*, v. 1, 61f.

more, access to citizenship now entailed transgressing their most deep-seated normative beliefs (i.e., participation in pagan civic duties).[316]

As anti-semitism became more visible, interaction with non-Jews became more precarious. The numerous clashes between Greeks and Jews (e.g., 38, 41, 66 and 72 A.D.), Claudius' edict[317] and his letter to the Alexandrians,[318] the closing of the Temple at Leontopolis[319] and *The Acts of the Alexandrian Martyrs*[320] all exemplify this tension. In the anti-Jewish revolts of 38 A.D. in Alexandria, Jews were deprived of the use of their synagogues[321] and many were destroyed.[322] They were classified as aliens without right of domicile[323] and were restricted to the Delta quarter which became *ipso facto* a ghetto.[324] Commercial life was severely curtailed as Greeks were warned "to beware of the Jews."[325] Even members of the *gerousia* were arrested and whipped for public entertainment.[326]

The period from the *Letter of Aristeas* (early second century B.C.) until Philo (early first century A.D.) can be demarcated as encompassing the limits of toleration between the Jewish and Greek communities in Egypt. During this period the Jewish population significantly increased, *politeumata* were established and Jewish religious institutions thrived. A number of Jews became landholders, were called Macedonians, claimed *epheboi* status, were granted citizenship and attained high social status. Hellenistic ideology and behaviour patterns were incorporated into Juda-ism and apocryphal literature flourished. However, in spite of the commu-nity's flowering into a strong ethnic force, Jewish secular institutions were never fully developed. They remained under the shadow of Ptole-maic-Roman institutions, which jurisdictionally regulated Jewish socio-economic behaviour. For the upwardly mobile, Hellenistically-oriented Jew the door to the Greek world was opened wide—in contrast to the lower class, more traditional Jew, who remained outside and became

---

[316]*3 Macc* 2:30.
[317]Josephus, *Ant.*, 19.279ff.
[318]*CPJ*, v. 2, no. 153.
[319]Josephus, *War*, 7.433ff.
[320]See *CPJ*, v. 2, nos. 154-159.
[321]Philo, *Flacc.*, 41ff. and *Leg. ad Gaium*, 132ff.
[322]Philo, *Leg. ad Gaium*, 133f.
[323]Philo, *Flacc.*, 53f.
[324]*Ibid.*, 55 and *Leg. ad Gaium*, 121ff.
[325]*CPJ*, v. 2, no. 152.
[326]See Philo, *Flacc.*, 78ff.

increasingly embittered. Philo is at the cross-roads. On the one hand he was the last great Jewish apologist accommodating Hellenism to Judaism. He attained Greek citizenship[327] and was respected in both Jewish and Greek communities. On the other hand, Philo observed the introduction of the *laographia,* experienced the revolt against the Jews of 38 A.D., and was asked to lead a delegation to persuade the Roman Emperor that Jews had legitimate rights, including religious liberty and the *politeuma.* It was during Philo's life that the Jewish lobby lost its effectiveness, that different Jewish interest groups appeared in Alexandria representing different ideological-cultural interests, and that Jews were classified as Egyptians for jurisdictional purposes. The Alexandrian Jewish community's solidarity was split over a variety of issues, of which two—secularization and assimilation—threatened the very essence of the community's future.[328]

The changes after Philo were swift and inevitable: there were further uprisings against the Jews and the leaders of the *politeuma* were increasingly unable to exercise control over the Alexandrian Jewish community. Even Tiberius Julius Alexander, the nephew of Philo and the governor of Egypt, was unable to prevent through negotiation the revolt of 66 A.D. Less than a decade later the Jewish tax was imposed.[329] Class divisions, country-city biases, anti-semitism and Roman economic changes coalesced in the first century A.D. Hellenistic Judaism, the product of secularization, re-surfaced in other forms.

3.4   Palestinian Contact

3.4.1   Introduction

In the pre-industrial world communication channels were slow

---

[327]See above 125 and fn. 299.

[328]Both Smallwood (*Jews,* 234ff.) and Tcherikover (*CPJ,* v. 2, 50ff.) have also viewed the period from the introduction of the *laographia* to the revolts of 38-41 A.D. as a turning point in the Jewish history of Egypt. Both have also suggested that by 41 A.D. the Alexandrian community was divided into two factions.

[329]Josephus, *War,* 7.218 and *CPJ,* v. 2, nos. 160-229. See also Wallace, *Taxation,* 170ff. Unlike the *laographia* which was a male per capita tax imposed on non-citizens, the Jewish tax was levied on all members of a household, whether citizens or non-citizens, including women, children and slaves. The tax was one half-*shekel* (equal to eight *drachmae*). With additional surcharges this tax approximated two weeks of wages for a Jewish peasant. See Chapter 2, 58 for the annual wages of a peasant.

and frequently unreliable. Nevertheless, Egyptian Jews had extensive socio-economic and religious contact with Palestine. Egypt and Palestine were adjacent countries. The distance from Alexandria to Jerusalem is approximately 375 miles, about the same as from Washington to Boston. Acceptance of novel normative prescriptions, innovative changes in ritual or even allegiance to a new High Priest may not have been quickly forthcoming. Marginal ideological developments would have remained unknown. From the Hasmonean revolt until the destruction of the Temple in Jerusalem in 70 A.D., Jerusalem and Alexandria were the two largest and most important Jewish centres in the Hellenistic-Roman world. Without first-hand knowledge, Alexandrian Jewish leaders would have been unable to decide which religious interest-group in Jerusalem to follow.

Psychologically, moreover, the Egyptian Jew's fate was tied to Palestine, and socially he was dependent on ethnic and religious solidarity with Palestinian Jewry. Abetted by a positive natural increase and proselytism, fertile social, economic, cultural and religious contacts between Palestinian and Egyptian Jewry could only have expanded.

3.4.2   Socio-economic Contact

Commercial contacts between Palestine and Egypt are documented during the Ptolemaic age. The Zenon papyri mention trade in slaves, oil, wheat, meat, fish and wine among an abundance of further items.[330] These goods were transported either from Gaza to Pelusium by water (a two-day journey) with coastal cities acting as trade links, or overland across the desert by camel caravans.[331] Egypt, on the other hand, exported manufactured goods such as papyrus, glass, pottery and textiles, with Alexandria playing the most prominent role.[332] In Hengel's assessment the Zenon papyri give "the picture of a very active, almost hectic commercial life . . . [with] agents [i.e., Greek administrators] and

---

[330]D. Sperber, "Objects of Trade," 113 and fn. 2. See also *CPJ*, v. 1, 115-146; V. Tcherikover, "Palestine in the Light of the Papyri of Zenon" (in Hebrew), *Tarbiz* 4/2-3 (1933), 226-247 and 5/2 (1933), 37-44; and Hengel, *Judaism and Hellenism*, v. 1, 37-47.

[331]For transportation and trade routes see M. P. Charlesworth, *Trade Routes and Commerce of the Roman Empire* (Cambridge, 1926[2]).

[332]See Hengel, *Judaism and Hellenism*, v. 1, 42f. and Rostovtzeff, *SEHHW*, v. 1, 366ff.

merchants flood[ing] the land [and pursuing trade with even] the last village of the country."[333]

That such trade activity occurred is not surprising, since Palestine was part of the commercial empire of the Ptolemies until 198 B.C.[334] The Ptolemies imposed their economic policies (e.g., state intervention, increased productivity, tax-farming) on all their foreign possessions and relied on an efficient centralized bureaucracy. Technological innovations were transplanted to Palestine, and new plants and methods of production were introduced.[335] Furthermore, the method of tax-farming was inaugurated to regulate all forms of production and to control the population. So thorough was the Ptolemaic domination of economic production that "its basic features continued down to Roman times."[336] Economic standardization translated into common Greek standards, weights, coins and trade terminology for all commercial transactions. And with this economic transition there developed a common language, *koine* Greek, dispersed by the merchant, the educated and the bureaucrat.[337] However, with regard to land, political considerations made it impracticable for all Palestinian land to be owned by the king. Consequently, state and private ownership of land co-existed with the latter remaining the norm.[338]

---

[333]Hengel, *Judaism and Hellenism*, v. 1, 43.

[334]For numismatic evidence indicating the extent of Palestinian integration with the Ptolemaic commercial empire, *ibid.*, 43ff., v. 2, fn. 341 and Table II, 208.

[335]For example, papyrus, mustard, lentils, beans and marrow were all introduced; see Josephus, *Ant.*, 14.33 (papyrus); *m. Kil.*, 1.2 (mustard); *m. Maas.*, 5.8 (lentils); *m. Kil.*, 2.11 (beans); and *m. Kil.*, 1.5 (marrow). New methods of production included the irrigation wheel and the plow, techniques for making oil and wine, the manufacture of dyes, and advances in building. See Hengel, *Judaism and Hellenism*, v. 1, 46f.

[336]Hengel, *Judaism and Hellenism*, v. 1, 23.

[337]The pervasiveness of Greek as the *lingua franca* is most clearly attested to by the adoption of Greek loan words, in particular those linked to trade in apocalyptic, Qumran and Mishnaic literature. Cf. 164 below and fn. 519.

[338]For state ownership of land see Rostovtzeff, *SEHHW*, v. 1, 342 and Hengel, *Judaism and Hellenism*, v. 1, 44ff. Applebaum has suggested that the Maccabean revolt was in part "generated by the actual existence of such [state-owned] land[s] and the oppressive regime by which they were characterized." (S. Applebaum, "Economic Life in Palestine," in Safrai and Stern, eds., *Jewish People*, v. 2, 634).

During this period there are few data regarding individual Jews engaged in commercial activities, but one can surmise that commercial traffic increased among Jews between the two countries as the Jewish population of Egypt increased. Trade among Jews may have been expedited as a result of Jews serving in the Egyptian army, which made occasional forays into Palestine.[339] In addition, there is evidence of Jewish slaves who had come to Egypt during the time of Ptolemy I as prisoners, and others who were sold as part of commercial transactions.[340] They too may have helped to establish commercial contacts. Still more important than these mercenaries and slaves would have been the role of the Jewish elite in Palestine (i.e., the large landholders, leaders of the priesthood, aristocratic families). The Ptolemies would have catered to these individuals and intimated that they shared mutual interests. The elites of both countries depended on the exploitation of those who were engaged in agricultural activity, and as such they were natural allies. The Ptolemies therefore skilfully induced them to participate in the risks and benefits of collecting the taxes and sharing in the commercial windfall. In time these shared interests and the profits that accrued with tax-farming evolved into wide-spread commercial contacts with both Jews and non-Jews in Egypt. However, the price of this co-operation and economic activity was expressed, in the spirit of the Hellenistic Age, through the process of secularization, and manifested itself in class, city-country and ideological conflicts that paralleled Egyptian-Jewish developments.[341] Hengel has summarized this development and the latent conflicts that were produced as follows:

> A relatively small, but rich and powerful upper class, which moreover had the confidence of their Greek masters and their immediate neighbours, faced on the one hand the representatives of a theocracy faithful to the Law, . . . and on the other those groups in which the prophetic tradition lived on and [the] apocalyptic [one] was coming to birth. . . . Both regarded the growth in the power of the aristocracy and the penetration of Greek customs into Jerusalem with the utmost distaste. On the other hand, their members had to face the

---

[339]For Jews serving in the Ptolemaic army, see above 78f.

[340]For Jewish prisoners of war and slaves, see above 77f.

[341]This argument has been presented by a number of authors although in different contexts. See, for example, Finkelstein, *The Pharisees* and Hengel, *Judaism and Hellenism*.

temptation to rise into the class of the privileged by compromising with the new masters and their way of life.[342]

Out of social and economic contacts, the seeds of the Hellenistic spirit evolved along with the impulse to re-interpret Greek ideas in terms meaningful to Judaism.

The most noteworthy example of accommodation by the aristocracy is that of Tobias, who according to Josephus was the brother-in-law of Onias II, the High Priest.[343] His commercial activity with the Ptolemies[344] and his kinship with the priesthood ultimately led to the Tobiad family's moving their principal residence from Transjordan to Jerusalem.[345] From this vantage point and their class standing the Tobiad family acquired a leading role in the secularization of Judaism. For nearly a century there is evidence of the family's inclination towards accommodation and maintaining profitable contact with Alexandrians.[346] Hengel, following Schlatter, has even postulated that Joseph and his family became the first Jewish bankers in Alexandria.[347] Among the Alexandrian contacts the Tobiad family would have nurtured would have been the leading Jewish families, to serve as their intermediaries. For example, the marriage of a niece of the Tobiad Joseph to a prominent Jew in Alexandria can be viewed from this perspective.[348] Similarly, Hezekiah's descendants may have acted as important commercial contacts as they most likely would have been men of means and well-placed in the Jewish community.[349] The Tobiad family would have sought out such individuals both in order to increase their credibility among Jews and to serve their own material interests. Such action would have been instrumental in establishing a sense of solidarity among aspiring Hellenistic Jews.

Over time the commercial class of Hellenistic Jews expanded. Patterns of trade became routinized and social contact more regular. Increased

---

[342]Hengel, *Judaism and Hellenism*, v. 1, 49.

[343]Josephus, *Ant.*, 12.160.

[344]See *CPJ*, v. 1, nos. 2a-e, 4, 5. The family also held credits in Alexandria in the third century B.C. (Josephus, *Ant.*, 12.199).

[345]Josephus, *Ant.*, 12.160, 222.

[346]*Ibid.*, 12.160ff.

[347]Hengel, *Judaism and Hellenism*, v. 1, 270 and v. 2, 80, fn. 86.

[348]Josephus, *Ant.*, 12.186ff.

[349]Josephus, *Apion*, 1.187.

social interaction was accompanied by the exchange of ideas with corresponding Hellenistic biases. Through regular contact, these ideas evolved, and were transformed. According to Hengel, it was intensive economic activity that "prepared the ground for apocalyptic speculation and the later revolts. . . ."[350]

After the Ptolemaic defeat and until the Hasmonean revolt, trade between Palestine and Egypt probably deteriorated, as Palestine was part of the commercial empire of the Seleucids. The change of political regime affected the direction of trade and the trade objects themselves. Arabian trade no longer passed from Gaza to Alexandria but found its way through Syria.[351] However, with the establishment of the Hasmonean dynasty and with the resulting access to the sea (141 B.C.)[352] commercial contacts expanded rapidly between Palestine and Egypt and continued under Roman domination.[353]

The Hasmoneans, and later the Herodians, left the fundamental features of social structure established by the Ptolemies intact. Private ownership of property remained the norm although several parcels of land passed into the royal household or later into Roman hands. Monopolistic practices receded and commerce became less controlled. Nevertheless, the state still intervened in the functioning of the economy in a variety of ways, such as through monetary and taxation policies. Technologically, the Hasmoneans and the Herodians followed a course similar to that of the Ptolemies. Consequently, the only way these dynasties were able to increase their economic productivity was by territorial expansion. This involved driving a wedge into the important Arabian trade route by controlling the Mediterranean, and in particular Gaza, which dominated the flow of merchandise from Arabia and the East to Alexandria. Conquests also brought parts of the *Via Maris* and the King's Highway under Jewish control for a period of time, as well as the Road of the Patriarchs, the artery that connected Jerusalem to Egypt via Beer Sheva. The Jewish commercial class took advantage of these transformations and the material and ideological bonds between the Jewish elite of Egypt and Palestine were further cemented.

The fact that Jews began to enter higher social strata in Egypt after

---

[350] Hengel, *Judaism and Hellenism*, v. 1, 56.
[351] Rostovtzeff, *SEHHW*, v. 2, 696.
[352] See *1 Macc* 13:11, 14:5 for access to Gaza and *1 Macc* 13:51 for the establishment of the Hasmonean dynasty.
[353] Baron, *Social*, v. 1, 255.

the Maccabean revolt (e.g., Onias, Dositheus, Helkias and Ananias)[354]
further facilitated the strengthening of mutual class interests between
aspiring Hellenistic Jews from the two respective countries. Although
individuals such as Onias were initially hostile to the Hasmoneans, they
too came to view the Hasmonean monarchy as compatible with their own
interests and felt "morally bound to defend it. . . ."[355] This also contributed to the development of trade links between the two countries, and at
times was manifested in the form of political loyalty. In 55 B.C. and again
in 48 B.C. the Jews guarding Pelusium permitted the Romans to enter
Eygpt unmolested.[356]

With the Roman conquest of Palestine and Egypt the Mediterranean
world was bound together, with Alexandria as the most important city in
the eastern sector of the Empire. The volume of trade and movement
substantially increased between cosmopolitan centres such as Alexandria
and Jerusalem. With Rome patrolling the seas and improving the high-
ways, travel by land or sea was easier than before. These transportation
changes further stimulated trade. One immediate effect was that goods
from the East could now pass through Palestine on the way to Alexandria,
while many western products could pass via Alexandria and Palestine on
their way eastward. Many Jews from both countries shared in this activity
as the increased volume provided employment for merchants, boat
builders and haulers as well as for a variety of other trades. Easier transportation also facilitated the dispersion of Jewish missionaries and served
indirectly to strengthen socio-economic and ideological links between
Palestinian and Egyptian Jewry.

An examination of imports and exports from the second century B.C. to
the second century A.D. attests to the depth of the economic relationship
between Egypt and Palestine (see Table 6). Sperber, for example, who has
investigated objects of trade in Roman times, has commented that "the
volume of trade between these two countries throughout the Roman
period was quite considerable."[357] In his opinion, even "much of the
shipping industry was in (partial) control of Alexandrian Jews, during the
early Roman Empire. . . ."[358] Although it is impossible to verify Sperber's
speculation, the fact that Jews were active in the Red Sea trade and in

---

[354] See above 80 and fn. 25.
[355] Tcherikover, *Hellenistic Civilization,* 284.
[356] See above 81.
[357] Sperber, "Objects of Trade," 146.
[358] Ibid., loc. cit.

Table 6
Objects of Trade Between Palestine and Egypt *

	Imports (Egypt to Palestine)				*Exports* (Palestine to Egypt)		
	2 and 1 cent. B.C.	1 cent. A.D.	2 cent. A.D.		2 and 1 cent. B.C.	1 cent. A.D.	2 cent. A.D.
beer			X	tar	X	X	X
wheat	X			bitumen		X	X
fish			X	hides			?
linen/cloth	X	X	X	oil	X	X	X
natron	X	X	X	balsam	X	X	
medicines	X						
rope	X	X					

* Source: D. Sperber, "Objects of Trade Between Palestine and Egypt in Roman Times," *Journal of the Economic and Social History of the Orient* 19 (1976), 147 with additional data included.

the movement of the *annona* lends it a certain degree of credibility. Indeed, the diverse interests of the wealthy commercial strata of Alexandria are well-attested to in the literature and the papyri.[359] Thus, it is quite possible that Egyptian Jews controlled parts of the Palestinian shipping coast under the Herodians and enjoyed a lucrative trade. If so, they probably constituted part of the Jewish *naukleroi* (i.e., shipowners), "the aristocracy among the Jewish merchants. . . ."[360]

Brief consideration of two of the objects of trade from Egypt to Palestine listed in Table 6 will demonstrate the relationship between class and economy. With the Roman conquest of Egypt the export of wheat to Palestine stopped. However, there are two pieces of evidence that suggest that during times of famine exceptions were made.[361] And these exceptions occurred only because of the fact that both Herod and Queen Helena were from the upper class, were able to make use of their personal networks in Egypt and had access to a large amount of cash. Moreover, if Sperber following Ginzberg is correct in his assumption that the reason there is no evidence for wheat imports is in large measure an economic boycott of Alexandrian wheat,[362] then such an undertaking would have been impossible without state (i.e., upper class) intervention in the economy. Since Egyptian wheat was substantially cheaper than Palestinian wheat,[363] the only means the Palestinian landowning elite had to safeguard their economic interests was to stop the importation of cheap (Egyptian) wheat. By introducing an economic boycott they were therefore able to control supply and keep the price artificially high. Only when supply-fluctuation, such as a famine, demanded additional wheat did they personally act to prevent civil unrest and economic disaster. Thus, an economic boycott seems plausible as it protected the home market and the interest of the large landowners. It accounts for the lack of trade in wheat between Egypt and Palestine after the first century B.C. and at the same time indicates that upper class had access, contacts (Jewish merchants) and cash to alleviate a potential problem.

Trade in linen is another example of how trade in commodities was class-related. In antiquity Pelusium linen was considered to be of excellent quality and was an expensive item. Considered a luxury, it "fetched

---

[359]See above 97 ff.

[360]*CPJ*, v. 1, 49f.

[361]Josephus, *Ant.*, 15.305ff. and 20.101.

[362]Sperber, "Objects of Trade," 118.

[363]D. Sperber, "Cost of Living in Roman Palestine," *Journal of the Economic and Social History of the Orient* 9 (1966), 190f.

premium prices and was bought only by the elite."[364] Hence its purchase can be viewed as an indicator of class position. The evidence in the Mishnah[365] that the robes of the High Priest on the Day of Atonement were made from Pelusium linen (i.e., the yarn) indicates that the High Priest had enough cash to purchase it. Although Sperber[366] has argued that this occurred only in the latter years of the Second Temple, it is unlikely that Herod and his elite, including the High Priests, would not have acquired such items nearly a century earlier. In spite of the fact that there are little data to substantiate this claim, the evidence regarding the upper class passion for luxury items in the Roman Empire is solid.[367] Conspicuous consumption allowed the aristocracy to enhance their status and to dramatize their differences from the lower class.

Geographical location also may have contributed to economic contacts between Palestine and Egypt. In addition to Alexandria, for which a great deal of evidence regarding trade exists, areas such as Wadi Natrun may have played an important role. Wadi Natrun was renowned for its natural deposits of natron (used for washing).[368] In the second century B.C. there is evidence of a Jewish community in this region[369] and, according to Sperber, natron was imported to Palestine from there two centuries later.[370] The fact that a *proseuche* was built in Wadi Natrun is a sign of a considerable concentration of Jews. Furthermore, the fact that Jewish communities existed in the *chora* between Alexandria and the Fayum until the revolt under Trajan suggests a continuity in community life for three centuries. If this assumption is correct then it is likely that the Jews of Wadi Natrun took advantage of the natural deposit and exploited it well before the second century A.D. Jews in Egypt would be keenly aware of the needs of Palestinian centres as potential markets and would have attempted to supply them when local markets could not meet the demand. Such was the case in the second century A.D., as noted by Sperber.[371]

---

[364]Hopkins, "Economic Growth," in Abrams and Wrigley, eds., *Towns*, 48.

[365] *M. Yoma*, 3.7.

[366]Sperber, "Objects of Trade," 123.

[367]See Chapter 2, 68 and fn. 235.

[368]See Pliny the Elder, *Natural History*, 31.109, 111 and Strabo, *Geog.*, 17.1.23.

[369] *CPJ*, v. 3, no. 1442; see also v. 1, 8.

[370]Sperber, "Objects of Trade," 128.

[371]Ibid., loc. cit.

The employment of key Egyptian Jews in the Palestinian Jewish aristocracy would also have contributed to an increase in the volume of trade between Egypt and Palestine. Jesus, son of Phiabi, and Simon, son of Boethus, were both of Egyptian stock and recruited by Herod to act as High Priests.[372] Moreover, an additional seven members of the Boethus family became High Priests, as did two from the family of Phiabi.[373] They and their descendants had the social contacts, extended capital base, and familial networks to facilitate commercial transactions between the two countries.

The importance of the Boethuseans, a synonym for the Sadducees, should be emphasized.[374] Originating from Alexandria they represented wealthy, urban, Jewish elite interests and would have catered to the needs and demands of this class. In fact, Josephus describes them as being able to have only "the confidence of the wealthy."[375] It is probable that Boethus was active in Alexandrian communal and religious life and his descendants therefore had intimate knowledge of two cosmopolitan markets and Jewish institutional contexts. Given their capital base[376] and wide social networks, the purchase of luxury items (such as the linen for the High Priest's robes mentioned above) is not unreasonable.[377] According to Jeremias, High Priestly families carried on a flourishing trade,[378] and the High Priest Ananias, according to Josephus, was infamous for his ability to procure money.[379] Consequently, it is not surprising that the Boethuseans came to exert enormous political influence as they dominated both the religious and economic sectors of society.[380] Without

---

[372]See above fn. 151. For evidence of other Jewish priestly families in Alexandria see *2 Macc* 1:10 and Josephus, *Apion*, 1.187.

[373]Jeremias, *Jerusalem*, 194.

[374]For a comprehensive survey of the sources see J. Le Moyne, *Les Sadducéens* (Paris, 1972).

[375]Josephus, *Ant.*, 13.298.

[376]*T. Yoma*, 1.6, suggests that the wealth of the High Priest exceeded that of the rest of the priesthood combined, although this is clearly exaggerated.

[377]The legendary story is told, for example, that Martha (of the High Priestly family of Boethus) carpeted the whole distance from her house to the Temple gate because she wanted to see her husband—Joshua b. Gamla—officiate on the Day of Atonement, and the law required everyone to go barefoot (*Lam. Rab.*, 1.50 on 1.16).

[378]Jeremias, *Jerusalem*, 31 and 49.

[379]Josephus, *Ant.*, 20.205.

[380]In part, the mechanism through which this entrenchment of power

doubt, their Alexandrian priestly and aristocratic heritage was an important contributing factor to this development. Not only did it provide the necessary social status but it also equipped them with the required Hellenistic *Weltanschauung*. Their Hellenistic roots coincided with Herod's aims: secularized policies that accommodated Judaism to Hellenism. Thus in the last century of the Temple, the spirit of the Hellenistic age fully matured with the Boethuseans, who were influenced by their Alexandrian heritage and instrumental in shaping for many the way Judaism should be conceptualized and practised.

Other sectors of the society, in addition to the commercial and priestly classes, had intimate contact with Palestine and Egypt. Jerusalem and Alexandria were both well-known centres of handicrafts and skilled artisans. Alexandrian Jewish artisans were considered exceptional: weavers, goldsmiths, silversmiths, wool-dressers, and dyers among others competed in a market of high demand, and the skills of individual workshops were acknowledged. If the several references in the Talmud to Palestinian Jewry requesting Jewish artisans from Alexandria are accepted,[381] then the evidence suggests that Egypt was viewed as a complementary market in time of need (e.g., a strike, scarcity of skilled labour, etc.). The advantage of hiring such artisans was that not only would they have the recommendation of the Alexandrian Jewish community but, more importantly, they would have first-hand knowledge of Judaism.[382] Knowledge of Judaism would have been especially relevant when the artisans were engaged in Temple construction or modifications, as such labour would have been viewed in part as a religious undertaking. Thus, artisans too were active

---

was achieved was nepotism. Jeremias (*Jerusalem*, 198) points out how the family of Annas controlled, through relatives, the Temple, the *cultus*, the priestly court, a number of seats on the *Sanhedrin* and the Temple's finances; and the family of Boethus would have behaved no differently. Support is provided by the famous rabbinical lament against them: "Woe unto me because of the house of Boethus" (*t. Menah.*, 13.21 and *b. Pesah.*, 57a), and Josephus' overall appraisal of them.

[381]For example, see *t. Yoma*, 2.5-6 (cf. *b. Yoma*, 38a) and *t. Arak.*, 2.3-4 (cf. *b. Arak.*, 10b). See also Tcherikover, *Hellenistic Civilization*, 519, fn. 22.

[382]A recent historical incident parallels the situation described in the Talmud. After the Al Aksa mosque in Jerusalem was bombed there was both a scarcity of labour in Israel as well as a need for individuals with the required legitimate Islamic knowledge. After the signing of the Camp David accords, one of the first requests of the Israeli government was for Egyptian artisans to repair the mosque.

participants in the economic development of Palestine and Egypt and carriers of Judaic and Hellenistic life-styles.

The material ties between the two countries depended on a variety of factors. However, at root was the desire of Jews to interact with fellow Jews. Ethnic and religious identification was an essential motivating force for Alexandrian Jews to seek Palestinian trade, to patronize Jewish establishments and to contribute to the Jewish nation's well-being by providing commodities or services; and similarly, ethnic and religious identification prompted Palestinian Jews to view Egypt as a complementary Jewish source of capital, labour and goods. Moreover, class ties between Jerusalem and Alexandria encouraged contact. The upper class, priests, artisans and merchants, continually interacted for social, economic and political reasons. Joseph, a tax-collector in Jerusalem, had an office in Alexandria managed by his steward.[383] Agrippa I borrowed money from Philo's brother Alexander,[384] and it was Alexander who commissioned the renovation of the wooden gates of Herod's Temple with silver and gold.[385] Thus it was not uncommon that different members of one family, workshop or business held managerial positions in various district offices outside their home country.[386] Sometimes this affiliation would have been expressed more generally, in a community context rather than one of class. Siegel, for example, has suggested that the Alexandrians bore the cost of a Torah scroll with gold *tetragrammata* for the Alexandrian community in Jerusalem.[387] Since the existence of such a community is well-established,[388] it is not difficult to subscribe to the opinion that those who emigrated maintained contact with their friends and kin. Nor is it hard to imagine that those who remained in Alexandria wanted their *polis* to stand out as unique and special in Jerusalem. Indeed this is exactly the situation in Israel today. New citizens of the State propagandize the benefits of living in a Jewish State to their home communities, while each home community attempts to outdo the other by dedicating something of significance to the State. The purchase and dedication of a scroll with gold *tetragrammata* would have been an obvious example of this trend.

---

[383]Josephus, *Ant.*, 12.160ff. and 199.
[384]Ibid., 18.159f.
[385]Josephus, *War*, 5.205.
[386]Cf. Sperber, "Objects of Trade," 146.
[387]J. P. Siegel, "The Alexandrians in Jerusalem and their Torah Scroll with the Gold *Tetragrammata*," *IEJ* 22/1 (1972), 39-43.
[388]Acts 6:9, and below fn. 394.

Close trade relations between Jerusalem and Alexandria would also have acted as a context for Jews in Palestine to be enticed by the wonders of Alexandria. The city's charms were alluring:

> For all that is and will be, can be found in Egypt [i.e., Alexandria]. Riches, stadiums, power, fine weather, reputation, theatres, philosophers, gold, young men . . . the museum, wine, every good thing, whatever you want, and women. . . .[389]

For the ruling elite and priestly aristocracy of Jerusalem, the ruling elite of the Jewish *politeuma* in Alexandria was a natural ally. For aspiring Hellenistic Jews who had become upwardly mobile, Alexandrian Jews served as a model of achievement. Compromise of beliefs for the promise of mobility and Hellenism was correspondingly appealing.

3.4.3 Religious Contact

Religious contact accompanied economic contact. Just as Jerusalem was the political and economic centre of Palestine so too was it the centre of devotion to Judaism. Jerusalem was the site of the Temple, the home of the Jewish *cultus,* where multitudes of pilgrims would converge to make sacrifice three times a year. In Jerusalem sat the *Sanhedrin,* the highest Jewish court of law. Jerusalem was the pivot for Jewish religious education and attracted scholars from abroad. It was the fulcrum of new religious movements and marginal sects and the axis for messianic expectations. It is understandable, therefore, that like all Diaspora Jews, Egyptian Jews were either pulled to Jerusalem or influenced by her attraction.

Egyptian Jews are well-documented as pilgrims to Jerusalem.[390] Philo writes that Jerusalem is the mother city not only for the Jews of Judaea but also those of Egypt[391] and that "thousands of men from thousands of cities stream to the Temple for every feast, some over land, others over sea, from the east and the west and from the north and the south."[392] Philo mentions that he himself visited Jerusalem as a pilgrim.[393] It is

---

[389]Herondas, cited in Hengel, *Judaism and Hellenism,* v. 1, 37.

[390]Philo, *De Spec. Leg.,* 1.69; Acts 2:9-11; and, less specifically, Josephus, *Ant.,* 17.214.

[391]Philo, *Leg. ad Gaium,* 281.

[392]Philo, *De Spec. Leg.,* 1.69.

[393]Philo, *De Prov.,* 2.64.

likely that many of these Egyptian pilgrims had contact with Egyptian Jews who were living in Jerusalem, because of common nationality, customs, and experience.[394] Social networks would have reduced accommodation problems and contributed to the strengthening of old socioeconomic relationships or the advancement of new ones. Hence "the economy of Jerusalem was based on a foreign trade which arose out of religion."[395]

Pilgrims came to Jerusalem to offer sacrifice for a number of reasons: *aliya le-regel*,[396] child birth,[397] the completion of a Nazirite's vow[398] and conversion.[399] For many it served not only as an opportunity to express their ethnic and religious solidarity but also to pursue the study of Torah.[400] Possibly the scribe, Hanan b. Abishalom, nicknamed the Egyptian, had come to Jerusalem in this fashion[401] as had the Egyptian proselyte called Minjamin.[402] Tcherikover has suggested that, once there, they continued to maintain "bonds of friendship with the Alexandrian Jew."[403] However, the majority of the Jews in Egypt did not fulfill the obligation of ritual sacrifice or come to Jerusalem to study Torah. Cost, secularization and lack of commitment would have reduced their observance. As well, women were not subject to the command to appear before the Lord during the *regalim*,[404] a fact which would have further reduced the total number of pilgrims. Jeremias has surmised that the total number of pilgrims during the Passover in the first century A.D. was over 60,000,[405] although Safrai has cast doubt on all such estimations.[406] Whatever the

[394]For evidence of an Alexandrian Jewish community in Jerusalem see 142 above and fn. 388. In addition see *t. Meg.*, 3.6 and *b. Meg.*, 26a (cf. Krauss, *Synagogale*, 201).

[395]Theissen, *First Followers*, 52.

[396]See Exod 23:14-17; Deut 16:16; *m. Hag.*, 1.1; and Josephus, *Ant.*, 4.203f.

[397]*M. Ker.*, 1.3-7, 2.1.

[398]Ibid., 2.1 and *m. Nazir*, 5.4.

[399]*M. Ker.*, 2.1.

[400]See *m. Neg.*, 14.13.

[401]*M. Ketub.*, 13.1-2.

[402]*T. Qidd.*, 5.4. Cf. Jeremias, *Jerusalem*, 322f.

[403]*CPJ*, v. 1, 106.

[404]*M. Hag.*, 1.1. However, in spite of the law not binding Jewish women to come to Jerusalem, many still undertook the journey. See Josephus, *Ant.*, 11, 109; Luke 2:42; *b. Hag.*, 6b and *b. Pesah.*, 89a.

[405]Jeremias, *Jerusalem*, 84.

[406]S. Safrai, "The Temple," in Safrai and Stern, eds., *Jewish People*, v.

number, many would have travelled from Alexandria, the Diaspora capital of Judaism, and returned home affected by their religious experience. Pilgrims travelled, as did merchants, by way of the *Via Maris*, or the Road of the Patriarchs, or by sea. Travel was differentiated by class. Those of the higher strata enjoyed a leisurely voyage with servants taking care of their needs while those of the lower class depended on their own means. Sea travel was more efficient, cheaper and faster, but cargo frequently took precedence over passengers and consequently foot travel to Palestine was more common.[407] In either case, however, during the Roman period travel included the purchase of an exit pass which had to be approved by the governor.[408] The Roman government therefore was able to control the movement of the population while at the same time filling its coffers by imposing a departure tax. Such a practice discriminated against those of the lower strata who wished to make the pilgrimage as they had neither the cash to spare nor the social networks to circumvent the tax.

After the pilgrims' arrival in Jerusalem class differences again discriminated against those from the lower classes. Travelling mercenaries, merchants and those of the upper strata may have obtained lodging with friends through their social contacts. Merchants who had regular contact with clients in Jerusalem, or who were affiliated with particular religious groups, also had the first opportunity to find lodging in synagogues (such as the one excavated on Mount Ophel)[409] or billeting with house-holders and innkeepers. Since in antiquity hired lodgings were costly and in short supply, those without ready cash would have been at a disadvantage.

2, 902. This also applies to Josephus' estimation of approximately three million (*War*, 2.280) and rabbinical accounts (e.g., *t. Pesah.*, 12 million). For modern comments, see Baron, *Social*, v. 1, 168, and 370, fn. 5.

[407]See L. Casson, *Travel in the Ancient World* (London, 1974), 149-162, 176-196, which provides an excellent overview of comparative modes of travel and costs. For travel to Palestine, see D. Sperber, "Social Legislation in Jerusalem During the Latter Part of the Second Temple Period," *JSJ* 6/1 (1975), 88. According to Jones (*Roman Economy*, 37), a *modius* of wheat could be transferred from Alexandria to Rome (1500 kms.) for 16 *denarii*, a sum which would not pay for a land journey of eighty kilometers.

[408]See Wallace, *Taxation*, 273 and Taubenschlag, *Law*, 642.

[409]*CII*, v. 2, no. 1404. The Greek inscription mentions a hostel and rooms "for needy travellers from foreign lands." Letters of recommendation were common and were frequently followed by offers of hospitality (e.g., 2 Cor 3:1).

Moreover, it should be noted that innkeeping was usually a woman's job, which would have offended many religious Jews.[410] The combination of these factors differentiates the kind of Jew who would have been more likely to frequent such inns: the aspiring, upwardly-mobile Hellenistic Jew rather than the lower class traditionalist, especially given that decor tended toward the erotic and that some offered the services of prostitutes.[411]

The rabbis, aware of the shortage of housing during the foot festivals and the practice of scalping the naïve and desperate pilgrim, devised a number of by-laws through *halachic* legislation to control the situation. Householders and innkeepers were forbidden to take a rental fee,[412] although in reaction to these laws, they began the custom of taking the hides of sacrificed animals in lieu of rent.[413] While it is impossible to plot accurately this change of practice, Sperber has suggested that this transition occurred in the first century A.D.[414] Egyptian Jews were subjected to this custom,[415] which paradoxically resulted in pilgrims from the lower classes suffering economically because of their inability to sell their valuable sacrificial skins.[416] On the other hand, pilgrims who were not fortunate enough to find lodgings had to depend on setting up camp in the countryside adjacent to Jerusalem.[417] This involved a significant number of pilgrims, particularly those from the lower class. Thus the Mishnah's

---

[410]Casson, *Travel*, 208.

[411]Ibid., 211ff. It is interesting to note that the association of innkeeping with eroticism continued well into the early Christian era. *The Apostolic Constitutions*, 54, for example, forbade the use of inns except in cases of emergency on account of their lack of morality.

[412]For example, *t. Neg.*, 6.2 and *Abot R. Nat.*, 1.35. Cf. Sperber, "Social Legislation," 91ff.

[413]*T. Maas.*, 1.12 and *b. Yoma*, 12a.

[414]Sperber, "Social Legislation," 93f.

[415]*Abot R. Nat.*, 1.35 uses the word *mizrim* (i.e., Egyptians) which suggests that the hides originally came from Egypt. Variant readings have *mezuyarim* (i.e., painted) and Sperber has postulated *mezumarim* (i.e., woolly). See Sperber, "Social Legislation," 94 and fn. 47.

[416]According to Jeremias, citing Krauss, the hides of Egyptian sheep were worth 4-5 *sela* each (= 16-20 *denarii*). Since the average Egyptian peasant's wage was just over one-half a *drachma* a day (4 *drachmae* = 1 *denarius*), his loss was considerable (64-80 *drachmae* or approximately one-third of his annual wage). See Jeremias, *Jerusalem*, 102 and fn. 6 and Philo, *De Spec. Leg.*, 1.151, for the high value of hides; and Chapter 2, 58 and fn. 162 for the annual wage of a peasant.

[417]*B. Pesah.*, 80a.

comment, that "no man ever said to his fellow, 'Too congested is the place for me that I should lodge in Jerusalem'"[418] can only be understood as supporting Sperber's earlier deduction that the *halachot* were affected by socio-economic conditions, and the rabbis extended the boundaries of Jerusalem to include the tent cities in order not to discriminate against the less fortunate.[419]

Contact between Egypt and Palestine substantially changed during the last two centuries of the Temple and peaked in the first century A.D. Whereas in the first century B.C., "the number of pilgrims that used to come to Jerusalem was relatively small, and . . . of the wealthier class, . . . [in the first century A.D.] the pilgrimage to Jerusalem became an event of considerable popularity. . . ."[420] The Mishnah's comment that certain craftsmen were able to work until noon on the eve of Passover (e.g., tailors, barbers) was changed to include shoemakers in the first century A.D. because many of the pilgrims came by foot and had to have their sandals repaired.[421] Contact also would have peaked in the first century A.D. between Palestine and Egypt for a variety of additional reasons as pointed out above: the fact that both countries were under Roman sovereignty; the relation between infrastructure (e.g., new roads) and the expansion of service facilities (e.g., new inns, regular patrols); the employment of key Egyptian Jews in the Palestinian priesthood and their extended kin and social network in Egypt; the increased volume of trade; the attempts of Palestinian rabbis to institutionalize Judaism; the pervasiveness of Jewish ideology disseminated by missionary preachers; and most importantly, the feeling in Egypt, and in particular Alexandria, of ethnic and religious identity. However, the increased popularity of pilgrimages did not alter the fact that those from the lower classes were discriminated against when leaving Egypt, travelling, or visiting Jerusalem. The volume of Egyptian pilgrims increased but those with means would have been disproportionately represented. The aspiring Hellenist would have had reasons equally valid as those of the traditional Jew for honouring the religious obligation. Not only would it reaffirm his identification with Judaism, however defined, but it would also create an opportunity for him to engage in economic transactions.

Jerusalem was the capital of Judaism for two main reasons: the presence of the Temple, and the fact that it was the locus of legitimate power

---

[418] *M. Abot*, 5.5.
[419] See *m. Menah.*, 11.2.
[420] Sperber, "Social Legislation," 88.
[421] *M. Pesah.*, 4.6. Cf. Sperber, "Social Legislation," 86ff.

over the direction of Judaism. After the Hasmonean revolt the institutionalized religion became progressively centralized through the policies of the *Sanhedrin, Beth Din,* priests, scribes and, in the last century of the Temple, the rabbis. Jews who lived in the Diaspora were dependent on Jerusalem for their religious practices. For the believing Egyptian Jew it meant continually looking East in order to comply with normative behavioural patterns. Jews in Egypt were dependent on envoys being sent from the *Sanhedrin* for the proclamation of a new month,[422] and for the intercalation of *Adar sheni*.[423] Josephus informs us that priests living in Egypt had to depend on the *Sanhedrin* legitimating the lawfulness of their marriages.[424] Similarly, when questions arose regarding the legitimacy of offspring of Alexandrian parents, Jews were dependent on Jerusalem to resolve the issue.[425]

Religious contact between Egyptian Jewry and Jerusalem was also supported by other norms. Jews of Egypt were obliged to give tithes to the priests[426] and to spend a tenth of the produce of their land in Jerusalem, the so-called 'second tithe.'[427] According to Alon, however, this custom declined near the beginning of Hyrcanus' reign.[428] Thereafter some followed the old *halacha* while others did not—hence Philo's report and his criticisms of fellow Egyptian Jews whom he perceived as negligent in their duties.[429] Yet in spite of the fulfillment of the Law by those who felt so obligated, once the tithes were brought to Jerusalem the *Beth Din* still had the authority to legislate which offerings would be considered ritually pure or impure. For example, the Mishnah comments, "the men of Alexandria brought their dough-offerings from Alexandria, but they did not accept them from them."[430] Regional differences sometimes resulted

---

[422] *M. Ros. Has.*, 1.3, 2.2 and *t. Pea,* 4.5.

[423] *T. Sanh.*, 2.6.

[424] Josephus, *Apion*, 1.33.

[425] *T. Ketub.*, 4.9.

[426] For example, see Jdt 11:13f.; 1 Macc 3:49f.; Heb 7:5; and Josephus, *Ant.*, 4.205, 241ff. For Philo see fn. 251 above.

[427] *M. Maas.*, 8. For evidence of payment see *Tob* 1:6-8 and *Jub* 32:8-12. Cf. Jeremias, *Jerusalem*, 134ff.

[428] Alon, *Jews, Judaism*, 89-102. For an alternative interpretation see Safrai ("Religion," 826) who has argued that Diaspora Jews were no less subject to the tithe than Palestinian Jews.

[429] Philo, *De Spec. Leg.*, 1.153ff. Cf. Alon, *Jews, Judaism*, 94 and fn. 13. After the destruction of the Temple some Egyptian Jews continued to pay this tithe (*m. Yad.*, 4.3).

[430] *M. Hal.*, 4.10.

in the Jews of Egypt having to choose between alternative practices (i.e., Egyptian versus Palestinian). From the above example regarding tithing and Philo's observations, it is evident that a range of alternatives existed. Similarly, religious ritual in Alexandria did not always follow the Palestinian format.[431] Religious observances may have been much more loosely defined and heterogeneous than previously postulated.

Regular religious contact between the two countries also existed on account of the payment of the half-*shekel*. Male Jews of Egypt between the ages of twenty and fifty, including proselytes, were obligated to forward to the Temple a half *shekel* for its upkeep.[432] These payments are first attested to in the Diaspora in 88 B.C. and in the Roman period there is abundant evidence for them.[433] In one sense the half-*shekel* can be viewed as membership dues—a statement of affirmation. The dating of these first payments provides further support for the argument that contact between Diaspora Jews and Jerusalem substantially changed during the last two centuries of the Temple and became more frequent, intensive and regular.

Religious contact manifested itself in a number of other ways that had political and even messianic overtones. So, for example, the endeavour by the Hasmoneans to entrench their political and religious power by dictating which Jewish festivals should be followed can be glimpsed in their attempt to persuade Egyptian Jewry to celebrate *Chanukkah* and *Purim*.[434] Although this undertaking proved futile it attests to Jerusalem's policy of centralizing and institutionalizing Judaism while, at the same time, attesting to the fact that Egyptian Jewry demanded more variability in religious practice. Moreover, the fact that the Hasmoneans sought out only the Jews in Egypt indicates that they viewed Egyptian Diaspora Jews as subject to the same religious duties. Political interventions are also observable in a variety of other situations. Agrippa's chance visit to Alexandria in 38 A.D. became a political event when his presence was exploited by the Jews for their own religious and political

---

[431]See above 116.

[432]Exod 30:11-16.

[433]See Josephus, *Ant.*, 3.194ff., 14.110ff., 16.28, 163, 169 and *War*, 7.218; Philo, *Quis Rerum Div. Heres*, 186; Matt 17:24; and *m. Seqal*. Cf. Smallwood, *Jews*, 125.

[434]For *Chanukkah* see 2 *Macc* 1.1-9. For *Purim* see the Greek text of *Esther*. Cf. *CPJ*, v. 1, 46 and fns. 118, 119 and Tcherikover, *Hellenistic Civilization*, 259 and fns. 61, 62.

purposes.[435] Basing their demands on ethnic and religious solidarity they prevailed on him to march through the streets and provide a rallying-point for the people. Again, for instance, appeal by the *sicarii* to Egyptian Jewry to participate in the revolt against Rome was similarly based on the perception that Egyptian Jews were bound by duty and had a share in Palestine. Even the political act of manumission was in part associated with the extent of religious contact. A number of Jews who had become slaves were manumitted by Jewish communities.[436]

The expectation of religious solidarity may have also kindled the flames of messianic movements. These movements flourished in the first century A.D., when contact between Palestine and Egypt was at its highest level, and continued to spread into the following century.[437] As a teacher, for example, Jesus was only one of many who acted as a catalyst for others to develop alternative understandings of Judaism. Wandering charismatics and radical theocratic movements that were messianic in orientation affected society, and in particular Judaism.[438] Josephus mentions several by name[439] and provides evidence, which is further supported by *Acts*,[440] that Egyptian Jews were accused of being in the forefront of religious changes.[441] Although plotting the chronological development of these changes and assessing their impact is highly speculative, frequent contact between Alexandria and Jerusalem concerning religious issues, and specifically the messiah, would have led to the cross-pollination of ideas and regional differences. If this exchange is related to Tacitus' and Suetonius' comments that Jews had a messianic wish to rule the world,[442] it would have further advanced popular belief in the Hellenistic-Roman world that the Jews of the Diaspora were more than just religiously united with Palestinian Jewry. This perception by non-Jews would have fueled further the conflict between Jew and Greek in

---

[435] See Philo, *Flacc.*, 25ff. and Smallwood's comments in *Jews*, 237ff.

[436] See above 82 and fn. 40.

[437] For example, the messianic movement led by Loukuas in Egypt during the reign of Trajan, and that of Bar Cochba in Palestine during the reign of Hadrian.

[438] Theissen, *First Followers*, 60.

[439] For example, Judas, Simon and Athronges (*Ant.*, 17.271ff. and *War*, 2.55ff.), Theudas (*Ant.*, 20.97ff.), Menachem (*War*, 2.433ff.) and Jonathan (*Ant.*, 20.167ff. and *War*, 7.438ff.).

[440] Acts 21:38.

[441] Josephus, *Ant.*, 20.169 and *War*, 2.261ff.

[442] Tacitus, *Histories*, 5.13.2 and Suetonius, *Vesp.*, 4.5.

Alexandria and between the aspiring Jewish Hellenist who wished to accommodate himself to Hellenism and the traditional believer who was apocalyptically inclined.

Finally, religious contact was instrumental in the translation of the Torah into Greek (*Septuagint*) in Egypt and the evolution and translation of the apocryphal and pseudepigraphical writings. According to the legend in Aristeas the translation of the Torah was due to Ptolemy II wishing a copy of all the books in the world to be housed in his library in Alexandria. In reality, the translation occurred piecemeal over a considerable period of time and was undertaken by Jews for the benefit of Jews in order to meet their religious needs in Greek-speaking countries such as Egypt.[443] Change of residence coupled with Hellenistic influence and social convention would have resulted in Greek becoming the language for socializing the new generation into Judaism.[444] It was not that Hebrew lost its sacred status;[445] rather it was that Hebrew came to be perceived as no longer the language of Jewish religious experience in Egypt.[446] Thus, the rabbis acknowledged the presence and importance of Greek.[447]

The *Septuagint* was only the vanguard of many ventures to bring contemporary and meaningful Palestinian literature to the attention of Diaspora Jews whose native language was Greek. Hengel has established firmly how Palestinian Greek literary and translation work rested on a tradition that was Hasmonean and has suggested that it may even have gone back to pre-Hasmonean times.[448] For example, Judas Maccabeus' invitation to the Jews of Egypt that if they required any of the books that had been lost during the revolt they should send representatives to get them[449] could be interpreted as an early Hasmonean indicator of this tradition. Consequently, two important developments occurred. First, complementary themes were developed in Egypt with a progressive growth towards the apocalyptic (e.g., *Sibylline Oracles, II Enoch, Wisdom of Solomon*). Second, books that were composed in Palestine in Hebrew or

---

[443]See Murray, "Aristeas," 337-371. See also Fraser, *Ptolemaic Alexandria*, v. 1, 689f., and v. 2, fns. 68, 71.

[444]There is a chronological relationship between the rapid Hellenization of the Jews in Egypt and the translation of the *Pentateuch*.

[445]See above 106f.

[446]Hengel, *Judaism and Hellenism*, v. 1, 100ff.

[447]See *m. Meg.*, 1.8 and 2.1; *m. Seqal.*, 2.2; *m. Git.*, 9.6, 8; and *Gen. Rab.*, 14.

[448]Hengel, *Judaism and Hellenism*, especially v. 1, Part 3, 107-254.

[449]2 *Macc* 2:14f.

Aramiac were translated in the natural course of events into Greek for the benefit of non-Palestinian Jewish communities, such as Alexandria, and enjoyed immense popularity. According to Russell, apocalyptic books in Alexandria "came to enjoy there a much wider reading public than they ever had in Palestine itself."[450] Russell's argument with regard to the apocalyptic directly supports the chronological hypothesis that from the Hasmonean era contact between Palestine and Egypt grew more regular and was intensely vibrant.[451] Moreover, the translations and compositions of apocalyptic literature by Egyptian Jewry for Egyptian Jewry appear to have peaked in the last two centuries of the Temple, when the Alexandrian Jewish community played a prominent role in the future of Judaism.[452]

The translation of Jewish religious literature into Greek had many latent consequences. The Greek-speaking Jew hereafter would view the cosmos and himself from a Hellenistic perspective. Greek would have become the nucleus of his cognition and all his associations would have been dependent on Hellenistic culture. The Torah would have been transformed from a Palestinian-Hebrew Jewish experience into a non-Palestinian Greek Jewish experience with significant alterations in a number of passages.[453] Thus Hellenistic awareness became *ipso facto* secularized consciousness, with the degree of secularization among the Jewish population in part a function of class. Except for those who learned Hebrew or visited Palestine, the general rule would be the higher the social strata the more visible the signs of secularized consciousness and the more refined the integration of Hellenism with Judaism.

The demand for translations of Palestinian literature can only be explained by continuous religious contact. For Palestinian Jewry it was, generally speaking, a means of cementing the bonds of religious solidarity among Greek-speaking Jews and, more particularly, of lobbying for religious groups that shared a common ground (e.g., the apocalyptic movement). On the other hand, for Egyptian Jewry it similarly was a means of affirming religious bonds but also, and more importantly, it expressed a

---

[450]D. S. Russell, *The Method and Message of Jewish Apocalyptic* (Philadelphia, 1964), 29.
[451]D. S. Russell, *Between the Testaments* (London, 1970), 95. Russell dates the flourishing of apocalyptic literature between 165 B.C. and 90 A.D.
[452]Fraser, *Ptolemaic Alexandria,* v. 1, 100f.
[453]See E. J. Bickerman, "The Septuagint as a Translation," *Proceedings of the American Academy for Jewish Research* 28 (1959), 30-35.

desire to assert their individuality while at the same time addressing Palestinian trends.

Religious contact between the Jewish communities in Egypt and Palestine implied that they shared and sought to maintain common interests. At issue is not whether the majority of Jews in Egypt became pilgrims or even whether they forwarded their tithes; rather it is whether there is evidence to demonstrate regular contact, communication, dialogue and standardization on important issues. It is continuity that is essential rather than monolithic uniformity. Continuity would have led Egyptian Jews to become knowledgeable about Judaism.

In spite of the fact that Alexandria was the capital of the Hellenistic world the Egyptian Jew remained under the shadow of Jerusalem. The Hasmonean victory facilitated the dominance of Jerusalem and accelerated the frequency of contact which continued until the destruction of the Temple in 70 A.D. Control over the normative definitions of Judaism remained in Jerusalem and those who offered alternative formulations had to be legitimated first and foremost by Palestinian Jewry. The institutionalization of Judaism from the Hasmonean revolt until the destruction of Jerusalem was circumscribed by an ideology that paradoxically attempted both to maintain the *status quo* and to address renewed interpretations of Judaism that incorporated Hellenistic philosophy.

3.5   Hellenistic Contact and Assimilation

3.5.1   Introduction

"There is always a measure of risk that with the acceptance of a technology the ethos of the technologue will be transmitted."[454] For many of the Jews of the Egyptian Diaspora during the Ptolemaic-Roman epoch, the adoption of Hellenistic technology was accompanied by the acceptance of Greek ideology. Technologies for the material reproduction of life had social, cultural and ideological expressions that at times blurred the lines of demarcation between Greeks with Jewish sympathies and Hellenized Jews with Greek aspirations. Jewish institutions, customs, beliefs and literary devices were affected by contact with Hellenism, and Greek philosophy was absorbed by Alexandrian Jews. Lieberman,[455]

---

[454]H. A. Fischel, ed., *Essays in Graeco-Roman and Related Talmudic Literature* (New York, 1977), xxi.

[455]S. Lieberman, *Greek in Jewish Palestine* (New York, 1942), and *Hellenism*.

Bickerman,[456] Smith,[457] Tcherikover[458] and Hengel[459] have demonstrated impressively how strong an influence Hellenization had on Palestine, and all assume that this influence was transmitted via Ptolemaic Egypt among other places. By the first century A.D. Palestine "was profoundly Hellenized and . . . the Hellenization extended even to the basic structure of much Rabbinic thought."[460]

Hengel has developed this line of reasoning further and argued that Hellenistic and Palestinian Judaism were not two distinct forms of Judaism since both had been deeply affected by Greek influence. Focusing on Palestine prior to the Maccabean revolt (330-c.168 B.C.), Hengel cites a panoply of evidence to support his argument: the use of the Greek language in Palestine for writing, for epitaphs and for synagogue dedicatory inscriptions; the modeling of the scribal schools after Greek educational methods; the adopting of Greek economic terminology, coinage, art and architecture; and the incorporation of Greek literary genres and styles by Palestinian Jewish writers in the interests of being contemporary and/or for purposes of propaganda. Frequently he looks to Egypt for analogies and illustrations to document how the Spirit of the Hellenistic Age had already penetrated the Jews of the Diaspora. Although several scholars have criticized his interpretations and extrapolations of the data,[461] and have voiced the opinion that his illustrations and resolutions depend on a variety of socio-cultural influences that go well beyond the period of his study (168 B.C.),[462] Hengel's premise remains uncontested: the spirit of the Hellenistic Age encountered in Judaism originates in large measure,

---

[456]E. J. Bickerman, *From Ezra to the Last of the Maccabees* (New York, 1962) and "La chaine de la tradition pharisienne," *RB 59* (1952), 44-54.

[457]M. Smith, "Palestinian Judaism in the First Century," in *Israel: Its Role in Civilization*, ed. M. Davis (New York, 1956), 67-91.

[458]Tcherikover, *Hellenistic Civilization*.

[459]Hengel, *Judaism and Hellenism*.

[460]Smith, "Palestinian Judaism," 71.

[461]For example, see A. Momigliano's review of Hengel's *Judaism and Hellenism* in *JTS 21* (1970), 149-153. Momigliano has expressed his doubts as follows: "It seems to me that he [Hengel] has proceeded to establish the degree of Hellenization of third-century Judaism without asking himself in a preliminary way what we know about that Judaism. His book really deals with the Hellenization of an unknown entity" (151).

[462]See, for example, L. H. Feldman's article, "Hengel's *Judaism and Hellenism* in Retrospect," *JBL 96/3* (1977), 371-382.

as a direct consequence of the Ptolemaic control of Palestine and of production. Economic ties led to social relations and the assimilation of the ethos of the conqueror. The Hellenization of Judaism is undisputed; it is the speed of its progression and the depth of its impact that is in contention. And this process is closely tied to the acculturative tendencies within the Egyptian Jewish community.

3.5.2   Assimilation and Apostasy

The assimilation of the Jews in Egypt can be described as a multivariate assimilation.[463] Multivariate assimilation involves a number of social processes which can be divided under two headings: the cultural and the social. Whereas the former signifies acceptance by an ethnic group (i.e., Jews) of certain cultural-behavioural patterns (e.g., language, dress, personal names, forms of art), the latter denotes structural acceptance by a dominant culture (i.e., Greeks) of an ethnic group (i.e., Jews) into their social institutions. The more a group has been structurally assimilated, the more likely all other types of assimilation will naturally follow.

Tcherikover[464] has cited extensive data to demonstrate the pervasiveness of cultural assimilation among Jews in Egypt. "The rapid process of Hellenization of the Egyptian Jews, reveal[s] itself . . . in the selection of proper names, in the substitution of the Greek language for the Aramaic, in the adoption of the principles of Hellenistic law, and in many other ways."[465] These data also reveal that the degree of cultural assimilation was not identical for all social classes. Jews frequently adopted Graeco-Roman personal names during the Ptolemaic-Roman period.[466] Tcherikover discusses several of them (e.g., Ptolemy, Alexander, Jason)[467] and notes that they also derived their names from Greek gods such as

---

[463]See M. Gordon, Assimilation in American Life (New York, 1964).

[464]CPJ, v. 1, 27-47, 74-78 and Tcherikover, Hellenistic Civilization, 344-377.

[465]CPJ, v. 1, 27.

[466]For the adoption of Graeco-Roman names in general by Jews during the Ptolemaic-Roman era, see Hengel, Judaism and Hellenism, v. 1, 63ff.

[467]See CPJ, v. 1, 29 and Tcherikover, Hellenistic Civilization, 346. For Ptolemy see CPJ, v. 1, nos. 24, 31, 34, 35, 96 and v. 3, nos. 1443, 1538; for Alexander, v. 1, nos. 13, 14, 18 and v. 3, 1490, and for Jason, v. 1, nos. 22 and 28.

Apollo[468] or Dionysus,[469] or elected Egyptian appellations.[470] The most common names, however, were theophoric, such as Dositheus.[471] On the one hand the adoption of a Hellenistic name by itself may mean nothing more than a superficial change in a cultural pattern to display conformity with the dominant culture. On the other hand, the choice of a name may reflect a degree of assimilation. Naming oneself or one's children after a Greek god indicates stronger assimilative tendencies than the choice of a Hebrew or theophoric name. Whereas the former indicates the presence of or the need for greater assimilation into Hellenistic culture, the latter can be taken as imputing a special meaning symbolizing one's ethnic identity. Faithfulness to tradition versus the desire to conform may well have been two opposing attractions that continually faced the Egyptian Jew in conjunction with choosing a personal name.

The tendency to adopt Graeco-Roman names traverses all social classes. It is first observable among the Jewish military settlers in the Fayum in the third century B.C., and approximately 75% of the names of settlers found in the papyri are Greek.[472] According to Tcherikover, this adoption of Greek names would have been a deliberate choice, one vehicle of many to accelerate their assimilation.[473] Their descendants, the *Epigone*, were among the first Jews to be part of the Ptolemaic landholding class and to be structurally assimilated (as indicated by their ability to enter the *gymnasium*). During the early Roman period, "the overwhelming proportion of Alexandrian Jews bore Greek names. . . ."[474] In fact, the adoption of Graeco-Roman names appears to be the norm. Only after the revolts of 70 A.D. is there a return to Hebrew names in Egypt.[475] Feelings of ethnic-religious identification appear to have increased in proportion to the increase in anti-semitism.

---

[468]For Apollo see *CPJ*, v. 1, no. 23.

[469]For Dionysus see *CPJ*, v. 2, nos. 241, 294 and v. 3, no. 1538.

[470]For Egyptian names see *CPJ*, v. 1, nos. 38, 46, 91 and v. 3, nos. 1480, 1484, 1486, 1489, 1493, 1496 and 1520.

[471]See *CPJ*, v. 1, Introduction and 27ff., and Tcherikover, *Hellenistic Civilization*, 346. The name Dositheus was almost exclusively used by Jews in the Hellenistic period (*CPJ*, v. 1, xix and fn. 7). For the use of Dositheus, see *CPJ*, v. 1, nos. 19, 21, 28, 29, 30, 43, 71, 76, 83 and 127.

[472]*CPJ*, v. 1, 27f. See *CPJ*, v. 1, nos. 18-32.

[473]*CPJ*, v. 1, 27.

[474]Ibid., 84.

[475]Ibid., 84f.

Language is another indicator of cultural assimilation.[476] Arriving in Egypt speaking Aramaic or Hebrew, the Jew was isolated and insulated until he learned Greek. Yet by the latter half of the Ptolemaic epoch Greek had become the dominant language for Egyptian Jews. The literature of the Ptolemaic-Roman period, the epitaphs and synagogue dedicatory inscriptions all testify to this transition. As indicated above, the Torah as well as numerous apocryphal and pseudepigraphical books had to be translated into Greek if the Egyptian Jew was to read or understand it. Although the more educated and commercial classes may have known Hebrew or Aramaic there is wide consensus that the majority of the Jewish population depended on Greek. If social class increased the opportunity for knowledge of Hebrew or Aramaic it also increased the likelihood that the individual would be familiar with non-Jewish classical literature and influenced by Hellenistic philosophy. Thus, phenomenologically speaking, the average Jew would have experienced Egypt through Greek perceptions.[477] As the Greek language permeated everywhere, so Greek thought, in one way or another, affected the synagogue and the school, the tavern and the *politeuma*. "The Greek Bible became Greek in concept as well as in language, . . . and religious and legal terms . . . evoked numerous associations with Greek classical literature and with Hellenistic legal practice."[478] One side-effect of this process was that the Egyptian Jew's cognition of Palestine and Palestinian Judaism was mediated by the Greek language.[479] Even the Jewish literature of the period (e.g., *Ecclesiasticus*) acknowledges this predicament and offers no solution:

> You are therefore asked to read this . . . and to show indulgence in those places where . . . we may seem to have failed to give an adequate rendering. . . . The fact is that you cannot find an equivalent for things originally written in Hebrew when you come to translate them into another language. . . . The Law itself, the Prophets and the other books differ considerably in translation. . . .[480]

---

[476]Ibid., 30f. Cf. Tcherikover, *Hellenistic Civilization*, 347f.

[477]Cf. Wilson, *Gnostic Problem*, 15, 32f.; and see 152 above.

[478]*CPJ*, v. 1, 31.

[479]For a sociological analysis of the relationship between language and cognition see Berger and Luckmann, *Social Construction*, especially 34-46; and J. Habermas, *Knowledge and Human Interests*, trans. J. Shapiro (Boston, 1971), 161-186.

[480]*Sir*, Foreword, 15-26.

Such difficulties in inter-cultural communication contributed further to
ethnic assimilation.

Jews also took Greek social structures as their institutional models.[481]
Official Jewish positions were identified by Greek titles (e.g., *ethnarch,
archon, gerousiarch*), and their daily behaviour was regulated exclusively
by Hellenistic law concerning non-religious matters. Contracts were
written in Greek and women were subject to the customs prevalent in the
Hellenistic culture.[482] Education followed Graeco-Roman pedagogical
methods and familial patterns appear similar to those of the Greeks.[483]
Since it was the upper strata and the intelligentsia who were responsible
for organizing and overseeing the institutional matrix, they may also have
been responsible for introducing a predisposition for cultural assimilation.
As spokesmen for the Jews they represented their interests in Hellenistic-
Jewish relations. These individuals tended to be more culturally assimilated and their decisions encouraged secularization. The handful of Jewish
leaders whose names have survived, such as Onias, Dositheus and Philo, all
gravitate towards accommodating Hellenistic behavioural patterns.

The development of figurative art by Egyptian Jews may be viewed as
another indicator of cultural assimilation. Although the Torah specifically
forbids the making of graven images or of any likeness of anything,[484]
Goodenough has amply shown that Jews created and enjoyed a variety of
images and amulets.[485] In contrast to Palestine where pagan objects of
art did not (with isolated exceptions) attain national status or dominate
the *polis* until after the destruction of Jerusalem, Egyptian Jews were
exposed to them as part of their daily lives. In Alexandria, for example,
all non-Jewish public institutions (e.g., bathhouses, courts, administrative
offices) as well as the majority of private homes housed forbidden images
and amulets. Festivals to honour the gods further exposed Jews to rituals
where figurative art was present. The degree of contact with Hellenistic

---

[481]See above Section 3.3.3, 117ff. Cf. *CPJ*, v. 1, 32ff. and Tcherikover,
Hellenistic Civilization, 348ff.

[482]See above 85.

[483]For pedagogical methods see above 110f. For familial patterns see
83f.

[484]Lev 26:1. Cf. *m. Abod. Zar.*

[485]See E. Goodenough, *Jewish Symbols in the Graeco-Roman Period*
(Bollingen Series 37, New York, 1953-1968), 13 vols. Cf. E. Urbach, *The
Sages*, trans. I. Abrahams (Jerusalem, 1975), 126f., 129f.; Trachtenberg,
Jewish Magic, 132f.; and above 113 and fns. 236 and 243.

art, therefore, can be understood as a function of class, employment and peer association.

Jews who aspired to upward mobility and had frequent contact with non-Jews (e.g., upper strata, intelligentsia, merchants, and artisans in non-Jewish workshops) were more likely to be influenced by Graeco-Roman cultural customs than those who had neither the opportunity nor the aspiration. Artisan apprentices, for example, were given time off to attend pagan festivals.[486] Peer pressure in combination with a desire for greater social acceptance may have prompted Jewish artisans to patronize these events, especially if they were named after the particular Greek or Roman god. Thus, a rift may have developed between different classes of Jews concerning the tolerance of figurative art and its modifications for Jewish contexts. The more a Jew adopted Hellenistic behavioural patterns the more likely he would be to appropriate the ornamentation and symbolism of the Hellenistic world and imbue it with new meaning.

During times of trouble with the Greeks this issue particularly mirrored different class interests. On several occasions there is evidence of Greeks purposefully erecting statues on Jewish property and of Jews destroying Greek property where forbidden images stood.[487] In these crisis situations the upper strata diplomatically attempted to accommodate themselves to their foreign administrators and to accept the *status quo,* in contrast to the lower strata and those more traditionally inclined who undertook to destroy the very idols themselves. The tolerant spirit adopted by the rabbis in Palestine in the second century A.D.[488] already existed in Egypt a century earlier.

Goodenough has suggested that this orientation may represent new religious values associated with a mystic movement of Hellenized Jews.[489] Although this thesis has been severely criticized by many scholars[490] the material assembled by Goodenough suggests that cultural assimilation was widely spread. Avigad has pointed out that some of Goodenough's arguments, if not the conclusions, are reasonable. Rather

---

[486]See H. C. Youtie, "The Heidelberg Festival Papyrus: A Reinterpretation," in Coleman-Norton, ed., *Studies,* 182.

[487]For example, see Philo, *Leg. ad Gaium,* 133ff. and Josephus, *Ant.,* 19.278ff., for the riots of 38-41 A.D.; for the riots of 66 A.D. see Josephus, *War,* 2.487ff.

[488]For example, see *m. Abod. Zar.,* 3.4.

[489]Goodenough, *Jewish Symbols.*

[490]For a summary of scholarly opinion see M. Smith, "Goodenough's 'Jewish Symbols' in Retrospect," *JBL* 86 (1967), 53-68.

than looking for Jungian insights Avigad proposes that Hellenistic themes could have become "devoid of all content and evolved into strictly decorative designs."[491] According to Avigad the development of winged Jewish mythological figures (i.e., angels) may have been a natural outgrowth of the fusion of Hellenistic art forms with Judaic themes.[492] Similarly, Gager has postulated that charms and amulets which make mention of Moses, the *tetragrammaton* or divine names such as *Iao, Sabaoth* or *Adonai*, may have combined Jewish tradition with Egyptian syncretism.[493] Pilgrims from Egypt may have worn such amulets when they travelled to Jerusalem.[494] Gager dates the image of Moses as magician as early as the first century A.D. and concludes that this would be possible only with the direct and active participation of Jews in the production of magical documents.[495] These kinds of developments could have materialized through the direct intervention of culturally assimilated Jews,[496] and in particular those from the upper strata.

Cultural assimilation is also evident in the Jews' desire to participate in athletic events as spectators or participants.[497] Attendance may be similar to the adoption of Graeco-Roman names: the more assimilated the spectator, the more likely his attendance. But whereas attendance may only indicate social conformity to the Hellenistic normative patterns, participation in athletic events is indicative of more than cultural assimilation: it testifies to structural assimilation as well. The chief function of Hellenistic education was to initiate youth "into the Greek way of life,

---

[491]N. Avigad, *Beth She'arim* (Jerusalem, 1976), v. 3, 284.

[492]Ibid., 285.

[493]See J. Gager, *Moses in Greco-Roman Paganism* (SBL Monograph Series 16, Nashville, 1972), 134-161. See also Goodenough, *Jewish Symbols*, v. 2, 154 for further examples of Jews who borrowed from the Egyptian religion. For amulets in general see C. Bonner, *Studies in Magical Amulets* (Ann Arbor, 1950) and E. A. W. Budge, *Amulets and Superstitions* (London, 1930). See also below Chapter 4, 187f.

[494]See *m. Seqal.*, 3.2. The baskets containing *terumah* were inscribed in Greek and the rabbis explicitly state that amulets could be used as a source of magical power. So inveterate was the belief in the efficacy of charms that later Christians of the early Church began to make amulets from portions of the Scriptures. See Paul Collart, "Psaumes et amulettes," *Aegyptus* 14 (1934), 463-467.

[495]Cf. Gager, *Moses,* 159f.

[496]For further examples see Feldman, "Orthodoxy," 234 and Goodenough, *Jewish Symbols*, v. 2, 194, 229, 237 and 291ff.

[497]For Jewish attendance see above 125f.

[and] above all to athletics, its most characteristic features."[498] Greek athletics involved participation in religious festivals and were under the patronage of Greek gods.[499] To participate in sports required a *gymnasium* education and, concomitantly, the acceptance by Greeks of Jews in their educational institutions.

Gymnasium education is the key measure of structural assimilation. According to Hengel the "unique fusion of Jewish and Hellenistic culture in Alexandria . . . is only understandable on the grounds of the unhindered access of Egyptian Jews to the treasures of Greek education."[500] Only through this door was it possible both for Jew and Greek alike to attain social status and mobility. If a Jew could be labelled an *ephebos* he potentially had access to Alexandrian citizenship. For many, this would be tantamount to negating the Law and submitting oneself to becoming uncircumcised.[501] In Applebaum's opinion, a *gymnasium* education "must have been purchased with the betrayal of Judaism."[502] Yet, as discussed above, Greeks in the early Roman Empire in Alexandria actively lobbied to prevent Jews from entering the ranks of the *epheboi*. Under the Ptolemies access to a *gymnasium* education was theoretically open to all including the *Epigone;* in contrast, under the Romans only those with influence, status or credentials had access. Consequently, a *gymnasium* education under the Romans became increasingly the prerogative of upper class Jews.[503] Not only did they have the power to lobby on their own behalf, they also accommodated themselves to a large extent to Hellenistic patterns of behaviour and were outwardly perceived as Greeks. Nevertheless, in spite of the Jews' ability to enter the ranks of the *epheboi*, the Greek community did not accept them willingly into their institutions and laboured to segregate them socially. This policy of social segregation was less visible under the Ptolemies; but with the Roman conquest, class and degree of cultural assimilation became important factors in distinguishing Jews from Greeks. The Jew who was a potential *ephebos* may have been

---

[498]Marrou, *Education*, 104.

[499]E. N. Gardiner, *Athletics of the Ancient World* (Oxford, 1930), 33.

[500]Hengel, *Judaism and Hellenism*, v. 1, 66.

[501]See *1 Macc* 1:15. For the omittance of circumcision altogether see *Jub* 15:33.

[502]S. Applebaum, "Review of V. Tcherikover and A. Fuchs," *Tarbiz* 28 (1958/59), English summary, xiii.

[503]See above 125ff. *CPJ*, v. 2, no. 153 explicitly prohibits the Jews from participating in athletic contests held by the city magistrates unless they had *epheboi* status.

more Greek than the Greek. Structural assimilation was the only way to avoid the *laographia* and other forms of discrimination.

In addition to a *gymnasium* education structural assimilation could be achieved by conversion. A Jew could convert to a pagan religion or accept the imperial cult and thereby gain non-Jewish social acceptance. He could intermarry[504] and publicly adopt Greek norms and achieve the same effect. However, the combination of conversion with a *gymnasium* education proved to be the most successful formula (e.g., Tiberius Julius Alexander). Only then would an individual's opportunities to become upwardly mobile increase and the doors to Graeco-Roman institutions open. For the majority of the Jews in Egypt religious beliefs and class position constrained them from following such a course.

Hellenistic contact also affected Jews in their ideological interpretations of Judaism and is another manifestation of cultural assimilation. Alexandria was a fertile meeting place for philosophers of every breed: Platonic, Stoic, Epicurean, Pythagorean, Sceptic, and Cynic. The intellectual elite of Egyptian Jewry did not escape their influence. Here the Jew encountered the world of the *sophos,* the rhetorician and the religious pedagogue. Influenced by these thinkers Jewish *literati* began to modify Jewish ideas and open the doors to the integration of Hellenistic concepts that, *ipso facto,* remoulded the normative interpretations of Judaism. Although Wilson has been generous in describing this process as "not so much [an attempt] to assimilate alien elements, but to present . . . [Judaism] in the form which approached most closely to current ideas,"[505] Jewish reaction throughout history has not been so lenient. The rabbis disassociated themselves from such writings (e.g., those of Artapanus, Aristeas, Aristobulus, Philo) and did not consider them as worthy of canonization (e.g., apocryphal writings). The legacy that remains is one that incorporates Hellenism to varying degrees.[506]

---

[504] Philo's disapproval of intermarriage (*De Spec. Leg.,* 3.29) is at the same time an acknowledgement of it. The main reason given for this disapproval is the likelihood that the children would be apostates. See also Josephus, *Ant.,* 8.191ff.; *Jub* 30:7-11; Tcherikover, *Hellenistic Civilization,* 353; *CPJ,* v. 1, 2f.; Juster, who has compiled a list of mixed marriages (*Juifs,* v. 2, 45ff., fn. 5); and Baron (*Social,* v. 2, 233), who writes: "intermarriage must have increased in direct ratio with the intimacy of social contacts with Gentiles. . . . Marriage outside the fold was quite common."

[505] Wilson, *Gnostic Problem,* 17.

[506] See Feldman, "Orthodoxy," 221ff. for Jewish Alexandrian writers accommodating Greek culture to Judaism.

The synthesis of Judaism with Hellenism was an exercise both in making Judaism intellectually respectable and in legitimizing its presence. It appealed to proselytes, acted as an apologetic, and met the needs of various segments of the Egyptian Jewish population. Its product resulted in the presentation of Semitic ideas in Greek dress. So, for example, the Hellenistic rhetorical style was employed in order to affirm God's saving action in history.[507] If an Alexandrian Jew did not know Hebrew or Aramaic he was dependent on these Greek forms of expression to understand his religion. For him the formulations of the problems, the aims and methods employed would be more akin to a Hellenized interpretation of the cosmos than those of the Pharisee or rabbi.

Cultural assimilation among the intelligentsia could take many forms. In many cases Alexandrian Jewish philosophers modeled themselves after particular Greek philosophical schools; they distinguished themselves by the styles of their speech and clothing; and they taught without pay, discussing the same questions as the Greek philosophers. When they attached themselves to particular teachers, it is more than likely that they were viewed by the teachers as more Greek than Jewish and were strongly assimilated into the prevailing Greek social structure.

Philo, the contemporary of Jesus, not only symbolizes this accommodating trend in Judaism in Alexandria but also represents an important link between Diaspora Judaism and Gnosticism.[508] "Philonic Judaism is the result of a hellenization which transcends mere language."[509] Its subsequent "disappearance from Judaism . . . may be attributed partly to reaction against his accommodating spirit. . . ."[510] This spirit depended on the allegorical method to find Hellenic ideas hidden in the *Pentateuch*.[511] Philo's interpretation of scripture, although an attempt to

---

[507] Hengel, *Judaism and Hellenism*, v. 1, 100.

[508] For the view that Philo was drawing on existing tradition see Wilson, *Gnostic Problem*, 35, 51f., and fns. 38, 39.

[509] Sandmel, *Philo's Place*, 211.

[510] Wilson, *Gnostic Problem*, 48.

[511] There is considerable debate as to whether Philo was essentially a Jewish thinker who clothed his ideas in Greek dress or a Hellenist. The former interpretation supposes that Philo was well-acquainted with Palestinian tradition and stresses the importance of rabbinic parallels. The latter plays down Philo's knowledge of Palestinian traditions and denies that the parallels are impressive or significant. For Philo the Jew see Wolfson, *Philo*; for Philo the Hellenist see E. R. Goodenough, *By Light, Light* (New Haven, 1935).

justify Judaism in terms of contemporary thought, ironically provided encouragement for other accommodating Jews to erode further the meaning of Torah. His identification of wisdom with the *logos* and his assignment of the *logos'* function as an intermediary between God and man would have driven a wedge between traditional and secular Jews. The former rejected him whereas the latter continued to spiritualize the law and ignore its observance, an act that Philo severely condemned.[512] Some even went on to derive antinomian conclusions.[513]

The impact of Hellenistic ideology and literary styles on rabbinical thought indirectly testifies to the importance of Alexandria as a centre for the development of accommodating trends in Judaism. Daube has suggested that the rabbinical system of interpretation derives many of its features from Hellenistic rhetoric in the first two centuries before Christ and that the method *seres* (ἀναστροφή) was probably borrowed from an Alexandrian model.[514] Kaminka asserts that "at least one of the seven rules (δὶς λεγόμενα = שוה גזרה) by which Hillel explained the Torah seems to be identical with a philological method known at the Alexandrian school. . . ."[515] Lieberman has commented that "it appears that Alexandria in Egypt supplied to the Rabbis a constant source of information about Greek wisdom. . . ."[516] Finally, Fischel has postulated that Azzai's statements regarding free will may have derived from Alexandrian Judaism.[517] In other words, Alexandrian Judaism not only had a symbiotic relationship with the Hellenistic philosophical schools but also had a significant influence on rabbinical Judaism in relation to topics such as cosmology, the immortality of the soul, and ethics.[518] In addition, the Talmud contains two thousand or more Greek words reflecting commercial relations.[519] Whatever the individual philosopher's inclination, it is his use of the method or the idea that reveals the extent of his assimila-

---

[512]Philo, *Migr. Ab.,* 89ff.

[513] *CPJ,* v. 1, 77 and below, Chapter 4, 199ff.

[514]D. Daube, "Alexandrian Methods of Interpretation and the Rabbis," *Festschrift Hans Lewald* (Basel, 1953), 28.

[515]Cited in Lieberman, *Hellenism,* 57.

[516]S. Lieberman, "How Much Greek in Jewish Palestine?", *Biblical and Other Studies,* ed. A. Altmann (Cambridge, Mass., 1963), 131.

[517]H. Fischel, *Rabbinic Literature and Greco-Roman Philosophy* (Studia Post-Biblica 1, Leiden, 1973), 96.

[518]Cf. Hengel, *Judaism and Hellenism,* who has also drawn attention to the analogies between rabbinic thought and Greek philosophy.

[519]Feldman, "Retrospect," 377.

tion. Writers such as Aristobulus and Philo, and the authors of *Pseudo-Orpheus* and Book Three of the *Sibylline Oracles,* created a bridge for the secular Alexandrian Jew to remain a Jew—in contrast, for example, to the author of *3 Maccabees,* who would have viewed Philo's work as crossing over into foreign territory by disguising Judaism under a Hellenistic mantle.

This symbiotic relationship between Jewish and Hellenistic philosophers also meant that the latter had to take account of the Jewish philosophical presence. In fact, most gentile authors of the period who speculated regarding Jewish origins connected them with Egypt.[520] Gager, for example, by examining Moses in Graeco-Roman literature, outlines how, according to one tradition, he was viewed as a native Egyptian. This perception arose in Alexandria and was developed by anti-Jewish writers primarily in the period from the Maccabean revolt until the end of the first century A.D.[521] As early as the third century B.C. an anti-Jewish version of the origin of the Jews and their expulsion from Egypt was formulated. Writers such as pseudo-Manetho,[522] Lysimachus, Chaeremon and Apion denigrate Moses and claim that he was morally debased. They inform the Egyptian population that Moses was a polluted Egyptian priest and that the Jews were expelled from Egypt on account of their leprosy. According to Gager, "the representation of Moses as the symbol and the founder of a godless and hateful nation expresses not so much local chauvinism or xenophobia as it does the more or less official attitude which resulted from violent conflicts between Jews and non-Jews."[523] This kind of Hellenistic literature presents another window into the material conflict between Alexandrian Jews and Greeks.[524] It is probable that these writings were composed in reaction to Jewish apologetic literature,[525] in response to Jewish claims that the wisdom of the Greeks was enshrined in the teachings of Moses. Anti-Jewish writers were reacting, for example,

---

[520]See Stern, *Authors,* for a chronological collection of Greek and Latin literature relating to Jews and Judaism in antiquity.

[521]Gager, *Moses,* 19 and 113-133.

[522]Stern credits Manetho as the only author (*Authors,* 63).

[523]Gager, *Moses,* 133.

[524]See above 126ff.

[525]Cf. Gager, *Moses,* 76ff., although in a different context. For an opposing view see R. McL. Wilson, ("Jewish Literary Propaganda" in *Paganisme, Judaisme, Christianisme: Mélanges offerts à Marcel Simon* (Paris, 1978), 61-74) who views the Jewish propaganda as a reaction to pagan slanders.

to Aristobulus' assertion that Plato borrowed his legislation from Moses;[526] to Eupolemus' representation of Moses as being indirectly responsible for transmitting the skill of writing to the Greeks;[527] to Artapanus' claim that Moses was the teacher of Orpheus and the founder of Egyptian ritual;[528] and to Philo's declaration that Heraclitus borrowed from Moses' teachings and that he was the ideal priest.[529] It should be emphasized, however, that these Hellenistic writers (prior to the influence of Christianity) rarely if ever had first-hand knowledge of the *Septuagint*. Gager, for example, comments that "there is no direct evidence that of Hecataeus of Abdera, Strabo or Pompeius Trogus possessed a first-hand knowledge of biblical writings. . . . [or that Apion] was familiar with the *Septuagint*."[530] As a result, their information at best could be only second-hand or oral. By contrast, the ideological integration of Hellenistic ideas into Judaism by Jews was first hand, and this borrowing further buttressed Hellenistic arguments that any attempt by Jews to become structurally assimilated should be viewed as contrary to their interests (e.g., Chaeremon, Apion). Hence it is not hard to imagine that accusations of Jews being atheistic (contempt of the gods) and misanthropic (hatred of mankind) would have naturally evolved.[531]

Yet in spite of these Hellenistic writers' claims that Judaism was contemptible, gentile adherents to Judaism are well-documented. In addition to the evidence noted above in the section on proselytism (3.2.3), there were God-fearers, those who accepted the monotheistic idea but not the Jewish law.[532] The Titus-Bernice scenario indicates how influential Romans feared the infiltration of Judaism into their social world and

---

[526] Aristobulus, apud: Eusebius, *Prep. Evang.*, 13.12.1.

[527] Eupolemus, apud: Eusebius, *Prep. Evang.*, 9.26.1.

[528] Artapanus, apud: Eusebius, *Prep. Evang.*, 9, 18, 23, 27. Cf. Wilson, *Gnostic Problem*, 28, fn. 147.

[529] Philo, *Leg. All.*, 1.108; and *Quis Rerum Div. Heres*, 214 and *De Vita Mosis* 1.1 and 2.2.

[530] Gager, *Moses*, 76 and 124. Cf. Zeitlin (*Rise and Fall*, v. 3, 465, fn. 30) who has commented: "it is evident that Roman intellectuals . . . knew about . . . Moses, the lawgiver. . . . However, these writings . . . show that the authors did not read the Septuagint. Even those . . . not hostile to Judaeans showed this ignorance. . . ." See also Hengel, *Judaism and Hellenism*, v. 1, 261 and S. Sandmel, *The First Christian Century in Judaism and Christianity* (New York, 1969), 115.

[531] See above 123 and fn. 291. See also N. Sevenster, *The Roots of Pagan Anti-Semitism in the Ancient World* (NovTSup 41, Leiden, 1975).

[532] Acts 13:16.

systematically lobbied for Bernice's dismissal.[533] Dio informs us in the late first century A.D. that non-Jews were drifting into Jewish ways;[534] and Josephus[535] and Philo[536] both comment that several individuals in the Hellenistic world were fascinated by the Sabbath and celebrated it regularly.[537] These Sabbath observers, *Sambathions*, were located throughout Egypt in the first century A.D. (e.g., Philadelphia, Oxyrhynchus, Karanis) and "even children playing dice in the streets of Alexandria knew that the seventh day was called Sabbath."[538] Tcherikover dates the rise of the *Sambathions* in Egypt to the late Ptolemaic and early Roman period.[539] Thus, the report by Josephus that the religion of the Jews was having a significant impact on both the educated classes and those who were uneducated appears to mirror the historical situation.[540]

Cultural assimilation therefore had two faces. On the one hand there were Jews who accommodated to Hellenistic behavioural patterns and became increasingly secularized. On the other hand, there were non-Jews who adopted Judaism or aspects of it and who were already culturally assimilated. The appropriation by Alexandrian Jewish writers of Greek ideological themes, the integration of cultural models in social institutions and the desire by Jews to be counted among the *epheboi* are strong indicators of cultural assimilation. The speed of their assimilation, however, is a function of their class position. Those from the upper strata, the intelligentsia, and the commercial class had a greater likelihood of becoming structurally assimilated and adopting cultural and behavioural patterns than those of the lower strata, the tenant farmers, wage labourers, and tillers of the soil.

The reaction by Hellenistic philosophers and the Greek population of Alexandria to Jewish assimilation was basically one of opposition. Their rhetoric of misanthropy and xenophobia accompanied policies of excluding Jews form their social institutions. The Greeks viewed the Jews as ideological and economic competitors and believed that structural assimila-

---

[533]See Smallwood's discussion (*Jews*, 385f.).
[534]Dio Cassius, *Hist. Rom.*, 67.14.2.
[535]Josephus, *Apion*, 2.282.
[536]Philo, *De Vita Mosis*, 2.20ff.
[537]See above fn. 181.
[538]*CPJ*, v. 3, 52.
[539]Ibid., 53.
[540]Josephus, *Apion*, 2.281ff.

tion accelerated the Jew's opportunities at the expense of their own.[541] This reaction towards the Jews flourished after the transition from Ptolemaic to Roman sovereignty and coincided with the Roman policy of private rather than state ownership of property. The *boule* papyrus and the *Acts of the Alexandrian Martyrs* point out the depth of this conflict after the introduction of Roman rule.[542]

For a Jew the greater his cultural assimilation the more likely that he would consider apostasy as a possibility. Hellenistic contact therefore also stimulated Jewish apologetic literature as a reaction to potential apostates. Tcherikover[543] and Feldman,[544] for example, have postulated that the pre-Christian Jewish apologetic literature of Egypt was directed at Jews who were secularly inclined or at apostates and not at the Greeks. Although few apostates are identified by name there is wide consensus that contact did encourage apostasy.[545] For example, *3 Maccabees* condemns Jews who traded away their faith in exchange for Alexandrian citizenship[546] and Philo castigates those who alter their traditional religion and betray Judaism for "the frivolous spirit of life's success."[547] For some this would have included the violation of "the covenant of Abraham" (i.e., by rendering themselves uncircumcised).[548] Elsewhere Philo speaks of certain Alexandrian Jews who allegorized the scriptures to the exclusion of the literal meaning.[549] In addition, Nock has suggested in reference to Strabo's sources that the excursus "reproduces the creation of a Jew familiar with the ideas of Poseidonius, a Jew whose hellenization

---

[541]Hengel would date the origin of this competition to the second half of the second century A.D. He viewed it as a "reaction to the political and military influence of the Jews in Ptolemaic Egypt. . . ." (*Judaism and Hellenism*, v. 1, 258). Also see 129 f. above.

[542]See *CPJ*, v. 2, nos. 150 and 156.

[543]V. Tcherikover, "Jewish Apologetic Literature Reconsidered," *EOS* 48 (1956), 169-193. See also his *Hellenistic Civilization*, 180: The apologetic literature was the product of "an inner need so characteristic of educated Jewish circles in Egypt . . . [who] found it easier to cling to Judaism as long as they knew that Judaism stood on an equal level with Hellenism."

[544]Feldman, "Orthodoxy," 218.

[545]For example, see Hengel, *Judaism and Hellenism*, v. 31 and v. 2, 25, fn. 224.

[546]*3 Macc* 2:31 and 7:10.

[547]Philo, *De Vita Mosis*, 1.30f. and *De Virt.*, 182.

[548]See *m. Abot*, 3.12, *t. Sabb.*, 15.9 and *2 Bar.*, 41.3.

[549]Philo, *Migr. Ab.*, 89ff.

was not, like Philo's, controlled by an over-powering loyalty to scripture."[550] Several scholars have suggested that Longinus was a Hellenized Jew and Goold has postulated that Longinus belonged to the same environment that produced Philo.[551] Gager assumes that such Jews existed in Alexandria and may have provided Strabo with "perhaps even the actual form of his excursus on Moses."[552] Thus, Jewish apologetic literature attempted to diffuse the momentum of Jews who attributed meanings to the Torah which were not according to *halakah*, who abandoned the behavioural norms of the community and who, in essence, rejected the Torah.

Mommsen has characterized this meeting of Jews with Hellenism in Alexandria as "the most acute and most palpable expression of a religious movement, not merely affecting but also attacking the essence of Judaism."[553] Their accommodating spirit affected Judaism and their apostasy attacked it. "The abundant use made of pagan material and traditions . . . alongside the strictly Jewish, is an indication . . . of the extent to which a Jew might assimilate. . . ."[554] In light of these renegades Jewish apologetic literature attempted to compromise Judaism in order to deter further defections. However, segments of the lettered elite and the wealthy of Alexandria had already begun the process which would turn Judaism on its head. Reacting to the barriers that socially and structurally segregated them from the Greek Alexandrian *polis*, upwardly mobile Jews and disenchanted intellectuals began to develop an alternative ideology to compensate for their anomie.[555]

---

[550] A. D. Nock, "Posidonius," *JRS* 49 (1959), 8. Cf. Gager, *Moses*, 47.

[551] G. Goold, "A Greek Professorial Circle at Rome," *Transactions of the American Philological Association* 92 (1961), 177. Cf. Gager, *Moses*, 63 and Stern, *Authors*, 362.

[552] Gager, *Moses*, 47.

[553] Mommsen, *Provinces*, v. 2, 183.

[554] Fraser, *Ptolemaic Alexandria*, v. 1, 714.

[555] See E. Durkheim, *Suicide*, trans. J. A. Spaulding and G. Simpson (London, 1952). Anomie arises in a period of abrupt social change and creates a form of psychological dislocation where members of a society or class are no longer able to function in accordance with established norms.

4

The Emergence of Gnosticism

4.1 Introduction

The preceding chapters have developed a number of themes which provide a foundation for the present argument. Chapter 2 described the Ptolemaic mode of production and the evolution of the Egyptian economy after the Roman conquest in 31 B.C. The changes in economic structure and legal status which resulted from the conquest provided both opportunities and obstacles for Egyptian Jews. As was discussed in Chapter 3, the educated, upwardly mobile Jews who were in a position to take advantage of these changes were already highly assimilated into the dominant Hellenistic culture; yet, with the removal of the Ptolemaic aristocracy they found themselves in conflict with the remainder of the Greek upper class. To gain citizenship for themselves or their children it became necessary to renounce their religion and sever their ties with the Jewish community. In such an anomic situation new ideologies and behaviour patterns were likely to emerge.

As Brunt has pointed out, the rate of technological change was relatively low during this period, and religion was the principal medium for the expression of new values and understandings. Gnosticism must be interpreted in this context. The main features of Gnosticism correspond symbolically to the social and economic conditions of Jews during the Ptolemaic-Roman period. For example, the Gnostic distinctions between the *pneumatic, psychic* and *hylic* levels of being correspond symbolically to the political categories of citizen, non-citizen and slave. In some respects Gnosticism can be read as the ideological expression of the trend towards the privatization of land-holding begun at the end of the Ptolemaic era and carried to fruition under the Romans.

It remains to be shown that Jewish influences were indeed crucial to the origins of Gnosticism. This will be demonstrated in this chapter by documenting the presence of numerous elements in the Gnostic texts derived from the Judaic tradition, to which Jews alone would have had ready access. There is little disagreement among modern Gnostic scholars that several of the earliest Gnostic texts show a marked Jewish influence, not only with regard to themes and images derived from (or developed in opposition to) the books of the Old Testament, but also in the form of references to traditional Jewish practices and constructions. Yet the argument presented in this chapter is a broader one: it is that the principal elements of the Gnostic ethos, and of the Gnostics' behaviour and patterns of charismatic authority, derived from the character of the individualism thrust upon Egyptian Jews by the circumstances of the Roman era.

To understand the situation that faced upwardly mobile assimilated Jews in the first century A.D. in Egypt it is necessary to bear in mind that the privatization of property was of relatively recent origin, and its potential for exacerbating class or ethnic conflict remained latent until the Roman period. It was only in the earlier part of the first century B.C. that land allotments became transferable. Two elements of the Jewish situation at the turn of the millenium stand out: the growing ethic of privatization and the fact of Hellenistic cultural assimilation.

On the one hand, the transformation of the mode of production provided opportunities for Jews to benefit from privatization. The Romans encouraged them to do so; and consequently a number of Jews came to play prominent roles in the agricultural, commercial, industrial and financial sectors of the economy. The status of many was significantly changed and *ephebos* and citizenship standing became a legal reality. Structural assimilation was the result of Jews becoming full members of the privileged class of Roman Egypt.

On the other hand, the Greeks viewed themselves as qualitatively different from the Jews and considered them a threat to their own socioeconomic interests. For Jews to become assimilated into the dominant class entailed an ideological rupture with the traditions of Judaism. Thus, Jews imbued with the spirit of privatization were thwarted in their attempts to fully capitalize on the opportunities resulting from membership in the Roman Empire. In time, Roman policy came to reflect the Greek perspective and many upper class Jews were both deprived of the right to enter the *gymnasium*—the gateway to the Hellenized world—and subject to the imposition of the *laographia*. For this select group of urban, educated and assimilated Jews a serious personal and social dislocation occurred. Having abandoned Judaism for the material benefits of assimilation into Graeco-Roman society, they adopted the behaviour of the

Greeks as their normative standard. Yet, these very Greeks, who for so long had constituted their cultural models, now demanded that Jews wishing to obtain citizenship abandon all connection to the Jewish community and the Jewish faith. Mere possession of land or of wealth was not sufficient; they had also to show their adoption of Hellenistic identity by becoming apostates.

The more culturally assimilated Jews of the period shared the ideological canopies of both Hellenism and Judasim. In all likelihood, many had visited Palestine, were familiar with Jewish learning and observed certain of the ritual Jewish prohibitions. At the same time, most would also have been trained in the Greek schools and would have shared the outlook of the Hellenized urban intelligentsia. These culturally assimilated, educated, urban, marginalized Jews possessed all the ingredients for the development of Gnosticism: a social cause (Greek rejection), a psychological dislocation (anomie), a knowledge of Judaism, and an ethos of individualism. Simultaneously allowed to possess wealth and property, but denied social and legal recognition as Jews, they turned inward for an understanding of their situation; cut off from the institutions of Judaism, they sought a more direct (and ultimately mystical) revelation. The following sections examine the Jewish origins and the ideology, behaviour and organizational expression of Gnosticism.

4.2   Model

A possible model of Jewish responses at the turn of the millennium to Hellenistic cultural assimilation is presented in Table 7 below. Upper class Jews, such as the wealthy commercial strata, landowners and the intelligentsia, faced a choice between seeking to accommodate Hellenism to Judaism, or rebelling against their Jewish identity, in order to become structurally assimilated into Graeco-Roman society. By contrast, lower class Jews, including both the rural peasantry and urban wage-labourers and artisans, either insulated themselves from Hellenistic cultural contacts, or developed variant forms within the confines of the Judaic structure. The former in each case can be regarded as traditionalists, the latter as innovators.

Consequently, different kinds of literature were produced as a response to different social locations and degrees of adherence to Judaism. For the lower class urban believer, innovation meant the inclusion of apocalyptic themes into the Jewish tradition without rejecting it (e.g., *2 Enoch*). From a sociological point of view this reflects reform rather than rebellion. There is no literature that is distinctively representative of the more

conservative inclination of the rural peasantry, although their social
location and tendency to conform to existing tradition suggests a literature reflecting more conventional forms of Judaism. In contrast, for upper
class Jews, accommodation meant the incorporation of Hellenism into
Judaism, both to make the latter more attractive to educated Jews and in
order to rationalize their position as outsiders within the Hellenistic
culture (e.g., Philo, Aristeas). Those who rebelled sought to reconstitute
elements of Judaism in Hellenistic terms as a mystical resolution of their
anomic situation. These four responses—accommodation, insulation,
reform and rebellion—indicate that Jews expressed their Judaism in a
variety of ways and that ideological formulations were, in part, a consequence of material conditions. In particular, rebellion implied the inversion of Judaism and a search for liberation in inward experience.

Table 7
Behavioural Response by Social Class

	Traditionalists	Innovators
Upper Class	Accommodation	Rebellion
Lower Class	Insulation	Reform

4.3   Jewish Origins

The innovative response of Jewish rebels was an attempt to
compensate for their social dislocation. Stigmatized and socially adrift
from their reference groups, they viewed similarly the Jewish community
and the privileged Hellenistic community. They regarded both communities as equally responsible for their marginal status. Apostasy no longer
provided a guarantee of mobility or a route to structural assimilation.
Such social and psychological dislocation was self-reinforcing, and these
Jews had ample motivation to reject their tradition and develop an
alternative ethos that reflected their deepest values and social experiences, to consider alternative behavioural patterns that were not

constrained by Jewish law, and to organize alternative institutional structures for their public presentation in the world.

From a sociological perspective, these conditions are ideal for a charismatic upsurge. The emergence of charisma reflects a shattering of what exists already and the articulation of an entirely new basis for normative obligation. Moreover, charisma has a strong individualistic emphasis that lends itself to mystical accents at the expense of traditionalism.[1] If Gnosticism is indebted to Judaism, then the movement away from tradition may well incorporate reconstituted elements of Judaism tending towards the charismatic.

One key variable which supports such an interpretation is the role of disenfranchised intellectuals. According to Weber, it is the distinctive character of disenfranchised intellectuals that they tend "to work in the direction . . . of seeking salvation through mystical channels."[2] The combination of inner tensions and social discontent leads to a search for mystical transformation. Thus, a religion of salvation may very well have its origin within a socially privileged group with a certain minimum of intellectual sophistication. In fact, Weber has postulated that a salvation religion "has the best chance of becoming permanent . . . when the noble [i.e., privileged] class has lost its political power to a bureaucratic, militaristic state."[3] If disenfranchised Egyptian Jews are identified as a privileged group then the social origins of Gnosticism as a salvation religion may in part be attributed to these lay intellectuals who had lost their social and political influence.[4] These protagonists had both the motivation and the knowledge to open up Jewish cosmic perspectives and

---

[1]For the general characteristics of charisma see H. H. Gerth and C. W. Mills, *From Max Weber Essays in Sociology* (New York, 1969), 245-252.

[2]Max Weber, *The Sociology of Religion,* trans. E. Fischoff (Boston, 1964), xliii.

[3]Ibid., 121f.

[4]Nearly a century ago, Max Weber suggested a link between Gnosticism and lay intellectuals, although he did not pinpoint any particular social group or conduct historical research into the origins of Gnosticism. See his *Sociology of Religion,* xliii. Today this link is assumed although there has been no systematic attempt to provide evidence to support it. See, for example, Pearson, "Friedländer Revisited," 35: "It is usually taken for granted that Gnosticism appeared primarily as an intellectual movement."

develop a complex soteriology. Moreover, the features of Gnosticism readily corresponded to their social position as marginal intellectuals.

Jonas, among others, has indicated that the Gnostic protest is a symbolic devaluation of the existing social order.[5] Further, scholars such as Kippenberg have interpreted the Demiurge as a symbolic accentuation of the negative experiences of earthly rule.[6] In other words, aggression against the Greeks and Romans is displaced and transferred to the Archons. Accordingly, mythological events come to reflect political events. Hence, the connection between socio-political events and salvation can be viewed as a direct consequence of socio-cultural tensions between competing privileged groups within the Jewish and Hellenistic communities.[7] The stigmatization by Greeks and Romans of Jewish lay intellectuals led them to devalue the world and simultaneously to segregate themselves from other Jewish groups. Cultural assimilation and apostasy became spiritualistic sectarianism.

To support the hypothesis that the presence of Jews was necessary (although not sufficient) for the development of Gnosticism, it will be shown that several features of the Gnostic texts derive from the Judaic tradition. These include quotations and echoes from the Old Testament, the use of the midrashic method and the theme of antinomianism. While some of these examples are related to early Gnostic writings, later writings are also referred to when appropriate to emphasize certain points. The results of this analysis will indicate that only Jews who were educated and familiar with their traditions could have passed on such highly specific aspects of their religion.

An examination of tractates considered as non-Christian suggests that Jewish content existed in sectarian Judaism independently of Christian influence. As indicated in the previous chapter, various individuals evolved traditions without seeking to replicate exactly what was said by earlier writers. Moreover, extra-scriptural traditions existed and were written down.[8] According to Neusner, with the exception of the Mishnah which was "formulated so as to facilitate [its] memorization . . ." other

---

[5]See Jonas, *Gnostic Religion,* especially 320-340.

[6]Kippenberg, "Versuch," 220f.

[7]Both Kippenberg ("Versuch," 222f.) and Rudolph ("Problem einer Soziologie," 41ff. and *Die Gnosis,* 310ff.), although in different contexts and without socio-economic evidence, have also suggested socio-cultural tensions between competing social groups.

[8]The Qumran library is the best example of extra-scriptural traditions that are both pre-Christian and pre-Gnostic.

rabbinical documents do not exhibit "the redactional as well as formulary mnemonic care revealed in the Mishnah. . . ."[9] He suggests that it was only "after the first writing down of a tradition in, e.g., . . . [the] Apocrypha and Pseudepigrapha or Philo or Josephus, [that] a rabbi heard the tradition from someone familiar with such literature . . . or learned it himself in its original location."[10] Thus parallels and similarities in Gnostic literature and in the Targum, Midrash, Mishnah, Talmud or Merkavah literature need not indicate a common derivation, but rather that similar ethnic and religious groups were involved in developing a variety of interpretations in response to the basic theological problems provoked by the Bible. The claim that certain traditions were not written down on account of their reference to secret doctrines (e.g., Qumran, New Testament and Gnostic literature) seems principally a means to legitimate innovative tendencies. Traditions are not monolithic, but must be continually reinterpreted. As Scholem has stated, "tradition is not simply the totality of that which the community possesses as its cultural patrimony and which it bequeaths to its posterity; it is a specific selection from this patrimony, which is elevated . . . with religious authority."[11]

Gnostic tractates that have been considered as non-Christian include *Eugnostos the Blessed* (NHC III, 3 and V, 1), *The Paraphrase of Shem* (NHC VII, 1), *The Three Steles of Seth* (NHC VII, 5), *The Apocalypse of Adam* (NHC V, 5) and *The Thunder, Perfect Mind* (NHC VI, 2). Two of the tractates, *Eugnostos* and *The Paraphrase of Shem* have some Jewish content, the latter in particular, including references to specific Jewish themes

---

[9]J. Neusner, *Method and Meaning in Ancient Judaism* (Brown Judaic Studies 10, Missoula, 1979), 66. Elsewhere Neusner, using form-critical methods, takes issue with the allegation that the rabbinic traditions were orally formulated and orally transmitted: "The characteristic medium for the preservation of Jewish traditions was writing, not oral formulation and transmission and preservation by memory. . . . The Qumran community wrote its traditions. Indeed it had a library and had a large room for the purpose of writing down its documents. Josephus wrote his histories. The apocryphal and pseudepigraphic books seem to have been written down at the outset. . . . In pre-70 writings we do not find memorizers [but] scribes." See *Rabbinic Traditions*, v. 3, 153.

[10]Neusner, *Method*, 75.

[11]G. Scholem, *The Messianic Idea in Judaism* (New York, 1971), 285f. For a sociological explanation of how traditions are institutionalized and serve those in authority see Weber, *Social and Economic Organization*, 56-77.

such as Sodom and the Sodomites, the flood and the tower of Babel.[12]
Both texts may have been composed in part or whole in the first or second
century A.D.[13] One of the tractates, *The Three Steles of Seth*, has clear
affinities with neo-Platonic writings and is an example of a non-Christian
text that can be dated well after the development of Christianity.[14]

---

[12]For Jewish features in *The Paraphrase of Shem*, see F. Wisse, "The
Redeemer Figure in the Paraphrase of Shem," *NovT* 12 (1970), 130-140.

[13]D. Parrott, the translator of *Eugnostos*, in Robinson, ed., *Nag Hammadi Library*, 207, suggests "sometime in the first two centuries C.E."
This suggestion is based on Parrott's conclusions that *Eugnostos* was both
non-Christian and preceded *The Sophia of Jesus Christ* (NHC III, 4 and BG
8502.3), and that the latter was dependent on the former. According to
Parrott, Christian interpolations changed *Eugnostos* from a dogmatic
epistle about the God of Truth to a Gnostic Christian book of revelation.
J. Doresse, "Trois livres gnostiques inédits: Évangile des Égyptiens, Epître
d'Eugnoste, Sagesse de Jesus Christ," *VC* 2 (1948), 150ff., Puech, "Gnostic
Gospels," in Hennecke and Schneemelcher, eds., *New Testament Apocrypha*, v. 1, 248, and M. Krause, "Das literarische Verhältnis des
Eugnostosbriefes zur Sophia Jesu Christi," in *Mullus, Festschrift Theodor
Klauser* (JAC 1, Münster, 1964), 215-223, similarly argue for the dependence of *Sophia* on *Eugnostos* and its non-Christian nature. In contrast, W.
Till, *Die gnostischen Schriften des koptischen Papyrus Berolinensis 8502*
(TU 60, Berlin, 1955), 54 and H.-M. Schenke, "Nag Hammadi Studien II:
Das system der Sophia Jesu Christi," *ZRGG* 14 (1962), 263-278 argue that
Sophia was the source of *Eugnostos* (i.e., *Eugnostos* was de-Christianized
rather than *Sophia* Christianized). For a brief summary of scholarly opinion see R. McL. Wilson, *Gnosis and The New Testament* (Oxford, 1968),
111ff., J. M. Robinson, "The Coptic Gnostic Library Today," *NTS* 14
(1967-1968), 374ff. and E. Yamauchi, *Pre-Christian Gnosticism* (London,
1973), 104ff. With regard to *The Paraphrase of Shem*, Robinson (*Nag
Hammadi Library*, 308 and "Coptic Gnostic Library," 380) and Wisse
("Redeemer Figure," 135), both argue that this tractate may provide
evidence of a pre-Christian Gnostic redeemer and therefore lend support
to the claims for a pre-Christian Gnosticism. However, several scholars
disagree and postulate that Christian traces are intentionally veiled and
that the Elchasaites were involved. See Jean-Marie Sevrin, "A propos de
la 'Paraphrase de Sem,'" *Le Muséon* 83 (1975), 89ff. and E. Yamauchi,
"Pre-Christian Gnosticism in the Nag Hammadi Texts," *CH* 48 (1979), 137.
Despite their differences with regard to non-Christian content, all would
agree that the work was most likely composed sometime in the first two
centuries A.D.

[14]Robinson has speculated that this tratate originated in part in
Jewish Egyptian apocalyptic circles that nurtured Sethian traditions

Consequently, only the *Apocalypse of Adam* and *The Thunder* provide significant evidence for associating Gnosticism with Judaism. The *Apocalypse of Adam* is frequently cited as evidence for first century Gnosticism.[15] This text relates a revelation received by Adam and passed on to his son Seth. The document is dependent on the Genesis story and according to Parrott, "its close dependence on Jewish apocalyptic traditions suggests that it may represent a transitional stage in an evolution from Jewish to Gnostic apocalyptic."[16] The apocalypse mentions Adam, Eve, Noah, the flood, Noah's sons Ham, Japheth and Shem; and there is a possible allusion to Sodom and Gomorrah.[17] All these characters and events suggest that the author(s) were familiar with

---

(*Jewish Nag Hammadi Gnostic Texts* (Berkeley, 1975), 6f.) and in part from Neoplatonism, during the life of Plotinus (c. 250 A.D.), on account of its similarity to *Zostrianos* (NHC VIII, 1), *Marsanes* (NHC X, 1) and *Allogenes* (NHC XI, 3). See his introduction to the tractate in Robinson, ed., *Nag Hammadi Library*, 362f. and his article, "The Three Steles of Seth and the Gnostics of Plotinus," in Widengren, ed., *Proceedings*, 132f. For criticism of Robinson's argument of an independent Sethian tradition prior to Christianity, see Yamauchi, "Pre-Christian," 140.

[15]For evidence of a pre-Christian or non-Christian origin and first or second century composition, see Böhlig, "Jüdisches und iranisches," in *Mysterion und Warheit*, 149-161, MacRae, "Coptic Gnostic Apocalypse," 27-35 and "The Apocalypse of Adam Reconsidered," in McGaughy, ed., *1972 Proceedings*, v. 2, 573-577, J. M. Robinson, "The Johannine Trajectory" in *Trajectories through Early Christianity*, ed. J. M. Robinson and H. Koester (Philadelphia, 1971), 234, fn. 4 and R. Kasser, "Bibliothèque gnostique V: Apocalypse d'Adam," *RTP* 17 (1967), 316-333. However, several scholars have suggested a later dating and a Christian provenience. See H.-M. Schenke, Book Review of A. Böhlig's and P. Labib's, *Koptisch-gnostische Apokalypsen aus Codex V von Nag Hammadi im koptischen Museum zu Alt-Kairo* (Halle-Wittenberg, 1966), in *OLZ* 61 (1966), 23-34, W. Beltz, *Die Adamapokalypse aus Codex V von Nag Hammadi* (Berlin, 1970), 204f., Stroumsa, *Another Seed*, 151 and Yamauchi, "Pre-Christian," 132-135. For a bibliographical summary see Charlesworth, *Pseudepigrapha and Modern Research*, 72ff.

[16]D. Parrott, ed., *Nag Hammadi Codices V, 2-5 and VI with Papyrus Berolinensis 8502, 1 and 4* (NHS 11, Leiden, 1979), 152.

[17]For the allusion to Sodom and Gomorrah see Wilson, *Gnosis*, 135.

Jewish traditions.[18] Genesis is never directly quoted[19] although several passages are near quotations—"And I breathed into you a breath of life as a living soul"[20] echoes Genesis 2:7; similarly, events are paraphrased—the story of Noah and the flood[21]—that would indicate that the author had access to a Genesis manuscript. Moreover, this paraphrasing can be interpreted as dependent on midrashic methods. For example, the passage "Therefore the days of our life become few"[22] can be viewed in relation to Genesis 6:3 where God limits human life to 120 years. Further, the role of the Illuminator as the suffering revealer-redeemer can be interpreted as a Gnostic midrash in the Deutero-Isaiah servant songs.[23] The fact that the Genesis narrative, the midrashic method and the apocalyptic tradition were utilized would point to Jews who were educated, literate, knowledgeable about midrashic methods and most likely urban dwellers. Moreover, the fact that Hellenistic writers rarely, if ever, had first-hand knowledge of the *Septuagint*,[24] whereas Jews had such knowledge, points to Jews as the most likely mediators of the Biblical elements in *The Apocalypse of Adam*. Thus, MacRae's suggestion that one might trace the origin of the apocalypse to late Jewish sectarian influences[25] can perhaps be supported by suggesting that the disenfranchised Alexandrian Jews were responsible for the transition from Jewish to Gnostic apocalyptic.[26]

A relationship between *The Apocalypse of Adam* and the *Hypostasis of the Archons* (NHC II,4), which in turn is closely related to *On the Origin*

---

[18]C. W. Hedrick, "The Apocalypse of Adam: A Literary and Source Analysis," in McGaughy, ed., *1972 Proceedings*, 581-590, suggests that two Jewish sources were later integrated by the tractate's editor.

[19]Parrott, ed., *Nag Hammadi Codices*, 152.

[20]NHC V,5:66,21-23.

[21]NHC V,5:69,2-71,8.

[22]NHC V,5:67,10-11.

[23]See MacRae, "Coptic Gnostic Apocalypse," 27-35.

[24]Cf. Chapter 3, 166.

[25]MacRae, "The Apocalypse of Adam Reconsidered," 575.

[26]The suggestion of Alexandrian Jewish influence made here should not be misconstrued as meaning that *The Apocalypse of Adam* should be considered an Alexandrian composition. Rather the suggestion is that Alexandrian Jews were involved in these events and that they could have carried their reinterpretations of Judaism to fertile geographical centers outside of Egypt. Indeed, this is the case with early Christian writers, such as Paul, who both reinterpreted Judaism and carried their reinterpretations outside of Palestine.

the *World* (NHC II,5 and XIII,2), has been noted by several scholars.[27]
Although both the *Hypostasis of the Archons* and *On the Origin of the World* have Christian features, Fallon has commented that they "share common gnostic traditions . . .[and] common mythologumena."[28] Focusing on the *Sabaoth* accounts, his conclusion is that the account in the *Hypostasis of the Archons* "represents the typologically earlier form . . . [and] derives from . . . Apocalyptic Judaism."[29] Still more important than the question of sharing Gnostic traditions is whether the *Hypostasis of the Archons* and *On the Origin of the World* reveal a Jewish hand at some

---

[27]See, for example, F. Fallon, *The Enthronement of Sabaoth* (NHS 10, Leiden, 1978) and I. Gruenwald, "Jewish Sources for the Gnostic Texts from Nag Hammadi," in *Proceedings of the Sixth World Congress of Jewish Studies* (Jerusalem, 1977), v. 3, 45-56. For the dating of the *Hypostasis of the Archons* see R. A. Bullard, *The Hypostasis of the Archons* (Berlin, 1970). Bullard suggests that it is a composite document consisting of at least two sources, the first cosmological and a reinterpretation of the first chapters of Genesis, and the second, soteriological with reminiscences of Valentinian doctrine, with the final date of redaction in the late second or third century A.D. in Egypt. The assumption that there was a fusion of independent literary sources sewn together by the author is also supported by A. Böhlig in the preface to Böhlig's and Labib's, *Koptisch-gnostische Schrift* and by M. Krause, "Zur 'Hypostasis der Archonten' in Codex II von Nag Hammadi," *Enchoria* 2 (1972), 1-20, although neither agree with Bullard's diagnosis. In contrast, see B. Layton, "The Hypostasis of the Archons or The Reality of the Rulers," *HTR* 67 (1974), 351-425 and 69 (1976), 31-101. Layton contends that the author and his addressee are Christian and that the *Hypostasis of the Archons* contains only one literary source. Nevertheless, he acknowledges that the author is indebted to Jewish sources and that his cultural milieu could not be too far removed from Jewish circles. Due to Neoplatonic influences in the text, Layton suggests the early third century A.D., in Egypt, for its final redaction. In addition see Fallon, *Enthronement*, 87f. For *On the Origin of the World*, see Böhlig and Labib, *Koptisch-gnostische Schrift*. Although they do not date the tractate they comment that the dominant style throughout the tractate is that of targum and midrashic commentary (35). Yet in spite of these traditions Tardieu only dates the final redaction to the late second century A.D., and Hans-Gebhard Bethge, in Robinson, ed., *Nag Hammadi Library*, 161, to the late third or fourth in Alexandria. For M. Tardieu, see *Trois mythes gnostiques* (Paris, 1974), 38. In addition, see Fallon, *Enthronement*, 115ff.

[28]Fallon, *Enthronement*, 71.

[29]Ibid., 8.

stage of their developments. Both tractates contain a Gnostic reinterpretation of the early chapters of Genesis, the former through the story of the flood[30] (in contrast to the latter which stops after the expulsion from Paradise). Both reflect Jewish haggadic and apocalyptic traditions. Fallon, moreover, has postulated that the primary context for *Sabaoth* is an early form of Jewish throne mysticism, through a combination of features of the Jewish God, Jewish angelic traditions, the enthronement ritual and the apocalyptic seer.[31] No influence from the New Testament has been discerned by Fallon.[32]

Gruenwald, although viewing the evidence of "judaizing Gnostics" as highly speculative,[33] nevertheless explains the incorporation of Genesis material in these tractates in terms of the Midrash and Targum. Contrary to Fallon, he is sceptical that the Gnostics were Jews "at some point in their career"; nonetheless, Gruenwald affirms that "their selection of material and the way they used it almost always displays a fairly good knowledge and understanding of the Jewish sources in question."[34] For example, in his discussion of veils,[35] Gruenwald draws parallels from Hekhalot literature, Merkavah mysticism and the Talmud and concludes that the Gnostic use does not indicate "a clear case of borrowing . . . [but] only of the working of Jewish material on the mind of the Gnostic writer in the manner of free association."[36] However, in spite of his insistence on pointing out differences in the function of the veil in Gnoticsm and Judaism he has implicitly argued that the composers of the *Hypostasis of the Archons* and *On the Origin of the World* were educated in midrashic methods, familiar with contemporary Jewish debates and had access to

[30]R. McL. Wilson has pointed out twenty-five references to Genesis. See "The Gnostics and the Old Testament," in Widengren, ed., *Proceedings*, 167.

[31]Fallon, *Enthronement*, 8f. In contrast, it should be noted that Gruenwald, although similarly pointing to common Jewish traditions, has suggested essential differences between the enthronement of *Sabaoth* in Gnostic and Jewish mystical texts. See Gruenwald, "Jewish Sources," in *Sixth World Congress*, 54f.

[32]Fallon, *Enthronement*, 133.

[33]In contrast to Gruenwald, see Pearson who attributes to "judaizing gnostics" Gnostic midrashes in the *Hypostasis of the Archons* and *On the Origin of the World*. See Pearson, "Haggadic Traditions," in Bergman et al., eds., *Ex Orbe*, v. 1, 457-470.

[34]Gruenwald, "Jewish Sources," in *Sixth World Congress*, 47.

[35]NHC II,4:94, 9-15 and NHC II,5:98,11-23.

[36]Gruenwald, "Jewish Sources," in *Sixth World Congress*, 52.

Jewish manuscripts. Moreover, his analysis points out how these Gnostic texts describe *Sabaoth* "in terms that approximate certain details of both the Merkavah literature and the *targumin* and *midrashim*."[37] Thus, it would appear that Jews may very well have been participants in the process as they and only they have had the necessary materials with which to restate Jewish events in Gnostic terms. Similarly, Layton has implicitly adopted this position with regard to the *Hypostasis of the Archons* by acknowledging that the author is deeply dependent on Jewish sacred texts. He suggests that the period of Philo and intertestamental Judaism may be the link between this tractate and Judaism.[38]

The *Thunder, Perfect Mind* has also received a great deal of attention due to Quispel's claim regarding its relationship to Judaism.[39] The *Thunder* is a revelation discourse by a female figure (Sophia?) who issues antithetical self-proclamations.[40] Quispel has associated *The Thunder* with the fallen Sophia by postulating that the descent of Sophia parallels that of Ishtar since both were designated as prostitutes. Furthermore, he situates the writing in Alexandria in either the first century B.C. or A.D.[41] Although Quispel's reconstruction has been criticized by a number of scholars,[42] Pearson has suggested affinities to Simonian Gnosticism,[43] thus concurring with Quispel that it is an example of first century A.D. Gnosticism and is indebted to Judaism.[44]

Yet in spite of the paucity of data in non-Christian Gnostic texts there is ample evidence that Jewish midrashic methods and content play an important role in the Nag Hammadi library as a whole. Old Testament echoes and passages appear frequently from the *Septuagint*, the Jewish bible for Greek-speaking Jews.[45] In addition to the opening chapters of

---

[37]Ibid., 55f.

[38]See above fn. 27.

[39]G. Quispel, "Jewish Gnosis," in Ménard, ed., *Les textes*, 82-122.

[40]For similar self-proclamations see NHC II,5:114,8-10.

[41]Quispel, "Jewish Gnosis," in Ménard, ed., *Les Textes*, 86 and 93.

[42]See, for example, "Die Bedeutung der Texte von Nag Hammadi für die moderne Gnosisforschung," by the Berliner Arbeitskreis, in Tröger, ed., *Gnosis*, 47 and R. Unger, "Zur sprachlichen und formalen Struktur des gnostischen Textes 'Der Donner: die vollkommene Nous,'" *OrChr* 59 (1975), 106 and E. Yamauchi, "The Descent of Ishtar, the Fall of Sophia, and the Jewish Roots of Gnosticism," *TynBul* 29 (1978), 148f.

[43]Pearson, "The Thunder."

[44]As discussed in Yamauchi, "Descent of Ishtar," 149.

[45]It should be remembered that it was only in due course that the *Septuagint* became the Christian Bible for Greek-speaking believers.

Genesis, quotations from or allusions to Exodus, Isaiah, Ezekiel and Psalms, among others, can easily be identified.[46] Ideas concerning the creation of the world, the hypostatization of wisdom and law are all rooted in Jewish contexts and many of the central characters (e.g., Adam, Eve, Cain, Seth) are Jewish figures. Several Gnostic sects are associated with Egypt, such as the Carpocratians, the Cainites and the Basilidians, all of whom cite Old Testament books. Of course, it would be futile to suggest that the majority of the Old Testament quotations or allusions in the tractates discovered at Nag Hammadi were mediated without Christian influences, as Christian elements are predominant in the versions which are available to us.[47] In spite of this difficulty, an examination of some of the studies focusing on Jewish haggadic elements may point to non-Christian Jewish roots of Gnosticism.

Birger Pearson has been the most prolific proponent of the thesis that Gnosticism is a Jewish heresy and has published several examples of Gnostic midrashes. For example, according to Pearson, a passage in *The Testimony of Truth* (NHC IX,3) is an Ophite Gnostic Midrash revolving around three Old Testament passages (Gen 2:7; 3:22; and Exod 20:5) and focuses on "the Gnostic affirmation of the φθόνος (envy) of the Demiurge."[48] Pearson bases his case on a combination of factors including the fact that within Philo there may be examples of polemics directed against specifically Gnostic *theologumena*.[49] He suggests that Philo in *Quaes. Gen.* 1.55 (re: Gen 3:22) counters such an interpretation of God by commenting that, "There is neither doubt nor envy in God."[50] Similarly he speculates that Philo in *Dec.* 63 (re: Exod 20:5) alludes to Gnostics since

---

[46]Wilson has pointed out seventeen Old Testament books in the Gnostic writings collected in Werner Foerster's anthology, *Gnosis* v. 2. See Wilson, "Gnostics," in Widengren, ed., *Proceedings*, 165. For specific examples see R. McL. Wilson, "Old Testament Exegesis in the Gnostic Exegesis on the Soul," in Krause, ed., *Essays*, 217-224 and R. Kasser, "Citations des grands prophètes bibliques dans les textes gnostiques coptes," in Krause, ed., *Essays*, 56-64.

[47]For the dating of the Nag Hammadi library see above Chapter 1, 9 and fn. 37.

[48]NHC IX,3:47,14-48,7. See Pearson, "Haggadic Traditions," in Bergman, et al., eds., *Ex Orbe*, 468 and "Friedländer Revisited," 31.

[49]Pearson continually refers to Philo as relevant to the background of Gnostic hermeneutics without asserting that Philo is himself a Gnostic. In addition to "Haggadic Traditions," see "Gnostic Interpretation," 317 and "Observations," in O'Flaherty, ed., *Critical Study*, 244.

[50]Pearson, "Friedländer Revisited," 31.

Exod 20:5 "is cited regularly in Gnostic texts as a proof for the envy of the Demiurge."[51] Unfortunately, these examples from Philo, although plausible, still seem to demand a due measure of caution. Philo chastised those Jews who spiritualized the Law at the expense of literal observance[52] as well as others who objected to sections of the Law outright without feigning allegorical interpretations.[53] The evidence suggests only that Judaism was interpreted in many ways; it does not provide concrete evidence that Philo's opponents were in fact Gnostics. Nevertheless, it does furnish confirmation that Alexandrian Judaism contained heretical elements which were co-terminous with the rise of Christianity.[54]

Pearson is on firmer ground when he examines haggadic materials in the Targum and rabbinical literature for parallels to Gnostic ideas. For example, in *Targum Neophiti* there exists an expanded version of Genesis 4:8, the story of Cain and Abel. Pearson has suggested that "although 'Cain' has been interpreted in this passage as a representative of 'Sadducean' heresy, the affirmation put into the mouth of Cain could also be seen as representing 'Gnostic' heresy."[55] The important phrases include, "—the world was not created by love, that it is not governed according to the fruit of good deeds. . . . There is no Judgment. . . . There is no other world. . . ."[56] Evidence to support Pearson's interpretation can also be found in *The Testimony of Truth*. In this tractate there are numerous polemical arguments against resurrection[57] and the fact that all the races of man (*pneumatic, psychic,* and *hylic*) are ontologically determined can be interpreted to mean that conduct is not important and that there is no Judgment.[58] Although the dating of the Targum literature is extremely

---

[51]Ibid., 32 and fn. 27.

[52]For example, see *Migr. Ab.*, 89ff. and above Chapter 3, 164.

[53]See *Conf.*, 2ff.

[54]For a thorough analysis of the relation between Gnosticism and the thought of Diaspora Judaism, especially in the wake of Philo, see Wilson, *Gnostic Problem*, who concludes that Philo was not a Gnostic.

[55]Pearson, "Friedländer Revisited," 33. Pearson bases his argument on the assumption that Cain "was interpreted as a prototype of heresy among scripture interpreters of Palestine" and that Philo, at times, employed Cain in a similar way (33f.).

[56]Ibid., 33.

[57]For example, see NHC IX,3:34,26-35,2 and 36,29-37,5.

[58]The ontological and anthropological distinction between *pneumatic, psychic* and *hylic* is prevalent in most Gnostic systems. Cf. below 212f.

difficult to assess, there is a consensus that some of the traditions underlying the extant Targums go back to the first century B.C.[59]

Elsewhere in *The Testimony of Truth* Pearson has indicated how certain
haggadic traditions (those of the serpent, the tree and the creator God)
reflect only Jewish, not Christian influences and are examples of "primitive" Gnosticism with numerous Old Testament passages quoted or paraphrased.[60] Similarly, in the *Apocryphon of John* (NHC II,1, III,1 and IV,1)
Pearson demonstrates how Jewish traditions of exegesis are basic to the
Gnostic creation-of-man narrative.

> These exegetical traditions include (1) the Hellenistic-Jewish
> (probably Alexandrian) tradition that God relegated the
> creation of man's mortal nature to the angels, (2) the Hellen-
> istic-Jewish (again probably Alexandrian) distinction based on
> the LXX text of Gen. 2.17, between man's lower and higher
> soul, i.e., his ψυχή and his πνεῦμα, and (3) the Palestinian
> tradition that Adam was created as a "formless mass" (Heb.
> golem) into which God breathed his life-giving breath.[61]

Given the preponderance of Jews using haggadic traditions in the first
century A.D. whether they were rabbis, Qumranites or early Christians,
there is reason to believe that Jews if primitive Gnostics did likewise.
What is certain is that by the end of the first century A.D. Jewish haggadic traditions had been employed by the Gnostics.

---

[59]In Macho's opinion, *Targum Neofiti*, although a first or second
century A.D. recension, was originally a Jerusalem targum of pre-
Christian origin. See A. D. Macho, "The Recently Discovered Palestinian
Targum," in *Congress Volume Oxford 1959* (*VT*Sup 7, Leiden, 1960), 237.
The existence of Aramaic targums in the intertestamental period has been
attested to by Jewish traditions since the Qumran discoveries. See, for
example, *Le Targum de Job de la grotte XI de Qumran*, ed. and trans.
J. P. M. van der Ploeg O.P. and A. S. van der Woude (Leiden, 1971), 4 and
8. M. Sokoloff, *The Targum to Job from Qumran Cave XI* (Ramat-Gan,
1974), 9-25, dates the targum on linguistic grounds to 100 B.C. or possibly
the late second century B.C. The rabbis mention, with disapproval, the
existence of a targum to Job as early as the beginning of the first century
A.D. (*t. Sabb.*, 13.2-3; *y. Sabb.*, 15c; and *b. Sabb.*, 115a; cf. see Sokoloff,
Targum to Job 4 and fn. 1).

[60]Pearson, "Haggadic Traditions," in Bergman, et al., eds., *Ex Orbe*,
470 and "Gnostic Interpretation," 314. Pearson suggests that these haggadic traditions are as early as the first century B.C. (470).

[61]Pearson, "Biblical Exegesis," in Stone, ed., *Armenian*, 75.

One Gnostic midrash in *The Testimony of Truth* is of particular rele-
vance.[62] The midrash centers on Solomon's reputation as a sorcerer.
Pearson[63] points out parallels in Jewish haggadic traditions and, in particular, in *The Testament of Solomon*,[64] *The Apocalypse of Adam*[65] and
On the Origin of the World,[66] The midrash reads: "when the Romans
[went] up to [Jerusalem] they discovered [the] waterpots, [and immedi-
ately] the [demons] ran out of the waterpots. . . ."[67] Pearson interprets
this allusion to the Romans and the release of the demons as perhaps a
reference to the destruction of the Second Temple in 70 A.D.[68] Since
Josephus is himself aware of traditions about Solomon's control over the
demons and his use of the Divine Name,[69] Pearson's dating of the midrash
to the late first century A.D. is plausible. Circles that made use of Jewish
divine names wrote Hebrew names in Greek transcriptions—as evidenced
in magical Greek papyri[70] as well as in the Nag Hammadi tractates[71]—
and some of these circles were composed of Hellenistic Jews living outside of Palestine.[72] According to Meeks and Wilken, Alexandria was one
of the "chief centres for the production of magic gems (and) Jews were
responsible for many, if not most of these objects."[73] Further, Gager
views the Greek transcriptions of divine names such as *Iao*, *Sabaoth* and
Adonai as "the greatest contribution of Judaism to the syncretistic world

---

[62]NHC IX,3:69,31-70,24.
[63]Pearson, "Gnostic Interpretation," 316f.
[64]*Testament of Solomon*, 15.9. C. C. McCown, *The Testament of
Solomon* (UNT 9, Leipzig, 1922), 42 has pointed out a possible reference to
Egypt in the text.
[65]NHC V,5:78,27-79,19.
[66]NHC II,5:106,19-107,17.
[67]NHC IX,3:70,14-18. Cf. Pearson, "Gnostic Interpretation," 317.
[68]Ibid., loc. cit.
[69]Josephus, *Ant.*, 8.42.
[70]See *Papyri Graecae Magicae*, ed. K. Preisendanz and A. Henrichs
(Stuttgart, 1973-1974), 2 vols. R. Pack, *The Greek and Latin Literary
Texts from Greco-Roman Egypt* (Ann Arbor, 1965^2) and Goodenough,
Jewish Symbols.
[71]For example, Ιαω (part of the Tetragrammaton) in NHC I,5:11,30
and 12,21; and NHC II,5:101,15 and 29.
[72]For Jews as magicians in antiquity outside of Palestine, see Gager,
Moses, 134-161 and above Chapter 3, 160.
[73]W. A. Meeks and R. Wilken, *Jews and Christians in Antioch in the
First Four Centuries of the Common Era* (SBL, Sources for Biblical Study
13, Missoula, 1979), 51, fn. 172.

of magic . . ." and suggests that at least the treatment of Moses as a
magician originated in Egypt and was established by the first century
A.D.[74] Culturally and structurally assimilated Jews in Alexandria, therefore, could have had knowledge of the legends concerning Solomon's
powers and consciously integrated their negative views of him into a new
midrash that can be dated to the late first century A.D.[75]

Pearson's analysis of Jewish haggadic traditions emphasizes the role of
Philo and marginal Jews in Egypt. Without addressing himself to sociological issues he acknowledges tacitly that there were structurally assimilated Jews in Egypt who were educated in Judaism and aware of midrashic
methods. Moreover, he suggests that their rebellion changed the direction
of Judaism and turned it upside down. If these Jews are viewed as anomic
and socially dislocated then their hermeneutics can be interpreted as an
attempt both to divorce themselves from Judaism and to seek out an
alternative sacred canopy that met their immediate needs. Thus,
Pearson's conclusion derived from an analysis of motifs, that "the Gnostic
phenomenon itself originates in a Jewish environment as an expression of
alienation from Judaism,"[76] supports the present thesis.

Recently, several studies have been undertaken regarding the role of
Seth and the Sethians.[77] This is not surprising since several of the Nag
Hammadi tractates have been identified as Sethian[78] and the Church

---

[74]Gager, *Moses*, 142 and 159.

[75]Pearson, "Gnostic Interpretation," 317 would similarly place the
author's provenance to Alexandria due to his hermeneutical theory and use
of the allegorical method. Elsewhere Pearson describes the hermeneutical
principle at work in the Gnostic synthesis as one of "revolt." "Biblical
Exegesis," in Stone, ed., *Armenian*, 79.

[76]Pearson, "Biblical Exegesis," in Stone, ed., *Armenian*, 80.

[77]For example, see Stroumsa, *Another Seed*, A. F. J. Klijn, *Seth in
Jewish, Christian and Gnostic Literature* (NovTSup 46, Leiden, 1977) and
B. Pearson, "Egyptian Seth and Gnostic Seth," in *Society of Biblical
Literature, 1977 Seminar Papers*, ed. P. J. Achtemeier (Missoula, 1977),
25-44.

[78]Stroumsa, *Another Seed*, 13, fn. 33 includes the following: *Apoc.
John, Hyp. Arch., Gos. Egy., Apoc. Adam, Steles Seth, Zost., Melch.,
Norea, Marsanes, Allogenes, Trim. Prot.* and *Paraph. Shem*. See also F.
Wisse, "The Sethians and the Nag Hammadi Library," in McGaughy, ed.,
1972 Proceedings, 601-607 and "The Nag Hammadi and the Heresiolo-
gists," *VC* 25 (1971), 209, fn. 22.

Fathers knew of them.[79] Pearson, for example, examined the relationship between the Egyptian god Typhon-Seth and the Gnostic Seth and concluded that "the Egyptian god Seth and the Gnostic Seth, son of Adam, are two altogether different entities."[80] On the other hand, both Klijn and Stroumsa focused on the relationship between Sethian Gnosticism and Judaism and concluded that "almost all the Gnostic ideas about Seth can be found in Jewish writings."[81] Sethian origins were traced to Jewish exegetical traditions. Moreover, according to Stroumsa "there is no reason to assume that the 'biblical' features of early Sethian mythology were mediated through Christianity . . . [or] that Christian influences are responsible for the *Historisierung* or the *Vergeschichtlichung* of the Gnostic saviour."[82]

Once again Alexandria can be viewed as the centre of innovation. Philo is the first Jewish author to develop the idea that Seth was 'another seed,' that from him came the generation of the righteous.[83] This theme is fundamental to Sethian Gnosticism. Sethians are the biological offspring and the spiritual heirs of Seth whom Eve conceived.[84] Stroumsa's exhaustive documentation of haggadic traditions in Sethian Gnostic writings indicates that the development of Sethian mythology would have been impossible without the input of heterodox Jews.[85] Man's origin and destiny in Sethian Gnosticism, the place of evil and the role of history are all indebted to Jewish haggadic material. "The Gnostic Demiurge emerges solely out of the Biblical son of Adam and Eve."[86] According to Stroumsa, Gnostic myths "emerge from their meditation upon the Greek texts of Genesis . . . [and in conjunction with] detailed interpretations in Jewish exegesis."[87]

---

[79]For the evidence of the heresiologists see Klijn, *Seth*, 82-90.

[80]Pearson, "*Egyptian Seth*," 35.

[81]Klijn, *Seth*, 116.

[82]Stroumsa, *Another Seed*, 300f.

[83]Ibid., 200 and fn. 179. See also Klijn, *Seth*, 26: In addition to Philo, only Samaritan writings take up the idea of Seth as 'another seed.'

[84]See Gen 4:25.

[85]Stroumsa, *Another Seed*. For Klijn's analysis see *Seth*, 90-107.

[86]Stroumsa, *Another Seed*, 18. Stroumsa, however, is unable to isolate the passage marking the transition from the Jewish God to the Gnostic Demiurge (300).

[87]Ibid., 45.

Stroumsa employs new texts—*The Midrash of Shemhazai and Azail* and the Armenian apocryphal book, *The Death of Adam*—to support Pearson's argument that "both the name and figure of the Gnostic Norea have their roots in the Jewish Naamah."[88] Moreover, Stroumsa dates the Jewish tradition identifying Seth's sister with the maiden Naamah as in place by the first century A.D. and postulates Jewish Hellenistic influences.[89] Similarly, Pearson has suggested Jewish Greek speaking communities in the first century A.D., and possibly Egypt, since 'Ωραία was a personal name for a Jewess in Leontopolis before 73 A.D.[90] Stroumsa also suggests that Bahenosh (daughter of man), Noah's mother, evolved into Barthenōs and finally became hypostasized in Barbelo.[91] In Stroumsa's opinion, the fall of Eve, the Gnostic Norea and Barbelo "must be rooted in Jewish exegetical traditions about Genesis."[92]

Stroumsa's thesis not only sheds light on the Jewish background of Gnosticism but also links the roots of Gnosticism to exegetical problems of the first chapters of Genesis.[93] His interpretation, like Pearson's, rests on the relationship between heterodox Jews who had access to and knowledge of Alexandrian and Palestinian traditions, and on the absence of Christian elements. Consequently, the disenfranchised Jewish intellectuals of Alexandria would have been well placed to have absorbed these exegetical traditions and to have acted as catalysts in passing them on in a revised form.

Alan Segal has also examined the relationship between Judaism and the origins of Gnosticism. Like Stroumsa, however, he does not address the historical connections between the rabbis and their opponents but rather chooses to examine the rabbinic evidence for two powers in heaven. According to Segal, the "two powers in heaven" heresy refers to an interpretation of "scripture to say that a principal angelic or hypostatic

---

[88]Ibid., 82. For B. Pearson, see "The Figure of Norea," in Widengren, ed., *Proceedings*, 143-152.

[89]Stroumsa, *Another Seed*, 85.

[90]Pearson, "Figure of Norea," 150. Cf. *CPJ*, v. 3, no. 1509.

[91]Stroumsa, *Another Seed*, 90ff.

[92]Ibid., 111.

[93]Stroumsa following Böhlig, sought to situate the origin of some Sethian texts in Palestinian or Syrian Jewish baptist sects but was unable to identify any precise social milieu.

manifestation in heaven was equivalent to God."[94] Segal understands this development to have begun in the first century A.D. Rabbis reacted to heretics (Christians, immature Gnostics, mystical sectarians) who believed in two complementary powers in heaven. Only later did this issue develop into that of two opposing powers which Segal argues is a post-Christian phenomenon.[95] In his view, the radicalization of Gnosticism "arose in Judaism out of the polarization of the Jewish community over the issue of the status of God's primary angel."[96] Segal therefore sees Christianity and Gnosticism as originating in Hellenized apocalyptic Judaism's speculation concerning a principal angelic messiah. However, the rabbis' method of attacking opponents was by allusion and polemic, rather than by identification and debate, and they did not distinguish between groups or concepts. There is no first century evidence to identify the particular heretical group (Gnostic, Christian or mystical sectarian) that the rabbis were attacking. Consequently, it is difficult to draw a firm conclusion from internal developments in rabbinical Judaism in the second century A.D. and suggest that radical Gnosticism can only be identified when the rabbis deemed it so. The evidence from the Gnostic midrashes in the first century A.D. may suggest that the seeds and evolution of the Gnostic movement were similar to those of early Christianity. Only in the second century A.D. do we hear of Gnostics or, for that matter, Christians[97] in non-Jewish texts but this has not deterred speculation about the evolution (ideologically and structurally) of early Christianity in the first century A.D. It is likely that the diffusion of Gnosticism from Egypt to Palestine and other locations (e.g., Syria) was gradual and uneven. It may very well be that the rate of diffusion was similar to that of Christianity (although Gnosticism rested on a less developed social structure) and that Philo and

---

[94] A. Segal, *Two Powers in Heaven: Early Rabbinic Reports about Christianity and Gnosticism* (Studies in Judaism in Late Antiquity 25, Leiden, 1977), x.

[95] Segal in an unpublished paper has tentatively suggested that the Johannine community may be a possible link in the creation of radical Gnosticism (i.e., the Gnostic concept of the Demiurge). See "Ruler of this World: Towards a Sociology of Gnosticism," mimeo, 32.

[96] Segal, *Two Powers*, 266.

[97] The two exceptions for Christianity in the first century A.D. are the passages in Tacitus, *Annals*, 15.44 and Suetonius, *Nero*, 16.2 which intimate knowledge of Christians only in passing. The first example in the second century A.D. is Pliny the Younger, *Epist.*, 10.96.

the rabbis are witnesses to particular exegetical issues at different historical stages of development. In fact, until after 70 A.D., Palestine may have been one of the least appealing places for intellectual Jewish apostates to proselytize.

Moreover, as Stroumsa has indicated in his analysis of the "sons of God" motif, two alternative interpretations could have co-existed in the first century A.D. in Judaism. In one case, "sons of God" referred to angels;[98] in the other, to certain righteous men.[99] Stroumsa also points out that Philo could have been aware of both interpretations and probably added further meanings to them.[100] In other words, Jewish intellectuals outside of the Palestinian community could have used Palestinian traditions to construct new interpretations which might subsequently be defined as heretical because of their ideological content. Thus, it is possible that Gnostics in the first century A.D. in Egypt could have identified the "sons of God" with the "sons of Seth," the righteous.[101] On the other hand, the rabbis drifted towards the identification of the "sons of God" with angels and rejected the doctrine that these angels had fallen.[102] Consequently, Sethian tendencies in Hellenistic Judaism may have been partly responsible for the rabbinic opposition to the "two powers" doctrine by providing the catalyst through which the heresy evolved.

Segal's analysis of the links between Judaism and Gnosticism emphasizes its evolutionary character. His comments above regarding the development of radical Gnosticism indicate this inclination as does his analysis of the ignorant Demiurge:

> It appears that the myth of the arrogance of the Demiurge was created to make Gnostic sense of particular scriptural references, especially those from Genesis. But the Gnostic

---

[98]For the identification of "sons of God" with angels before Christ see P. Alexander, "The Targumim and Early Exegesis of 'Sons of God' in Genesis 6," *JJS* 23 (1972), 60-71. Cf. Stroumsa, *Another Seed,* 198ff.

[99]Stroumsa, *Another Seed,* 198ff.

[100]Ibid., 200. Cf. B. Bamberger, "Philo and the Aggadah," *HUCA* 48 (1977), 163.

[101]See also Stroumsa, *Another Seed,* 200.

[102]Ibid., 198f. See also Bamberger, *Fallen Angels* (Philadelphia, 1952), 92 and Alexander, "Targumim," 60-71. R. Simeon b. Yohai is the first piece of identifiable evidence of this rejection. R. Simeon flourished in the mid-second century A.D. and thus is more or less a contemporary of Aher. See *Gen. Rab.,* 26.5.2.

interpretation appears to have been transmitted in elements,
. . . rather than as a single exegetical interpretation.[103]

Like other scholars, Segal gives special attention to Philo in this development. He comments that Philo speculated on the same passages in the Old
Testament as the heretics who were opposed by the rabbis. Moreover,
Philo discusses the concept of a second deity (a deuteros theos) and is
indebted to mystical and apocalyptic traditions concerning the divine
name of God as a separate hypostasis. The concept of two divine powers
in heaven was therefore known in Alexandria in the mid first century A.D.
Thus, Gnostic midrashes of the second god may have emerged from
Alexandria for, according to Segal, "there is nothing specifically Christian
about [them]. . . . rather [they] depend on Jewish exegesis of Genesis."[104]

Segal's analysis of the links between Judaism and Gnosticism also
points to Jews (unspecified) revolting against Jews. Although he does not
develop the historical and social connections between the rabbis and their
opponents, he emphasizes the fact that Gnostic evolution is developmen-
tal and that the patterns of Gnostic mythology began to evolve in the first
century A.D. and are indebted to Jewish exegesis. Thus, Segal's analysis,
like those of Pearson and Stroumsa, associates Gnosticism with intellectually heterodox Jews who had knowledge of Judaism, were non-
Palestinian, felt alienated and advocated segregation from other Jewish
groups. All indirectly identify them as the innovators who transformed the
creator of the world into an arrogant ruler as a means of divorcing themselves from Judaism and of negating the value of Old Testament scripture
for believers.

Finally, in addition to Pearson, Stroumsa and Segal, Gruenwald has
continued the studies of Scholem on the relationship between Gnosticism
and Merkavah mysticism. Scholem had argued that there existed a Jewish
Gnosticism that fought to preserve its non-dualist character prior to a
Christian Gnosticism; and that Christian converts from Judaism could
have transmitted Jewish esoteric doctrines.[105] For Scholem, the world of

---

[103]A. Segal, "Rabbinic Polemic and the Radicalization of
Gnosticism," mimeo, 28.

[104]Ibid., loc. cit.

[105]G. Scholem, *Jewish Gnosticism, Merkabah Mysticism and Talmudic
Tradition* (New York, 1960) and also his *Major Trends in Jewish Mysticism*
(New York, 1969), 40-79.

Merkavah is closely connected to the *pleroma* of the Gnostics.[106] In contrast, Gruenwald views "Gnosticism and Jewish Merkavah [as] two parallel though strictly separate lines of development emanating from apocalypticism."[107] Although both are the offspring of apocalypticism, their cosmological and soteriological features separate them. Like Scholem, Gruenwald documents the fact that mystical speculations about the Merkavah existed in the second half of the first century A.D. and that the *Ma'aseh Merkavah* (theosophy) is intrinsically related to *Ma'aseh Bereshit* (cosmology). Apocalypticism is a widely spread literary phenomenon[108] in which several themes such as knowledge, vision and salvation are developed. However, as he points out, different Jewish groups focused on different exegetical traditions. Thus, although "the relation between knowledge and salvation was one of the major elements which Jewish apocalyptic contributed to the development of Gnosticism,"[109] the interpretation developed varied considerably depending on the degree of assimilation of this time.

Gruenwald, like Stroumsa and Segal, indicates how the Jewish Apocrypha and Pseudepigrapha contain different traditions regarding particular exegetical interpretations. For example, Gruenwald points out two traditions concerning the revelation of cosmological secrets. The first (e.g., Enoch) permits man to receive supernatural revelations; the second does not (e.g., *The Testament of Job*).[110] Dissident Jews such as those in Egypt therefore would have based their views on scripture but only developed one of the two exegetical apocalyptic traditions. The *Apocalypse of Adam*,[111] the *Hypostasis of the Archons*,[112] and *On the Origin of the World*[113] all contain Gnostic midrashes and in essence say that knowledge

---

[106]G. Scholem. *Ursprung und Anfänge der Kabbala* (Berlin, 1962), 19.

[107]I. Gruenwald, "Knowledge and Vision: Towards a Clarification of Two 'Gnostic' Concepts in the Light of their Alleged Origins," *Israel Oriental Studies* 3 (1973), 101.

[108]In contrast see Hengel, *Judaism and Hellenism*, v. 1, 58ff. who views apocalypticism much more narrowly and within the framework of *Hasidism*.

[109]I. Gruenwald, *Apocalyptic and Merkavah Mysticism* (AGJU 14, Leiden, 1980), 16.

[110]Ibid., 16ff.

[111]See, for example, NHC V,5:64,1-4 and 85,19-24.

[112]See, for example, NHC II,4:86,26-27 and 93,33-94,2.

[113]See, for example, NHC II,5:97, 24-30.

(*gnosis*) is possible only through revelation of the cosmological secrets.[114] Jews probably would have been responsible for the exegetical innovations regarding supernatural revelations, since until the late first century A.D. they and only they would have had not only a direct link to the mystical tendencies in Judaism (including the use of the secret names of the Deity and his angels and hence interpretations of the Merkavah[115]), but also access to marginal Jewish writings in Greek such as the play by Ezekiel the Tragedian which, among other things, contains a Merkavah vision.[116] Familiar with Merkavah traditions, the disenfranchised elite of the privileged class had the knowledge and the motivation to transform Jewish apocalyptic into Gnostic apocalyptic.

The studies referred to above have shown that Jewish haggadic traditions are intrinsic to the development of Gnosticism. It has also been pointed out that Jews in Alexandria had the necessary knowledge to reflect on and to develop a number of these traditions. Also, as indicated in the previous chapter, it is evident from the writings of the Graeco-Romans that they were acquainted neither with the original Hebrew *Pentateuch* nor with the *Septuagint*.[117] As Zeitlin has noted, "only with the rise of Christianity did the Hebrew Bible become known to Greek and Roman intellectuals through the Septuagint."[118] Other scholars have also indicated important connections between Judaism and Gnosticism. Rudolph in several publications mentions the indebtedness of Gnosticism to Jewish sceptical, apocalyptic and wisdom literature.[119] Perkins has concluded that the origins of the Gnostic revelation dialogue is to be found

---

[114]Gruenwald suggests that "the preoccupation of Gnosticism with cosmological matters could well be the central contribution of Jewish apocalypticism." See "Knowledge and Vision," 73.

[115]According to Gruenwald, magico-theurgic practices in Judaism "bear strong resemblance to practices and symbolism known from the various gnostic writings." See *Apocalyptic*, 110. Cf. Pearson's discussion above concerning Solomon as a sorcerer, and Jews as magicians (187f.).

[116]Ezekiel the Tragedian is usually situated in Alexandria in the second century B.C. See Hengel, *Judaism and Hellenism*, v. 1, 109 and v. 2, 109 fn. 396. For a dissenting viewpoint see Gutman, *Jewish-Hellenistic Literature*, v. 2, 66ff. who places Ezekiel in Berenice in Cyrenaica in the first century B.C.

[117]Chapter 3, 165f.

[118]Zeitlin, *Rise and Fall*, v. 3, 280 and 465, fn. 30. Cf. Gager, *Moses*, 23f., 76f., 111 and 124.

[119]See, for example, Rudolph, *Die Gnosis*, 294ff. and "Problem einer Soziologie," 43.

in Jewish apocalyptic literature.[120] Turner has suggested that "Jewish wisdom literature forms the pre-Gnostic prototype for the descent motif of *The Apocryphon of John* and *Trimorphic Protennoia* [CG XIII,1]."[121] In addition, both MacRae and Quispel have contributed a number of studies indicating how the Gnostic Sophia is derived from Jewish wisdom literature. MacRae, for example, links the traditions of wisdom and creation by attributing the fall of Sophia to Jewish traditions of the fall of celestial beings.[122] Elsewhere MacRae has pointed out that the ἐγώ (I-am) style of self-proclamation in *The Thunder, Perfect Mind* is indebted to the wisdom hymns of Jewish literature as well as to Egyptian Isis aretalogies.[123] For MacRae, "Gnosticism arose as a revolutionary reaction in Hellenized Jewish wisdom and apocalyptic circles."[124] On the other hand, Quispel not only supports MacRae in principle, but further suggests that Jews were among the first to develop the Gnostic conception of the Demiurge.[125] By combining Segal's argument concerning the doctrine of the two powers in heaven with the argument that the Orphic view of the Demiurge was integrated into Gnosticism by heterodox Jews "even before the redaction of the myth contained in the present *Apocryphon of John*,"[126] Quispel suggests Alexandria as the location where these views were formulated for the first time.[127]

Another scholar, Vermes, in arguing that the *minim* were responsible for the removal of the Decalogue in Jewish worship, utilizes the Palestinian Targum to argue that the Decalogue was removed to elude those who would take Deuteronomy 5:2 literally and in an all-encompassing fashion, and avoid the suggestion that "God proclaimed no laws beyond the

---

[120]As noted by F. Fallon, "The Gnostic Apocalypses" in J. Collins, ed., *Apocalypses: The Morphology of a Genre (Semeia* 14, Missoula, 1979), 124.

[121]J. D. Turner, "The Gnostic Threefold Path to Enlightenment," *NovT* 22 (1980), 342, fn. 11.

[122]See MacRae, "Jewish Background," 98 and 100.

[123]G. MacRae, "Discourses of the Gnostic Revealer," in Widengren, ed., *Proceedings,* 115f. For the Isis aretologies see D. Müller, *Ägypten und die griechischen Isis-Aretalogien* (Berlin, 1961).

[124]MacRae, "Nag Hammadi and the New Testament," in Aland, ed., *Gnosis,* 150.

[125]See Quispel, "Origins of the Gnostic Demiurge," in *Gnostic Studies,* v. 1, 218.

[126]G. Quispel, "The Demiurge in the Apocryphon of John," in Wilson, ed., *Nag Hammadi and Gnosis,* 22.

[127]Ibid. loc. cit.

Decalogue."[128] He then identifies these *minim* with Jewish Gnostics from the ranks of Hellenistic Judaism, that is, "from among the progressive, enlightened intellectual elite of the Mediterranean and especially Egyptian Diaspora."[129] Vermes bases his conclusion on the fact that Philo and those in the Jerusalem Church all agreed on the superiority of the Decalogue and none would have argued against the divine origin of the Torah.[130] Similarly, Segal dates the term *min* to the late first century A.D. and suggests it was formulated in response to those who speculated on divine mediation.[131] Further, S. Lieberman has contended that "in many cases the *minim* mentioned in Rabbinic literature designates Gnostics."[132] In Jewish liturgy the term מינים is used to designate heretics, those who did not believe in the true Torah or in an afterlife. Once again, this may refer to Jewish Gnostics.[133] Moreover, it is to such groups of *minim* and *Toe'ime* that Scholem attributes the production of the secret name of *Yaldabaoth*,[134] a name that is central to several Nag Hammadi tractates including *The Apocryphon of John*,[135] *The Hypostasis of the Archons*,[136] *On the Origin of the World*,[137] *The Second Treatise of the Great Seth*,[138] *Trimorphic Protennoia*[139] and *The Sophia of Jesus Christ*.[140] There is a high degree of probability that this development had

---

[128]G. Vermes, "The Decalogue and the Minim," in *Post-Biblical Jewish Studies* (Leiden, 1975), 174.

[129]Ibid., 177.

[130]Ibid., 176f.

[131]Segal, "Ruler."

[132]Lieberman, "How Much Greek" in Altmann, ed., *Biblical and Other Studies*, 135. In contrast, Segal, rather than labelling these *minim* as Gnostics, would claim only that they were part of that amorphous heretical group chastised by the rabbis for speculating on divine mediation and compromising Judaism's monotheistic principles. See his "Two Powers."

[133]Gruenwald, "Knowledge and Vision," 82 and fn. 51.

[134]Scholem, "Jaldabaoth Reconsidered," in *Mélanges*, 405-421. Also see the variations of *Yaldabaoth—Yaltabaoth* and *Aldabaoth*.

[135]NHC II,1:24,12.

[136]NHC II,4:95,11 and 96.4.

[137]NHC II,5:100,14.19.24; 102,11; 103,1 and 33.

[138]NHC VII,2:53,13 and 68,29.

[139]NHC XIII,1:39,27.

[140]BG 8502,3:119,15.

taken place by the time the benediction known as *birkhath ha-minim* had been composed.[141]

Jewish heretics, whether believing in two opposing powers in heaven or in personal revelatory knowledge, can still be distinguished from Gnostics by their lack of antinomian attitudes. In contrast to the situation in Judaism and Christianity, antinomianism is fundamental to Gnosticism. In Gnostic ideology, it signifies opposition to the Mosaic Law, and in particular, to the obligations of moral law as defined in the Old Testament.[142]

---

[141]This prayer excluded heretics from participating in the synagogue liturgy. See *b. Ber.*, 28b and Jerome, *On Isaiah*, 5.18. Tradition claims that Samuel the Small, a contemporary of Gamaliel II (c. 100 A.D.), composed this prayer.

[142]At the time the early Church Fathers and the Gnostics wrote their treatises the word antinomian (ἀντινομία), meaning opposition to the Law of Moses, did not exist. It was first coined by John Chrysostom (*Homily*, 62.1 in Matt) who was a contemporary of Epiphanius, although Epiphanius himself never used the term. See *A Patristic Greek Lexicon*, ed. G. W. H. Lampe (Oxford, 1961), v. 1, 155. ἀντινομία for the Greeks during the period of history under consideration was a legal term and meant a conflict of laws. See H. G. Liddell and R. Scott, eds. *A Greek-English Lexicon* (Oxford, 1940[9]), 159. The Greek word to convey a sense of lawlessness was ἀνομία (*Greek-English Lexicon*, 146). This term can be found in Philo, Josephus, the *Septuagint*, the New Testament and in Gnostic literature. According to H. Kleinknecht and W. Gutbrod in "Nomos" in Kittel, ed., *Theological Dictionary*, v. 4, 1022-1091, ἀνομία had three general meanings: no law, violation of the law and against the law. The third meaning is less frequent and is not used for opposing the moral imperatives of the Mosaic Law. In the *Septuagint* ἀνομία frequently refers to pagans and sinners but has no Hebrew equivalent. The most frequently recurring words used are פשע (sin), אין (there is not . . .), עין (antagonistic) and תועבה (horrible deed), all of which are supposedly synonomous to ἀνομία. In contrast, the Greek word νόμος (law), in a Jewish context, was an ethical term and more or less identical with the Hebrew word תורה (Torah). In the *Septuagint* νόμος kept its primary Jewish denotation of Law (i.e., Torah/*Pentateuch*) but could also connote instruction or revelation. In the New Testament, the most frequent meaning is also that of Torah, that is, Mosaic Law or Old Testament scripture. See also Dodd, *The Bible and the Greeks*, 25-41. In summary, ἀνομία, meaning "against the Law," is rare and never means against the moral imperatives of the Mosaic Law. In spite of this vacuum one should not assume that the Gnostic antinomian attitude was absent as will become obvious in the following presentation. Rather it attests to the

This theme provides the basis for exploring further the Jewish background of Gnosticism.

It has been argued that Paul introduced antinomian practices in his refusal to accept the imperatives of the Torah.[143] It is true that Paul, in an eschatological context, contended that the Jewish Law was no longer the way of salvation because Christ had replaced it. Jesus, and not the Torah, became the mediator between God and man.[144] Righteousness before God became manifested by Jesus on the cross. To Paul, it was not necessary that a believing Gentile become a Jew according to the rituals of the Mosaic Law. Jesus' death freed the Christians from these ritualistic bonds and from the necessity of obeying Mosaic Law as interpreted by the rabbis of the period.[145] "Man is justified by faith and not by doing something the Law tells him to do."[146] In other words, Paul rejected the specific precepts of Jewish Law and proposed to put in their place not a new set of rules but Christ himself.[147]

---

fact that patterns of behaviour precede intellectual classification and appellation. For example, the term hippie, used in the late 1960's, referred to individuals who manifested cultural behaviour that was non-normative. Their attitudes toward society, cultural conventions and life-styles were given wide publicity. But it is obvious if one reads novelists in the genre of Tom Wolfe, and in particular his book *The Electric Kool-Aid Acid Test* (New York, 1968) that the hippie phenomenon long preceded public acknowledgement. The same can be seen if one traces the evolution of modern art movements. The various artists responsible for the growth of new developments conceive and create the changes long before they are recognized or labelled.

[143]See especially Rom 3:8 and Gal 3:13f.

[144]See, for example, Matt 10:32ff. and Rom 8:2.

[145]See Gal 2:16-21 and Phil 3:9.

[146]Rom 3:28. See also J. F. Bottorff, "The Relation of Justification and Ethics in Pauline Epistles," *SJT* 26 (1973), 421-430.

[147]It is not my intention to examine the question of Paul and the Law. Such an undertaking is beyond the scope of this study. Rather, the aim is only to indicate that Paul was not antinomian in an ethical sense, and that Christ, and not the Law, became the means to salvation. For Paul's position with regard to the Law, see, among others, W. D. Davies, *Paul and Rabbinic Judaism* (London, 1955); J. Munck, *Paul and the Salvation of Mankind*, trans. F. Clark (Richmond, 1959); H. J. Schoeps, *Paul: The Theology of the Apostle in the Light of Jewish Religious History*, trans. H. Knight (Philadelphia, 1961); L. Cerfaux, "L'antinomie paulinienne et la vie apostolique," *RevScRel* 39 (1951-1952), 221-234; J. W. Drane, "Tradition, Law and Ethics in Pauline Theology," *NovT* 16 (1974), 167-178;

Paul's theology was shaped by the pressures of historical events. How could he reconcile on the one hand, his theology, and on the other, the differences between Jewish Christians who practised the laws of Judaism and non-Jewish Christians who had no reason to do so? Was circumcision of the Gentile Christians necessary as a sign of their subjection to the Mosaic Law, and consequently for salvation?[148] The issue came to a head at the Council of Jerusalem. The result of the Council was that Paul and Peter were able to break away from James and those wishing to adhere to the practices of Jewish Law and simultaneously to secure the principle of salvation through faith in Christ. In other words, Gentile Christians no longer needed to be circumcised nor obey the rituals of Mosaic Law, whereas Jewish Christians were still bound by what is now known as pre-Mishnaic Law.[149] In due course non-Jewish Christianity would become the norm, and Jewish Christians who observed the requirements of pre-Mishnaic Law were relegated to minor sects such as the Ebionites or the Nazarenes.

Paul minimized the role of Judaism in the development of early Christianity and curtailed the practice of pre-Mishnaic Law among the non-Jewish Christians. Yet Paul did not preach antinomianism in an ethical sense, that is, that one should abrogate the moral code of the Mosaic Law.[150] This is explicitly stated in Romans 6:15: "Does the fact that we

---

C. F. D. Moule, "Obligation in the Ethic of Paul" in *Christian History and Interpretation: Studies Presented to John Knox*, ed. W. R. Farmer, C. F. D. Moule and R. R. Niebuhr (Cambridge, 1967), 389-406; and F. F. Bruce, "Paul and the Law of Moses," *John Rylands University Library of Manchester 57* (1974-1975), 259-279.

[148]See Acts 15:1ff. and Gal 2:1ff.

[149]Gal 2:7-9 and Acts 15:28f. Although this attempts to encapsulate a very critical and problematic period in the early Church it has certain shortcomings. There are problems of chronology, the reliability of Acts, its relation to Galatians, etc. The aim is only to indicate that (1) Paul's theology is dependent on his historical context and (2) that the controversy over who could be a Christian centered on the issue of salvation through faith in Christ. See among others, E. Haenchen, *The Acts of the Apostles*, trans. R. McL. Wilson (Oxford, 1971), 440ff. and H. M. Feret, *Pierre et Paul: à Antioche et à Jerusalem* (Paris, 1955). For a brief summary and evaluation of opinions, see C. H. Talbert, "Again: Paul's Visits to Jerusalem," *NovT 9* (1967), 26-40.

[150]It might be argued that Paul advocated antinomian behaviour in Rom 3:8ff. but the following context does not warrant such an interpretation. At most, it may suggest that Paul's opponents could have been

are living by grace and not by law mean that we are free to sin? Of course not."[151] So far as it is known Paul himself continued to observe the Law as a guide to conduct but not as a means to salvation. Nor did Paul deny the validity of the Mosaic Law by proposing that the Old Testament God was in fact the evil Demiurge. Similarly, Jesus did not repudiate the moral obligations of the Mosaic Law; on the contrary, he kept them and demanded that others do likewise.[152] Jesus advocated a more liberal and accountable observance in contrast to the ritualistic Jewish observances. In Burrows' words, "Jesus taught the ethics of the Old Testament, with some shift in emphasis, but with no change of substance."[153] Paul's displacement of Torah for the word of Christ was not a call for non-Jewish Christians to become opposed to the obligations of moral law in general or Mosaic Law in particular. Rather it was a call to share in the salvation of Christ and to disregard the ritualistic practices of Judaism. Later Christian theologians would argue that Paul's historical opponents misunderstood this emphasis on grace through faith as opposed to the Mosaic Law[154] and were led to deviant antinomian practices by subjective exegesis.

In the history of early Christianity some of these opponents became identified with the Gnostic heresy. The Gnostics deprecated the cosmic world and conceived of it as evil. This rejection of the world and its creator manifested itself in various ways but frequently involved the identification of evil with the God of the Old Testament. As previously postulated by Quispel, this concept of the Demiurge may have been produced in the first century A.D. by Alexandrian Jews.[155]

---

antinomian, or according to certain scholars, Gnostics. Cf. 1 Peter 2:16. For the opinion that they were Gnostics, similar to those in Corinth, see W. Schmithals, *Gnosis in Korinth* and *Paul and the Gnostics,* trans. J. Steely (Nashville, 1972). For dissenting opinions that there were Gnostics in Corinth see R. McL. Wilson, "How Gnostic were the Corinthians?," *NTS* 19 (1972-1973), 65-74 and R. A. Horsley, "Gnosis in Corinth: I Corinthians 8.1-6," *NTS* 27/1 (1980), 32-51.

[151]Cf. Acts 21:24 and 25:8; Rom 2:12f. and 7:7ff.; Gal 3:21; and 1 Cor 5:1ff.

[152]For example, see Matt 5:17 and 21; 8:4 and 19:18 and Mark 10:19.

[153]M. Burrows, "Old Testament Ethics and the Ethics of Jesus" in *Essays in Old Testament Ethics,* ed., J. L. Crenshaw and J. T. Willis (New York, 1974), 242. For example, see Mark 3:4, Luke 14:4 and Matt 15:10-20 and 23:23-32.

[154]For example, see Eph 2:8 and 6:6 and Rom 6:14.

[155]See above, 196.

In general, the Gnostics believed that the cosmic world was created by a Demiurge who was an inferior being to the supreme being, creator of the divine world. Between the supreme being and our world there existed a series of levels among which were the Archons inhabiting the planets and ruling our world. The letter of *Eugnostos the Blessed* and *The Gospel of the Egyptians* (NHC III,2 and IV,2) provide detailed descriptions of the complexity of stratification between the supreme being and the Demiurge, and of the Gnostic anti-cosmic attitude. One version of *The Apocryphon of John* lists the names of the angels who created each individual part of the human body, and one is able to deduce their relative positions in the hierarchy of the celestial world.[156] This individualization of angels occurs for the first time in Jewish history during the intertestamental period. It is only then that "angels are given personal names which are associated with specific duties. . . ."[157] By the time of Gnosticism, according to Jonas, "concrete personal agents, individual divinities" are fundamental.[158]

There are numerous Gnostic systems explaining the origin of man and his ontological nature. Those Gnostic systems which posit the fall of a divine being usually begin with one principle and the Demiurge is identified with the creator God of the Old Testament. As head of the Archons he holds mankind in subjection. The entity which is responsible for this fall can be either male or female. Among the Naassenes it is Adam, a male, who has fallen from the primal man. It may be a female entity such as Prunikos who fell due to an erotic impulse, or Sophia, who fell because of her pride and ignorance, which is common in Valentinianism. The consequence of the Fall is that mankind has a dual ontological nature. The radical dualism between the good God and the bad God, the divine world and the material world, was believed by the Gnostics to be reflected in man himself. Man's body and soul are shaped by the cosmic powers and fasten him irreparably to the material world. On the other hand, man also contains a portion of the divine substance, the *pneuma*, which has fallen into the world and which is necessary for *gnosis*. Man is seen as the vessel created by the Archons in which to keep the *pneuma* captive.

From a sociological perspective antinomian tendencies constitute the

---

[156]NHC II,1:15,1-19,14. See also S. Giverson, *Apocryphon Johannis* (Copenhagen, 1963), 245ff. and 280f.

[157]Russell, *Method and Message*, 243. Cf. W. Schmithals, *The Apocalyptic Movement*, trans. J. Steely (Nashville, New York, 1975), 20.

[158]Jonas, "Delimitation," in Bianchi, ed., *Origini*, 93.

eruption of the assimilative elements in Alexandrian Judaism. The imposition of barriers for Jews wishing to be structurally assimilated suggests a connection between foreign rule and the rule of demons.[159] The Demiurge and his Archons are a symbolic accentuation of the negative experiences of Roman rule.[160] Gnostic mythological events reflect the socio-political conditions. For example, in *The Paraphrase of Shem* Derdekeas descends to save the *pneumatic* and is persecuted by powers, symbolized by the forces of nature.[161] In the *Hypostasis of the Archons* it is the Archons who are responsible for casting man into the toils and troubles of life.[162] Thus, Gnostic ideology is not only structurally similar to the Jewish experiences but at least in part arises out of it. Just as the Jew has fallen so has the *pneuma*. Just as the *pneuma* is held captive so too has the Jew been held prisoner to his former identity.

The fact that Gnosticism is dominated by dualism is quite predictable within the context of other contemporary ideas. R. McL. Wilson has noted that the dualist conception of the world as divided into regions of sense and spirit is common to Platonic, Stoic, Philonic and Orphic systems. "The world is evil because matter is evil."[163] In Qumran literature there is a dualism of light and darkness; and dualism also exists in early rabbinical tradition although it never contradicts Judaism's monotheistic principles.[164] However, unlike these other systems, Gnosticism denies the validity of the material world, the God who created the world and the societal laws that contribute towards maintaining its social structures. Gnostic antinomianism reverberates therefore on both the cosmological and anthropological planes.

For the disenfranchised Jewish intellectual the cosmic world alienated man from God and consequently God in turn became alien from the cosmic world.[165] As a Gnostic his only choice was to purge the cosmic world of its power. Hence, the Demiurge and his laws were jettisoned,[166] new

---

[159]For a similar analysis in Palestine with regard to Jewish renewal movements see Theissen, *First Followers*, 101ff.
[160]Cf. Kippenberg, "Versuch," 220f.
[161]NHC VII,1:36,2-24.
[162]NHC II,4:91,7-11.
[163]Wilson, *Gnostic Problem*, 45.
[164]See above 193 and Scholem, *Jewish Gnosticism*, 42: "Jewish Gnosticism was striving equally hard to maintain a strictly monotheistic character."
[165]See also Jonas' discussion in the *Gnostic Religion*, 250-253.
[166]R. McL. Wilson has presented an hypothesis that the Gnostics trans-

patterns of behaviour were encouraged to decrease the Demiurge's power, and a new ideology was developed to re-interpret creation. For the majority of the Gnostics who were indebted to the Jewish story of creation, antinomianism was in fact opposition to the Mosaic Law, the cosmic law. All law became identical to oppressive cosmic fate.[167] *Pneumatic* morality, determined by hostility towards the cosmic world and the law which governed the cosmic world, concentrated on liberating the Gnostic from Mosaic Law and Jewish morality.

During this historical epoch there is plausible evidence for the development of antinomian attitudes within Judaism. Philo may have referred to antinomians when he chastised Alexandrian Jews for allegorizing the Scriptures.[168] Jewish movements such as the Sibyllists[169] and the Hellenians[170] may also have represented innovative responses that resulted in non-normative, antinomian ideas and behaviour. Furthermore, the evidence in the rabbinical literature concerning *minim*, and in particular Elisha b. Abuya (Aher) may refer to heterodox Jewish movements that

---

formed the laws of the State, which subjected man to those in political power, from the initiative of earthly rulers to that of the rulers of the cosmos. In other words, the Gnostics not being able to change the condition of man politically, developed a rationalization that no longer made them responsible for man's fate. The cosmic powers were to blame and in particular, the Demiurge, all of whom were beyond man's control. Man's only choice, given his condition, was disobedience—an antinomian attitude (*Gnostic Problem*, 105f.). Hans Kippenberg's sociological thesis is an extension of Wilson's suggestion. See "Versuch," 211-232 and Chapter 1, 1f.

[167] See Jonas, *Gnostic Religion*, 253.

[168] See above Chapter 3, 164.

[169] See Pearson, "Friedländer Revisited," 24. Although Pearson's source is late (Origen, *Contra Celsum*, 5.61ff.) Pearson suggests a link to the "pious ones" in *Sib. Or.*, 4. Taken in conjunction with John Collins' conclusions that the third and fifth book of the *Sibylline Oracles* originated on Egyptian territory and incorporated heterodox Jewish traditions from the first centuries B.C. and A.D., Pearson's hypothesis adds further weight to the argument that Jewish assimilation and behaviour took many forms. For Collins, see *The Sibylline Oracles of Egyptian Judaism* (Society of Biblical Literature, Dissertation Series 13, Missoula, 1974).

[170] See Pearson, "Friedländer Revisited," 24 in reference to Justin Martyr, *Dialogue*. Pearson places the Hellenians in the first century A.D. and identifies them as a Diaspora group.

leaned towards antinomian doctrines.[171] Pearson, for example, has adopted the position earlier put forward by Graetz that Aher was the model antinomian Gnostic;[172] and Stroumsa views Aher as not only a converted Gnostic but as a Gnostic proselytizer who "cut down the saplings" (i.e., caused apostasy among youth).[173] Still as Segal has concluded in his discussion of the two powers doctrine, "Aher functions as the heretic *par excellence,* as Simon Magus does in Christian anti-heresiological writings."[174] Rather than explain Elisha b. Abuya as an antinomian Gnostic, Segal suggests that Aher was used as a model by later sages to argue against heresy. However, in spite of Segal's caution, Scholem's attribution of the secret name of *Yaldabaoth* to groups such as the *minim,* his designation of Aher as a Gnostic[175] and the inclusion of the *birkhath ha'minim* by the turn of the first century A.D. would suggest a correlation between heterodox Judaism, antinomianism and Gnosticism. Allegorical interpretations of the Mosaic Law or its rejection in part or whole could easily have led to heterodox movements characteristic of the rebel's response. Expressing the viewpoint of the anomic, disenfranchised Jew, Greek ethics and attitudes could surface openly, stripped of the Jewish God and his Laws.

There is a great deal of evidence from both the Church Fathers and the Nag Hammadi library that the Gnostics opposed the Mosaic Law. Basilides, an Egyptian Gnostic, states that anything made by the Jewish God is deceptive, "that even the prophecies themselves came from the rulers who made the world, and that the law in particular came from their chief, him who led the people out of the land of Egypt."[176] Similarly, according to Clement of Alexandria's description of another Egyptian Gnostic's system, that of Carpocrates, it was the Law that taught mankind to transgress: "for the private property of the laws cut up and nibbled away the fellowship of the divine law . . . 'mine' and 'thine' were introduced

---

[171]See especially Segal, *Two Powers.*
[172]Pearson, "Friedländer Revisited," 33. For H. Graetz see *Gnosticismus und Jüdentum* (Westmead 1971 [1846]).
[173]Stroumsa, *Another Seed,* 291. It should also be noted that Fischel is in agreement with Stroumsa that Aher was a corruptor of youth even though he has reinterpreted the passage (*b. Hag.,* 14b) in terms of Epicurean thought. See Fischel, *Rabbinic Literature,* 19f.
[174]Segal, *Two Powers,* 60.
[175]Scholem, "Jaldabaoth Reconsidered," 418f.
[176]Irenaeus, *Adv. Haer.,* 1.24.5.

through the laws. . . ."[177] Epiphanes, the son of Carpocrates, taught that all things were given in common by the Father of the All without distinction between male or female, man and animal. Law is a manifestation of the cosmic world, introduced by man, and contrary to nature. For Epiphanes, in the beginning all were "not governed by any law, but harmoniously present. . . ."[178] In a passage describing the ascent of the *pneumatics* in Orphian thought (which may have developed in Egypt),[179] the following is written: "Ruler of the fifth power, commander Sabaoth, advocate of the law of your creation . . . by a mightier pentad let me pass. . . ."[180] Again the Archons are associated with the God "of the Jews . . . the creator of this world, the God of Moses and of his cosmology. . . ."[181] One of the clearest statements equating the God of the Old Testament with the Demiurge, claiming that all Law is evil, is made by Heracleon, a disciple of the Egyptian Gnostic Valentinus:

> the mountain represents the Devil or his world. . . . The world is the total mountain of evil . . . to which all before the law and all the Gentiles render worship. But Jerusalem (represents) the creation. . . . The *Pneumatics* will worship neither the creation nor the Demiurge, (i.e., the Devil), but the Father of truth.[182]

Other writings by Valentinians are similar. Hippolytus claims that the Valentinians believed that "all the prophets and the law spoke from the Demiurge, . . . and they were foolish and knew nothing."[183] In the Letter of Ptolemaeus to Flora, Flora's initiation into Valentinianism involved her understanding of the spiritual significance of the Old Testament commandments:

---

[177]Clement of Alexandria, *Strom.* 3.7.2-3.

[178]Ibid., 3.6.4.

[179]According to Stroumsa (*Another Seed*, 11), "Sethianism has taken the place of 'Ophitism' as a generic heading for some of the central and perhaps the earliest trends of mythological Gnosticism." And as indicated above (188f.), these earliest trends stem from a Jewish background that has Egyptian roots.

[180]Origen, *Contra Celsum*, 6.31.

[181]Ibid., 6.27.

[182]Origen, *In Joannem*, 13.16.

[183]Hippolytus, *Ref.*, 6.35.1.

It is evident that this [i.e., the Law ordained through Moses]
was not ordained by the perfect God. . . . The entire law
which is contained in the Pentateuch of Moses was not
decreed by . . . God alone. . . . It is divided into three parts.
There is a section attributed to God himself . . . [a] division
belonging to Moses . . . and the third part [is attributed] to
the elders. . . .[184]

In this letter the Decalogue is seen as the work of the divine God but still
requires fulfillment by Jesus. All the other Laws in the Pentateuch are
considered either to be evil or to have been misinterpreted by the Jews.

The Nag Hammadi library also bears witness to the development of
opposition to the Mosaic Law. In *The Tripartite Tractate* (NHC I,5), a
work attributed to the Valentinian school, the Hebrews are identified as
the *psychics* and the Greeks as *hylics*. The context describes how the
Hebrews, by comparison with the Gnostics, have "accepted the scriptures
in an altered way," and that this has resulted in "heresies which have
existed to the present among the Jews."[185] Although the Jews are *psychics* they are still considered to be under the power of the Demiurge.[186]
Hippolytus' account of the Valentinians is reinforced by this tractate.[187]
In both versions, the Old Testament is seen to be derived from the Demiurge. And in another section of *The Tripartite Tractate*, Archons are
specifically identified with the Law.[188]

In *On the Origin of the World* all *hylic* men are identified with the
earthly Adam, the "man of law"[189] and Moses is called the ἀρχαγγελικός
(archangel-like).[190] *The Apocalypse of Peter* (NHC VII,3) contains a
polemical discussion arguing that the Law is relative[191] and that even the
Catholic Christians are in error in pursuing their Law.[192] This misunder-

---

[184]Epiphanius, *Pan.*, 33.3.4-4.2.
[185]NHC I,5:112,14-22.
[186]With the exception of Heracleon, Valentinians considered *psychics*
to be Catholic Christians and *hylics* to be Jews.
[187]Cf. fn. 183.
[188]NHC I,5:100,19-30.
[189]NHC II,5:117,35.
[190]NHC II,5:102,8-9.
[191]NHC VII,3:77,22-32.
[192]NHC VII,3:78,23-31.

standing of the true Law has a parallel in the above mentioned Letter of Ptolemaeus to Flora.[193]

In *The Gospel of the Egyptians* there is a passage that reads as follows: "and Jesus who possesses the life came and crucified that which is in the law."[194] Although influenced by the Pauline tradition,[195] a hostile attitude toward the Law is present.[196]

The best example of the Gnostic antinomian attitude is to be found in *The Testimony of Truth*. In this tractate the Pharisees and the Scribes are seen to be submissive to the Archons.[197] Anyone who follows their ways is unable to receive *gnosis:* "no one who is under the Law will be able to look up to the truth."[198] The defilement of the Law is manifest. Those who are from the generation of Adam (i.e., the Mosaic generation) are subservient to law. "The [book of the] generation of Adam [is written for those] who are in the [generation] of [the Law]. They follow the law [and] they obey it."[199] In contrast, those who are from the generation of the Son of Man are *pneumatic* and undefiled. The distinctions between *hylics* and *pneumatics,* the Son of Adam and of Man, the cosmic world and the *pleroma,* the Judaic Law and Gnostic conventions, are explicit.

In the above mentioned Nag Hammadi tractates, although Christian, as well as in the writings of the heresiologists concerning the Gnostics, the Jewish God is never recognized as the righteous God of creation; on the contrary, he is the unjust and evil creator God of the material world. He is continually described as a "malicious envier," a "jealous God."[200] "I am a jealous God, besides me there is no other."[201] The Prophets and the Scribes are considered as misunderstanding scripture. Mosaic Law, identified as the law of the cosmic world, is rejected and corrected by the

---

[193]Cf. fn. 184.

[194]NHC III,2:65,17-18 and IV,2:77,13-15.

[195]For example, Gal 6:14; Eph 2:15f.; and Col 2:14.

[196]See A. Böhlig and F. Wisse, *Nag Hammadi Codices III, 2 and IV, 2. The Gospel of the Egyptians* (NHS 4, Leiden, 1975), 37 and 196. Böhlig and Wisse are interpreting the *Gospel of the Egyptians* in the light of Colossians.

[197]NHC IX,3:29,18-21.

[198]NHC IX,3:29,22-24.

[199]NHC IX,3:50,5-9.

[200]See, for example, NHC IX,3:47,29-48,5; NHC II,5:103,11-12,107, 30-31 and 112,28-29; NHC II,4:86,30-31 and 94,21-22 and Irenaeus, *Adv. Haer.,* 1.29.4 and 30.5ff.

[201]BG 8502,2:44,14 and NHC II,1:13,8-9.

introductory phrase, "Not as Moses wrote."[202] The Mosaic Law is thus discredited as a way of ethical purification, and is viewed as the psychic analogue to the physical law: "Just as the law of the physical world, . . . integrates the individual bodies into the general system [society], so the moral law does with the souls, and thus makes them subservient to the demiurgical scheme."[203] In other words, ideologically, the Gnostic is asserting that the norms of the non-spiritual realm are not binding on him, as he is of the spirit.

Hence it was not this antinomian attitude alone that was a threat to those in authority; more importantly, it was the behavioural manifestations of this acosmic ideology and its opposition to the Mosaic Law. The Gnostic movements which chose libertine or ascetic behaviour as alternative modes of expression collided head-on with the moral code of the Mosaic Law. Abandoning all obligations of Law and becoming libertine, or preparing oneself for the ascent by becoming a disciplined ascetic, were basically comparable patterns of individualistic behaviour moving toward the same Gnostic end: to decrease the power of the Demiurge in the world. The realization of *gnosis* meant access to the hidden world of divine light and, consequently, liberation from the Laws Mosaic reality.

The Gnostic's battle to decrease the power of the Demiurge was an attempt to sever himself from his Jewish identity and to curtail the power of Rome. Antinomianism as an ideology therefore expressed social and political values. It rejected the established beliefs and de-legitimized the institutions of Judaism. If antinomian social movements develop in times of socio-economic transition[204] then the blockage of mobility for status-hungry, well-placed Jewish intellectuals in Alexandria could well have turned them toward such a course of action. Resenting the fact that established bureaucrats and Greeks were disproportionately rewarded, upper class marginal Jews deprecated the established system and responded to their frustration by constructing new mythologies.[205] Alienated from political and social power, denied access to the *gymnasium* and

---

[202]For example, see NHC II,1:22,22-23.

[203]Jonas, *Gnostic Religion*, 272.

[204]For a theoretical account see N. Adler, *The Underground Stream: New Life Styles and the Antinomian Personality* (New York, 1972). For an historical application see G. Scholem, *Sabbatai Sevi*, trans. R. J. Z. Werblowsky (Princeton, 1973).

[205]Pearson, in a different context, has arrived at the same conclusion. The Gnostic myth "reflects an intellectual and 'elitist' attempt to put the basic Gnostic revelation into religious language." See his "Observations," in O'Flaherty, ed., *Critical Study*, 248.

opposed to policies preventing them from being structurally assimilated, they sought refuge in an alternative ideology. Consequently, the apocalyptic ethos was expanded and embraced by Jews seeking to be liberated from fate and to reaffirm their freedom. For the wealthy, disenfranchised Jews of Alexandria, anomie and its theological counterpart, antinomianism, went hand in hand. The moral code institutionalized evil and bound them to a society that had to be transcended.

4.4   Individualism and Gnosticism

4.4.1   Introduction

The preceding section has described a variety of interconnections between Judaism and Gnosticism. It has indicated that a marginal, upper class, but powerless social group could have acted as a significant catalyst in the origins of Gnosticsm by rebelling against its cultural heritage. However, the conclusions presented do little more than support working hypotheses. Further research in other geographical centres defined as Jewish and Gnostic and with other social groups will need to be undertaken if this reconstruction is to be accepted.

The Jewish evidence indicates the possible social origins of Gnosticism but does not answer the sociological problems addressed in Chapter 1 concerning the correlation between changes in mode of production and the manifestation of new ideologies. It posits only that a certain social group could have provided the necessary elements through its collective social experiences. In the following sections, the theme of social change will be explored by positing structural similarities between the ideology and behaviour of the Gnostics and the transformation of the Ptolemaic mode of production introduced by the Romans. As indicated in Chapter 2, the transformation from state to private ownership of property in Egypt led to a socio-economic transformation and a fragmentation of the dominant (Ptolemaic) ideology. And as indicated in Chapter 3, this led to the social dislocation of dispossessed groups, such as the Jews. The emergence of a new ideology (Gnosticism) can therefore be viewed, on the one hand, as a reflection of material change, and on the other hand, as a means to create a new identity and to forge new bonds of social cohesion. By examining Gnostic ideas, behaviour and organization, a correlation is suggested between the essence of Gnosticism (individualism) and that of the Ptolemaic mode of production under Rome (privatization).

4.4.2   The Gnostic Ethos

The goal of all Gnostic systems is to reveal to man his 'true inner nature' and thereby liberate him from the fetters of the cosmic world. *Gnosis* brings man knowledge of his divine origin and his present state of being.

> He who is to have knowledge . . . knows where he comes from and where he is going.[206]

> Know your birth. Know yourself, that is, from what substance you are, or from what race.[207]

> [He has come to] know [himself. This] is the perfect life, [that] man knows [himself].[208]

Gnosis releases man from the shackles of the cosmic (material) world and all its manifestations including its laws.

> Knowledge is freedom.[209]

> He who has the knowledge of the truth is a free man.[210]

> [Knowledge] makes us free, . . . the knowledge of who we were, what we became, what we were, where into we have been thrown; where to we hasten, where from we are redeemed, what birth is, and what rebirth.[211]

Thus, the Gnostic "is no longer retained here but rises above the Archons."[212]

---

[206]NHC I,3:22,13-15.
[207]NHC VII,4:92,11-14.
[208]NHC IX,3:35,25-28.
[209]NHC II,3:84,10-11.
[210]NHC II,3:77,15-16.
[211]Clement of Alexandria, *Exc. ex Theod.*, 78.2.
[212]Jonas, *Gnostic Religion*, 60.

From a sociological perspective, an ideal typification[213] of Gnostic consciousness focuses on individualism and entails the following: a sense of calling, an I that is *pneumatic*, a hostility to the material world, an absence of internalized Mosaic Law and a personal concern for otherworldly retributions. Gnostics were called.[214] "How is one to hear if his name has not been called?"[215] Those who responded were *pneumatic*. According to the dominant Gnostic ideology, there were three classes of men: the material (*choic* or *hylic*), the *psychic* and the *pneumatic*. The *pneumatic* or spiritual man possessed Spirit and was therefore saved; the *psychic* man possessed soul and free will but not spirit; and the *choic* man was of the earth, earthy and ontologically evil. Irenaeus describes the system of salvation as follows: "They [the Gnostics] assume three types of men; the spiritual, the *choic* and the *psychic*, ... in order that they may represent by these the three natures, not with reference to an individual, but with reference to kinds of men."[216] Membership in these three categories of men is determined at birth and each type manifests certain caste-like characteristics. Relationships within and between castes are prescribed by their belonging to the *pneumatic*, *psychic* or *choic* categories. Again Irenaeus demonstrates this assertion: "for it is not conduct that brings men into the *pleroma*, but the seed which was sent out from it in its infancy."[217]

Although in some systems there is mobility for the *psychic* whereby he can also be saved, this salvation is still hierarchically lower and not in the abode which the *pneumatics* enter.[218] On the other hand, there is no

---

[213]For a sociological interpretation of ideal types see Max Weber, *Methodology of the Social Sciences*, 91ff. Ideal types are a configuration of characteristic elements abstracted from the phenomena under study and employed as a methodological technique to test hypotheses.

[214]For an excellent analysis of these 'calls of awakening' see Jonas, *Gnostic Religion*, 74ff. See also Foerster, *Gnosis*, v. 1, 9ff.

[215]NHC I,3:21,32-34.

[216]Irenaeus, *Adv. Haer.*, 1.7.5. Cf. Irenaeus, *Adv. Haer.*, 1.8.3, Clement of Alexandria, *Exc. ex Theod.*, 54.1-2, Hippolytus, *Ref.*, 5.6.7, and Epiphanius, *Pan.*, 31.7.8-11.

[217]Irenaeus, *Adv. Haer.*, 1.6.4.

[218]Elaine Pagels would disagree. She would argue that in Clement of Alexandria's *Exc. ex Theod.*, 63.2, "all who are saved" refers to both *psychics* and *pneumatics* being equally saved. See her "Conflicting Versions of Valentinian Eschatology: Irenaeus' Treatise Vs. The Excerpts from Theodotus," *HTR* 67 (1974), 45.

mobility between the other castes. For example, Irenaeus describes the mobility patterns of the three castes as follows:

> The *psychic* men have been instructed in psychic matters; they are strengthened by works . . . and do not have perfect knowledge. . . . Therefore they [the Gnostics] affirm that for us [Christians] good conduct is necessary—for otherwise it would not be possible to be saved—but they themselves, in their opinion, will be for ever and entirely saved, not by means of conduct, but because they are spiritual by nature. For just as it is impossible that the *choïc* should participate in salvation—since, they [the Gnostics] say, it is incapable of receiving it—so again it is impossible that the spiritual—and by that they mean themselves—should succumb to decay, regardless of what kind of actions it performs.[219]

Thus in Gnosticism we have a stratified system that closely resembles a caste system. This system of stratification is an hierarchical ordering of salvation with inferior and superior grades that are eternally sustained. This hierarchical ordering is seen as being ontologically determined and anthropologically present in this world. Caste membership is only by ascription. The rewards in Gnosticism are not material but metaphysical— entrance into the *pleroma* and transformation into noetic aeons.[220] The intrinsic superiority of the Gnostic in this world is due to his membership in the *pneumatic* caste which is entirely exclusive.

Yet the paradox with the Gnostic system of stratification is that it is tautological: only he who has been called knows he is *pneumatic*; on the other hand, he knows he has been called only because he is *pneumatic*. For example, in *The Gospel of Thomas* (NHC II,2), the paradox is expressed as follows: "When you come to know yourselves, then you will become known."[221] Thus, while in principle it is available to all to be called ("I am the hearing which is attainable to everyone";[222] "I cry out in everyone"[223]), the ideology suggests that in fact only a few are *pneumatic*— "not many can know these (doctrines), but one in a thousand and two in

---

[219]Irenaeus, *Adv. Haer.*, 1.6.2. See also Origen, *In Joannem*, 20.24 and Epiphanius, *Pan.*, 31.7.6-11.
[220]Irenaeus, *Adv. Haer.*, 1.2.6.
[221]NHC II,2:32,26-27.
[222]NHC VI,2:19,20-22.
[223]NHC XIII,1:36,15.

(two thousand)."[224] For each individual, "his deed and his knowledge will reveal his nature."[225] The individualistic calling of the Gnostic therefore democratizes him in the broadest sense, by providing him with the freedom to experience the divine without mediators, traditional values or Mosaic Law. Moreover, it allows the individual a vehicle to escape repressive social controls. Once a Gnostic "no one will persecute you, nor will anyone oppress you, other than yoursel[f]."[226] Not confined by *Gesellschaft* bonds, the Gnostic could sever his commitments to particular social institutions by proclaiming that they were material artefacts and therefore evil. Individualism and universalism are basic experiences for the Gnostic.

The liberation of the Gnostic through a calling structurally resembles and chronologically fits the liberation of the landholder in Egypt from the State through privatization. Both developments occur in the first century A.D. and exacerbate the conflict between the individual and society. Moreover, as expressed by Rivkin, the disintegration of the Hellenistic monarchies (e.g., the Ptolemaic) "unloosed the moorings that had underpinned the security of the individual."[227] For Jews, in particular, the ensuing crisis in identity was accentuated by the Roman policy of encouraging private ownership of production and land but simultaneously refusing Jews the opportunity of becoming structurally assimilated. Socially and politically isolated, Jews seeking an escape from historical and cosmic fate alleviated the painful burden that reality imposed by explaining it in mystical terms.[228] Creating a counter-ideology to Judaism and Hellenistic philosophy, they developed an alternative belief system that justified their position in the world. "Alienation from the

---

[224]Irenaeus, *Adv. Haer.*, 1.24.6.

[225]NHC II,5:127,16-17.

[226]NHC I,2:9,20-23. Pagels, in response to Aland's paper at the Yale Conference, has suggested a similar idea although in a different context. See B. Aland, "Gnosis und Christentum," in Layton, ed., *Rediscovery*, v. 1, 350.

[227]E. Rivkin, "Pharisaism and the Crisis of the Individual in the Greco-Roman World," *JQR* 61 (1970), 43. For the psychological dislocation of identity in the first several centuries of our era see E. R. Dodds, *Pagan and Christian in an Age of Anxiety* (New York 1970, [1965]).

[228]Cf. Kippenberg, "Versuch," 221. "Das kosmische Modell, das der Gnostiker entwirft, scheint mir die Projecktion einer bestimmten sozialen Wertung zu sein: der Ablehnung des autoritären römischen Verwaltungsstaates."

world goes closely with alienation from one's empirical, this-worldly self."[229]

For the Gnostic, revealed knowledge confers present salvation.[230] It awakens the individual to the recognition that he is already divine—that he bears within himself a spark of the divine.[231]

> But I say to [you, as for what], you seek after [and] inquire about, [it is] within you.[232]

> And what you see outside of you, you see inside of you.[233]

> Cease to seek after God and creation . . . and seek after yourself of yourself. . . . And if you carefully consider . . . you will find yourself within yourself. . . .[234]

The eye ("I") through which the Gnostic sees himself is the eye ("I") through which he sees God. Even for Gnostic Christians the encounter with Christ is a recognition of one's own hidden, unknown true identity. It is the discovery of self. "Liberation is not due to grace, but to knowledge."[235] Only by choosing liberty over domination can this experience be actualized. Thus, man is obliged to be an active participant in his own redemption and self-realization.[236] Only then can he be liberated from worldly (Roman) power and from cosmic determinism (fate). "The starting

---

[229]A. H. Armstrong, "Gnosis and Greek Philosophy," in Aland, ed., *Gnosis*, 92f.

[230]According to Fallon, the Gnostic emphasis upon present salvation through knowledge is "strikingly different from the emphasis in the Jewish apocalypses" (*Gnostic Apocalypses*, 136). Since Judaism is community and historically oriented in contrast to Gnosticism, which is individualistic and ahistorical, the differing emphasis on this world and the next is perfectly logical.

[231]The idea of the consubstantiality of man and God is common to all Gnostic systems.

[232]NHC III,5:128,2-5.

[233]NHC VI,2:20,22-24.

[234]Hippolytus, *Ref.*, 8.15.1-2.

[235]Munz, "Problem," 45.

[236]G. Quispel has described this process of self-realization also in terms of individuation. See "Gnosis and Psychology" in Layton, ed., *Rediscovery*, v. 1, 22.

point for Gnosis is an infinite feeling of freedom,"[237] an authentic freedom which "is a matter not of the 'soul' [*psyche*], which is ... determined
by the moral law ... but wholly a matter of the 'spirit' [*pneuma*]."[238]

In Gnosticism religious individualism meant that an individual had the
primary responsibility (identical to ownership) for his own spiritual (or
material) destiny. As a result, its radically individualistic doctrine of
inner illumination created spiritual aristocrats. The development of this
elite coincides with the individualization of angels,[239] and the perceived
need for greater self-knowledge. Thus, spiritual aristocrats by claiming
gnosis were in effect granting themselves higher status in the world. They
were saying to both Jews and Romans that apostasy could itself be
redemptive. "When man knows himself ... he will be saved."[240] For those
identified as spiritual aristocrats knowledge meant "the immediate and
definitive liberation of the knower."[241]

4.4.3   Gnostic Behaviour

4.4.3.1   Introduction

The evidence from the Nag Hammadi texts and the Church
Fathers indicates that the Gnostics engaged in two extreme forms of
behaviour, asceticism and libertinism.[242] These writings also reveal that
women engaged in these practices, thus violating traditional norms of
female subservience and dependence. In other words, sex roles became
diffused when social and psychological dislocation occurred.[243] This is not
surprising since, in Hopkins' view, the growth of individualism is
associated with the sexual freedom of women amongst the upper

---

[237]Aland, "Gnosis und Christentum" in Layton, ed., *Rediscovery*, v. 1,
349. Cf. Chapter 1, 2.
[238]Jonas, *Gnostic Religion*, 333.
[239]See above Chapter 4, 202.
[240]NHC IX,3:45,1-4.
[241]H.-Ch. Puech, "The Concept of Redemption in Manichaeism," in J.
Campbell, ed., *The Mystic Vision* (Bollingen Series 30-6, New York, 1970),
250.
[242]Not all Gnostic sects translated antinomian tendencies into ascetic
or libertine behaviour. Valentinus, for example was neither an ascetic nor
a libertine, and adhered to conventional codes of moral conduct.
[243]Pagels (*Gnostic Gospels*, 48-69) has developed the consequences of
this social transformation for women in Gnosticism.

classes.[244] While asceticism is the behavioural response most often
supported by Gnostic writings, it will be argued that libertinism was also
practised.

These behavioural extremes arose from a *pneumatic* morality, that
reflected an antinomian ideology and was hostile to the cosmic world. For
some, the possession of *gnosis* meant the obligation to avoid contamination by the world; for others, the possession of *gnosis* granted them the
licence of absolute freedom in the world. Once they were saved (by definition), their behaviour was no longer bound by the moral law. Whereas
the ascetic's behaviour is rigid and highly structured and proscribes
worldly activities, the libertine's is unstructured and open-ended.

To the Gnostic, antinomianism was an expression of individuality and
freedom. On this foundation was erected an alternative social construction of reality that explained and justified man's position vis-à-vis God
and the world. By opposing the Mosaic Law and abandoning the normative
frame of reference, the Gnostic was able to define spiritual existence
more immediately and to manifest his ideology through an individualistic
life-style. This is consistent with the psycho-historical perspective of
Adler, according to which the consequences of antinomianism affect both
behavioural patterns and personality configurations. From this perspective, the renunciation of family and traditional marriage; the establishment of small communities and new rituals; the validation of visions and
gnosis; passivity and activity, control and release, discipline and pleasure,
asceticism and libertinism, are all alternative modes for meeting social
and psychological stress.[245] While it can be argued that neither asceticism nor libertinism is intrinsically individualistic, adopting either entails
an individual choice to stand outside social convention. In the first case
the individual turns inward, away from the world and the company of men;
in the second, the individual turns outward, but is nonetheless 'possessed'
by a form of personal ecstasy that sets him apart from others. Sociologically and psychologically, the Gnostic forged a new identity that forced
him to abandon traditional community loyalties. It counterbalanced the
power of the Archons and repudiated his former identity with Judaism.
The Gnostic hostility to the cosmic world entailed a negation of the
moral and social perspectives of Judaism and later Christianity. For all
these reasons, these religions regarded Gnostic ethics as unequivocally

---

[244]See K. Hopkins, "Contraception in the Roman Empire," *Comparative Studies in Society and History* 8 (1965-1966), 149.

[245]Adler, *Underground Stream*, 20-25, 76-79.

deviant and heretical. In a fundamental sense, the Gnostic spiritual pride overran the limits of conventional reason.

4.4.3.2   Libertinism

In the context of Gnostic antinomianism, libertinism involved attitudes and practices that reflected an expanded conception of moral freedom and a rejection of conventional standards of behaviour. In light of the Gnostics' contempt for the cosmic world and the Mosaic Law it can be argued that libertinism is a direct outgrowth of Gnostic ideology. Still, Gnostic libertinism can also be interpreted as a mirror image of the society in which it arose. Temple prostitution was an accepted ritual. Sexual exploitation of female slaves was acceptable as was adultery among equals. Pornographic displays during circuses were frequent. Cults such as that of Dionysus (Bacchus) encouraged the consumption of wine and orgiastic practices while others such as that of Isis had erotic elements.[246] Moreover, these cults were widespread among the Jews during the Hellenistic-Roman period. Baron, for example, comments that Jews living in Egypt "felt the strange attraction of the mysterious Egyptian practices."[247] And Tcherikover points out that Jews [in Egypt] did not scruple to give their children names recalling Greek or Egyptian gods, . . . [such as] Dionysus, . . . Isis, . . . and Serapis."[248] Moreover, Goodenough has painstakingly indicated how Jews incorporated Greek and Egyptian symbols from mystery religions such as the Dionysian ones, not as ornaments, but as living symbols.[249] According to Nock, the cult of Dionysus

---

[246]The bibliography with regard to mystery religions and cults in antiquity is very large. The more important works include, U. Bianchi, *The Greek Mysteries* (Leiden, 1976), J. Ferguson, *The Religions of the Roman Empire* (London, 1974), F. Cumont, *Oriental Religions in Roman Paganism* (London, 1956), H. J. Bell, *Cults and Creeds in Graeco-Roman Egypt* (Liverpool, 1955), and M. P. Nilsson, *A History of the Greek Religion,* trans. F. J. Fielden (New York, 1952). For Dionysus, in particular, see M. P. Nilsson, *The Dionysiac Mysteries of the Hellenistic and Roman Age* (Lund, 1957), and W. F. Otto, *Dionysus: Myth and Cult,* trans. R. B. Palmer (Bloomington, 1965). For Isis, see R. E. Witt, *Isis in the Graeco-Roman World* (Ithaca, 1971) and F. Dunand, *Le culte d'Isis dans le bassin oriental de la Méditerranée* (Leiden, 1973), 3 vols.

[247]Baron, *Social,* v. 2, 16ff. See Philo, *De Spec. Leg.,* 1.319ff.

[248]Tcherikover, *CPJ,* v. 1, 29. Cf. Chapter 3, 155f.

[249]See Goodenough, *Jewish Symbols,* v. 6, 92. Cf. Chapter 3, 159f. and fn. 490 for reservations regarding Goodenough's claim.

"assumed dimensions sufficient to cause government regulation" in Ptolemaic Egypt;[250] it is probable that Jews were also initiates, given that they comprised 10% to 15% of the total population.

The evidence regarding Gnostic libertinism comes almost exclusively from the heresiologists' writings. Many of the accounts of the early forms of Gnosticism—including those of Simon, Carpocrates and Basilides— describe them as libertines. But were the Church Fathers describing authentic religious movements or were they denigrating Gnostic behaviour in order to undermine its popularity?[251]

According to Hippolytus, Simon Magus, the purported originator of the

---

[250]A. D. Nock, *Early Gentile Christianity and it Hellenistic Background* (New York, 1964), 114. On Jews and the mystery religions generally, see Hengel, *Judaism and Hellenism*, v. 1, 158f., 297f., Lieberman, *Hellenism*, F. Cumont, "Les Mystères de Sabazius et le Judaisme," in *Comptes-Rendus de l'Académie des inscriptions et belles-lettres* (Paris, 1906), 63-67, Pokorný, "Hintergrund" in Tröger, ed., *Gnosis*, 77-87, J. H. Levy, *Studies in Jewish Hellenism* (in Hebrew, Jerusalem, 1960), and A. Tzarichobar, *The Jews in the Greek-Roman World* (in Hebrew, Jerusalem, 1961).

[251]The credibility of the heresiologists' evidence of libertinism in Gnosticism is a much debated issue. Scholars are divided more by their own ideological inclinations than by the empirical evidence. Morton Smith, for example, in his book, *Clement of Alexandria and a Secret Gospel of Mark* (Cambridge, 1973) argues for the prevalence of libertinism in Gnosticism. Other scholars such as Jonas (*Gnostic Religion*), Grant (*Gnosticism*), Pokorný ("Hintergrund") and Rudolph (*Die Gnosis*) also accept the accounts of the heresiologists but with careful reservations. Still others endorse the opinion that the libertine traditions are suspect. These scholars support their position with reference to the Gnostics' silence or disapproval of libertinism, and the fact that the heresiologists' writings are polemical and do not reflect first-hand observations. Wisse contends, for example, that the heresiologists only extrapolated those aspects of Gnostic teachings that had negative moral implications in order to demean them in the eyes of Catholic Christians. See F. Wisse, "Die Sextus-Sprüche und das Problem der gnostischen Ethik" in A. Böhlig and F. Wisse, *Zum Hellenismus in den Schriften von Nag Hammadi* (Göttinger Orientforschungen 6, Reihe: Hellenistica, Band 2, Wiesbaden, 1975), 55-86. Similarly, K. Koschorke, *Die Polemik der Gnostiker gegen das kirchliche Christentum* (NHS 12, Leiden, 1978) suggests that the imputation of libertinism to Gnosticism is purely ideological rhetoric.

Gnostic heresy according to Church tradition,[252] advocated that "one must engage in intercourse without consideration. . . . It makes no difference where a man sows, if only he sows."[253] This indiscriminate intercourse brings "perfect love."[254] Irenaeus adds further that the Simonians used "love-potions and erotic magic."[255] Vice could not affect them because they had already been redeemed.[256] Being *pneumatic* assured eternal salvation. The report by Hippolytus of Simon is set in the context of Simon's interpretation of the Mosaic Law and in particular, his anticosmic attitude.

Carpocrates, an early Egyptian Gnostic, taught that sin was a means of salvation. Only by participating in all kinds of experience could the soul satisfy the demands of the rulers of this world and be allowed to ascend to the heavens. "If a man does not in one life do at one and the same time all that is not merely forbidden for us to speak or hear but may not even enter into the thoughts of our minds . . . [he will] be compelled to be sent

---

[252]Simon Magus is a problematic figure for those trying to assess the origins of Gnosticism. There are many Simons that have to be reconciled. These include Acts 8:9-25, Justin Martyr, *Apol.*, 1.26.1-3, Irenaeus, *Adv. Haer.*, 1.23.1-7, Hippolytus, *Ref.*, 6.19-20, Epiphanius, *Pan.*, 21.2, Pseudo-Clementine, *Hom.*, 2.22.1-26.5, Origen, *Contra Celsum*, 1.57, as well as other references. For a list and commentary of all the sources see K. Beyschlag, *Simon Magus und die christliche Gnosis* (WUNT 16, Tübingen, 1974), 7-78. For recent attempts at understanding Simon's role in Gnosticism see G. Lüdemann, *Untersuchungen zur simonianischen Gnosis* (Göttingen, 1975); K. Rudolph, "Gnosis und Gnostizismus, ein Forschungsbericht. Simonianische Gnosis," *TRu* 37 (1972), 322-347; and E. Haenchen, "Simon Magus in der Apostelgeschichte" in Tröger, ed., *Gnosis*, 267-279. For a brief overview see Yamauchi, *Pre-Christian Gnosticism*, 58-65, W. A. Meeks, "Simon Magus in Recent Research" *Religious Studies Review* 3 (1977), July, 137-142, and R. McL. Wilson, "Simon and Gnostic Origins" in J. Kremer, ed., *Les Actes des Apôtres* (BETL 48, Leuven, 1979), 485-491. It would appear that whatever his origin, authenticity or role as a pre-Christian Gnostic redeemer, Simon became the model for the Church Fathers (like Aher for the rabbis) to argue against heresy (cf. above 205, fn. 174). And within this model a libertine Simonian tradition, among others, is conspicuous.

[253]Hippolytus, *Ref.*, 6.19.5.

[254]Ibid., loc. cit.

[255]Irenaeus, *Adv. Haer.*, 1.23.4.

[256]Hippolytus, *Ref.*, 6.19.5.

again in [a body],"[257] is the way Irenaeus describes Carpocrates' beliefs.

In a recently discovered fragment of a letter purported to be from Clement of Alexandria, Morton Smith has provided further evidence that Carpocrates and his teachings were regarded as unspeakable, wandering "from the narrow realm of the commandments into a boundless abyss of the carnal and bodily sins."[258] Elsewhere, Clement of Alexandria writes of the Carpocratian law of licentiousness and promiscuity, "in such a love-feast, they [men] demand even by day from the women of whom they wish it, obedience toward the Carpocratian law [i.e., sexual intercourse on demand]."[259] Clement of Alexandria's refutation of Carpocrates focused almost exclusively on his ethics and according to Chadwick, "offers a surely trustworthy portrait of licence."[260]

Love is Carpocrates' central doctrine. Through love one can disdain the Mosaic Law, transgress it, and become free. Thus, the love feasts of Carpocrates can be interpreted as sacraments. The heresiologists' attack on Carpocrates can be viewed as a determined attempt to disassociate themselves from so-called Christians who would pollute their developing Orthodoxy and tarnish their tenuous peace with Rome.

Basilides, an Alexandrian Gnostic and a contemporary of Carpocrates, was also accused by Irenaeus of licentiousness: "they enjoy the other (pagan) festivals and all (that) appetite (prompts)."[261] Elsewhere Irenaeus writes, "Others following upon Basilides and Carpocrates, have introduced promiscuous intercourse and a plurality of wives. . . ."[262] In contrast to Irenaeus' account, Hippolytus' report of Basilides' son Isidore does not mention libertinism, and according to Clement of Alexandria's version, some of Basilides' followers were eunuchs while others were libertine.[263] Although there are contradictory traditions for Basilides, both Irenaeus and Clement of Alexandria support a libertine tradition.

The Cainites, who perversely honoured Cain, Korah, Esau and the

---

[257]Irenaeus, Adv. Haer., 1.25.4.

[258]Smith, Clement of Alexandria, 446.

[259]Clement of Alexandria, Strom., 3.10.

[260]H. Chadwick, "The Domestication of Gnosis" in Layton, ed., Rediscovery, v. 1, 5.

[261]Irenaeus, Adv. Haer., 1.24.5.

[262]Ibid., 1.28.2.

[263]Clement of Alexandria, Strom., 3.1ff. To reconcile the various traditions is beyond the scope of this study. For an attempted reconciliation of the varying accounts see W. Foerster, "Das System des Basilides," NTS 9 (1962-1963), 233-255.

Sodomites, held an ethical position similar to that of Basilides and
Carpocrates.

> And at every sinful and base action an angel is present . . .
> [and] they say in the angel's name: '. . . O thou power, I
> accomplish thy deed.' And this is the perfect 'knowledge', to
> enter without fear into such operations, which is not lawful
> even to name.[264]

Reports on Naassene behaviour are conflicting. There is evidence that
they forbade intercourse with women: "they urge most severely . . . that
one should abstain . . . from intercourse with women."[265] In one passage
from Hippolytus there is even a close parallel to *The Gospel of Thomas*, in
which all Gnostics become bridegrooms, "having been made male through
the virgin spirit."[266] This parallel is extremely important given that *The
Gospel of Thomas* is part of a Gnostic tradition that shows itself to be the
most ascetic. On the other hand, Hippolytus comments that the Naassenes
gave up "natural intercourse with women, having been inflamed with
passion for one another; men behaving shamelessly with men. . . ."[267] This
homosexual practice, from the point of view of Judaism, is libertine and
contrary to moral law. Thus although one tradition suggests that the
Naassenes were ascetic, another indicates homosexual behaviour.[268]

---

[264]Irenaeus, *Adv. Haer.*, 1.31.2.

[265]Hippolytus, *Ref.*, 5.9.11.

[266]See R. McL. Wilson, *Studies in the Gospel of Thomas* (London,
1960), 31f. Hippolytus, *Ref.*, 5.8.44 and NHC II,2:51,21-26.

[267]Hippolytus, *Ref.*, 5.7.18.

[268]It is a well-known fact that many Greek and Romans were bi-sexual
and that among the upper classes it was considered permissable behaviour.
For example, see K. J. Dover, *Greek Homosexuality* (Cambridge, 1978). In
contrast, for Jews who adhered to the Mosaic Law to choose such behaviour would be considered immoral and they would be severely chastised. In
Lev 18:22 and 20:13 Jews who engage in homosexual activity are threatened with capital punishment and in the Mishnah homosexuality brings
stoning (*m. Sanh.*, 7.4). See L. M. Epstein, *Sex Laws and Customs in Judaism* (New York, 1948). Those in authority in the nascent Church also
prescribed Mosaic Law with regard to sexual morality. Those who chose
homosexuality were excluded from the Kingdom of God. See Rom 1:27,
1 Cor 6:9-10 and 1 Tim 1:9-10. Also see D. S. Bailey, *Homosexuality and
Western Christian Tradition* (New York, 1955) and R. W. Wood, "Homosexual Behaviour in the Bible," *One Institute Quarterly* 5 (1962), 10-19.

Although Valentinus and his school are reputed to have encouraged neither libertinism nor asceticism, there are some examples to the contrary. Marcus the Magician, a disciple of Valentinus, is chastised by Irenaeus for deceiving and leading women astray by claims of perfection and boasting that as a result he is free to do anything without fear.[269] Irenaeus' description is placed partly within a ritual context which further enhances his concern over Marcus' misinterpretation of developing Christian orthodoxy; and partly within the context of Marcus' allegorical interpretation of the *Pentateuch* and the New Testament. In another passage describing the system of Valentinus, Irenaeus mentions that the most perfect Valentinians engage in sexual promiscuity, and among other things, frequent the circus:

> the most perfect among them freely practise everything that is forbidden. . . . Some of them do not even avoid the murderous spectacle of fights. . . . And some of them secretly seduce women. . . .[270]

In addition to those mentioned above there were other Gnostic sects which purportedly practised libertinism. These Gnostic sects are described only in the writings of Epiphanius in the fourth century A.D. and are of doubtful validity both because of his fanatical fervour to destroy the Gnostic movements and because of the lack of additional evidence to corroborate his testimony. These sects include, among others, the Archontics who "polluted their bodies by licentiousness"[271] and the Phibionites.[272]

When a comparison is made between the heresiologists' accounts and the writings of Nag Hammadi, the latter are surprisingly silent concerning libertine behaviour.[273] The only piece of supportive evidence is in *The*

---

[269]Irenaeus, *Adv. Haer.*, 1.13.6.

[270]Ibid., 1.6.3.

[271]Epiphanius, *Pan.*, 40.2.4. Epiphanius also reports that certain Archontics were ascetics: "Others pretend to an affected abstinence and deceive the simpler sort of man by making a show of withdrawal from the world in imitation of the monks" (40.2.4).

[272]Epiphanius, *Pan.*, 26.4.1-11.9.

[273]MacRae has recently suggested that inherent in Gnostic language and speculation one may find "examples of Gnostic authors' own formulations of a principle underlying such conduct." See G. MacRae, "Why the Church Rejected Gnosticism," in Sanders, ed., *Jewish and Christian Self-Definition*, v. 1, 129.

Testimony of Truth and it is conjectural at best because of the *lacunae*. Basilides and his son are mentioned and the context of the few remaining words may refer to a libertine situation.[274] Similarly, the discussion of the Simonians which directly follows suggests libertine behaviour.[275] Koschorke has speculated that these references refer to the seed of Adam and may be libertine because of the words, "they have not ceased [from desire which is wicked . . .]."[276] These passages that refer to the Son of Adam are polemical outbursts against those who are bound by the Law and the cosmic world in contrast to those who follow the ascetic practices of the Son of Man. This particular passage in the tractate indicates how varied and contradictory the Gnostic movements were in historical reality. Gnostics could deprecate the cosmic world, reject the Old Testament God, consider themselves *pneumatic* and exhibit libertine behaviour as complementary to their ideology.

In spite of the lack of evidence in the Nag Hammadi texts, other clues may point to libertine behaviour within Gnostic sects. For example, Smith has analysed all the traditions and sources with regard to Carpocratian libertinism and has concluded that in pre-Pauline Christianity "alongside the legalistic interpretation of the religion we must set the libertine. . . . It was dominant in the Jerusalem Church in the earliest days, but lost its hold."[277] In Smith's opinion, a libertine tradition was initially present in both Gnosticism and early Christianity,[278] but whereas Gnosticism expanded this tradition, Christianity divorced itself from it and adopted Mosaic Law. Although Smith's reconstruction is highly conjectural, if he is correct it would have been Christian Jews who participated in these libertine practices and contributed to this development. The triumph of the legalist party (James) in Jerusalem over the libertines was, in effect, the victory of the Mosaic Law over antinomianism. Thus, the heresiologists' attack on Carpocrates was an attempt not only to impose social control over deviant behaviour within the nascent Church but also to counter ideological developments that eroded social cohesion.

The accounts by Irenaeus may provide another clue. Hippolytus, Epiphanius and other heresiologists depended on Irenaeus for their information. Not only was he the earliest heresiologist but according to Wisse,

---

[274]NHC IX,3:57,6-58,2.
[275]NHC IX,3:58,2-4.
[276]NHC IX,3:67,12-13. See Koschorke, *Die Polemik*, 116f.
[277]Smith, *Clement of Alexandria*, 263.
[278]Ibid., 266-278 and Appendix B, 295-350.

"the agreements [between the Nag Hammadi texts and the Church Fathers] are mainly with Irenaeus."[279] Sagnard,[280] in particular, has vindicated the essential reliability of Irenaeus, by comparing the *Apocryphon of John* with his account of the *Barbelo-Gnostics*.[281] It is Irenaeus who cites Simon, Carpocrates and Basilides as libertine; but if the fragmentary evidence of *The Testimony of Truth* can be employed as corroboration of libertine traditions (as suggested by Pearson and Koschorke), then it would appear that there are additional references to Simon and Basilides as libertines. There are also data in the *Pistis Sophia* and the second book of *Jeu*.[282]

A further clue arises from the nature of libertine cults themselves in antiquity, which rarely codified their behaviour. Consequently, it is impossible to compare the heresiologists' report with the libertine Gnostics or cultists themselves. Even the slight evidence of the non-Gnostic libertine traditions that exists is fragmentary and rarely describes in detail rituals and other practices.[283] These cults were frequently considered to be mystery religions and the requirements for initiation included oaths of secrecy.[284]

---

[279]Wisse, "Nag Hammadi," 208.

[280]F. M. M. Sagnard, *La gnose Valentinienne et le témoignage de saint Irénée* (Paris, 1947).

[281]See Foerster, *Gnosis*, v. 1, 100-120.

[282]Cited in S. Benko, "The Libertine Gnostic Sect of the Phibionites according to Epiphanius," *VC* 21 (1967), 112.

[283]See, for example, the evidence collected by A. Henrichs in *Die Phoinikika des Lollianos* (Bonn, 1972), 44-47 and D. Rice and J. Stambaugh, *Sources for the Study of Greek Religion* (SBL, Sources for Biblical Study 14, Missoula, 1979), 195-209 with regard to the cult of Dionysus.

[284]B. Metzger makes a similar point when discussing problems in estimating the amount of influence of the mysteries upon early Christianity: "The nature and amount of the evidence of the Mysteries create certain methodological problems. Partly because of a vow of secrecy imposed upon the initiates, relatively little information concerning the teaching imparted in the Mysteries has been preserved. Furthermore, since a large part of the scanty evidence regarding the Mysteries dates from the third, fourth and fifth Christian centuries, it must not be assumed that beliefs and practices current at that time existed in substantially the same form during the pre-Christian era. . . . Pagan doctrines would differ somewhat from place to place and from century to century." See "Methodology in the Study of the Mystery Religions and

Lastly, it should be emphasized that the Nag Hammadi library, if associated with the Pachomian monasteries, would have been biased towards the collection of ascetic works.[285] Libertine behaviour would have been considered heretical. Consequently, it may well be that just as the heresiologists were biased in their descriptions of the Gnostics (libertinism), so too the Nag Hammadi library may present a biased account of Gnostic tendencies towards asceticism.

The demise of Gnostic libertinism was due not only to the integration of Christian elements into its superstructure but also to the fact that the institutionalization of orthodox Christianity made it more difficult for libertine Gnostics and Catholic Christians to co-exist. Competing for the same audience, the libertine Gnostics lacked a viable social structure to keep pace with their opponents. Without an institutional base to buttress their position, these Gnostics' sole weapon was verbal censure. The Apocalypse of Peter, for example, gives us insight into the limitations of even ascetic Gnostics' reaction to orthodox Christian institutionalization.

> And there shall be others of those who are outside our number who name themselves bishop and also deacons, as if they have received their authority from God. They bend themselves under the judgement of the leaders. Those people are dry canals.[286]

These Gnostics, although they regarded Catholic Christians as morally lax and were contemptuous of their hierarchical structures, were able to express their opposition only through withdrawal and verbal censure. Given that the libertine Gnostics had less social structure and that their rites were secret, their ability to discredit Catholic Christianity would have been even less effective. Moreover, the fact that Gnosticism, according to the Nag Hammadi tractates, was more ascetically inclined by the end of the second century A.D., would have made it extremely difficult for libertine Gnostics to co-exist socially in a community that condemned their behaviour.

Early Christianity" in B. Metzger, *Historical and Literary Studies: Pagan, Jewish and Christian* (Leiden, 1968), 6.

[285]For the association of the Library with Pachomian monasteries see Robinson, *Nag Hammadi Library*, 16ff. and more recently, Hedrick, "Gnostic Proclivities," 78-95.

[286]NHC VII,3:79,22-31.

One Gnostic tractate refers to Catholic Christians persecuting ascetic Gnostics because of ideological differences.

> We were hated and persecuted, not only by those who are ignorant, but also by those who think that they are advancing the name of Christ. . . . They persecuted those who have been liberated by me, since they hate them.[287]

Libertine Gnostics who engaged in immoral acts and simultaneously claimed elements of Christianity, would have been all the more suspect from the perspective of orthodox Christians. In all probability this too would have led to conflict and persecution.

Finally, it should be noted that the conflicting reports of the heresiologists and the Nag Hammadi tractates concerning libertine and ascetic traditions represent only one of many points of contention between the Church Fathers and the Gnostics. For example, Pagels has argued that the Valentinian interpretation of the Pauline letters is at odds with the Church Fathers' interpretation.[288] She suggests that the Apostle was not anti-Gnostic although according to the heresiologists he was. Pagels' view is that orthodox Christianity developed the Pastoral letters, interpreting Paul as the antagonist of 'false teachers', whereas the Valentinians "ignored the Pastorals and concentrated on Romans, I-II Corinthians, Galatians, Ephesians, Philippians, Colossians, I Thessalonians and Hebrews."[289] In other words, the Valentinians, according to Pagels, viewed Paul as the originator of a secret oral esoteric tradition[290] that passed from Theudas (Paul's disciple)[291] to Valentinus. She comments on these conflicting traditions as follows:

> When we compare the heresiological accounts with the newly available evidence, we can trace how two antithetical traditions of Pauline exegesis have emerged from the late first century through the second. Each claims to be authentic, Christian and Pauline: but one reads Paul *antignostically,* the other *gnostically.* Correspondingly, we discover two conflicting images of Paul: on the one hand, the antignostic Paul

---

[287]NHC VII,2:59,22-32.
[288]Pagels, *Gnostic Paul.*
[289]Ibid., 5.
[290]Irenaeus, *Adv. Haer.,* 3.2.1. Cf. Pagels, *Gnostic Paul,* 4-6.
[291]Acts 5:36. Cf. Pagels, *Gnostic Paul,* 5.

familiar from church tradition, and, on the other, the gnostic
Paul, teacher of wisdom to gnostic initiates.[292]

These extreme divergencies suggest that some caution must be exercised in attributing behavioural patterns on the basis of such polemical
writings; nonetheless, if these polemics have some basis in fact, the
presence of libertine sects within Gnosticism would support the
individualistic character of Gnostic antinomianism. Gnostic libertines may
simply have adopted behavioural patterns that mirrored the society
around them. However, as Gnosticism developed, it acquired Christian
elements and the ascetic tradition became more pronounced.

4.4.3.3   Asceticism

Gnostic libertinism had its polar opposite in asceticism. Just as
libertinism repudiated allegiance to the cosmic world through excess,
asceticism repudiated allegiance through abstention. In Jonas' words,
"freedom by abuse and freedom by non-use . . . are only alternative
expressions of the same acosmism."[293] Asceticism, in an antinomian
context, advocated a denial of physical desires as an affirmation of *pneumatic* morality. Like libertinism, ascetic behaviour decreased the power
of the Demiurge and demonstrated Gnostic contempt for Mosaic Law. The
hylic body and *psychic* soul bound to passion and appetites were expunged.
The more one was 'at rest' from the world, the more awake one became to
the 'call.'

Asceticism was in fact less prevalent than libertinism in the Graeco-
Roman world as a whole in spite of the attempts by the Stoics, Pythagoreans and Orphics to create a system of practices that would combat vice
and develop virtues. In Greek ἄσκησις (ascetic practice) had long been
used to denote both the training of the body and the exercise of the mind.
The Stoics, for example, believed that it was possible to train the will
against a life of sensuous pleasure and thereby enhance the dignity of
man. Platonic asceticism inspired a moral conversion by the practice of
virtue and contemplation. The Pythagoreans considered life a purifying
ritual and taught moderation of desires and resignation to the inescapable
sufferings of the present. The Orphics abstained from sexual intercourse
and had strict rules of purity including abstinence from animal food and

---

[292]Pagels, *Gnostic Paul*, 5.
[293]Jonas, *Gnostic Religion*, 275.

avoidance of polluting actions, which were similar to those practised by the Levites.[294] In the Old Testament, there is a great deal of evidence to suggest that ritual purity was very important, but there is little evidence of asceticism apart from the Nazirites and the Rechabites, who constituted special groups.[295] The only consistent practice mentioned is fasting,[296] which was instituted on special occasions to aid prayer, rather than as a religious experience in and of itself. Except for limited data concerning the Essenes and the Therapeutae, there is little further information.[297] Urbach maintains that the reason for this lies in the differing world-views of Hellenic and Jewish thought. The basis of Hellenic asceticism, according to Urbach, was the opposition between body and soul, flesh and spirit, which was more or less absent from the Jewish literature of that period.[298] It is unusual in Judaism to find acts of self-denial contrary to human nature—and God's commandments (e.g., Gen 1:28). The asceticism of the Qumran community, the Essenes, is an aberration, although it is well-documented in the literature of antiquity. Except for a handful of references,[299] the sources describe them as principally a male desert community.[300] The Essenes had strict ascetic practices, disdained

---

[294]For Stoicism see L. Edelstein, *The Meaning of Stoicism* (Cambridge, 1966) and F. H. Sandback, *Stoics* (London, 1975); for Neoplatonism F. C. Grant, ed., *Hellenistic Religions: the Age of Syncreticism* (Indianapolis, 1953) and P. Merlan, *From Platonism to Neoplatonism* (The Hague, 1960); and for Orphism E. R. Dodds, *The Greeks and the Irrational* (Berkeley, 1951) and W. K. C. Guthrie, *Orpheus and Greek Religion* (London, 1935). See also W. K. C. Guthrie, *A History of Greek Philosophy* (Cambridge, 1962-1975), 4 vols.

[295]For the Nazirites see Num 6:2-21; Judg 13:5; and Amos 2:11. For the Rechabites, see Num 10:29-32; Judg 1:16; 2 Kgs 10:15 and 23 and 1 Chr 2:55

[296]Lev 23:27.

[297]For the Essenes see Josephus, *Ant.*, 13.171f., 18.18ff. and *War*, 2.120ff. and the Dead Sea Scrolls. For the Therapeutae, see Philo, *De Vita Cont.*

[298]E. E. Urbach, "Ascesis and Suffering in Talmudic and Midrashic Sources" in *Yitzhak F. Baer Jubilee Volume* (in Hebrew, Jerusalem, 1969), 48-68.

[299]For example, see Josephus, *War*, 2.124 and Philo, *Hypothetica*, 11.1.

[300]See Josephus, *War*, 2.120-161, and *Ant.*, 18.18ff.; Philo, *De Vita Cont.*, 1, *Quod Omn. Prob.*, 75-91, and *Hypothetica*, 11.1-18; and Pliny the Elder, *Natural History*, 5.73. For the designation as predominately a male

material goods, were bound by strict oaths, and abstained from sexual gratification.[301] The Therapeutae, by contrast, were situated near Alexandria and included both men and women as participants. They abstained from wine and spent most of their waking hours in study and contemplation.[302] However, asceticism in the Graeco-Roman world or in Judaism was not the norm, and it was not a means of negating the cosmic world. Rather it was a means to ritual purity or an exercise to fortify the will. In contrast, the Gnostic asceticism of the Nag Hammadi library is normatively prescribed as a means of denying the cosmic order. Through spiritual asceticism the initiate could achieve *gnosis* and be absolved of obligation to moral law. For the Gnostic, asceticism reflected a detachment from the world, and its main characteristic was a marked individualism.

The evidence of Gnostic asceticism in the heresiologists' reports is not abundant. Saturninus, the first Gnostic to be labelled as an ascetic, was from Syria and active in the early second century A.D. He held that "the God of the Jews . . . was one of the angels. . . . Christ came for the destruction of the God of the Jews. . . . [And that] marriage and procreation . . . are of Satan."[303] Procreation was a device of the angels to increase their number of subjects. Saturninus thought that by encouraging celibacy he could reduce the number of mankind and thereby reduce the power of the Demiurge. According to Irenaeus, his followers also abstained from eating meat.[304]

Marcion also forbade marriage and the eating of meat since these acts would only increase the influence of the Demiurge. According to Hippolytus, Marcion forbade "marriage, the procreation of children and the eating

---

desert community see M. Black, *The Scrolls and Christian Origins* (New York, 1961). However, Josephus also comments in passing that the Essenes could marry and have children (*War*, 2.160) and many of the secondary cemeteries of Qumran held the remains of women. See R. de Vaux, *Archaeology and the Dead Sea Scrolls* (London, 1973), 45ff., 57f., 88ff. For a brief discussion of the status of women among the Essenes see E. and F. Stagg, *Woman in the World of Jesus* (Philadelphia, 1978), 36-40.

[301]For example, fasting, *Dam. Doc.*, VI.19; non-ownership of property, *IQS* I.10-11, VI.13-23; rules of strict conduct *IQS* VI.24-VII.25; vigils, *IQS* VI.6-7; oaths *IQS* II.19-23; rules of precedence *IQS* VI.8-13; and sexual abstinence *IQS* aII.3-9.

[302]Philo, *De Vita Cont.*, 2ff.

[303]Irenaeus, *Adv. Haer.*, 1.24.2.

[304]Ibid.,loc. cit.

from meats." Moreover, he "dissolved marriages that had been cemented by the Demiurge."[305] Marcion regarded celibacy as a positive act against the power of the Demiurge, the God of the Old Testament. Although it is questionable whether Marcion was a Gnostic, his asceticism is sympathetic to the Gnostics.[306] Finally, there is a reference in Ptolemaeus' description of the Valentinian school that fasting was observed by many of its followers.[307]

Until the discovery of the Nag Hammadi library, the Church Fathers' descriptions of Gnostic behaviour suggested that many of the Gnostics were morally depraved, libertines run wild. However, when a comparison is made between the heresiologists' accounts and the Nag Hammadi tractates, comparable examples of libertine behaviour are not present. Doresse, the first to observe this incongruity, voiced his astonishment as follows: "one finds oneself almost disappointed at this, so freely had the heresiologists given us to understand that mysteries of that description were common practice in the principal sects."[308]

Far from libertinism, the Nag Hammadi library bears witness to ascetic ethics and behaviour. This asceticism is most pronounced in those tractates that belong to the Thomas tradition. For example, in *The Book of*

---

[305]Hippolytus, *Ref.*, 7.18. Cf. Clement of Alexandria, *Strom.*, 3.12 and 17.

[306]There is considerable debate over the question of Marcion's Gnosticism. Gager has pointed out that: "Marcion's thought is totally devoid of mythological and cosmological speculation, that his higher god is absolutely unrelated to the creator and finally that Marcion has no idea of kinship between man's inner self or spirit and the highest god." See "Marcion and Philosophy" *VC* 26 (1972), 59, fn. 20. A. Harnack, concentrating on these points of contention, among others, was one of the first to tackle these problems. He expressed the view that Marcion stood within the Catholic Christian tradition, a second century Paulinist, who misunderstood Paul. See *Marcion* (Leipzig, 1924). R. S. Wilson, *Marcion: A Study of a Second-Century Heretic* (London, 1933) and E. U. Schüle, "Der Ursprung des Bösen bei Marcion" *ZRGG* 16 (1964), 23-42 have also adopted this position. But the more general trend today is for scholars to support Marcion's Gnostic tendencies, while at the same time affirming the significant influence of Paul. For an overview see Turner, *Pattern of Christian Truth*, 117-124 and E. C. Blackman, *Marcion and his Influence* (London, 1948).

[307]Epiphanius, *Pan.*, 33.5.13.

[308]Doresse, *Secret Books*, 251.

Thomas the Contender (NHC II,7), which is the most ascetic tractate found at Nag Hammadi, a negative attitude towards sex is conspicuous:

Woe to you who hope in the flesh;[309]

Woe to you who love intimacy with womankind and polluted intercourse with it;[310]

Woe to you who beguile your limbs with the fire;[311]

Everyone who seeks the truth from the truly wise one will make himself wings so as to fly, fleeing the lust that scorches the spirits of man.[312]

According to Turner's commentary, the anthropology of *Thomas the Contender* is ascetic and anti-*hylic*.[313] "The moral teaching of Thomas the Contender . . . (is predicated upon) its ascetic character."[314] Turner's interpretation of section 139.2-6 suggests that Thomas condemned the eating of meat.[315] Partaking of the flesh of a lustful body would only propagate bestiality (i.e., a *hylic* nature) because anything deriving from intercourse is itself bestial. Only strict abstinence can free man from the flesh. The polemic of the book of *Thomas the Contender* is directed toward Catholic Christians and their worldly ways, who were viewed by these Gnostics as morally lacking; they were seen as succumbing to profligacy and perishing.[316] Moreover, ideologically these Gnostics rejected the Catholic form of resurrection and accepted a docetist position, arguing that they would be saved by their *pneumatic* ascetic actions.

According to Turner's analysis *The Book of Thomas the Contender* is composed of two sections, A and B, with the final redaction occurring during the latter half of the third century A.D. Section A is in the form of a dialogue and Turner believes it was composed about 200 A.D., whereas

---

[309]NHC II,7:143,10-11.
[310]NHC II,7:144,8-10.
[311]NHC II,7:144,14.
[312]NHC II,7:140,1-4.
[313]J. D. Turner, *The Book of Thomas the Contender* (Society of Biblical Literature, Dissertation Series 23, Missoula, 1970), 226f.
[314]Ibid., 232.
[315]Ibid., 131-136 and 232.
[316]See NHC II,7:140,20-37; 142,10-19; 143,32-39 and 144,37-145,1. Cf. Koschorke, *Die Polemik*, 124f.

he dates the sayings of Jesus (section B) during the first half of the third century.[317] Turner places the dialogue section (section A) in a median position between *The Gospel of Thomas* and *The Acts of Thomas* because of the various literary traditions it contains and the nature of the language used.[318] In contrast, Turner speaks of section B as "a collection of sayings expanded with an (ascetic) interpretation" and says "the interpretation has outgrown the sayings far more than has the gnosticizing interpretation of *The Gospel of Thomas* outgrown the sayings therein."[319]

If Turner's chronological reconstruction is accepted, then *The Acts of Thomas*, tentatively dated between 200-250 A.D.,[320] were composed after section A of *Thomas the Contender*. Here, sexual abstinence is more pronounced.

> Men and women, boys and girls, youths and maids, vigorous and aged, whether you are slaves or free, abstain from fornication and avarice and the service of the belly.[321]

In the bridal chamber Thomas speaks these words: "remember my children. . . . If you abstain from this filthy intercourse, you become holy temples. . . . If you obey, and keep your souls pure for God, you shall have living children."[322] The morning following the bridal night the bride was interrogated by her father because of her unveiled face. She responded, "and I have not had intercourse . . . the end of which is lust and bitterness of soul. . . ."[323] In the Third Act Thomas says, "unless you raise yourselves up from your former conduct and unprofitable practices and the lusts that do not last, from the wealth that is left behind here, from the earthly possessions . . . from the clothes that rot, from the beauty that ages and vanishes . . . [you will be condemned]."[324]

---

[317]Turner, *Thomas the Contender*, 232-238.

[318]Ibid., 236f.

[319]Ibid., 233.

[320]See A. F. J. Klijn, *The Acts of Thomas, Introduction, Text, Commentary* (NovTSup 5, Leiden, 1962). Klijn denies its Gnostic character. See also G. Bornkamm, "The Acts of Thomas" in Hennecke and Schneemelcher, eds., *New Testament Apocrypha*, v. 2, 425-531.

[321]Klijn, *Acts of Thomas*, Second Act, 28.

[322]Ibid., First Act, 12.

[323]Ibid., First Act, 14.

[324]Ibid., Third Act, 37. The predominance of the ascetic strain in Thomas literature is not confined solely to Gnostic tradition, but it is

The Gospel of Thomas is the earliest Thomist piece of literature and thus the least ascetic.[325] Nevertheless, in this gospel several logia center on the rejection of the sexual life as well as on the rejection of the world.[326] For example, logion 27 (NHC II,2:38,17-18) advocates total detachment from the world: "if you fast not from the world, you will not find the kingdom."[327] Logion 112 (NHC II,2:51,10-12) rejects the flesh outright:

Woe to the flesh that depends on the soul;
woe to the soul that depends on the flesh.

And logion 114 (NHC II,2:51,21-22) emphasizes the "obliteration of sex" in which the phrase "I shall make her (Mary) . . . male" is interpreted as referring to the original androgynous unity of mankind.[328] In The Gospel of Thomas the elect are called in Coptic "OUA" (ογα), one (i.e.,

---

indicative of a much more general phenomenon within both Gnostic and Catholic Christianity in Syria. See A. Vööbus, Celibacy, a Requirement for Admission to Baptism in the Early Syrian Church (Papers of the Estonian Theological Society in Exile 1, Stockholm, 1951) and History of Asceticism in the Syrian Orient. A Contribution to the History of Culture in the Near East (CSCO 184, Louvain, 1958-1960), 2 vols.

[325]For the dating of The Gospel of Thomas as early as the mid-second century A.D., see G. Quispel, Makarius. Das Thomasevangelium und das Lied von der Perle (NovTSup 15, Leiden, 1967), A. F. J. Klijn, "Christianity in Edessa and the Gospel of Thomas," NovT 14 (1972), 70-77, H. Koester, "GNŌNAI DIAPHORI: The Origin and Nature of Diversification in the History of Early Christianity" in Robinson and Koester, eds., Trajectories, 114-157 and H.-Ch. Puech, "The Gospel of Thomas" in Hennecke and Schneemelcher, eds., New Testament Apocrypha, v. 1, 278-307. Concerning its doctrinal background, however, there is a wide range of opinion. Puech calls it Gnostic, Quispel Encratite, and Grobel Jewish-Christian (K. Grobel, "How Gnostic is the Gospel of Thomas?," NTS 8 (1961-1962), 367-373). The Gospel of Thomas resembles the synoptic sayings (source 'Q') and some have argued (e.g., Koester) that it has preserved the early traditions independent of the canonical Gospels. For an overview see B. Lincoln, "Thomas-Gospel and Thomas-Community: A New Approach to a Familiar Text," NovT 19 (1977), 65-76, and especially fn. 1.

[326]See Turner, Thomas the Contender, 235.

[327]See Wilson, Gospel of Thomas, 132.

[328]Ibid., 32. Cf. above 222 and fn. 266.

androgynous), which can be equated to the Greek "MONACHUS" (μονα-χος), solitary one, in the sense of a celibate person. [329]

The three Thomas writings mentioned above embrace ascetic themes in varying degrees during the second and third centuries. Ascetic ethics become more prominent in the movement from Tatian (fl. 160 A.D.) to Mani (fl. 260 A.D.). Celibacy is emphasized as a means of decreasing the power of the Archons. The final goal of redemption is the liberation of the Gnostic from his entanglement in earthly appetites.

In *The Paraphrase of Shem*, the theme of asceticism appears several times as a means of liberation: "Those who have a free conscience distance themselves from the babbling of Nature," indicating that those who have chosen Gnosticism and have been 'called' separate themselves from the world.[330] Similarly, the passage "they who will prove to be from her root will strip off the Darkness and the chaotic fire" indicates abstinence from sex since fire is identified with lust.[331] Nature is considered under the domain of the Archons and 'fire' is conceived as their instrument. The need for celibacy is emphasized if man is to curtail the work of the Demiurge.

In *The Gospel of Philip* (NHC II,3) sex is regarded as evil. The separation of woman from man begins the process of death. It is only Christ who can reunite the two in their original androgynous state.[332] Other forms of union (i.e., sexual intercourse) are considered unclean and a distinct antilibertine trend is observed.[333] Even human marriage is considered unclean.[334] Only marriage in the bridal chamber, that is, spiritual

---

[329] Yamauchi, *Gnostic Ethics*, 32.
[330] NHC VII,1:42,24-27.
[331] NHC VII,1:43,21-24.
[332] NHC II,3:70,9-17. There are a great number of Nag Hammadi tractates that emphasize that man and woman were one before the Old Testament God intervened. In addition to *The Gospel of Philip*, see, among others, *The Exegesis on the Soul*, *The Apocalypse of Adam*, *The Letter of Eugnostos the Blessed*, *The Hypostasis of the Archons*, *The Apocryphon of John* and *On the Origin of the World*. For an analysis of the androgynous theme in early Christianity see W. A. Meeks, "The Image of the Androgyne: Some Uses of a Symbol in Earliest Christianity" *HR* 13 (1974), 165-208.
[333] NHC II,3:64,35-65,26.
[334] NHC II,3:82,4-14.

marriage, is legitimate.[335] A similar statement also occurs in *The Exegesis on the Soul* (NHC II,6).[336]

In *The Acts of Peter and the Twelve Apostles* (NHC VI,1) Peter can only obtain the pearls from Christ if he submits to severe asceticism.[337] And a similar theme is present in *Authoritative Teaching* (NHC VI,3) as indicated by the following phrase:

> We go about in hunger (and) in thirst . . . not clinging to the things which have come into being, but withdrawing from them.[338]

So, too, the *Sentences of Sextus* (NHC XII,1) advocate austerity and forbid the indulgence of any bodily appetite beyond what is necessary for life.

The theme of fire as a metaphor for lust mentioned both in *The Book of Thomas the Contender* and in *The Paraphrase of Shem* is a common image in Gnostic asceticism. Yet another example is *The Teachings of Silvanus* (NHC VII,4), which states:

> Do not burn yourself, O miserable one, with the fire of lust.[339]

Along with *The Book of Thomas the Contender,* there are several tractates which emphasize that the Catholic Christians are attached to this material world and will be destroyed with it unless they become ascetic. This ascetically-oriented criticism of the Church is very clearly exhibited, for example, in *The Testimony of Truth.* In this tractate the Gnostics are ideologically opposed to many of the basic tenets of orthodox Christianity (e.g., baptism, carnal resurrection and the value of martyr- dom). "It is by renunciation of [the] world that it (i.e., the baptism of truth) is found."[340] Ignorance traps those who are not ascetic in the cosmic world, and as a result "the pleasures which defile rule over

---

[335]NHC II,3:82,23-26. In other words, the reunion of the *pneumatic* with his heavenly counterpart.

[336]NHC II,6:132,27-35.

[337]See P. Perkins, "Peter in Gnostic Revelation" in *Society of Biblical Literature, 1974 Seminar Papers,* ed. G. MacRae (Cambridge, 1974), v. 2, 1-13. Cf. NHC VI,1:1,1-8,6.

[338]NHC VI,3:27,14-21.

[339]NHC VII,4:108,4-6.

[340]NHC IX,3:69,23-24.

them."[341] For according to these Gnostics, "no one knows the God of truth except solely the man who will forsake all of the things of the world."[342] Only those who are from the generation of the Son of Man are not in ignorance: "he who is able to renounce them (i.e., women) shows [that] he is [from] the generation of the [Son of Man]."[343] The Mosaic Law is discredited as a way of ethical purification. *The Testimony of Truth* is an attempt to convince an audience to adopt the only logical pattern of behaviour capable of destroying the creator God.[344]

Ascetic Gnostics focused on abstention from sexual intercourse in order to purge the world of the Archons and thereby decrease their hold over mankind. By renouncing the cosmic world and the Mosaic Law, including the Old Testament God, the ascetic Gnostic hoped to avoid contamination. The command to be fruitful and multiply (Gen 1:28) was repudiated. Passion, desires and material goods bound man to the cosmic world. Laws, rather than forbidding desires, promoted them. The abstention from meat or wine likewise circumscribed the power of the Demiurge. In other words, the ascetic Gnostic abstained from any act that would perpetuate matter. Unlike the later orthodox Christians who would become ascetic in order to keep their bodies pure for resurrection, the sole purpose of the Gnostic's asceticism was to avoid becoming an accomplice of the Demiurge. The Essenes or later ascetic Christians purified their bodies in order to attain spiritual perfection. It was a positive act. In contrast, the Gnostics were making a negative statement. They were showing total contempt for their bodies and the world. For in negating matter, and in denying procreation, the Gnostics were negating society and its continuation. The ascetic as much as the libertine devalued the world and devoted his efforts to entering the *pleroma*.

Hence, asceticism and libertinism can be seen as complementary rebellious responses, arising from the rejection of the God of the Old Testament and the commandments of Mosaic Law. The fact that both heresiological and Gnostic writings condemned libertinism in no uncertain terms makes it difficult to determine the extent of such practices in either group, but suggests that they must have been present at some time. In either case, the rebellion against Jewish moral law took the form of an

---

[341]NHC IX,3:38,29-39,1.

[342]NHC IX,3:41,4-8.

[343]NHC IX,3:68,8-11.

[344]For ascetic antinomianism in *The Testimony of Truth*, see Koschorke, *Die Polemik*, 108ff.

individualistic ethos which corresponded to the increasing privatization of social and economic life.

4.4.4 Social Structure and Institutionalization

4.4.4.1 Introduction

The combined influence of privatization and individualism can be observed further in the evolution of Gnostic social structures. However, this investigation involves a judicious weighing of incomplete evidence, partially contradictory trends and the internal paradox that Gnosticism as a form of institutionalized belief rests on radically individualist and anti-institutional theological premises. There were numerous Gnostic sects, and they remained disunited, sharing no common framework of doctrinal interpretation. The dualism of spirit and matter preached by Gnostics denied the doctrine of incarnation, and so was heretical from a Catholic Christian standpoint. Their belief that the Old Testament God was evil evoked a similar response from those in rabbinic authority. Yet the Gnostics collectively refused to be identified with a common ideology. Doctrinal orthodoxy was lacking, since Gnostic leaders arose spontaneously from amongst those who had received a 'calling.' Consequently, new directions and interpretations were dependent more on individual charismatic teachers than on authoritative prescription.

In this sense, the experience of *gnosis* was radically anti-institutional. Despite this, however, the fundamental elements of social organization are present both in Gnosticism as an overall movement and in its particular sectarian forms. These elements of Gnostic social structure reflect the interplay between belief, behaviour, communal identity and social position. Using the sociological concept of institutionalization, this section describes those forms of social organization that were considered appropriate by the Gnostics in order to sustain Gnostic behaviour and spread the Gnostic ethos.

4.4.4.2 Institutionalization

Institutionalization is a sociological concept used to explain the process through which habitual actions become socially objectified. It denotes that process through which patterns of behaviour become normative, ideologies become legitimate, and structures to maintain these ideologies permanent. For Gnosticism, this took the form of sectarian development, based on the emergence of charismatic leadership.

For the Gnostics, charisma was manifested in the attribution of extraordinary qualities to certain individuals on the basis of their revelations. The emergence of charisma as a source of new ideas and obligations can be seen as a response to psychic and social dislocation.[345] Gnosticism reflects just such a shattering of normative conventions. Alienated from the dominant social order and marked by spiritual sectarianism, Gnostic sects can be identified as religious groupings characterized by the belief that the spirit is immediately present.[346]

The Gnostic orientation was individualistic, both personally and socially. As a unique vessel of the divine, each individual Gnostic claimed membership in a brotherhood of equals. Gnostic leaders, such as Simon, Basilides, Carpocrates, Valentinus, Heracleon, Ptolemaeus, Marcus and Marsanes all appealed to each person's capacity to receive *gnosis* directly and acquire spiritual independence. Consequently, any form of social organization had to be conceived in terms of a growing individualism, in which emphasis was placed on the continuous exercise of freedom. This meant resolving the tension involved in realizing mystical values through a social institution. This tension was resolved in Gnosticism through rituals, which at the same time structured the experience, ordered the mystical values revealed in *gnosis*, and defined the brotherhood of believers as an organic community with an identifiable social structure.

Gnostic sects reflect a form of *Gemeinschaft* social organization. Formalization, although present, was relatively weak, as social bonds were based on personal ties and emphasis was placed on consensus and informality. For ascetic Gnostics in particular, other sect members became the primary group for all social interaction. Thus, two significant elements stand out in shaping the institutionalization process within Gnosticism: its emphasis on individualism, and its break with religious tradition by attributing authority to 'calling' rather than to office.

Sociologically, sects are defined by the following characteristics: membership is by voluntary association and by proof to those in authority of some special merit; exclusivity is emphasized and there is a self-conception of being part of an elite by virtue of a particularistic claim to

---

[345]Gerth and Mills, eds., *From Max Weber*, 245 and 249. See also Bryan Wilson, *Magic and the Millennium: A Sociological Study of Religious Movements of Protest Among Tribal and Third World Peoples* (London, 1973) and *The Noble Savages: The Primitive Origins of Charisma and its Contemporary Survival* (Berkeley, 1975). Cf. above 174f.

[346]See P. Berger, "The Sociological Study of Sectarianism," *Social Research* 21/4 (1954), 474.

the truth; and there is theoretically a high level of lay participation offering equal priestly status to all believers, although in reality this may not prove to be the case.[347] Bryan Wilson has commented that those sects which lack a centralized structure of community allegiance as a basis for solidarity "must necessarily rely on some form of devised organizational structure,"[348] and has described the minimal criteria needed to regulate the activities of a sectarian movement. These include: criteria to determine who will call meetings, the location of meetings, who will preside over meetings, how new members will be accepted and their worthiness assessed; arrangements for the dissemination of teachings and the socialization of members, both new and old, as well as for making decisions about purely administrative and instrumental concerns; and agencies to maintain solidarity in beliefs and practices, to discipline members for deviance and to deal with external authorities. In other words, the sect has to internalize its own authority and have its members remain apart from the world. Commitment has to be total and identification as a sectarian has to supersede all other role identities. All of these features, both individually and collectively, indicate varying degrees of institutionalization.

Rituals, in particular, are illustrative of the institutionalization process. Rituals are prescriptions for the performance of habitual actions. These actions ground religious ideation in experience, and in turn are legitimized by religious ideology which justifies, explains and reinforces these patterns of behaviour.

Specifically, rituals are designed both to express belief and to bring about desired ends (e.g., salvation). Frequently they connote transitions from one social status to another which are referred to as *rites de passage*. In these rituals, the individual is 'stripped' of his former status and reintegrated into the community with a new status that marks his acceptance. Conversion is probably the most important *rite de passage* that an individual can experience. On the one hand, it is a solitary experience that marks the rebirth of an initiate, bringing him to a more sacred level of existence. From this viewpoint, the ritual produces an ontological transformation in the life of the initiate and constitutes a fundamental

---

[347] These characteristics are taken from Bryan Wilson, "An Analysis of Sect Development," *American Sociological Review* 24 (1959), 3-15. For typologies of religious organization, and in particular sects, see M. Hill, *A Sociology of Religion* (London, 1973), 71-97.

[348] Bryan Wilson, "Introduction" in Bryan Wilson, ed., *Patterns of Sectarianism* (London, 1967), 13.

existential experience.[349] On the other hand, conversion in its institutional form is preeminently a social phenomenon. It demonstrates a disciplinary and preparatory function through which members learn the ideology of the religious movement. It provides for social integration by reinforcing communal solidarity. This implies not only encouraging the integration of the initiate into a new community of believers, but also strengthening the beliefs of fellow worshippers who witness the ritual. Thus, it is misleading to focus attention solely on the act of conversion of the initiate, for the heart of the conversion ritual lies in the collective celebration of all who have participated.[350]

In addition, rituals demonstrate the division of labour within the collectivity and denote the existence of hierarchy and status stratification. Some members will have a greater degree of authority than others, and be more influential in defining the rules governing organizational behaviour and formulating ideology. Usually, several of these members with higher status will help prepare the specialized educational programs for initiates who are to be converted and guide members who wish to acquire further knowledge of their religion. The educational programs as well as the rituals may become codified in order that they may be passed from generation to generation, thereby avoiding ideological conflicts over oral interpretations. Through such a process, those in authority are able to exercise social control. Finally, mention should be made of the fact that rituals also involve sacred objects, special symbols, prayers, words, and locations, as well as specific behavioural roles, all of which further legitimate the prescribed order of habitual actions. Rituals, therefore, are instrumental in the continual socialization processes of new and old participants. They reiterate right attitudes, reinforce the solidarity of the group and heighten the member's state of self-consciousness concerning his own identity.

By comparison with Gnostic Christian sects, the rituals of non-Christian Gnostics show little structure and provide only sparse evidence of institutionalization. In Gnostic Christianity, the data reveal an institutional structure that reinforced the developing ideology; it may be inferred that whereas Gnostic Christian sects tended towards asceticism

---

[349]See M. Eliade, *Rites and Symbols of Initiation*, trans. W. R. Trask (New York, 1965) and *The Sacred and the Profane*, trans. W. R. Trask (New York, 1959).

[350]See V. Turner, *The Ritual Process: Structure and Anti-Structure* (London, 1970).

and well-developed social structures, non-Christian Gnostic sects, especially if they gravitated towards libertinism, would by definition have been less structured.

From a sociological viewpoint, Gnostic Christianity was better organized, more stratified, had a greater degree of social solidarity and was more ideologically standardized than non-Christian Gnosticism. Its structure was supported by established rituals, and social cohesion was strengthened by the development of a common ideology. These were the means for the social control of its members. The lack of data prevents a reliable comparative analysis of non-Christian Gnostic and Gnostic Christian institutionalization processes or even of Sethian and Valentinian social organization. Consequently, the following section will explore only Valentinian Gnosticism (i.e., Gnostic Christianity), and in particular its rituals, as a means of probing the Gnostic institutionalization process.

4.4.4.3   Valentinian Social Structure

Valentinus, the reputed founder of the movement that bears his name, flourished in Alexandria and Rome c. 135 A.D.-c. 160 A.D. Little is known of the man except for a few mutilated scraps which the heresiological polemics provide. Circumstantial evidence suggests that Valentinus was born in Egypt c. 100 A.D. and was raised in Alexandria where he absorbed Hellenisitic culture, Jewish and Christian beliefs and Gnostic ideology. In c. 140 A.D., he migrated to Rome and shortly thereafter, according to Tertullian, was nearly declared bishop.[351] Although it is impossible to assess the historical accuracy of Tertullian's account, Hippolytus states that Valentinus maintained that he had experienced a revelation and that the *logos* had appeared to him. Valentinus "saw a newborn child, and when he asked who he might be, the child answered, 'I am the *Logos*.'"[352] As a result, Valentinus had been 'called' and possessed *gnosis*. Valentinus' conviction that he had *gnosis* made him a fervent missionary of the Gnostic cause, a cause which appropriated Christian territory yet identified itself as Gnostic. Moreover, according to Clement of Alexandria, Valentinus asserted that his interpretation of Christianity was part of a legitimate tradition that stretched from his teacher, Theudas, a disciple of Paul.[353] It would be reasonable to postulate that

---

[351]Tertullian, *Adv. Val.*, 4.
[352]Hippolytus, *Ref.*, 6.42.2.
[353]Clement of Alexandria, *Strom.*, 7.17. Cf. Above 227 and fn. 291.

Valentinus acted as an irritant to many Catholic Christians and weakened his own opportunities to advance hierarchically in the second century Catholic Church. Consequently, even if Tertullian's account is disregarded, there is reason to believe that Valentinus' ideological beliefs and practices were perceived by many as marginal or deviant to the growing normative consensus of Catholic Christianity.

Yet in spite of his marginal Christian status, Valentinus was a charismatic leader who was able to attract and mobilize numerous pupils and disciples.[354] Over time, these disciples both developed and transformed the tradition that had begun with Paul and was modified by Valentinus. These disciples have been classified into two categories—Oriental (i.e., Eastern Mediterranean) and Western (i.e., Italian)—depending on the content of their works.[355] For example, of the many charismatic disciples listed by Tertullian,[356] Ptolemaeus and his student Heracleon would be representative of the Western sub-group, whereas Theodotus, who is mentioned by Clement of Alexandria in the *Excerpta ex Theodoto*, would be representative of the Oriental. In addition to these disciples, other followers include Florinus, a teacher in Rome, and Marcus, a magician who may have lived in Asia Minor. All these disciples, as well as Valentinus himself, use Paul extensively but selectively.[357]

The Nag Hammadi library further reinforces the heresiologists' observations that the influence of the Valentinians was widespread throughout the Mediterranean world. Approximately twenty-five per cent of the library has been identified by several scholars as being tentatively of Valentinian origin or as having affinities to Valentinianism.[358] A handful

---

See also *The Gospel of Philip for reference to a historical tradition that stretches from Jesus to the apostles and the Valentinians (NHC II, 3:74, 16-18).*

[354]See, for example, Tertullian, *Adv. Val.,* 4, Irenaeus, *Adv. Haer.,* 1.11.1-13.6 and Hippolytus, *Ref.,* 6.35.5.

[355]This is based on Hippolytus' account in *Ref.,* 6.35.5.

[356]Tertullian, *Adv. Val.,* 4.

[357]See Pagels, *Gnostic Paul.*

[358]These include *The Prayer of the Apostle Paul* (NHC I,1), *The Apocryphon of James* (NHC I,2), *The Gospel of Truth* (NHC I,3), *The Treatise on Resurrection* (NHC I,4), *The Tripartite Tractate* (NHC I,5), *The Gospel of Philip* (NHC II,3) *The Exegesis on the Soul* (NHC II,6), *The First Apocalypse of James* (NHC V,3), *Authoritative Teaching* (NHC VI,3), *The Second Treatise of the Great Seth* (NHC VII,2) *The Interpretation of Knowledge* (NHC XI,1) and *A Valentinian Exposition* (NHC XI,2). There is debate over whether several of these tractates, given the evidence, can be jus-

of scholars have suggested that two of these tractates may have been written by Valentinus himself, *The Gospel of Truth* (NHC I,3 and XII,2) and *The Treatise on Resurrection* (NHC I,4),[359] while for a third, the hypothesis has been advanced that the author may be Heracleon (*The Tripartite Tractate*),[360] a disciple of Valentinus. The dates offered for the Valentinian tractates from the library range from the mid-second century to the close of the third century A.D.

In brief, the influence of Valentinus was widespread from Egypt eastward to Syria and Asia Minor, and westward to Rome and North Africa. Valentinus appeared before there was a New Testament canon and his

---

tifiably identified as Valentinian or even as having affinities to Valentinianism. Among those who favour a Valentinian interpretation of the disputed texts, see *The Apocryphon of James* (H.-Ch. Puech and G. Quispel, "Les écrits gnostiques du codex Jung," *VC* 8 (1954), 21-22); *The Gospel of Truth* (H.-Ch. Puech and G. Quispel, "Les écrits gnostiques," 31 and 39 as well as W. C. van Unnik, "The 'Gospel of Truth' and the New Testament" in *The Jung Codex*, ed. F. L. Cross (London, 1955), 79-129); *The Exegesis on the Soul* (M. Krause, "The Exegesis on the Soul" in Foerster, ed., *Gnosis*, v. 2, 102-109; M. Krause, "Die Sakramente in der 'Exegese über die Seele,'" in Ménard, ed., *Les textes*, 47-55 and J. E. Ménard, "L'Évangile selon Philippe et l'Exégèse de l'Âme," in Ménard, ed., *Les textes*, 56-67); *The First Apocalypse of James* (W. R. Schoedel, "Scripture and the Seventy-Two Heavens of the First Apocalypse of James," *NovT* 12 (1970), 118-129); *Authoritative Teaching* (J. E. Ménard, *L'Authentikos Logos* (Bibliothèque Copte de Nag Hammadi 2, Laval, 1977), 4ff.); and *The Second Treatise of the Great Seth* (J. Gibbons, "The Second Logos of the Great Seth: Considerations and Questions" in Society of Biblical Literature, 1973 Seminar Papers, ed. G. MacRae (Cambridge, 1973), v. 2, 242-261.

[359] For *The Gospel of Truth* with Valentinus as author, see W. C. van Unnik, "Gospel of Truth" in Cross, ed., *Jung Codex*, 99 and 103; K. Grobel, *The Gospel of Truth* (New York, 1960), 27; and Grant, *Gnosticism*, 128ff. For *The Treatise on Resurrection* only H.-Ch. Puech and G. Quispel, the first editors, have offered the hypothesis that Valentinus may have been the author. See M. Malinine, H.-Ch. Puech, G. Quispel, W. C. Till, eds., *De Resurrectione. Epistula ad Rheginum* (Zurich, 1963), xxxiii. Cf. G. Quispel, "The Jung Codex and its Significance" in *Gnostic Studies*, v.1, 12ff.

[360] See R. Kasser, M. Malinine, H.-Ch. Puech, G. Quispel, J. Zandee, W. Vycichl and R. McL. Wilson, eds., *Tractatus Tripartitus, Pars I, De Supernis* (Bern, 1973), 37 for Quispel's and Puech's hypothesis. Cf. Quispel, "Jung Codex" in *Gnostic Studies*, v. 1, 16.

disciples were still active in the fourth century A.D. after Constantine had proclaimed the Roman Empire to be Christian.

This sketch of the historical and geographical setting of Valentinianism is pieced together from incomplete evidence; data on individual biographies, historical developments and particular social contexts are scattered and disjointed. Nevertheless, it is possible to view Valentinian Gnosticism as an umbrella under which several Gnostic sects developed. These would include those founded by Valentinus, Ptolemaeus, Heracleon, Theodotus and Marcus, as well as others (in the Nag Hammadi writings) that have yet to be classified, but which demonstrate affinities to Valentinian ideology. Thus, all these religious movements, although uncoordinated, have a standard reference point—Valentinus—and have been collectively identified as Valentinian both by the Church Fathers and by modern religious scholars.

This situation may be compared to that of Protestantism. Like Protestantism, Valentinian Gnosticism may have served as an umbrella for several religious movements that shared a common ideology but were uncoordinated in practice. To be labelled a Protestant is to be defined as a non-Catholic. Similarly, to be labelled a Valentinian was to be identified as non-Catholic. 'Protestant' is a generic term that refers to members of any of the Christian sectarian off-shoots which separated from the Roman Catholic community in and after the Reformation. Similarly, 'Valentinian' was a generic term that referred to Christian sectarian movements that separated from the Catholic Christian community in the wake of Valentinus and shared ideological affinities with his Gnostic system. Many Protestant movements were small and localized, their affiliation to each other being minimal or non-existent. Similarly, even though the evidence is sparse, it appears that the various Valentinian off-shoots were localized and lacked associational links to a regional or universal community.

In both cases, this may be explained in part through a sociological interpretation. Ethnicity and communal identity are important determinants of sectarian allegiance and solidarity.[361] In both Protestant and Valentinian religious movements, an initial lack of centralization

---

[361]For an excellent historical-sociological study of how ethnicity and communal identity are important determinants of sectarian allegiance and solidarity, see N. Cohn, *The Pursuit of the Millennium* (London, 1970) who has investigated millenarian movements between the eleventh and sixteenth centuries.

encouraged strong lay involvement and a tradition of independent religious thinking. Yet in spite of the diversity of the Protestant movements, Protestantism is frequently considered and examined as a self-contained entity. It is not that scholars have ignored or lost sight of the fact that 'Protestant' is a generic term and that each movement may have evolved in a completely unique manner depending on its particular historical, socio-structural circumstances; rather, it is the common origins that are being stressed. This may be in order to explore common features, structural characteristics or ideologies, to understand the institutionalization process, or to compare other religions to Protestantism. Similarly, Valentinian Gnosticism can be studied as an integrated whole, without dismissing the differences among particular Valentinian Gnostic movements.

Valentinus was the leading Gnostic figure in the period of mid-second century A.D. spiritual sectarian developments.[362] Valentinus and his disciples represent a body of sectarian movements within the developing Christian Church. If these movements are combined for analytical purposes, they exhibit a mosaic of features that provide evidence of Valentinian sectarian institutionalization. From this perspective each Valentinian movement may have evolved in a different way, while at the same time developing the structural characteristics of an institutionalized sect. Unlike Catholic Christianity, however, which increasingly solidified and emphasized the office as paramount, Valentinian Gnosticism continued to place emphasis on the charismatic individual within the institutionalized sect.

The Letter of Ptolemaeus to Flora provides a starting point for examining Valentinian Gnosticism as an institutionalized sect. Throughout this letter, it is implied that Flora is voluntarily seeking information about Valentinianism; this is explicitly stated at the end of the letter when Ptolemaeus encourages Flora to continue her pursuit of Valentinian doctrines.[363] An individual's voluntary choice to become a member of a Valentinian sectarian movement is also disclosed in *The Apocryphon of James* and *The Gospel of Philip*. In *The Apocryphon of James*, one saves oneself from Satan only through individual choice.[364] Thus, if James was to be saved, he had to make the appropriate decision voluntarily.

---

[362]See Hippolytus, *Ref.*, 6.42.2 in Foerster, *Gnosis*, v. 1, 243: "Then he [i.e., Valentinus] added to this an imposing myth and on this he wants to base the 'sect' that was founded by him."
[363]Epiphanius, *Pan.*, 33.7.10.
[364]NHC I,2:5,6.

Similarly, in *The Gospel of Philip*, potential members attain Valentinian Christian membership only if "they have acquired it on their own."[365]

In Valentinian Gnosticism, all potential adherents had to be perceived as having *gnosis* if they were to be accepted as members. In practical terms, this meant an acquaintance with a special body of esoteric teaching which offered a new interpretation of Christian doctrine. For example, in *The Gospel of Truth*, the author speaks of "Knowledge of the living book" and of letters which are not merely vowels and consonants, but "letters of the truth which one does not pronounce unless one knows them."[366] Having *gnosis* resulted in being identified by fellow believers as *pneumatic* and part of a spiritual elite.

> We are elected to salvation and redemption since we are predestined from the beginning not to fall into the foolishness of those who are without knowledge, but we shall enter into the wisdom of those who have known the truth.[367]

> If one has knowledge, he is from above. If he is called, he hears, he answers, and he turns to him who is calling him, and ascends to him.[368]

Thus Valentinian Gnostics viewed their relationships to God as exclusive and denied spiritual legitimacy to those who did not reinforce and publicly affirm their ideological beliefs.

> But if there is one who does not believe, he does not have the (capacity to be) persuaded.[369]

> It remains for us who have been counted worthy of the knowledge . . . to provide you with an accurate and clear account of the nature of the law. . . .[370]

> Truth, . . . is sown everywhere . . . but few are they who see it as it is reaped.[371]

---

[365]NHC II,3:67,19-21.
[366]NHC I,3:22,38-23,10.
[367]NHC I,4:46,25-32.
[368]NHC I,3:22,3-7.
[369]NHC I,4:46,3-5.
[370]Epiphanius, *Pan.*, 33.3.8.
[371]NHC II,3:55,19-22.

Finally, concerning the high level of lay participation, attention should be drawn to the writings of Irenaeus and Tertullian. Irenaeus' description of the Marcosians drawing lots to see who will prophesy has led Pagels to suggest that "the drawing of lots demonstrates . . . that no such distinctions of fixed orders divide the participants . . . within a hierarchy of spiritual authority."[372] Similarly, Tertullian notes that the heretics enjoyed a high degree of lay participation: "it is uncertain who is a catechumen, and who is a believer; they all have access equally. . . ."[373] These comments by Tertullian are followed by an even more revealing passage:

> today one man is bishop and tomorrow another; the person who is deacon today, tomorrow is a reader; the one who is a presbyter today is a layman tomorrow; for even on the laity they impose the functions of priesthood.[374]

Pagels has interpreted Tertullian's remarks to intimate that the Valentinian Gnostics upheld "the principles of equal access, equal participation and equal claims to gnosis. . . ."[375]

This brief description identifies the sectarian features of Valentinian Gnosticism. These characteristics not only indicate that Valentinian Gnosticism can be classified as a sect, but, more importantly, provide clues that the institutionalization process generated organizational structures. For example, if Valentinian sectarian movements were to flourish, they needed members to survive. Consequently, like the Catholic Christians, they must have been engaged in activities such as missionary work to "teach those who will receive teaching."[376] However, different Valentinian movements applied different degrees of control in determining how this knowledge could be shared. In The Interpretation of Knowledge (NHC XI,1), it is stated that this teaching should be passed on indiscriminately:

---

[372]E. Pagels, "'The Demiurge and his Archons'—A Gnostic View of the Bishop and Presbyters," HTR 69 (1976), 317f.

[373]Tertullian, De Praescriptione Haereticorum 41. Cf. Pagels, "Demiurge and his Archons," 318.

[374]Tertullian, De Praescriptione Haereticorum 41. Cf. Pagels, "Demiurge and his Archons," 318f.

[375]Pagels, "Demiurge and his Archons," 318.

[376]NHC I,3:21,2.

"Does someone have a prophetic gift? Share it without hesitation."[377] In contrast to *The Interpretation of Knowledge* is *The Apocryphon of James*, where, on the surface, it appears that missionary activity is more discriminate. In this tractate, the teaching is secret and the recipient of the letter is told explicitly to "take care not to rehearse this text to many. . . ."[378] This passage may indicate that the recipient of the letter should be careful as to whom he approaches and must judge the quantity of knowledge that he can surrender in his missionary work, until he is absolutely certain of the initiate's commitment to the religion. Thus, what seems to be lack of missionary activity is in fact a combination of precautionary advice regarding the selection of prospective initiates, and an indication of appropriate recruitment procedures. As Etzioni has stated, sectarian selectivity is "positively associated with the intensity of commitment of the average participant."[379]

The effort by Valentinians to acquire new members in all likelihood led to some degree of consensus within each sect regarding ideological development and the codification of writings. Irenaeus intimates as much when he comments that "they bring forward an innumerable quantity of apocryphal and spurious writings, which they themselves have forged. . . ."[380] Similarly, Epiphanius, as an aside, informs us that they (i.e., the Valentinians) follow "the order of their [own] books."[381] In *The Interpretation of Knowledge,* there is a reference to "another school [that] indeed [sets apart many] writings," writings through which initiates are taught about their death.[382] And in *The First Apocalypse of James* (NHC V,3) James is to transmit the revelations to Addai, who will "sit and write them down" and pass them on.[383] In addition, some of the Valentinians, such as Ptolemaeus and Marcus, utilized portions of the Evangelists and the Apostles, the Torah and the Prophets, according to their own allegorical principles. This is not only attested to by the Church Fathers,[384] but is

---

[377]NHC XI,1:15,35-37.

[378]NHC I,2:1,21-22.

[379]A. Etzioni, *A Comparative Analysis of Complex Organizations* (New York, 1961), 156.

[380]Irenaeus, *Adv. Haer.,* 1.20.1.

[381]Epiphanius, *Pan.,* 31.5.1.

[382]NHC XI,1:9,23-27.

[383]NHC V,3:36,22-23.

[384]For example, Irenaeus, *Adv. Haer.,* 1.3.6 and 1.20.2 and Epiphanius, *Pan.,* 33.3.1-7.10.

also confirmed by the Valentinian Nag Hammadi tractates.[385] These codified writings (i.e., the Old and New Testaments, as well as Gnostic literature) imply that the Valentinian Gnostic movements had a sacred literary tradition.

The most visible reason for creating such a literary tradition is to promote religious cohesion. However, a sacred literary tradition also reveals that certain individuals felt the need to regulate the activities of members within their respective movements. A sacred literary tradition ensures transmission from generation to generation, a *Begrundung*, for later interpretation by those who will gravitate to become the movement's spokesmen. In addition, it implies that there is some arrangement for the dissemination of teachings and agencies in order to control who receives knowledge and in what manner. Thus, in spite of the fact there there may have been a high degree of lay participation in several of the Valentinian movements, there must also have been some form of hierarchical authority to make administrative, instrumental and ideological decisions.[386] Of particular importance would be those individuals who educated the new initiates and assisted members who wished to deepen their knowledge of the sect's beliefs. For example, The Letter of Ptolemaeus to Flora may represent an instructional manual on certain theological themes required for all initiates. Moreover, if this assumption is correct, this letter may provide evidence that the instruction period was systematized and standardized in a manner which involved progressive stages prior to and after the initiation ritual. It is in this context that a more general meaning may be given to the following words:

> If God permit, you will learn in the future about their origin [of different natures] and generation, when you are counted worthy of the apostolic tradition which we also have received by succession, because we can prove all our statements from the teaching of the Saviour.[387]

The notion of succession further reinforces the assumption that there were both organizational and hierarchical structures. Similarly, one can

---

[385]For example, see NHC I,3, NHC I,4 NHC II,3 and NHC XI,1.

[386]For the relationship between hierarchical authority and charismatic leadership see Gerth and Mills, eds., *From Max Weber*, 245-252.

[387]Epiphanius, *Pan.*, 33.7.9.

postulate that this is the case in *The Apocryphon of James,* because Cerinthos is advised to be careful of how he instructs new initiates.[388]

The above discussion has shown that the Valentinian Gnostic evidence supports the argument that there was a need to teach the new initiates the ideology of Valentinianism and the appropriate patterns of behaviour before they became *bona fide* members. Additional data further support this contention. Along with the various statements by Ptolemaeus to Flora,[389] in *The Tripartite Tractate* those who are not instructed "are unable to know the course of things which exist."[390] It is only instruction that brings freedom, and "freedom is the knowledge of the truth which existed before."[391] Thus, in spite of the Gnostic emphasis on direct knowledge—"[salvation] is due not to rote phrases or to professional skills or to book learnings"[392]—when religious ideology is translated into everyday practice, the *pneumatics,* the elect, need instruction. Consequently, Valentinian instruction can appeal to all kinds of people:

> a way for those who were lost and knowledge for those who were ignorant, a discovery for those who were searching, and a support for those who were wavering.[393]

Further, should they not understand the instruction, they are encouraged to probe deeper and ask questions. Thus, in *The Treatise on Resurrection* should Rheginos or his fellow-believers not understand "one thing written . . . [the author] shall interpret it for you when you ask,"[394] and thereby further teach them about death and the afterlife. In all of these examples, there is evidence of a teacher who knows and an initiate who does not, a person who is considered authoritative and another who is labeled a novice.

An example of the use of instruction and the existence of organizational and hierarchical structure exists in *The Gospel of Philip.* In one saying, an analogy is created between a householder who knows the foods

---

[388]NHC I,2:1,18-28. Cf. H.-M. Schenke, "Der Jakobusbrief aus dem Codex Jung," *OLZ* 66 (1971), 119 for the identification of the instructor as Cerinthos.

[389]For example, Epiphanius, *Pan.,* 33.3.8; 4.1; and 7.10.

[390]NHC I,5:109,3-4.

[391]NHC I,5:117,28-29.

[392]NHC II,6:134,30-32.

[393]NHC I,3:31,28-34.

[394]NHC I,4:50,5-8.

appropriate for his animals and the members of his household and provides accordingly for them, and the disciple who knows the spiritual needs of men and gives to each accordingly. Following this analogy, beasts represent the *hylics*, slaves the *psychics* and children the *pneumatics*, each receiving the elements of doctrine according to their level of understanding.[395] From a sociological perspective, this is suggestive evidence that those in authority in a Valentinian movement may have differentiated between different kinds of members-to-be, and in so doing established a series of stages of ideological instruction. Only those who were identified as *pneumatic*, that is, as having special merit, and whose commitment was total, earned the opportunity to become sect members with the accompanying social status. Thus, the exclusive nature of the sect is reinforced, while at the same time those in authority are able to exercise social control by maintaining that there are different stages of instruction and achievement for potential members.

Ritual in many ways typifies and best exemplifies these developments. It accentuates the transition from random, undifferentiated behaviour to behaviour where there is a prescribed order for performing habitual actions. Moreover, rituals support socialization processes by requiring actions that symbolically reaffirm man's sacred level of existence, as well as his membership in the collectivity.

There is a great deal of evidence concerning the rituals employed in Valentinian Gnosticism. Baptism, chrism, redemption, eucharist and bridal chamber rituals were present, as well as special prayers. The most informative list of rituals exists in *The Gospel of Philip*. "The Lord [did] everything in a mystery, a baptism and a chrism and a eucharist and a redemption and a bridal chamber."[396] There is evidence in this gospel of rites dealing with the descent and divesting of clothes before water baptism:

> When he is about to go down into the water, he unclothes himself, in order that he may put on the living man[397]

and the investing of baptismal robes upon ascent.[398] The rituals were also

---

[395]NHC II,3:80,23-81,14. See R. McL. Wilson, *The Gospel of Philip* (London, 1962), 178f. for this interpretation.

[396]NHC II,3:67,27-30.

[397]NHC II,3:75,23-24.

[398]NHC II,3:57,11-22. Cf. E. Segelberg, "The Baptismal Rite According to Some of the Coptic-Gnostic Texts of Nag Hammadi," in *Studia Patristica*, ed., F. L. Cross (TU 80, Berlin, 1962), 126.

stratified: chrism was more important than baptism;[399] the redemption was also more important than baptism, and the bridal chamber was considered the most important of all:

> Baptism is 'the Holy' building. Redemption is 'the Holy of Holy'. The 'Holy of the Holies' is the bridal chamber. Baptism includes the resurrection [and the] redemption; the redemption (takes place) in the bridal chamber. But the bridal chamber is in that which is superior to [it and the others]. . . .[400]

This suggests a standardized and traditional procedure with which to initiate novices and instruct members through different stages of Gnostic teaching. Moreover, *The Gospel of Philip* reveals many small details: that the oil of chrism was from the olive tree;[401] that the trinitarian formula was recited with the anointing;[402] that the eucharist involved the use of bread, cup (i.e., wine and water) and oil;[403] that a kiss may have been instrumental with the bridal chamber ritual;[404] and that a collection of prayers may have been recited.[405]

As mentioned previously, conversion is probably the most important *rite de passage* that an individual experiences. In *The Exegesis on the Soul* conversion is identified with baptism and compared to the washing of a dirty garment.

> When the womb of the soul . . . turns itself inward, it is baptized and is immediately cleansed of the external pollution . . . just as [garments, when] dirty, are put into the [water and] turned about until their dirt is removed and they become clean. . . . The cleansing of the soul is to regain the [newness] of her former nature. . . .[406]

In *The Gospel of Philip,* it is the chrism ritual which separates the initiate

---

[399]NHC II,3:74,12-18.

[400]NHC II,3:69,22-28.

[401]NHC II,3:73,18-19.

[402]NHC II,3:67,19-27.

[403]NHC II,3:75,1 and 14-21.

[404]NHC II,3:59,2-6. Cf. E. Segelberg, "The Coptic-Gnostic Gospel According to Philip and Its Sacramental System," *Numen* 7 (1960), 198.

[405]See E. Segelberg, "Prayer Among the Gnostics" in *Gnosis and Gnosticism*, ed. M. Krause (NHS 8, Leiden, 1977), 56ff.

[406]NHC II,6:131,27-132,1.

from his former status. The novice is transformed from the flesh to one who "possessed everything. He possesses the resurrection, the light, the cross, the Holy Spirit."[407] The conversion experience is dependent both on the novice's sharing the symbolic universe of beliefs and experiencing the rite before the community who collectively celebrate it. Both the proper instruction (i.e., knowing what to do) and participation in the ritual is mandatory. Without them, "it is not possible for anyone to see anything of the things that actually exist."[408] In *The Gospel of Philip*, the chrism ritual confers the status of membership on the initiate and reinforces the ideology and status of old members through their participation in the ritual. The sacrament itself testifies that the initiate has achieved special merit and that he has exhibited and subscribed to Valentinian normative patterns of behaviour. Thus, the initiate passes from the secular to the sacred religiously and socially. Conversion offers a metamorphosis in social identity whereby one's identification as a sectarian supersedes all other role identities, and provides a new reference group for support.

It is clear that initiates needed to learn specific patterns of behaviour, appropriate attitudes and proper procedures for membership in the sect. This in turn implies an hierarchical division of labour within each movement to convey the necessary information and to exercise social control. Each ritual would require teachers who were knowledgeable and who could prepare and administer the appropriate sacrament to those who were less than perfect. How and whether the initiate in Valentinian Gnosticism became socially equal to the person who administered the sacrament is not explained. It is evident, however, that different individuals have varying social status even within a priesthood of all believers and the devaluation of status distinctions. Thus, in summary, it would appear that Valentinianism possessed a structure similar to that of developing Catholic Christianity and may have posed a real threat to it.

Two other Valentinian Nag Hammadi tractates also merit attention as they provide further information about the Valentinian institutionalization process. In *The Gospel of Truth*, chrism again is given foremost importance, and the anointing of initiates is described.[409] Segelberg believes not only that *The Gospel of Truth* is a confirmation homily which focuses on chrism, but also "that there are some ceremonies belonging to baptism-chrism which are certain: divesting, baptism in water, investiture, unction

---

[407]NHC II,3:74,19-21.
[408]NHC II,3:61,20-21.
[409]NHC I,3:36,13-20.

with holy oil, raising up. . . .[And] other rites which are more or less likely to have belonged to the ritual: exorcism, turning, stretching out of the hand, insufflation. . . ."[410] Although caution is required in accepting Segelberg's assessment,[411] several ritualized elements are present which are indicative of organizational and hierarchical structure.

The second Valentinian Nag Hammadi tractate is *A Valentinian Exposition* (NHC XI,2), which contains baptismal, anointing and eucharist benedictions. According to Pagels, the Valentinian exposition "offers a kind of secret catechism for candidates being initiated into gnosis."[412] It is obvious when reading these Valentinian Gnostic benedictions that they were standardized and that the conferring of a new status by conversion through participation in the ritual was an important feature of the attainment of *gnosis*.

Evidence of rituals in other Valentinian writings, whether by the Church Fathers describing the Gnostics, or by the Gnostics themselves, is also available. For example, in *The Tripartite Tractate,* baptism is referred to as "the redemption into God, Father, Son and Holy Spirit, when confession is made through faith in those names."[413] It is from this ritual that it has been suggested by the first editors that the sacrament of redemption is derived.[414] In the *Excerpta ex Theodoto,* baptism is considered to be part of the process that brings freedom,[415] and the following context suggests that it is also linked to the revealing of Divine Names.

He who has been sealed by the invocation of the Father and the Son and the Holy Spirit will not be attacked by other powers, and by the three Names he is cleansed from the triad of corruption.[416]

---

[410]Segelberg, "Baptismal Rite," 123f.

[411]See Wilson's comments in *Gnosis,* 92.

[412]See E. Pagel's introduction to this tractate in Robinson, ed., *Nag Hammadi Library,* 435.

[413]NHC I,5:127,30-34.

[414]R. Kasser, M. Malinine, H.-Ch. Puech, G. Quispel, J. Zandee, W. Vycichl and R. McL. Wilson, eds., *Tractatus Tripartitus, Pars II, De Creatione Hominis, Pars III, De Generibus Tribus,* (Bern, 1975), 229f.

[415]Clement of Alexandria, *Exc. ex Theod.,* 78.1-2.

[416]Clement of Alexandria, *Exc. ex Theod.,* 80.3.

Heracleon mentions the need to baptize,[417] and according to Clement of Alexandria's description of Heracleon's system, the ritual involved marking "with fire the ears of those who are sealed."[418]

Pagels has commented that the water-baptism outlined by Heracleon is only for those of the prophetic order,[419] and that this should be interpreted solely on the *somatic* level. According to Pagels, the Valentinians applied a threefold (i.e., *somatic, psychic, spiritual*) distinction between the sacraments of baptism as a polemic against the *psychic* Christians (i.e., Catholic Christians). In her view, the Valentinians differentiated between *psychic* baptism and *pneumatic* redemption. Only those who were *pneumatic* could receive the "higher baptism of Christ" which is redemption. "This higher baptism 'of Christ' has nothing whatever to do with either the physical washing or the psychic cleansing from sins. Instead it 'perfects the spirit' in those who are the elect. . . . It consists of initiation into the highest gnosis. . . ."[420] By employing Irenaeus' account of Marcus and applying this in an analogous fashion to Heracleon in order to suggest the formulae for redemption, Pagels was able to conclude that there was a liturgical tradition common to several Gnostic groups.[421] She then goes on to demonstrate how the eucharist ritual has been similarly reinterpreted by Heracleon and that behind it also lay a common Gnostic tradition.[422] Thus, although it is tangential to her argument, Pagels has endorsed the thesis that there may have been a common liturgical and cult tradition for several Valentinian Gnostic sects. Moreover, if Pagels' suppositions are accepted, Heracleon would have had to employ rituals that involved a complex structure and required instruction to learn; and if this is the case then organizational and hierarchical structure would have gone hand in hand with the arrangements for the dissemination of teachings.

Prayers also played a significant role in Valentinianism. The formulae

---

[417] Origen, *In Joannem*, 6.23.

[418] Clement of Alexandria, *Eclogae Propheticae*, 25.1.

[419] Pagels, "A Valentinian Interpretation of Baptism and Eucharist—and its Critique of 'Orthodox' Sacramental Theology and Practice," *HTR* 65/2 (1972), 154.

[420] Ibid., 157.

[421] Ibid., 158-161. Cf. Irenaeus, *Adv. Haer.*, 1.13.1-21.5.

[422] Pagels, "A Valentinian Interpretation," 165-168. Cf. Pagels, *Johannine Gospel*, 51-82.

in *The First Apocalypse of James*[423] are similar to those passed on by Irenaeus in his description of the Marcosians[424] although, as pointed out by Schoedel, "the cultic context provided by the heresiologists is lacking [in the former]."[425] In the *Exegesis on the Soul* the act of praying is mentioned several times:

> It is therefore fitting to pray to the Father and to call on him with all our soul—not externally with the lips, but with the spirit . . . repenting for the life we lived; confessing our sins. . . .[426]

> It is fitting to pray to God night and day, as one who is afloat in the middle of the sea prays to God with his whole heart.[427]

The Gospel of Philip also expresses the need to pray[428] as does *The Prayer of the Apostle Paul*[429] and *The Apocryphon of James*.[430] And as mentioned above, *A Valentinian Exposition* provides detailed evidence of anointing, baptismal and eucharist prayers.

> [We give] thanks [to thee and we celebrate the eucharist]. . . . [Glory] be to thee through the Son [and] thy offspring Jesus Christ [forever and] forever. Amen.[431]

Mention should also be made of Irenaeus' account of Marcus and of Clement of Alexandria's report on Valentinian rituals, which may refer to the practices of Theodotus. Marcus can be viewed as a prototypical charismatic leader. His system of salvation and the rituals he formulated were, in all likelihood, interpretations of those practised by Christians. Nevertheless, they facilitated the development of his charisma and ensured the maintenance of his authority. For example, his eucharist consisted of invocations and magical ceremonies that encouraged

---

[423]NHC V,3:33,11-35,25.

[424]Irenaeus, *Adv. Haer.*, 1.21.5.

[425]W. Schoedel, "The (First) Apocalypse of James" in Parrott, ed., *Nag Hammadi Codices*, 66.

[426]NHC II,6:135,4-10.

[427]NHC II,6:136,16-20.

[428]For example, see NHC II,3:68,10-12.

[429]NHC I,1:A,1-B,10.

[430]NHC I,2:11,30-32.

[431]NHC XI,2:43,20-38.

everyone, and in particular women, to prophesy. This in turn led to the use of aphrodisiacs with which he seduced women. Irenaeus, while describing this ritual, furnishes many of the formulae chanted, including those used in the performance of the initiation, or by the initiates in response, as well as the appropriate responses by the congregation.[432] There are data about various rituals, including baptism, redemption and prayers for the dying, in addition to a great many details about sacred objects and language. The format of these rituals implies that there existed status differentiation and organizational structure. Moreover, Marcus had disciples and Irenaeus tells how Marcus communicated to his female disciples the gift of prophecy.[433]

Irenaeus' description of Marcus as "another of those among them [i.e., Gnostics] who prides himself on being an improver of his master's teaching"[434] presents the Marcosian system as an example of a revisionist Valentinian Gnosticism position. Marcus was only one of the disciples of Valentinus who developed his master's teachings into a new sectarian movement exhibiting both organizational and ritualistic characteristics.

Finally, Clement of Alexandria's account of Valentinian rituals has led Sagnard to postulate that these Valentinians employed formulae.[435] Sagnard suggests that these rituals were institutionalized and attempts to reconstruct the complete baptismal initiation ritual. His reconstruction includes preparatory features, such as fastings, prayers, invocations, impositions of hands and genuflections,[436] as well as the baptismal act itself and anointing by oil.[437] If his reconstruction of this ritual is accepted, then like Pagels' analysis, it implies an organizational and hierarchical structure, standardized behavioural patterns and an historical tradition.[438]

---

[432]Irenaeus, Adv. Haer., 1.21.3-5.

[433]Ibid., 1.13.3. For an excellent account of the role of prophecy and eucharist in Marcus see J. Reiling, "Marcus Gnosticus and the New Testament" in T. Baarda, A. F. J. Klijn and W. C. van Unnik, eds., Miscellanea Neotestamentica (NovTSup 47, Leiden, 1978), 161-179.

[434]Irenaeus, Adv. Haer., 1.13.1.

[435]Sagnard, La gnose Valentinienne.

[436]Ibid., 234.

[437]Ibid., loc. cit.

[438]The process of institutionalization can also be pointed to in other ways. For example, Paul Finney has indicated that Gnostics made images and venerated them. Moreover, he postulates that this iconography may have become common currency in the second century A.D. in Egypt. The

4.4.4.4   Summary Comments

The development of institutionalized structures enabled the Gnostic to escape from a disenchanting world and to pursue his own special interests in ways complementary to Gnostic ideology. Rituals developed into traditions and were sanctified as social truth. They represented the practical articulation of the Gnostic experience of redemption. These structures allowed the Gnostic a framework for realizing his mystical values and simultaneously distinguishing himself from the larger society. They conferred on him a new identity and status and provided him with a surrogate community.

The evidence for Gnostic structure not only indicates that Gnosticism was not merely an ideology, but also that, in its Christian dress, it offered a competing form of legitimacy to that of Catholic Christianity. The process of institutionalization, although less formalized than that of Catholic Christianity, nevertheless reflects group structures and shared values, symbols and language. At the same time, the idea of a continuous apostolic tradition whereby each individual was able to receive *gnosis* and thereby be equal to Paul the apostle raised the individual to prime importance. Every initiate had direct access to God within himself.

Liturgy, rituals, sacraments and prayers are all indicative of Gnostic institutionalization. As such they testify to a religious community with a corporate identity. Their character refects, however, the anti-institutional beliefs of the Gnostics, their extreme individualism, and their spiritual reaction to the processes of demonopolization and privatization in the secular world.

---

production of icons, amulets and charms is highly indicative of the existence of social structure. See Finney, "Did Gnostics Make Pictures?" in Layton, ed., *Rediscovery*, v. 1, 434-454.

5

Conclusion

This study has focused on the social origins of Gnosticism. It has emphasized economic and cultural phenomena, locating the precursors of Gnosticism within a specific geographical and historical context. By applying social-scientific models to an understanding of the emergence of Gnosticism, it has been shown that the key ideological, behavioural and organizational features of Gnosticism are rooted in the material reality of the period.

The argument has examined two central theses: (1) that the transformation in the Ptolemaic mode of production towards privatization was structurally related to the ideology of individualism embodied in Gnosticism; and (2) that certain Jews in Egypt, experiencing this change in the mode of production, acted as catalysts in the sectarian development of Judaism, and hence played a pivotal role in the emergence of Gnosticism.

The transformation in the Ptolemaic mode of production from state to private ownership has been seen as a radical departure in Egyptian economic organization. A flowering of individualism occurred as new patterns of landowning, production and economic management were established under Roman rule in the first century A.D. These changes not only indicate abrupt social and economic change but also correspond to a radical transformation in consciousness.

The Jews in Egypt were particularly affected by the changes in the Ptolemaic mode of production. The Jewish community was well established in Egypt in the first century A.D., with both secular and religious institutions in Alexandria, and the opportunities for well-placed Jews to take advantage of these economic changes were manifold. However, the price of upward mobility was compromise and accommodation. Upwardly mobile Jews aspired to a *gymnasium* education, *ephebos* status and ultimately citizenship. They sought to become assimilated, both culturally and structurally. Nonetheless, the rise of anti-semitism amongst the

Greek population made this increasingly difficult; many Jews who had acquired unofficial status as *epheboi* were henceforth defined as Egyptian for purposes of the *laographia*. The restricted access to Greek education curtailed the opportunities for occupational mobility of many Jews and contributed to their social stigmatization. Despite their acceptance of accommodation, secularization and assimilation, their social status was significantly lowered. Thus, the economic and social aspirations of Jews endowed with the spirit of privatization were thwarted; and for urban, educated , upper class Jews, this created a profound sense of personal and social dislocation.

The consciousness of these Jews was thus radically altered. Educated in both Jewish and Greek educational institutions, fully literate in a largely illiterate world, and familiar with Alexandrian and Palestinian Jewish traditions, they no longer saw Hellenism and Judaism as reconcilable. In contrast to their earlier ethnic and religious solidarity with Palestinian Jewry, they now viewed their Judaism as an impediment. Allowed to possess wealth and property, but denied social and legal recognition as Jews, they turned inward for an understanding of their position, and in the process came to see Judaism as a negative force. The emergence of Gnosticism can be interpreted partly as a response to the disruption of the Alexandrian upper class Jewish community in the wake of Roman social change.

The transformation in the Ptolemaic mode of production directly contributed to structural differentiation and increased mobility on the one hand, and to a shift in the status of Jewish intellectuals on the other. Egyptian Jewish intellectuals became disenfranchised, both legally and socially. To compensate for their alienation, these Jews rebelled against Judaism and founded spiritualistic sectarian movements which in turn contributed to the development of Gnostic mythology. Hence, the hypothesis that a Jewish sectarian milieu was a necessary, although not sufficient, ingredient in Gnostic origins (as postulated previously by Quispel, Pearson and MacRae, among others) has been supported in this thesis. Only Jews familiar with Judaism both in Alexandria and in Jerusalem would have had the necessary knowledge and cosmic outlook to develop a complex soteriology and provide the impetus for the reinterpretation of biblical passages. Thus, disenfranchised Egyptian upper class Jewish intellectuals became the catalysts for a new salvation religion. Over the next century, the Hellenistic (non-Jewish) contribution would come to dominate Gnosticism; but this is beyond the subject of this dissertation.

Gnostic ideas, behaviour and organization have been described as individualistic. The radically individualistic doctrine of inner illumination created spiritual elitism; libertine and ascetic forms of behaviour reflected individualistic rebellious responses; the anti-institutional character of Gnosticism represented a particular resolution of the tension between mystical values and social organization. In all these aspects the individualistic ethos of Gnosticism reflected the increasing privatization of social and economic life.

Cosmology and theology are united in Gnosticism. The search for divine revelation (i.e., transcendence) implies a search for meaning, order and authority outside the institutionalized structures of society. It constitutes, by definition, an implicit challenge to traditional authority. In its place, individuals possessing charismatic authority emerge to legitimate an alternative vision. For the Gnostic, this vision is acquired through a personal 'calling' which transforms him.

> You saw the Spirit, you became Spirit. You saw Christ, you became Christ. You saw [the Father, you] shall become the Father. . . . [What] you see [is] yourself; and what you see you shall [become].[1]

Receiving *gnosis*, the individual is awakened and knows that he is already divine. The acquisition of self-knowledge becomes the soteriological solution to the problem of evil. Consequently, Gnosticism reflected not only the anomic state of a marginalized Jewish intellectual elite but also constituted a redefinition of the nature of man as a spiritual being.

The Gnostic response to social and psychological dislocation was mystical, not political. Although Gnosticism was grounded in a dissatisfaction with the existing social order, this dissatisfaction was not expressed in political terms. A mystical search for salvation is by nature individualistic and apolitical. As a result, Gnostic institutional forms developed in isolation from the dominant culture. The discrepancies between societal ideology and lived experience could not be resolved by political change. As a transcendental experience, *gnosis* provided a liberation from conventional normative structures, and hence from the attempt to reform these structures in the world.

It is not possible to say that Judaism alone gave rise to Gnosticism, or that Gnosticism was solely the result of privatization in the Egyptian economy. An exhaustive account of the sources of the Gnostic phenomenon would, at the very least, need to examine the influences at work in

---

[1]NHC II, 3:61,29-35.

Asia Minor, in Syria, and in Palestine itself. Nonetheless, the association of Gnosticism with Egypt is prominent for most modern scholars and is extensively supported by the available literature.

To view the origins of Gnosticism in terms of a particular Alexandrian elite is not exceptional. Böhlig, for example, assumes that the Egyptian social stratum "in which Gnosticism was able to blossom . . . was an upper middle class. . . ."[2] Nor is it revolutionary to say that Gnosticism and Judaism are associated. In order to justify linking these two hypotheses, however, it is necessary to examine the evidence for attributing the Gnostic inversion of the Old Testament God to a Jewish privileged class in Alexandria. The above analysis has shown that the habitual use of Jewish material in Gnostic midrashes can only be explained by postulating that the early Gnostics were intimately acquainted with the Old Testament, Palestinian and Alexandrian exegetical methods and midrashim. Even Jonas has stated that a "group discriminated against, rejected and despised" would have had the necessary motivation for "*ressentiment,* aggression and spite."[3] The disenfranchised Jewish lay intellectuals in Alexandria would meet these criteria. They would be the logical candidates for the creation of a Gnosticism that was "the greatest case of metaphysical anti-Semitism."[4] If Gnosticism, in its negative aspects, is seen as a manifestation of Jewish self-denial, the circumstances giving rise to this self-denial—the anomie and marginality of the Jewish intelligentsia, brought about as a result of changes in the economic and social conditions prevailing in Egypt in the first century A.D.—can be seen as a necesssry precondition for the emergence of Gnosticism.

In terms of the model presented at the beginning of Chapter 4, the types of responses available to the Jews in Egypt were adherence to traditional values, through political accommodation or insulation from non-Jewish influences, and innovation in terms of reform or rebellion. The attempt by upwardly-mobile Jews to become assimilated into the dominant social order required apostasy and the acceptance of Hellenistic culture; but this means of adaptation was progressively blocked after the Roman conquest. The resulting conflict found its ideological expression in the pitting of the Demiurge against Man. Ideologies are the products of

---

[2]A. Böhlig, "Report on the Coptological Work Carried out in the Context of the Tübingen Research Project," in Wilson, ed., *Nag Hammadi and Gnosis,* 131.

[3]H. Jonas, "Response to G. Quispel's 'Gnosticism and the New Testament,'" in Hyatt, *Bible in Modern Scholarship,* 291.

[4]Ibid., 288.

human experience and of the material conditions which structure this experience; consequently, changes in the mode of production are historically correlated to the rise of new *Weltanschauungen*.

Both Christianity and Gnosticism represent fusions of Hellenism and Judaism, arising in a period of profound social upheaval and spiritual turmoil. They embody salvific reactions to the shattering of religious values. Although offering different historical interpretations, both Grant's thesis that Gnosticism emerged in the wake of the destruction of Judaism in 70 A.D. from "the debris of apocalyptic-eschatological hopes"[5] and Yamauchi's argument that Gnosticism arose after the Jewish revolts of 135 A.D.[6] point to the importance of social upheaval. It would have been in the context of such cataclysmic events that the early Gnostics would have proselytized and recruited members. They would have found fertile ground throughout the Empire. Although Hellenized Jews may have been the first social group to recoil from the conditions imposed by Rome, it is not unreasonable to think that just as they re-interpreted Jewish values and ideology, others in similar social situations, demoralized and estranged by Roman conquest, would have adopted and expanded their re-evaluation of the cosmos as a means of escaping the social order.[7] For all these individuals, the Gnostic world view provided a means of self-transcendence.

Although the explanatory models of the social scientist are restricted to the domain of historical experience, they can contribute to the study of religion by explicating the material circumstances in which particular spiritual manifestations arise. From a sociological point of view, the emergence of Gnosticism can be interpreted as a reaction to socio-economic conditions by a socially privileged group, with a particular ethnic and religious identity which was experiencing social conflict. From a Gnostic viewpoint, perhaps, this social conflict served merely as the context for individual transformation, the experience of socio-economic alienation being but a necessary catalyst for mystical awakening.

---

[5]Grant, *Gnosticism*.

[6]Yamauchi, "Descent of Ishtar," 162ff.

[7]Thus, both Kippenberg's ("Versuch") and Rudolph's ("Problem einer Soziologie") arguments can, in part, be placed within this analysis.

Bibliography

Achtemeier, P. J., ed., *Society of Biblical Literature, 1977 Seminar Papers (Missoula, 1977)*.

Actes du Colloque 1971 sur l'esclavage (Annales Littéraires de l'Université de Besançon 140, Paris, 1972).

Actes du Colloque 1973 sur l'esclavage (Annales Littéraires de l'Université de Besançon 182, Paris, 1976).

Adler, N., *The Underground Stream: New Life Styles and the Antinomian Personality* (New York, 1972).

Aland, B., ed., *Gnosis: Festschrift für Hans Jonas* (Göttingen, 1978).

_____, "Gnosis und Christentum," in B. Layton, ed., *The Rediscovery of Gnosticism* (NumenSup 41, Leiden, 1980), v. 1, 319-350.

Aland, K., et al., eds., *The Greek New Testament* (New York, 1975[3]).

Alexander, P., "The Targumim and Early Exegesis of 'Sons of God' in Genesis 6," *JJS* 23 (1972), 60-71.

Alon, G., *Jews, Judaism and the Classical World*, trans. I. Abrahams (Jerusalem, 1977).

_____, *The Jews in Their Land in the Talmudic Age*, ed. and trans. G. Levi (Jerusalem, 1980).

Altmann, A., ed., *Biblical and Other Studies* (Cambridge, Mass., 1963).

Anderson, P., *Lineages of the Absolutist State* (London, 1974).

_____, *Passages from Antiquity to Feudalism* (London, 1974).

Applebaum, S., "Review of V. Tcherikover and A. Fuchs" (English summary), *Tarbiz* 28 (1958/59), i-xiii.

_____, "The Legal Status of the Jewish Communities in the Diaspora," in S. Safrai and M. Stern, eds., *The Jewish People in the First Century* (Assen, 1974), v. 1, 420-463.

_____, "The Organization of the Jewish Communities in the Diaspora," in S. Safrai and M. Stern, eds., *The Jewish People in the First Century* (Assen, 1974), v. 1, 464-503.

_____, "Economic Life in Palestine," in S. Safrai and M. Stern, eds., *The Jewish People in the First Century* (Philadelphia, 1976), v. 2, 631-700.

_____, "The Social and Economic Status of the Jews in the Diaspora," in S. Safrai and M. Stern, eds., *The Jewish People in the First Centuiry* (Philadelphia, 1976), v. 2, 701-727.

Arkin, M., *Aspects of Jewish Economic History* (Philadelphia, 1975).

Armstrong, A. H., "Gnosis and Greek Philosophy," in B. Aland, ed., *Gnosis: Festschrift für Hans Jonas* (Göttingen, 1978), 87-124.

Augustine, *The City of God Against the Pagans*, ed. G. E. McCracken et al. (LCL, London, Cambridge, Mass., 1957-1968), 7 vols.

Avigad, N., *Beth She'arim* (Jerusalem, 1973-1976), 3 vols.

Avi-Yonah, M., "Historical Geography of Palestine," in S. Safrai and M. Stern, eds., *The Jewish People in the First Century* (Assen, 1974), v. 1, 78-116.

_____, *Hellensim and the East* (Jerusalem, 1978).

Bailey, D. S., *Homosexuality and the Western Christian Tradition* (New York, 1955).

Bamberger, B., *Fallen Angels* (Philadelphia, 1952).

_____, *Proselytism in the Talmudic Period* (New York, 1968).

_____, "Philo and the Aggadah," *HUCA* 48 (1977), 153-185.

Barns, J. W. B., "Greek and Coptic Papyri from the Covers of the Nag Hammadi Codices," in M. Krause, ed., *Essays on the Nag Hammadi Texts in Honour of P. Labib* (NHS 6, Leiden, 1975), 9-17.

Baron, S. W., *A Social and Religious History of the Jews* (New York, London, 1952²), vols. 1 and 2.

Barr, J., *The Semantics of Biblical Language* (Oxford, 1961).

Barthélemy, D. and Milik, J. T., eds., *Discoveries in the Judaean Desert I: Qumran Cave I* (Oxford, 1955).

Baynes, Charlotte, ed. and trans., *A Coptic Gnostic Treatise Contained in the Codex Brucianus* (Cambridge, 1933).

Bell, H. J., *Cults and Creeds in Graeco-Roman Egypt* (Liverpool, 1955).

Bellet, P., "The Colophon of the Gospel of the Egyptians: Concessus and Marcarius of Nag Hammadi," in R. McL. Wilson, ed., *Nag Hammadi and Gnosis* (NHS 14, Leiden, 1978), 44-65.

Beloch, K. J., *Die Bevölkerung des griechisch-römanischen Welt* (Leipzig, 1886).

Beltz, W., *Die Adamapokalypse aus Codex V von Nag Hammadi* (Berlin, 1970).

Benko, S., "The Libertine Gnostic Sect of The Phibionites according to Epiphanius," *VC* 21 (1967), 103-119.

Benz, E., "On Understanding Non-Christian Religions," in J. Kitagawa and M. Eliade, eds., *The History of Religions: Essays in Methodology* (Chicago, 1959), 115-131.

Berger, Peter, "The Sociological Study of Sectarianism," *Social Research* 21/4 (1954), 467-485.

_____ and Luckmann, Thomas, *The Social Construction of Reality* (New York, 1967).

Bergman, J., Drynjeff, K., and Ringgren, H., eds., *Ex Orbe Religionum: Studia Geo Widengren oblata* (NumenSup 21, Leiden, 1973), v. 1.

Berliner Arbeitskreis für koptisch-gnostische Schriften, "Die Bedeutung der Texte von Nag Hammadi für die moderne Gnosisforschung," in Karl-Wolfgang Tröger, ed., *Gnosis und Neues Testament* (Berlin, 1973), 13-76.

Bevan, E. R., *A History of Egypt under the Ptolemaic Dynasty* (Chicago, 1968 [1927]).

Beyschlag, K., *Simon Magus und die christliche Gnosis* (WUNT 16, Tübingen, 1975).

Bianchi, U., ed., *Le Origini dello Gnosticismo* (NumenSup 12, Leiden, 1967).

_____, "The Definition of Religion. On the Methodology of Historical-Comparative Research," in U. Bianchi, C. J. Bleeker, and A. Bausani, eds., *Problems and Methods of the History of Religions* (NumenSup 19, Leiden, 1972), 15-34.

_____, *The Greek Mysteries* (Leiden, 1976).

_____, Bleeker, C. J., and Bausani, A., eds., *Problems and Methods of the History of Religions* (NumenSup 19, Leiden, 1972).

Bickerman, E. J., "La chaîne de la tradition pharisienne," *RB* 59 (1952), 44-54.

_____, "The Septuagint as a Translation," *Proceedings of the American Academy for Jewish Research* 28 (1959), 30-35.

_____, *From Ezra to the Last of the Maccabees* (New York, 1962).

Biezunska-Malowist, I., "L'Esclavage dans l'Égypte Gréco-Romaine," in *Actes du Colloque 1971 sur l'esclavage* (Annales Littéraires de l'Université de Besançon 140, Paris, 1972), 81-92.

_____, "L'Esclavage à Aléxandrie dans la période Gréco-Romaine," in *Actes du Colloque 1973 sur l'esclavage* (Annales Littéraires de l'Université de Besançon 182, Paris, 1976), 291-312.

Birnbaum, N., "Conflicting Interpretations of the Rise of Capitalism: Marx and Weber," *British Journal of Sociology* 4/2 (1953), 125-141.

Black, M., *The Scrolls and Christian Origins* (London, New York, 1961).

Blackman, E. C., *Marcion and his Influence* (London, 1948).

Blackman, P., *Mishnah* (New York, 1964), 7 vols.

Bleeker, C. J., *The Sacred Bridge* (NumenSup 7, Leiden, 1963).

_____, "The Contribution of the Phenomenology of Religion to the Study of the History of Religions," in U. Bianchi, C. J. Bleeker and A. Bausani, eds., *Problems and Methods of the History of Religions* (NumenSup 19, Leiden, 1972), 35-54.

Böhlig, A., "Der jüdische und jüdenchristliche Hintergrund in gnostischen Texten von Nag Hammadi," in U. Bianchi, ed., *Le Origini dello Gnosticismo* (NumenSup 12, Leiden, 1967), 109-140.

_____, "Jüdisches und iranisches in der Adamapokalypse des Codex V von Nag Hammadi," in *Mysterion und Warheit (AGJU 6, Leiden, 1968), 149-161.*

_____, *Mysterion und Warheit* (AGJU 6, Leiden, 1968).

_____, "Report on the Coptological Work Carried Out in the Context of the Tübingen Research Project," in R. McL. Wilson, ed., *Nag Hammadi and Gnosis* (NHS 14, Leiden, 1978), 131-138.

_____ and Labib, P., *Die koptisch-gnostische Schrift ohne Titel aus Codex II von Nag Hammadi im koptischen Museum zu Alt-Kairo* (Berlin, 1962).

_____ and Labib, P., *Koptisch-gnostische Apocalypsen aus Codex V von Nag Hammadi in koptischen Museum zu Alt-Kairo* (Halle-Wittenberg, 1963).

_____ and Wisse, F., *Nag Hammadi Codices III, 2 and IV, 2. The Gospel of the Egyptians* (NHS 4, Leiden, 1975).

_____ and Wisse, F., *Zum Hellenismus in den Schriften von Nag Hammadi* (Göttinger Orientforschungen 6, Reihe: Hellenistica, Band 2, Wiesbaden, 1975).

Bonneau, D., "Esclavage et irrigation d'après la documentation papyrologique," in *Actes du Colloque 1973 sur l'Esclavage* (Annales Littéraires de l'Université de Besançon 182, Paris, 1976), 313-332.

Bonner, C., *Studies in Magical Amulets* (Ann Arbor, 1950).

Bornkamm, G., "The Acts of Thomas," in E. Hennecke and W. Schneemelcher, eds., *New Testament Apocrypha*, trans. R. McL. Wilson (London, 1965), v. 2, 425-531.

Bousset, Wilhelm, *Hautprobleme der Gnosis* (Göttingen, 1907).

Bottorff, J. F., "The Relation of Justification and Ethics in Pauline Epistles," *SJT* 26 (1973), 421-430.

Box, H., *Philonis Alexandrini: In Flaccum* (London, 1939).

Brightman, F. E., *Liturgies Eastern and Western* (Oxford, 1896), 2 vols.

Bromehead, C. N., "Mining and Quarrying to the Seventeenth Century," in C. Singer et al., eds., *A History of Technology* (Oxford, 1956), v. 2, 1-40.

Brooks, C. E. P., *Climate through the Ages* (New York, 1970[2]).

Bruce, F. F., "Paul and the Law of Moses," *John Rylands University Library of Manchester* 57 (1974-1975), 259-279.

Brunt, P. A., review of K. D. White's *Roman Farming*, in *JRS* 62 (1972), 156.

_____, "The Administrators of Roman Egypt," *JRS* 65 (1975), 124-147.

Budge, E. A. W., *Amulets and Superstitions* (London, 1930).

Bullard, R. A., *The Hypostasis of the Archons* (Berlin, 1970).

Bultmann, Rudolph, "Die Bedeutung der neuerschlossenen mandäischen und manichäischen Quellen für das Verständnis des Johannesevangeliums," *ZNW* 24 (1925), 100-146.

_____, "Urchristliche Religion (1915-1925)," *ARW* 24 (1926), 83-164.

_____, "Mythus und Mythologie in Neuen Testament," *RGG* 4 (1930), 390-394.

_____, *Das Urchristentum im Rahmen der antiken Religionen* (Zurich, 1949).

_____, *Das Evangelium des Johannes* (Göttingen, 1950).

_____, *Theology of the New Testament*, trans. K. Grobel (London, 1952, 1955), 2 vols.

_____, *Kerygma and Myth*, trans. R. H. Fuller (London, 1957, 1962), 2 vols.

_____, "Gnosis," in G. Kittel, ed., *Theological Dictionary of the New Testament*, trans. G. Bromiley (Grand Rapids, 1964), v. 1, 689-714.

Burford, A., *Craftsmen in Greek and Roman Antiquity* (London, 1972).

Burke, P. *Sociology and History* (London, 1980).

Burrows, M., "Old Testament Ethics and The Ethics of Jesus," in J. L. Crenshaw and J. T. Willis, eds., *Essays in Old Testament Ethics* (New York, 1974), 225-243.

Casey, R. P., "Gnosis, Gnosticism and the New Testament," in W. D. Davies and D. Daube, eds., *The Background of the New Testament and its Eschatology* (Cambridge, 1956), 52-81.

Casson, L., *Travel in the Ancient World* (London, 1974).

Centre d'études et de recherches marxistes, *Sur le 'mode de production asiatique'* (Paris, 1969).

Cerfaux, L., "L'antinomie paulinienne et la vie apostolique," *RevScRel* 39 (1951-1952), 221-234.

Chadwick, H., "The Domestication of Gnosis," in B. Layton, ed., *The Rediscovery of Gnosticism* (*Numen*Sup 41, Leiden, 1980), v. 1, 3-16.

Charles, R. H., *The Apocrypha and Pseudepigrapha of the Old Testament* (Oxford, 1913).

Charlesworth, J. H., *The Pseudepigrapha and Modern Research* (Septuagint and Cognate Studies 7, Missoula, 1976).

Charlesworth, M. P., *Trade Routes and Commerce of the Roman Empire* (Cambridge, 1926²).

_____, "Roman Trade with India: A Resurvey," in P. R. Coleman-Norton, ed., *Studies in Roman Economic and Social History* (Princeton, 1951), 131-143.

Cicero, *De Officiis*, ed., W. Miller (LCL, London, Cambridge, Mass., 1951).

Clement of Alexandria, *The Excerpta ex Theodoto of Clement of Alexandria*, ed. R. P. Casey (London, 1934).

_____, *Werke*, ed. O. Stählin (GCS 12, 15, 17, Leipzig, 1936-1970), 3 vols.

Cohen, A., ed., *Soncino Books of the Bible* (London, 1945-1962), 14 vols.

Cohn, N., *The Pursuit of the Millennium* (London, 1970).

Coleman-Norton, P. R., ed., *Studies in Roman Economic and Social History* (Princeton, 1951).

Collart, Paul, "Psaumes et amulettes," *Aegyptus* 14 (1934), 463-467.

Collins, J., *The Sibylline Oracles of Egyptian Judaism* (Society of Biblical Literature, Dissertation Series 13, Missoula, 1974).

_____, ed., *Apocalypses: The Morphology of a Genre* (Semeia 14, Missoula, 1979).

Colpe, C., *Die religionsgeschichtliche Schule* (Göttingen, 1961).

Cowley, A. E., ed., *Aramaic Papyri of the Fifth Century B.C.* (Oxford, 1923).

Crawford, D. J., *Kerekeosiris* (Cambridge, 1971).

Cross, F. L., ed., *The Jung Codex* (London, 1955).

Cross, F. M. et al., *Scrolls from Qumran Cave I: The Great Isaiah Scroll, The Order of the Community, The Pesher to Habakkuk* (Jerusalem, 1972).

Cumont, F., "Les Mystères de Sabazius et le Judaisme," in *Comptes-Rendus de l'Académie des inscriptions et belles-lettres* (Paris, 1906), 63-67.

_____, *Oriental Religions in Roman Paganism* (London, 1956).

Danby, H., *The Mishnah* (London, 1933).

Daniel, J. L., "Anti-Semitism in the Hellenistic Roman Period," *JBL* 98/1 (1979), 45-65.

Daniélou, J., *The Theology of Jewish-Christianity*, trans. J. H. Baker (London, 1964).

Daube, D., "Alexandrian Methods of Interpretation and the Rabbis," *Festschrift Hans Lewald* (Basel, 1953), 27-44.

Davies, W. D., *Paul and Rabbinic Judaism* (London, 1955).

de Ste. Croix, G. E. M., "Why Were the Early Christians Persecuted?," *Past and Present* 26 (1963), 6-39.

de Vaux, R., *Archaeology and the Dead Sea Scrolls* (London, 1973).

Delling, G., et al., *Bibliographie zur jüdisch-hellenistischen und intertes-tamentarischen Literatur 1900-1965* (TU 106, Berlin, 1969).

Dio Cassius, *Dio's Roman History*, ed. E. Cary (LCL, London, New York, 1914-1927), 9 vols.

Dio Chrysostom, *Dio Chrysostom*, ed. J. W. Cohoon and H. L. Crosby (LCL, London, New York, 1932-1951), 5 vols.

Diodorus, *Diodorus of Sicily*, ed. C. H. Oldfather et al. (LCL, London, Cambridge, Mass., 1933-1967), 12 vols.

"Discussion sur les formations économiques et sociales dans l'Antiquité," in *Actes du Colloque 1973 sur l'esclavage* (Annales Littéraires de l'Université de Besançon 182, Paris, 1976), 49-98.

Dodd, C. H., *The Bible and the Greeks* (London, 1935).

Dodds, E. R., *The Greeks and the Irrational* (Berkeley, 1951).

_____, *Pagan and Christian in an Age of Anxiety* (New York, 1970 [1965]).

Doresse, J., "Trois livres gnostiques inédits: Évangile des Egyptiens, Epître d'Eugnoste, Sagesse de Jesus Christ," *VC* 2 (1948), 137-160.

_____, *The Secret Books of the Egyptian Gnostics*, trans. P. Mairet (London, 1960).

Douglas, Mary, *Natural Symbols* (London, 1970).

Dover, K. J., *Greek Homosexuality* (Cambridge, Mass., 1978).

Drane, J. W., "Tradition, Law and Ethics in Pauline Theology," *NovT* 16 (1974), 167-178.

Drazin, N., *The History of Jewish Education from 515 B.C.E. to 220 C.E.* (Johns Hopkins University Studies in Education 29, Baltimore, 1940).

Dunand, F., *Le culte d'Isis dans le bassin oriental de la Méditerranée* (Leiden, 1973), 3 vols.

Duncan-Jones, R. P., "Some Configurations of Land-Holding in the Roman Empire," in M. Finley, ed., *Studies in Roman Property* (Cambridge, 1976), 7-24.

Durkheim, E., *Suicide*, trans. J. A. Spaulding and G. Simpson (London, 1952).

Edelstein, L., *The Meaning of Stoicism* (Cambridge, 1966).

Eliade, M., "Methodological Remarks on the Study of Religious Symbolism," in J. Kitagawa and M. Eliade, eds., *The History of Religions: Essays in Methodology* (Chicago, 1959), 86-107.

_____, *The Sacred and the Profane*, trans. W. R. Trask (New York, 1959).

_____, *Rites and Symbols of Initiation*, trans. W. R. Trask (New York, 1965).

_____, The Quest: History and Meaning in Religion (Chicago, 1969).

Epiphanius, *Ancoratus und Panarion*, ed. Karl Holl (CGS 25, 31, 37, Leipzig, 1915-1933), 3 vols.

Epstein, I. et al., *The Babylonian Talmud* (London, 1935-1952), 20 vols.

Epstein, L. M., *Sex Laws and Customs in Judaism* (New York, 1948).

Erickson, K. T., "Sociology and the Historical Perspective," *The American Sociologist* 5 (1970), 331-338.

Etzioni, A., *A Comparative Analysis of Complex Organizations* (New York, 1961).

Eusebius, *Preparatio Evangelica*, ed., G. H. Clifford (Oxford, 1903).

Evans, J. A. S., "A Social and Economic History of an Egyptian Temple in the Graeco-Roman Period," *Yale Classical Studies* 17 (1961), 149-283.

The Facsimile Edition of the Nag Hammadi Codices (Leiden, 1972-1979), 11 vols.

Fallon, F., *The Enthronement of Sabaoth* (NHS 10, Leiden 1978).

_____, "The Gnostic Apocalypses," in J. Collins, ed., *Apocalypses: The Morphology of a Genre* (*Semeia* 14, Missoula, 1979), 123-158.

Feldman, L. H., "The Orthodoxy of the Jews in Hellenistic Egypt," *Jewish Social Studies* 22 (1960), 215-237.

_____, "Hengel's Judaism and Hellenism in Retrospect," *JBL* 96/3 (1977), 371-382.

Feret, H. M., *Pierre et Paul: à Antioche et à Jerusalem* (Paris, 1955).

Ferguson, J., *The Religions of the Roman Empire* (London, 1974).

Finkelstein, L., *The Pharisees* (Philadelphia, 1962³), 2 vols.

Finley, M. I., ed., *Slavery in Classical Antiquity* (Cambridge, 1960).

_____, "Technical Innovation and Economic Progress in the Ancient World," *The Economic History Review,* second series 18/1 (1965), 29-45.

_____, *The Ancient Economy* (Berkeley and Los Angeles, 1973).

_____, ed., *Studies in Roman Property* (Cambridge, 1976).

_____, "The Ancient City: From Fustel de Coulanges to Max Weber and Beyond," *Comparative Studies in Society and History* 19 (1977), 305-327.

_____, *Ancient Slavery and Modern Ideology* (London, 1980).

Finney, Paul, "Did Gnostics Make Pictures?," in B. Layton, ed., *The Rediscovery of Gnosticism* (*Numen*Sup 41, Leiden, 1980), v. 1, 434-454.

Fischel, H., *Rabbinic Literature and Graeco-Roman Philosophy* (Studia Post-Biblica 1, Leiden, 1973).

_____, ed., *Essays in Graeco-Roman and Related Talmudic Literature* (New York, 1977).

Foerster, Werner, "Das System des Basilides," *NTS* 9 (1962-1963), 233-255.

_____, *Gnosis,* trans. R. McL. Wilson (Oxford, 1972, 1974), 2 vols.

Forbes, R. J., "Food and Drink," in C. Singer et al., eds., *A History of Technology* (Oxford, 1956), v. 2, 103-146.

_____, "Power," in C. Singer et al., eds., *A History of Technology* (Oxford, 1956), v. 2, 589-622.

_____, *Studies in Ancient Technology* (Leiden, 1964-1966[2]), 7 vols.

Frank, T., "On Augustus and the Aerarium," *JRS* 23 (1933), 143-148.

_____, *An Economic History of Rome* (New York, 1962[2] rev.).

Fraser, P. M., *Ptolemaic Alexandria* (Oxford, 1972), 2 vols.

Frazier, A., "Models for a Methodology of Religious Meaning," *Bucknell Review* 18 (1970), 19-28.

Freedman, H., *Midrash Rabbah* (London, 1939), 10 vols.

Frend, W. H. C., "The Failure of the Persecutions in the Roman Empire," *Past and Present* 16 (1959), 10-30.

Frey, J.-B., *Corpus Inscriptionum Judaicarum* (Vatican, 1936, 1952), 2 vols.

Friedländer, M., *Der vorchristliche jüdische Gnosticismus* (Göttingen, 1898).

Fromm, E., *Das Christusdogma und andere Essays* (München, 1965).

Gager, J., "Marcion and Philosophy," *VC* 26 (1972), 53-59.

_____, *Moses in Greco-Roman Paganism* (SBL Monograph Series 16, Nashville, 1972).

_____, *Kingdom and Community: The Social World of Early Christianity* (Englewood Cliffs, N.J., 1975).

Gardiner, E. N., *Athletics of the Ancient World* (Oxford, 1933).

Geffcken, Johannes, ed., *Oracula Sibyllina* (Leipzig, 1902).

Gerth, H. H. and Mills, C. W., *From Max Weber: Essays in Sociology* (New York, 1969).

Gibbons, J., "The Second Logos of the Great Seth: Considerations and Questions," in G. MacRae, ed., *Society of Biblical Literature, 1973 Seminar Papers* (Cambridge, Mass., 1973), v. 2, 242-261.

Ginzberg, Louis, *The Legends of the Jews*, trans. H. Szold (Philadelphia, 1909-1913), 7 vols.

Giverson, S., *Apocryphon Johannis* (Copenhagen, 1963).

Godlier, M., "The Concept of the 'Asiatic Mode of Production' and Marxist Models of Social Evolution," in D. Seddon, ed., *Relations of Production* (London, 1978), 209-257.

Goodenough, E. R., *The Jurisprudence of the Jewish Courts in Egypt* (New Haven, 1929).

_____, *By Light, Light* (New Haven, 1935).

_____, *Jewish Symbols in the Graeco-Roman Period* (Bollingen Series 37, New York, 1953-1968), 13 vols.

Goold, G., "A Greek Professorial Circle at Rome," *Transactions of the American Philological Association* 92 (1961), 168-192.

Gordon, M., *Assimilation in American Life* (New York, 1964).

Gordon, M. L., "The Nationality of Slaves under the Early Roman Empire," in M. Finley, ed., *Slavery in Classical Antiquity* (Cambridge, 1960), 171-189.

Graetz, H., *Gnosticismus und Judentum* (Westmead, 1971 [1846]).

Granfield, P. and Jungmann, J. A., eds., *Kyriakon* (Münster, 1970).

Grant, F. C., ed., *Hellenistic Religions: The Age of Syncretism* (Indianapolis, 1953).

_____, *Roman Hellenism and the New Testament* (New York, 1962).

Grant, R. M., review of Hans Jonas' *Gnosis und spätantiker Geist*, in *JTS* 7 (1956), 308-313.

_____, *Gnosticism and Early Christianity* (New York, 1966[2]).

_____, "Les êtres intermédiaires dans le judaisme tardif," in U. Bianchi, ed., *Le Origini dello Gnosticismo* (*Numen*Sup 12, Leiden, 1967), 141-161.

Green, H. A., "Gnosis and Gnosticism: A Study in Methodology," *Numen* 24 (1977), 95-134.

Grobel, K., *The Gospel of Truth* (New York, 1960).

_____, "How Gnostic is the Gospel of Thomas?," *NTS* 8 (1961-1962), 367-373.

Gruenwald, I., "Knowledge and Vision: Towards a Clarification of Two 'Gnostic' Concepts in the Light of their Alleged Origins," *Israel Oriental Studies* 3 (1973), 63-107.

_____, "Jewish Sources for the Gnostic Texts from Nag Hammadi," in *Proceedinqs of the Sixth World Congress of Jewish Studies* (Jerusalem, 1977), v. 3, 45-56.

_____, *Apocalyptic and Merkavah Mysticism* (AGJU 14, Leiden, 1980).

Guthrie, W. K. C., *Orpheus and Greek Religion* (London, 1935).

_____, *A History of Greek Philosophy* (Cambridge, 1962-1975), 4 vols.

Gutman, Y., *The Beginnings of Jewish Hellenistic Literature* (in Hebrew, Jerusalem, 1958, 1963), 2 vols.

Gutmann, J., ed., *The Synagogue: Studies in Origins, Archaeology and Architecture* (New York, 1975).

Haardt, R., *Die Gnosis: Wesen und Zeugnisse* (Salzburg, 1967).

_____, "Bemerkungen zu den Methoden der Ursprungsbestimmung von Gnosis," in U. Bianchi, ed., *Le Origini dello Gnosticismo* (*Numen*Sup 12, Leiden, 1967), 161-174.

_____, "Zur Methodologie der Gnosisforschung," in Karl-Wolfgang Tröger, ed., *Gnosis und Neues Testament* (Berlin, 1973), 183-202.

Habermas, J., *Knowledge and Human Interests,* trans. J. Shapiro (Boston, 1971).

Hadas, M., *Hellenistic Culture, Fusion and Diffusion* (New York, 1959).

Haenchen, E., *The Acts of the Apostles,* trans. R. McL. Wilson (Oxford, 1971).

_____, "Simon Magus in der Apostelgeschichte," in Karl-Wolfgang Tröger, ed., *Gnosis und Neues Testament* (Berlin, 1973), 267-279.

Hagedorn, R., ed., *Sociology* (Toronto, 1980).

Harden, D. B., "Glass and Glazes," in C. Singer et al., eds., *A History of Technology* (Oxford, 1956), v. 2, 311-346.

Harnack, A., *The Mission and Expansion of Christianity in the First Three Centuries,* trans. J. Moffatt (London, 1908[2]), 2 vols.

_____, *Marcion* (Leipzig, 1924).

Harrington, D. J., "Sociological Concepts and the Early Church: A Decade of Research," *TS* 41 (1980), 181-190.

Hedrick, C. W., "The Apocalypse of Adam: A Literary and Source Analysis," in L. C. McGaughy, ed., *Society of Biblical Literature, 1972 Proceedings* (Missoula, 1972), v. 2, 581-590.

_____, "Gnostic Proclivities in the Greek Life of Pachomius and the Sitz im Leben of the Nag Hammadi Library," *NovT* 22 (1980), 78-95.

Heer, D. M., *Society and Population* (Englewood Cliffs, N.J., 1968).

Heichelheim, F. M., *An Ancient Economic History*, trans. J. Stevens (Leiden, 1958-1970), 3 vols.

Hempel, C. G., "Typological Methods in the Social Sciences," in M. Natanson, ed., *Philosophy of the Social Sciences: A Reader* (New York, 1963), 210-231.

Hengel, M., *Judaism and Hellenism*, trans. J. Bowden (London, 1974), 2 vols.

_____, "Proseuche und Synagoge," in J. Gutmann, ed., *The Synagogue: Studies in Origins, Archaeology and Architecture* (New York, 1975), 27-54.

Hennecke, E. and Schneemelcher, W., eds., *New Testament Apocrypha*, trans. R. McL. Wilson (London, 1963, 1965), 2 vols.

Henrichs, A., *Die Phoinikika des Lollianos* (Bonn, 1972).

Hill, M., *A Sociology of Religion* (London, 1973).

Hippolytus, *Werke*, ed. Paul Wendland (GCS 26, Leipzig, 1916).

_____, *Philosophumena*, ed. F. Legge (London, New York, 1921), 2 vols.

Holmberg, B., *Paul and Power: The Structure of Authority in the Primitive Church as Reflected in the Pauline Epistles* (Lund, 1978).

Hombert, M. and Préaux, C., "Note sur la durée de la vie dans l'Égypte Gréco-Romaine," *Chronique d'Égypte* 20 (1945), 139-146.

_____, *Recherches sur le recensement dans l'Égypte Romaine* (Leiden, 1952).

Hopkins, K., "The Age of Roman Girls at Marriage," *Population Studies* 18 (1964-1965), 309-327.

_____, "Elite Mobility in the Roman Empire," *Past and Present* 32 (1965), 12-26.

_____, "Contraception in the Roman Empire," *Comparative Studies in Society and History* 8 (1965-1966), 124-151.

_____, "On the Probable Age Structure of the Roman Population," *Population Studies* 20 (1966-1967), 245-264.

_____, *Conquerors and Slaves* (Sociological Studies in Roman History 1, Cambridge, 1978).

_____, "Economic Growth and Towns in Classical Antiquity," in P. Abrams and E. A. Wrigley, eds., *Towns in Societies* (Cambridge, Mass., 1978), 35-77.

_____, "Taxes and Trade in the Roman Empire," *JRS* 70 (1980), 101-125.

Horace, *Satires, Epistles and Ars Poetica,* ed. H. R. Fairclough (LCL, London, Cambridge, Mass., 1947).

Horsley, R. A., "Gnosis in Corinth: I Corinthians 8.1-6," *NTS* 27/1 (1980), 32-51.

Hughes, H. Stuart, *Consciousness and Society* (New York, 1961).

Hyatt, J. P., ed., *The Bible in Modern Scholarship* (Nashville, New York, 1965).

Irenaeus, *Against the Heresies,* ed. W. W. Harvey (Cambridge, 1857), 2 vols.

Jeremias, J., *Jerusalem in the Time of Jesus,* trans. F. H. and C. H. Cave (London, 1969).

Jerome, *Oeuvres complètes de Saint Jérome,* ed. L'Abbé Boreille (Paris, 1877-1885), 18 vols.

Johnson, A. C., *An Economic Survey of Ancient Rome: Roman Egypt* (Paterson, N.J., 1959).

_____ and West, L. C., *Byzantine Egypt: Economic Studies* (Amsterdam, 1967).

Johnson, Roger A., *The Origins of Demythologizing* (*Numen*Sup 28, Leiden, 1974).

Jolowicz, H. F., *Historical Introduction to the Study of Roman Law* (Cambridge, 1954).

_____, *Roman Foundations of Modern Law* (Oxford, 1957).

282   Origins of Gnosticism

Jonas, Hans, *Der Begriff der Gnosis* (Göttingen, 1930).

_____, *Gnosis und spätantiker Geist* (Göttingen, 1954², 1966²), 2 vols.

_____, *The Gnostic Religion* (Boston, 1963²).

_____, "Response to G. Quispel's 'Gnosticism and the New Testament,'" in J. P. Hyatt, ed., *The Bible in Modern Scholarship* (New York, 1965), 279-293.

_____, "Delimitation of the Gnostic Phenomenon—Typological and Historical," in U. Bianchi, ed., *Le Origini dello Gnosticismo* (*Numen*Sup 12, Leiden, 1967), 92-109.

Jones, A. H. M., "Slavery in the Ancient World," in M. Finley, ed., *Slavery in Classical Antiquity* (Cambridge, 1960), 1-15.

_____, *The Cities of the Eastern Roman Provinces* (Oxford, 1971²).

_____, *The Roman Economy*, ed. P. A. Brunt (Oxford, 1974).

Jope, E. M., "Agricultural Implements," in C. Singer et al., eds., *A History of Technology* (Oxford, 1956), v. 2, 81-102.

Jordan, Z. A., *Karl Marx: Economy, Class and Social Revolution* (London, 1972).

Josephus, *Josephus*, ed., H. St. J. Thackeray et al. (LCL, London, Cambridge, Mass., 1961-1965), 9 vols.

Judéo-Christianisme. Recherches historiques et théologiques offertes en hommage au Cardinal Jean Daniélou (Paris, 1972).

Judge, E. A., "The Social Identity of the First Christians: A Question of Method in Religious History," *JRH* 7/2 (1980), 201-217.

Juster, J., *Les Juifs dans l'empire romain* (New York, 1914), 2 vols.

Justin Martyr, *Justin Martyr*, ed., T. B. Falls (New York, 1949).

Juvenal, *Juvenal's Satires*, ed., W. Gifford (London, New York, 1954).

Kasser, R., "Bibliothèque gnostique V: Apocalypse d'Adam," *RTP* 17 (1967), 316-333.

_____, "Citations des grands prophètes bibliques dans les textes gnostiques coptes," in M. Krause, ed., *Essays on the Nag Hammadi Texts* (NHS 6, Leiden, 1975), 56-64.

_____, Malinine, M., Puech, H.-Ch., Quispel, G., Zandee, J., Vycichl, W., and Wilson, R. McL., eds., *Tractatus Tripartitus, Pars I, De Supernis* (Bern, 1973).

_____, Malinine, M., Puech, H.-Ch., Quispel, G., Zandee, J., Vychichl, W., and Wilson, R. McL., eds., *Tractatus Tripartitus, Pars II, De Creatione Hominis, Pars III, De Generibus Tribus* (Bern, 1975).

Kee, H. C., *Christian Origins in Sociological Perspective: Methods and Resources* (Philadelphia, 1980).

Kippenberg, Hans, "Versuch einer soziologischen Verortung des antiken Gnostizismus," *Numen* 17 (1970), 211-232.

Kisch, Guido, ed., *Pseudo-Philo's Liber Antiquitatum Biblicarum* (Publications in Mediaeval Studies 10, Notre Dame, 1949).

Kitagawa, J. and Eliade, M., eds., *The History of Religions: Essays in Methodology* (Chicago, 1959).

Kittel, G., ed., *Theological Dictionary of the New Testament*, trans. G. Bromiley (Grand Rapids, 1964-1976), 10 vols.

Kleinknecht, H. and Gutbrod, W., "Nomos," in G. Kittel, ed., *Theological Dictionary of the New Testament*, trans G. Bromiley (Grand Rapids, 1967), v. 4, 1022-1090.

Klijn, A. F. J., *The Acts of Thomas, Introduction, Text, Commentary* (*NovT*Sup 5, Leiden, 1962).

_____, "Christianity in Edessa and the Gospel of Thomas," *NovT* 14 (1972), 70-77.

_____, "The Study of Jewish-Christianity," *NTS* 20 (1974), 419-431.

_____, *Seth in Jewish, Christian and Gnostic Literature* (*NovT*Sup 46, Leiden, 1977).

Koester, H., "GNŌMAI DIAPHOROI: The Origins and Nature of Diversification in the History of Early Christianity," in J. M. Robinson and H. Koester, eds., *Trajectories through Early Christianity* (Philadelphia, 1971), 114-157.

Koschorke, K., *Die Polemik der Gnostiker gegen das kirchliche Christentum* (NHS 12, Leiden, 1978).

Kraeling, E. G., ed., *The Brooklyn Museum Aramaic Papyri* (New Haven, 1953).

Kraft, R. A., "In Search of 'Jewish-Christianity' and its 'Theology,'" in *Judéo-Christianisme* (Paris, 1972), 81-92.

Krause, M., "Das literarische Verhältnis des Eugnostosbriefes zur Sophia Jesu Christi," in *Mullus, Festschrift Theodor Klauser* (JAC 1, Münster, 1964), 215-223.

_____, "Zur 'Hypostasis der Archonten' in Codex II von Nag Hammadi," *Enchoria* 2 (1972), 1-20.

_____, "The Exegesis on the Soul," in W. Foerster, ed., *Gnosis*, trans. R. McL. Wilson (Oxford, 1974), v. 2, 102-109.

_____, "Die Sakramente in der 'Exegese über die Seele,'" in J. E. Ménard, ed., *Les textes de Nag Hammadi* (NHS 7, Leiden, 1975), 47-55.

_____, *Essays on the Nag Hammadi Texts in Honour of P. Labib* (NHS 6, Leiden, 1975).

_____, ed., *Gnosis and Gnosticism* (NHS 8, Leiden, 1977).

_____ and Labib, P., eds. and trans., *Die drei Versionen des Apocryphon des Johannes im koptischen Museum zu Alt-Kairo* (Wiesbaden, 1962).

Krauss, S., *Synagogale Altertümes* (Berlin-Wien, 1922).

Krueger, P., *Corpus Iuris Civilis* (Berlin, 1929).

La Leche League, *The Womanly Art of Breastfeeding* (Franklin Park, 1963[2]).

Lampe, G. W. H., *A Patristic Greek Lexicon* (Oxford, 1961, 1968), 2 vols.

Layton, B., "The Hypostasis of the Archons or The Reality of the Rulers," *HTR* 67 (1974), 351-425, and 69 (1976), 31-101.

_____, ed., *The Rediscovery of Gnosticism* (NumenSup 41, Leiden, 1980, 1981), 2 vols.

Le Moyne, J., *Les Sadducéens* (Paris, 1972).

Lenski, G., *Power and Privilege* (New York, 1966).

Leon, H. J., *The Jews of Ancient Rome* (Philadelphia, 1960).

Levy, I., *The Synagogue* (London, 1963).

Levy, J. H., *Studies in Jewish Hellenism* (in Hebrew, Jerusalem, 1960).

Lewis, N., *Papyrus in Classical Antiquity* (Oxford, 1974).

Liddell, H. G. and Scott, R., eds., *A Greek-English Lexicon* (Oxford, 1940[9]).

Lieberman, Saul, *Greek in Jewish Palestine* (New York, 1942).

_____, *The Tosefta* (New York, 1955-1973), 4 vols.

_____, *Hellenism in Jewish Palestine* (New York, 1962²).

_____, "How Much Greek in Jewish Palestine?," in A. Altmann, ed., *Biblical and Other Studies* (Cambridge, Mass., 1963), 123-141.

Lincoln, B., "Thomas-Gospel and Thomas-Community: A New Approach to a Familiar Text," *NovT* 19 (1977), 65-76.

Lipset, S. M., "History and Sociology: Some Methodological Considerations," in S. M. Lipset and R. Hofstadter, eds., *Sociology and History: Methods* (New York, 1968), 20-58.

Lüdemann, G., *Untersuchungen zur simonianischen Gnosis* (Göttingen, 1975).

Lukács, G., *History and Class Consciousness*, trans. R. Livingstone (Cambridge, 1971).

Lukes, Steven, *Individualism* (Oxford, 1973).

Macho, A. D., "The Recently Discovered Palestinian Targum," in G. W. Anderson et al., eds., *Congress Volume Oxford 1959* (*VT*Sup 7, Leiden, 1960), 222-245.

MacLennan, H., *Oxyrhynchus: An Economic and Social Study* (Amsterdam, 1968).

MacMullen, R., *Roman Social Relations* (New Haven and London, 1974).

Macquarrie, J., *The Scope of Demythologizing* (London, 1960).

MacRae, G., "The Coptic Gnostic Apocalypse of Adam," *HeyJ* 6 (1965), 27-35.

_____, "The Jewish Background of the Gnostic Sophia Myth," *NovT* 12 (1970), 86-101.

_____, "The Apocalypse of Adam Reconsidered," in L. C. McGaughy, ed., *Society of Biblical Literature, 1972 Proceedings* (Missoula, 1972), v. 2, 573-579.

_____, ed., *Society of Biblical Literature, 1973 Seminar Papers* (Cambridge, 1973), v. 2.

_____, ed., *Society of Biblical Literature, 1974 Seminar Papers* (Cambridge, 1974), v. 2.

_____, "Discourses of the Gnostic Revealer," in G. Widengren, ed., *Proceedings of the International Colloquium on Gnosticism* (Stockholm, 1977), 111-122.

_____, "Nag Hammadi and the New Testament," in B. Aland, ed., *Gnosis: Festschrift für Hans Jonas* (Göttingen, 1978), 144-157.

_____, "Why the Church Rejected Gnosticism," in E. P. Sanders, ed., *Jewish and Christian Self-Definition* (London, 1980), v. 1, 126-133.

Macuch, R., "Anfänge der Mandäer," in F. Altheim and R. Stiehl, eds., *Die Araber in der Alten Welt II* (Berlin, 1965), 76-190.

_____, "Der gegenwärtige Stand der Mandäerforschung und ihre Aufgaben," *OLZ* 63 (1968), 5-14.

Mahé, J. P., "Remarques d'un latiniste sur l'Asclepius Copte de Nag Hammadi," *RSR* 48 (1974), 136-155.

Malherbe, A. J., *Social Aspects of Early Christianity* (Baton Rouge and London, 1977).

Malinine, M., Puech, H.-Ch., Quispel, G. and Till, W. C., eds., *De Resurrectione. Epistula ad Rheginum* (Zurich, 1963).

_____ et al., eds. and trans., *Epistula Jacobi Apocrypha: Codex Jung f.I-VIII* (Zurich, Stuttgart, 1968).

Marcus, R., "Rashe perakim beshitat ha-hinnukah shel Philon ha-Alexandroni," in *Sefer Touroff* (Boston, 1938), 225-231.

Marrou, H. I., *A History of Education in Antiquity*, trans. G. Lamb (Toronto, 1964).

Martial, *Epigrams*, ed. W. C. A. Ker (LCL, London, Cambridge, Mass., 1961), 2 vols.

Marx, K., *Pre-Capitalist Economic Formations*, ed. E. Hobsbawm (London, 1964).

_____, *Capital* (New York, 1967), 2 vols.

_____ and Engels, F., *Selected Correspondence* (New York, 1942).

McCown, C. C., *The Testament of Solomon* (UNT 9, Leipzig, 1922).

McGaughy, L. C., ed., *Society of Biblical Literature, 1972 Proceedings* (Missoula, 1972), v. 2.

Meeks, W. A., "The Image of the Androgyne: Some Uses of a Symbol in Earliest Christianity," *HR* 13 (1974), 165-208.

_____, "Simon Magus in Recent Research," *Religious Studies Review* 3 (1977), July, 137-142.

_____ and Wilken, R., *Jews and Christians in Antioch in the First Four Centuries of the Common Era* (SBL, Sources for Biblical Study 13, Missoula, 1979).

_____, *The First Urban Christians* (New Haven and London, 1983).

Mélanges d'histoire des religions offerts à H.-Ch. Puech (Paris, 1974).

Ménard, J. E., *L'Évangile selon Philippe* (Strasbourg, 1967).

_____, *L'Évangile de vérité* (NHS 2, Leiden, 1972).

_____, *L'Évangile selon Thomas* (NHS 5, Leiden, 1975).

_____, "L'Évangile selon Philippe et l'Exégèse de l'âme," in J. E. Ménard, ed., *Les textes de Nag Hammadi* (NHS 7, Leiden, 1975), 56-67.

_____, ed., *Les textes de Nag Hammadi* (NHS 7, Leiden, 1975).

_____, *L'Authentikos Logos* (Bibliothèque Copte de Nag Hammadi 2, Laval, 1977).

Mendelson, E. M., "Some Notes on a Sociological Approach to Gnosticism," in U. Bianchi, ed., *Le Origini dello Gnosticismo* (*Numen*Sup 12, Leiden, 1967), 668-676.

Merlan, P., *From Platonism to Neoplatonism* (The Hague, 1960).

Metzger, B., *Historical and Literary Studies: Pagan, Jewish and Christian* (Leiden, 1968).

Meyers, E. M., "Ancient Synagogues in Galilee: Their Religious and Cultural Setting," *BA* 43/2 (1980), 99-108.

Mickwitz, G., "Economic Rationalism in Graeco-Roman Agriculture," *The English Historical Review* 52 (1937), 577-589.

Milik, J. T., *Ten Years of Discovery in the Wilderness of Judea*, trans. J. Strugnell (London, 1958).

Mills, C. W., *The Sociological Imagination* (Oxford, 1959).

Momigliano, A., review of M. Hengel's *Judaism and Hellenism*, in *JTS* 21 (1970), 149-153.

Mommsen, T., *The Provinces of the Roman Empire*, trans. W. P. Dickson (New York, 1899), v. 2.

Mossé, Claude, The Ancient World at Work, trans. J. Lloyd (London, 1969).

Moule, C. F. D., "Obligation in the Ethic of Paul," in W. R. Farmer, C. F. D. Moule and R. Niebuhr, eds., Christian History and Interpretation: Studies Presented to John Knox (Cambridge, 1967), 389-406.

Müller, D., Ägypten und die griechischen Isis-Aretalogien (Berlin, 1961).

Munck, J., Paul and the Salvation of Mankind, trans. F. Clark (Richmond, 1959).

_____, "The New Testament and Gnosticism," in W. Klassen and G. Snyder, eds., Current Issues in New Testament Interpretation (London, 1962), 224-238.

Munz, Peter, "The Problem of 'Die soziologische Verortung des antiken Gnostizismus,'" Numen 19 (1972), 41-51.

Murray, O., "Aristeas and Ptolemaic Kingship," JTS 18 (1967), 337-371.

Mussies, G., "Greek in Palestine and the Diaspora," in S. Safrai and M. Stern, eds., The Jewish People in the First Century (Philadelphia, 1976), v. 2, 1040-1064.

Musurillo, H., ed., The Acts of the Pagan Martyrs: Acta Alexandrinorum (Oxford, 1954).

Neusner, Jacob, The Rabbinic Traditions about the Pharisees before 70 A.D. (Leiden, 1971), 3 vols.

_____, Method and Meaning in Ancient Judaism (Brown Judaic Studies 10, Missoula, 1979).

Nilsson, M. P., A History of the Greek Religion, trans. F. J. Fielden (New York, 1952).

_____, The Dionysiac Mysteries of the Hellenistic and Roman Age (Lund, 1957).

Nock, A. D., "Posidonius," JRS 49 (1959), 1-15.

_____, Conversion (London, 1961).

_____, Early Gentile Christianity and its Hellenistic Background (New York, 1964).

_____ and Festugière, J. A., Hermès Trismégiste: Corpus Hermeticum (Paris, 1945-1954), 4 vols.

Origen, Commentary on John, ed. A. E. Brooke (Cambridge, 1896), 2 vols.

_____, *Origen: Contra Celsum*, trans. Henry Chadwick (Cambridge, 1965).

Otto, W. F., *Dionysus: Myth and Cult*, trans. R. B. Palmer (Bloomington, 1973).

Ovid, *The Art of Love and Other Poems*, ed., J. H. Mozley (LCL, London, Cambridge, Mass., 1962).

Pack, R., *The Greek and Latin Literary Texts from Greco-Roman Egypt* (Ann Arbor, 1965²).

Pagels, E., "A Valentinian Interpretation of Baptism and Eucharist—and its Critique of 'Orthodox' Sacramental Theology and Practice," *HTR* 65/2 (1972), 153-169.

_____, *The Johannine Gospel in Gnostic Exegesis* (Nashville, 1973).

_____, "Conflicting Versions of Valentinian Eschatology: Irenaeus' Treatise vs. the Excerpts from Theodotus," *HTR* 67 (1974), 35-53.

_____, *The Gnostic Paul* (Philadelphia, 1975).

_____, "'The Demiurge and his Archons'—A Gnostic View of the Bishop and Presbyters," *HTR* 69 (1976), 301-324.

_____, *The Gnostic Gospels* (New York, 1979).

Parassoglou, G. M., "On *Idios Logos* and Fallen Trees," *Archiv für Papyrusforschung und verwandte Gebiete* 24-25 (1976), 91-99.

_____, *Imperial Estates in Roman Egypt* (American Studies in Papyrology 18, Amsterdam, 1978).

Parekh, Bhikhu and Berki, P. N., "The History of Political Ideas: A Critique of Q. Skinner's Methodology," *Journal of the History of Ideas* 34 (1973), 163-184.

Parrott, D., ed., *Nag Hammadi Codices V, 2-5 and VI with Papyrus Berolinensis 8502, 1 and 4* (NHS 11, Leiden, 1979).

Pavlovskaia, A. I., "On the Discussion of the Asiatic Mode of Production in *La Pensée* and *Eirene*," *Soviet Studies in History* 4/4 (1965), 38-45.

Pearson, B., "Friedländer Revisited: Alexandrian Judaism and Gnostic Origins," *Studia Philonica* 2 (1973), 23-39.

_____, "Jewish Haggadic Traditions in the Testimony of Truth from Nag Hammadi (CG IX.3)," in J. Bergman, K. Drynjeff and H. Ringgren, eds., *Ex Orbe Religionum: Studia Geo Widengren oblata* (NumenSup 21, Leiden, 1973), v. 1, 457-470.

_____, "The Thunder: Perfect Mind (CG VI.2)," paper given at the Graduate Theological Union, Berkeley,1973.

_____, "The Figure of Melchizedek in the First Tractate of the Unpublished Coptic-Gnostic Codex IX from Nag Hammadi," in *Proceedings of the XIIth International Congress of the International Association for the History of Religions* (Leiden, 1975), 200-208.

_____, "Biblical Exegesis in Gnostic Literature," in M. Stone, ed., *Armenian and Biblical Studies* (Jerusalem, 1976), 70-80.

_____, "Egyptian Seth and Gnostic Seth," in P. J. Achtemeier, ed., *Society of Biblical Literature, 1977 Seminar Papers* (Missoula, 1977), 25-44.

_____, "The Figure of Norea in Gnostic Literature," in G. Widengren, ed., *Proceedings of the International Colloquium on Gnosticism* (Stockholm, 1977), 143-152.

_____, "Some Observations on Gnostic Hermeneutics," in W. D. O'Flaherty, ed., *The Critical Study of Sacred Texts* (Berkeley, 1979), 243-256.

_____, "Gnostic Interpretation of the Old Testament in the Testimony of Truth," *HTR* 73 (1980), 311-319.

_____, "Jewish Elements in Gnosticism and the Development of Gnostic Self-Definition," in E.P. Sanders, eds., *Jewish and Christian Self-Definition* (London, 1980), v. 1, 151-160.

Perkins, P., "Peter in Gnostic Revelation," in G. MacRae, ed., *Society of Biblical Literature, 1974 Seminar Papers* (Cambridge, 1974), v. 2, 1-13.

Petronius, *Petronius. Seneca, Apocolocyntosis,* ed. M. Heseltine (LCL, London, Cambridge, Mass., 1961).

Philo, *Philo,* ed. F. H. Colson, G. H. Whitaker and R. Marcus (LCL, London, Cambridge, Mass., 1929-1962), 10 vols. and 2 sups.

Pliny the Elder, *Natural History,* ed. H. Rackham et al. (LCL, London, Cambridge, Mass., 1938-1963), 10 vols.

Pliny the Younger, *Letters,* ed. W. Melmoth (LCL, London, Cambridge, Mass., 1952, 1957), 2 vols.

Plotinus, *Plotinus,* ed. A. H. Armstrong (LCL, London, Cambridge, Mass., 1966-), 3 vols.

Pokorný, Petr, *Die Epheserbrief und die Gnosis: Die Bedeutung des Haupt-Glieder-Gedankens in der entstehenden Kirche* (Berlin, 1965).

_____, "Der Ursprung der Gnosis," *Kairos* 9 (1967), 94-105.

_____, "Der soziale Hintergrund der Gnosis," in Karl-Wolfgang Tröger, ed., *Gnosis und Neues Testament* (Berlin, 1973), 77-87.

Porten, B., *Archives from Elephantine* (Berkeley 1968).

Préaux, C., "La Taxe des bains dans l'Égypte Romaine," *Chronique d'Égypte* 9 (1934), 128-132.

_____, *L'Économie royale des Lagides* (Brussels, 1939).

Preisendanz, K. and Henrichs, A., eds., *Papyri Graecae Magicae* (Stuttgart, 1973, 1974), 2 vols.

Pseudo-Clementine, *Recognitions,* ed. B. Rehm (GCS 51, Berlin, 1965).

_____, *Homilies,* ed. B. Rehm (GCS 42.2, Berlin, 1969).

Puech, H.-Ch., "Gnostic Gospels and Related Documents," in E. Hennecke and W. S. Schneemelcher, eds., *New Testament Apocrypha,* trans. R. McL. Wilson (London, 1963), v. 1, 231-362.

_____, "The Gospel of Thomas," in E. Hennecke and W. Schneemelcher, eds., *New Testament Apocrypha,* trans. R. McL. Wilson (London, 1963), v. 1, 278-307.

_____, "The Concept of Redemption in Manichaeism," in J. Campbell, ed., *The Mystic Vision* (Bollingen Series 30-6, New York, 1970), 247-314.

_____ and Quispel, G., "Les écrits gnostiques du Codex Jung," *VC* 8 (1954), 1-51.

Pummer, Reinhard, "Religionswissenschaft or Religiology," *Numen* 19 (1972), 91-128.

_____, "Recent Publications on the Methodology of the Science of Religion," *Numen* 22 (1975), 161-182.

Quispel, G., *Gnosis als Weltreligion* (Zurich, 1951).

_____, "Der gnostische Anthropos und die jüdische Tradition," *ErJb* 22 (1953), 195-234, reprinted in G. Quispel, *Gnostic Studies* (Istanbul, 1974), v. 1, 173-195.

_____, "Gnosticism and the New Testament," in J. P. Hyatt, ed., *The Bible in Modern Scholarship* (Nashville, New York, 1965), 252-271.

_____, *Makarius. Das Thomasevangelium und das Lied von der Perle* (NovTSup 15, Leiden, 1967).

_____, "The Origins of the Gnostic Demiurge," in P. Granfield and A. Jungman, eds., *Kyriakon* (Münster, 1970), v. 1, 271-276, reprinted in G. Quispel, *Gnostic Studies* (Istanbul, 1974), v. 1, 213-220.

_____, "The Jung Codex and its Significance," in G. Quispel, *Gnostic Studies* (Istanbul, 1974), v. 1, 3-26.

_____, *Gnostic Studies* (Istanbul, 1974, 1975), 2 vols.

_____, "Jewish Gnosis and Mandaean Gnosticism," in J. E. Ménard, ed., *Les textes de Nag Hammadi* (NHS 7, Leiden, 1975), 82-122.

_____, "The Demiurge in the Apocryphon of John," in R. McL. Wilson, ed., *Nag Hammadi and Gnosis* (NHS 14, Leiden, 1978), 1-33.

_____, "Gnosis and Psychology," in B. Layton, ed., *The Rediscovery of Gnosticism* (Leiden, 1980), v. 1, 17-31.

Rabin, Ch., *The Zadokite Documents* (Oxford, 1958).

_____, "Hebrew and Aramaic in the First Century," in S. Safrai and M. Stern, eds., *The Jewish People in the First Century* (Philadelphia, 1976), v. 2, 1007-1039.

Reiling, J., "Marcus Gnosticus and the New Testament," in T. Baarda, A. F. J. Klijn and W. C. van Unnik, eds., *Miscellanea Neotestamentica* (*NovT*Sup 47, Leiden, 1978), 161-179.

Reinhold, M., "Historian of the Classic World: A Critique of Rostovtzeff," *Science and Society* 10 (1946), 361-391.

Reitzenstein, Richard, *Poimandres* (Leipzig, 1904).

_____, *Das Iranische Erlösungsmysterium* (Bonn, 1921).

_____, *Die Hellenistischen Mysterienreligionen* (Leipzig, 1927[3]).

Rice, D. and Stambaugh, J., *Sources for the Study of Greek Religion* (SBL, Sources for Biblical Study 14, Missoula, 1979).

Rivkin, E., "Pharisaism and the Crisis of the Individual in the Greco-Roman World," *JQR* 61 (1970), 27-53.

Robert, L., "Épigramme d'Égypte," *Hellenica* 1 (1940), 18-24.

Roberts, A. and Donaldson, J., *The Anti-Nicene Christian Library* (Edinburgh, 1866-1872), 24 vols.

Roberts, R. C., *Bultmann's Theology* (Grand Rapids, 1976).

Robinson, J. M., "The Coptic Gnostic Library Today," *NTS* 14 (1967-1968), 356-401.

_____, "The Johannine Trajectory," in J. M. Robinson and H. Koester, eds., *Trajectories through Early Christianity* (Philadelphia, 1971), 232-268.

_____, *Jewish Nag Hammadi Gnostic Texts* (Berkeley, 1975).

_____, ed., *The Nag Hammadi Library in English* (New York, 1977).

_____, "The Three Steles of Seth and the Gnostics of Plotinus," in G. Widengren, ed., *Proceedings of the International Colloquium on Gnosticism* (Stockholm, 1977), 132-142.

_____ and Koester, H., eds., *Trajectories through Early Christianity* (Philadelphia, 1971).

Rosenbloom, J. R., *Conversion to Judaism* (Cincinnati, 1978).

Rostovtzeff, M., *Studien zur Geschichte des römischen Kolonates* (Archiv für Papyrusforschung und verwandte Gebiete 1, Leipzig, Berlin, 1910).

_____, *A Large Estate in the Third Century B.C.* (New York, 1979 [1922]).

_____, "Roman Exploitation of Egypt in the First Century A.D.," *Journal of Economic and Business History* 1/3 (1929), 337-364.

_____, *The Social and Economic History of the Hellenistic World* (Oxford, 1959 [1941]), 3 vols.

_____, *A History of the Ancient World* (Oxford, 1945²), 2 vols.

_____, *The Social and Economic History of the Roman Empire* (Oxford, 1957²), 2 vols.

Rudolph, K., *Die Mandäer I: Das Mandäerproblem* (Göttingen, 1960).

_____, "Stand und Aufgaben in der Erforschung des Gnostizismus," *Sonderheft des Wissenchaftlichen Zeitschrift der Friedrich Schiller-Universität* (Jena, 1963), 89-102.

_____, "Die Problematik der Religionswissenschaft als akademisches Lehrfach," *Kairos* 9 (1967), 22-42.

_____, "Randerscheinungen des Judentums und das Problem der Entstehung des Gnostizismus," *Kairos* 9 (1967), 105-122.

_____, "Problems of a History of the Development of the Mandaean Religion," *HR* 8 (1969), 210-235.

_____, "Soziologische Bemühungen," *TRu* 36 (1971), 119-124.

_____, "Gnosis und Gnostizismus, ein Forschungsbericht. Simonianische Gnosis," *TRu* 37 (1972), 322-347.

_____, review of E. Yamauchi's *Gnostic Ethics and Mandaean Origins,* in *TLZ* 97 (1972), 733-737.

_____, *Die Gnosis* (Göttingen, 1977).

_____, "Das Problem einer Soziologie und 'sozialen Verortung' der Gnosis," *Kairos* 19/1 (1977), 35-44.

Russell, D. S., *The Method and Message of Jewish Apocalyptic* (Philadelphia, 1964).

_____, *Between the Testaments* (London, 1970).

Saad, A. S., "Le Mode de production asiatique et les problèmes de la formation social Égyptienne," *La Pensée* 189 (October, 1976), 19-36.

Safrai, S., "Education and the Study of the Torah," in S. Safrai and M. Stern, eds., *The Jewish People in the First Century* (Philadelphia, 1976), v. 2, 945-970.

_____, "Religion in Everyday Life," in S. Safrai and M. Stern, eds., *The Jewish People in the First Century* (Philadelphia, 1976), v. 2, 793-833.

_____, "The Synagogue," in S. Safrai and M. Stern, eds., *The Jewish People in the First Century* (Philadelphia, 1976), v. 2, 908-944.

_____, "The Temple," in S. Safrai and M. Stern, eds., *The Jewish People in the First Century* (Philadelphia, 1976), v. 2, 865-907.

_____ and Stern, M., eds., *The Jewish People in the First Century* (Assen, 1974), v. 1, (Philadelphia, 1976), v. 2.

Sagnard, F. M. M., *La gnose Valentinienne et le témoignage saint Irénée* (Paris, 1947).

Salmon, P., *Population et dépopulation dans l'empire romain* (Latomus 137, Brussels, 1974).

Samuel, A. E., *Death and Taxes* (American Studies in Papyrology 10, Toronto, 1971).

Sandback, F. H., *Stoics* (London, 1975).

Sanders, E. P., ed., *Jewish and Christian Self-Definition* (London, 1980), v. 1.

Sandmel, S., *Philo's Place in Judaism* (Cincinnati, 1956).

_____, *The First Christian Century in Judaism and Christianity* (New York, 1969).

Schechter, Solomon, ed., *Abot de Rabbi Nathan* (Vienna, 1887).

Schenke, H.-M., *Der Gott 'Mensch' in der Gnosis* (Göttingen, 1962).

Schenke, H.-M., "Nag Hammadi Studien II: Das system der Sophia Jesu Christi," *ZRGG* 14 (1962), 263-278.

Schenke, H.-M., review of A. Böhlig's and P. Labib's *Koptisch-gnostische Apokalypsen aus Codex V von Nag Hammadi im Koptischen Museum zu Alt-Kairo* in *OLZ* 61 (1966), 23-34.

_____, "Der Jakobusbrief aus dem Codex Jung," *OLZ* 66 (1971), 117-128.

_____, "Die neutestamentliche Christologie und der gnostische Erlöser," in Karl-Wolfgang Tröger, ed., *Gnosis und Neues Testament* (Berlin, 1973), 205-231.

Schmidt, Carl, ed., *Gnostische Schriften in koptischen Sprache aus dem Codex Brucianus* (TU 8, Leipzig, 1892).

_____, ed. and MacDermot, V., trans., *The Books of Jeu and the Untitled Text in the Bruce Codex* (NHS 13, Leiden, 1978).

Schmithals, W., *Paulus und die Gnostiker: Untersuchungen zu den kleinen Paulusbriefen* (Hamburg, 1965).

_____, *An Introduction to the Theology of Rudolph Bultmann*, trans. J. Bowden (Minneapolis, 1968[2]).

_____, *Die Gnosis in Korinth* (Göttingen, 1969[3]).

_____, *The Office of Apostle in the Early Church*, trans. J. E. Steely (New York, 1969).

_____, *Paul and the Gnostics*, trans. J. E. Steely (Nashville, 1972).

_____, *The Apocalyptic Movement*, trans. J. E. Steely (Nashville, New York, 1975).

Schoedel, W., "Scripture and the Seventy-Two Heavens of the First Apocalypse of James," *NovT* 12 (1970), 118-129.

_____, "The (First) Apocalypse of James," in D. Parrott, ed., *Nag Hammadi Codices V, 2-5 and VI with Papyrus Berolinensis 8502, 1 and 4* (NHS 11, Leiden, 1979), 65-103.

Schoeps, H. J., *Paul: The Theology of the Apostle in the Light of Jewish Religious History,* trans. H. Knight (Philadelphia, 1961).

Scholem, G., *Jewish Gnosticism, Merkabah Mysticism and Talmudic Tradition* (New York, 1960).

_____, *Ursprung und Anfänge der Kabbala* (Berlin, 1962).

_____, *Major Trends in Jewish Mysticism* (New York, 1969).

_____, *The Messianic Idea in Judaism* (New York, 1971).

_____, *Sabbatai Sevi,* trans. R. J. Zvi Werblowsky (Princeton, 1973).

_____, "Yaldabaoth Reconsidered," in *Mélanges d'histoire des religions offerts à H.-Ch. Peuch* (Paris, 1974), 405-421.

Scholer, David M., *Nag Hammadi Bibliography: 1948-1969* (NHS 1, Leiden, 1971), with annual supplements in *NovT.*

Schüle, E. U., "Der Ursprung des Bösen bei Marcion," *ZRGG* 16 (1964), 23-42.

Schürer, E., *The History of the Jewish People in the Age of Jesus Christ,* rev. and ed. G. Vermes, F. Millar and M. Black (Edinburgh, 1973-), 2 vols.

Schütz, J. H., "Steps Toward a Sociology of Primitive Christianity: A Critique of the Work of Gerd Theissen," paper presented at the annual meeting of the Society of Biblical Literature/American Academy of Religion, San Francisco, 1977.

Scroggs, R., "The Social Interpretation of the New Testament: The Present State of Research," *NTS* 26 (1980), 164-179.

Seddon, D., ed., *Relations of Production* (London, 1978).

Segal, A., "Ruler of this World: Towards a Sociology of Gnosticism," unpublished paper, 1976.

_____, *Two Powers in Heaven: Early Rabbinic Reports about Christianity and Gnosticism* (Studies in Judaism in Late Antiquity 25, Leiden, 1977).

_____, "Rabbinic Polemic and the Radicalization of Gnosticism," paper presented at the Canadian society for Biblical Studies, Ottawa, June, 1982.

Segelberg, E., "The Coptic-Gnostic Gospel According to Philip and its Sacramental System," *Numen* 7 (1960), 189-201.

_____, "The Baptismal Rite According to Some of the Coptic-Gnostic Texts from Nag Hammadi," in F. L. Cross, ed., *Studia Patristica* (TU 80, Berlin, 1962), v. 3, 117-128.

_____, "Prayer Among the Gnostics," in M. Krause, ed., *Gnosis and Gnosticism* (NHS 8, Leiden,1977), 55-69.

Segré, A., "Anti-semitism in Hellenistic Alexandria," *Jewish Social Studies* 8 (1946), 127-136.

Seneca, *Ad Lucilium Epistulae Morales*, trans. R. M. Gummere (LCL, London, Cambridge, Mass., 1953), 3 vols.

Septuaginta (Stuttgart, 1935), 2 vols.

Sevenster, N., *The Roots of Pagan Anti-Semitism in the Ancient World* (*NovT*Sup 41, Leiden, 1975).

Sevrin, Jean-Marie, "A propos de la 'Paraphrase de Sem,'" *Le Muséon* 83 (1975), 69-96.

Sherwin-White, A. N., "Why Were the Early Christians Persecuted: An Amendment," *Past and Present* 27 (1964), 23-27.

Siegel, J. P., "The Alexandrians in Jerusalem and their Torah Scroll with the Gold Tetragrammata," *IEJ* 22/1 (1972), 39-43.

Simon, Marcel, "Histoire des religions, histoire du Christianisme, histoire de l'église: réflexions méthodologiques," in *Liber Amicorum: Studies in Honour of Professor Dr. C. J. Bleeker* (*Numen*Sup 17, Leiden, 1969), 194-207.

_____, "The *Religionsgeschichtliche Schule*, Fifty Years Later," *RelS* 11 (1975), 135-144.

Singer, C., Holmyard, E., Hall, A. and Williams, T., eds., *A History of Technology* (Oxford, 1954, 1956), vols. 1 and 2.

Sjoberg, G., *The Pre-Industrial City* (New York, 1960).

Skinner, Quentin, "Meaning and Understanding in the History of Ideas," *History and Theory* 8 (1969), 3-53.

Smallwood, Mary, *The Jews Under Roman Rule* (Leiden, 1976).

Smith, M., "Palestinian Judaism in the First Century," in M. Davis, ed., *Israel: Its Role in Civilization* (New York, 1956), 67-91.

_____, "Goodenough's 'Jewish Symbols' in Retrospect," *JBL* 86 (1967), 53-68.

_____, *Clement of Alexandria and the Secret Gospel of Mark* (Cambridge, Mass., 1973).

Sokoloff, M., *The Targum to Job from Qumran Cave XI* (Ramat-Gan, 1974).

Sombart, W., *Der moderne Kapitalismus* (Leipzig, 1902), 2 vols.

Sperber, D., "Cost of Living in Roman Palestine," *Journal of the Economic and Social History of the Orient* 9 (1966), 182-211.

_____, "Social Legislation in Jerusalem During the Latter Part of the Second Temple Period," *JSJ* 6/1 (1975), 86-95.

_____, "Objects of Trade Between Palestine and Egypt in Roman Times," *Journal of the Economic and Social History of the Orient* 19 (1976), 113-147.

Stagg, E. and Stagg, F., *Woman in the World of Jesus* (Philadelphia, 1978).

Stone, M., ed., *Armenian and Biblical Studies* (Jerusalem, 1976).

Stern, M., *Greek and Latin Authors on Jews and Judaism* (Jerusalem, 1974, 1980), 2 vols.

Strabo, *Geography*, ed. H. L. Jones (LCL, London, Cambridge, Mass., 1917-1932), 8 vols.

Stroumsa, G., *Another Seed: Studies in Sethian Gnosticism* (Cambridge, 1978), Harvard doctoral thesis.

Suetonius, *Suetonius*, ed. J. C. Rolfe (LCL, London, Cambridge, Mass., 1913, 1914), 2 vols.

Tacitus, *Histories and Annals*, ed. C. H. Moore and J. Jackson (LCL, London, Cambridge, Mass., 1925-1937), 4 vols.

Talbert, C. H., "Again: Paul's Visits to Jerusalem," *NovT* 9 (1967), 26-40.

Talmud Bavli (in Hebrew, Jerusalem, 1958-1959), 20 vols.

Talmud Yerushalmi (in Hebrew, Jerusalem, 1971-1972), 7 vols.

Tardieu, M., "Les Trois Steles de Seth," *RSPT* 57 (1973), 545-575.

_____, *Trois Mythes Gnostiques* (Paris, 1974).

_____, "Le Congrès de Yale sur le Gnosticisme," *Revue des études augustiniennes* 24 (1978), 188-209.

Tarn, W. W. and Griffith, G. T., *Hellenistic Civilization* (London, 1952[3]).

Taubenschlag, R., *The Law of Graeco-Roman Egypt in the Light of the Papyri* (Warsaw, 1955²).

Tcherikover, V., "Palestine in the Light of the Papyri of Zenon" (in Hebrew), *Tarbiz* 4/2-3 (1933), 226-247 and 5/2 (1933), 37-44.

_____, "Jewish Apologetic Literature Reconsidered," *EOS* 48 (1956), 169-193.

_____, *Hellenistic Civilization and the Jews* (New York, 1979 [1959]).

_____, *The Jews in Egypt in the Hellenistic and Roman Age in the Light of the Papyri* (in Hebrew, Jerusalem, 1963²).

_____, Fuks, A. and Stern, M., eds., *Corpus Papyrorum Judaicarum* (Cambridge, Mass., 1957-1964), 3 vols.

Tertullian, *Apologeticum; De praescriptione haereticorum; Scorpiace*, ed. F. Oehler (Leipzig, 1853).

_____, *De praescriptione haereticorum*, ed. R. F. Réfoule (SC 46, Paris, 1957).

Theissen, G., *The First Followers of Jesus*, trans. J. Bowden (London, 1978).

_____, *Studien zur Soziologie des Urchristentums* (Tübingen, 1979).

Theodor, J. and Albeck, C., eds., *Bereshit Rabba* (Berlin, 1903-1929), 2 vols.

Till, W., *Die gnostischen Schriften des koptischen Papyrus Berolinensis 8502* (TU 60, Berlin, 1955).

Topitsch, E., *Sozialphilosophie zwischen Ideologie und Wissenschaft* (Luchterhand, 1961).

Trachtenberg, J., *Jewish Magic and Superstition* (New York, 1970).

Tröger, Karl-Wolfgang, ed., *Gnosis und Neues Testament* (Berlin, 1973).

_____, "Die sechste und siebte Schrift aus Nag-Hammadi Codex VI," *TLZ* 98 (1973), 495-503.

Tuma, E., *Economic History and the Social Sciences* (Berkeley and Los Angeles, 1971).

Turner, H. E. W., *The Pattern of Christian Truth* (London, 1954).

Turner, J. D., *The Book of Thomas the Contender* (Society of Biblical Literature, Dissertation Series 23, Missoula, 1970).

_____, "The Gnostic Threefold Path to Enlightenment," *NovT* 22 (1980), 324-351.

Turner, V., *The Ritual Process: Structure and Anti-Structure* (London, 1970)

Tzarichabar, A., *The Jews in the Greek Roman World* (in Hebrew, Jerusalem, 1961).

Unger, R., "Zur sprachlichen und formalen Struktur des gnostischen Textes 'Der Donner: die vollkommene Nous,'" *OrChr* 59 (1975), 78-107.

Urbach, E., *The Sages*, trans. I. Abrahams (Jerusalem, 1975), 2 vols.

_____, "Ascesis and Suffering in Talmudic and Midrashic Sources," in *Yitzhak F. Baer Jubilee Volume* (in Hebrew, Jerusalem, 1969), 48-68.

van Baaren, P., "Towards a Definition of Gnosticism," in U. Bianchi, ed., *Le Origini dello Gnosticismo* (*Numen*Sup 12, Leiden, 1967), 174-180.

van der Ploeg, J. P. M., van der Woude, O. P. and van der Woude, A. S., eds. and trans., *Le Targum de Job de la grotte XI de Qumran*, (Leiden, 1971).

van Groningen, G., *First Century Gnosticism* (Leiden, 1967).

van Unnik, W. C., "The 'Gospel of Truth' and the New Testament," in F. L. Cross, ed., *The Jung Codex* (London, 1955), 79-129.

Varro, *Marcus Porcius Cato On Agriculture, Marcus Teratius Varro on Agriculture*, ed. W. D. Hooper (LCL, London, Cambridge, Mass., 1954).

Vermes, G., *Post-Biblical Jewish Studies* (Leiden, 1975).

_____, *The Dead Sea Scrolls* (London, 1977).

Vööbus, A., *Celibacy, a Requirement for Admission to Baptism in the Early Syrian Church* (Papers of the Estonian Theological Society in Exile 1, Stockholm, 1951).

_____, *History of Asceticism in the Syrian Orient. A Contribution to the History of Culture in the Near East* (CSCO 184, Louvain, 1958, 1960), 2 vols.

Waardenburg, J., "Religion between Reality and Idea," *Numen* 19 (1972), 128-203.

Wallace, S. LeRoy, *Taxation in Egypt* (Oxford, 1938).

Weaver, P. R. C., *Familia Caesaris: A Social Study of the Emperor's Freedmen and Slaves* (Cambridge, 1972).

Weber, Max, *The Theory of Social and Economic Organization*, trans. T. Parsons (New York, 1947).

_____, *The Methodology of the Social Sciences*, trans. E. Shils and H. Finch (New York, 1949).

_____, *Ancient Judaism*, trans. H. H. Gerth and D. Martindale (New York, 1952).

_____, *The Protestant Ethic and the Spirit of Capitalism*, trans. T. Parsons (New York, 1958).

_____, *The Religion of India-The Socioloy of Hinduism and Buddhism*, trans. and ed. H. H. Gerth and D. Martindale (Glencoe, 1958).

_____, *The Religion of China—Confucianism and Taoism*, trans. and ed. H. H. Gerth (New York, 1964).

_____, *The Sociology of Religion*, trans. E. Fischoff (Boston, 1964).

_____, *The Agrarian Sociology of Ancient Civilizations*, trans. R. I. Frank (London, 1976).

Werblowsky, R. J. Zvi, "Marburg—and After?," *Numen* 7 (1960), 215-220.

Westermann, W. L., "Apprentice Contracts and the Apprentice System in Roman Egypt," *Classical Philology* 9 (1914), 295-315.

_____, "The "Uninundated Lands' in Ptolemaic and Roman Egypt," Part I, *Classical Philology* 15 (1920), 120-137.

_____, "The 'Uninundated Lands' in Ptolemaic and Roman Egypt," Part II, *Classical Philology* 16 (1921), 169-188.

_____, "The 'Dry Land' in Ptolemaic and Roman Egypt," *Classical Philology* 17 (1922), 23-36.

_____, *The Slave Systems of Greek and Roman Antiquity* (Philadelphia, 1955).

White, K. D., *Roman Farming* (London, 1970).

Whittaker, C. R., "Agri Deserti," in M. Finley, ed., *Studies in Roman Property* (Cambridge, 1976), 137-165.

Widengren, G., "Les origines du gnosticisme et l'histoire des religions," in U. Bianchi, ed., *Le Origini dello Gnosticismo* (*Numen*Sup 12, Leiden, 1967), 28-60.

_____, "La méthode comparative: entre philologie et phénoménologie," *Numen* 18 (1971), 161-172.

_____ ed., *Proceedings of the International Colloquium on Gnosticism* (Stockholm, 1977).

Wilkinson, John, "Christian Pilgrims in Jerusalem during the Byzantine Period," *PEQ* 108 (1976), 75-101.

Wilna, ed., *Midrash Rabbah on the Five Books of the Torah and the Five Megillot* (Jerusalem, 1961 [1878]), 2 vols.

Wilson, Bryan, "An Analysis of Sect Development," *American Sociological Review* 24 (1959), 3-15.

_____, ed., *Patterns of Sectarianism* (London, 1967).

_____, *Magic and the Millennium: A Sociological Study of Religious Movements of Protest Among Tribal and Third-World Peoples* (London, 1973).

_____, *The Noble Savages: The Primitive Origins of Charisma and its Contemporary Survival* (Berkeley, 1975).

Wilson, J. A., "Buto and Hierakonpolis in the Geography of Egypt," *Journal of Near Eastern Studies* 14/4 (1955), 209-236.

Wilson, R. McL., *The Gnostic Problem* (London, 1958).

_____, *Studies in the Gospel of Thomas* (London, 1960).

_____, *The Gospel of Philip* (London, 1962).

_____, *Gnosis and the New Testament* (Oxford, 1968).

_____, "How Gnostic were the Corinthians?," *NTS* 19 (1972-1973), 65-74.

_____, "From Gnosis to Gnosticism," in *Mélanges d'histoire des religions offerts à Henri-Charles Puech* (Paris, 1974), 423-429.

_____, "Old Testament Exegesis in the Gnostic Exegesis on the Soul," in M. Krause, ed., *Essays on the Nag Hammadi Texts* (NHS 6, Leiden, 1975), 217-224.

_____, "The Gnostics and the Old Testament," in G. Widengren, ed., *Proceedings of the International Colloquium on Gnosticism* (Stockholm, 1977), 164-168.

_____, "Jewish Literary Propaganda," in *Paganisme, Judaisme, Christianisme: Mélanges offerts à Marcel Simon* (Paris, 1978), 61-74.

_____, ed., *Nag Hammadi and Gnosis* (NHS 14, Leiden, 1978).

_____, "Simon and Gnostic Origins," in J. Kremer, ed., *Les Actes des Apôtres* (BETL 48, Leuven, 1979), 485-491.

Wilson, R. S., *Marcion: A Study of a Second-Century Heretic* (London, 1933).

Wisse, F., "The Redeemer Figure in the Paraphrase of Shem," *NovT* 12 (1970), 130-140.

_____, "The Nag Hammadi Library and the Heresiologists," *VC* 25 (1971), 205-223.

_____, "The Sethians and the Nag Hammadi Library," in L. C. McGaughy, ed., *Society of Biblical Literature, 1972 Proceedings* (Missoula, 1972), v. 2, 601-607.

_____, "Die Sextus-Sprüche und das Problem der gnostischen Ethik" in A. Böhlig and F. Wisse, *Zum Hellenismus in den Schriften von Nag Hammadi* (Göttinger Orientforschungen 6, Reihe: Hellenistica, Band 2, Wiesbaden, 1975), 55-86.

_____, "Do the Jewish Elements in Gnostic Writings Prove the Existence of a Jewish Gnosticism?," paper presented at the annual meeting of the Society of Biblical Literature/ American Academy of Religion, New York, 1979.

Witt, R. E., *Isis in the Graeco-Roman World* (Ithaca, 1971).

Wolfe, Tom, *The Electric Kool-Aid Acid Test* (New York, 1968).

Wolfson, H. A., *Philo* (Cambridge, Mass., 1947), 2 vols.

Wood, R. W., "Homosexual Behaviour in the Bible," *One Institute Quarterly* 5 (1962), 10-19.

Yadin, Y., *Tefillin from Qumran* (Jerusalem, 1969).

Yamauchi, E., *Gnostic Ethics and Mandaean Origins* (Harvard Theological Studies 24, Cambridge, Mass., London, 1970).

_____, *Pre-Christian Gnosticism* (London, 1973).

_____, "The Descent of Ishtar, the Fall of Sophia, and the Jewish Roots of Gnosticism," *TynBul* 29 (1978), 143-175.

_____, "Pre-Christian Gnosticism in the Nag Hammadi Texts," *CH* 48 (1979), 129-141.

Youtie, H. C., "The Heidelberg Festival Papyrus: A Reinterpretation," in P. R. Coleman-Norton, ed., *Studies in Roman Economic and Social History* (Princeton, 1951), 178-208.

_____, "ΑΓΡΑΜΜΑΤΟΣ: An Aspect of Greek Society in Egypt," *Harvard Studies in Classical Philology* 75 (1971), 161-176.

Zeitlin, I., *Ideology and the Development of Sociological Theory* (Englewood Cliffs, N.J., 1968).

Zeitlin, S., *The Zadokite Fragments* (Philadelphia, 1952).

_____, *The Rise and Fall of the Judaean State* (Philadelphia, 1962-1978), 3 vols.

Zuckermandel, M. S., *Tosephta* (Jerusalem, 1963 [1875]).

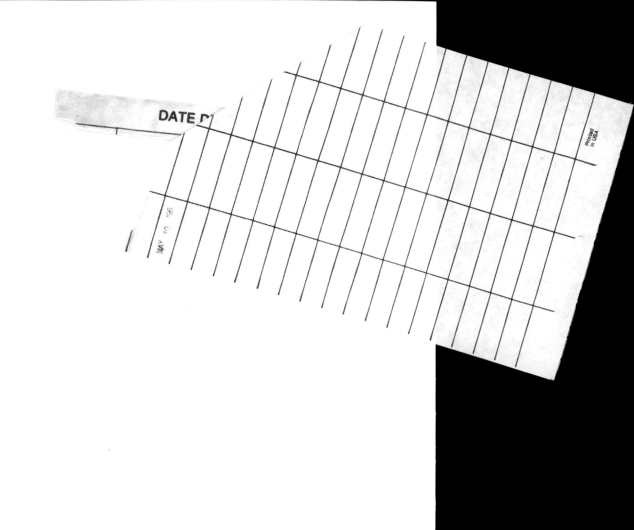

DATE D

MAY 19 '96

Printed in USA